D1345558

Frontiers of
Game Theory

Frontiers of
Game Theory

edited by Ken Binmore,
Alan Kirman, and Piero Tani

The MIT Press
Cambridge, Massachusetts
London, England

© 1993 Massachusetts Institute of Technology

All rights reserved. No part of this book may be reproduced in any form by any electronic or mechanical means (including photocopying, recording, or information storage and retrieval) without permission in writing from the publisher.

This book was set in Palatino by Asco Trade Typesetting Ltd., Hong Kong, and was printed and bound in the United States of America.

Library of Congress Cataloging-in-Publication Data

Frontiers of game theory / edited by Ken Binmore, Alan Kirman, Piero Tani.
  p. cm.
Includes bibliographical references and index.
ISBN 0-262-02356-3
1. Social sciences—Mathematics—Congresses. 2. Game theory—Congresses.
I. Binmore, K. G. II. Kirman, A. P. III. Tani, Piero.
H61.25.F76   1993   93-1742
300'.1'5193—dc20   CIP

Contents

Introduction:
Famous Gamesters

Ken Binmore, Alan Kirman, and Piero Tani

There was no game but what he was an absolute artist at, either upon the Square or foul Play: as at English Ruff and Honours, Whist, French Ruff, Gleek, L'Ombre, Lanterloo, Bankafalit, Beast, Basset, Brag, Piquet; and he was dextrous also at Verquere, Tick-Tack, Grand Trick-Track, Irish and Back-Gammon; which are all games play'd within Tables; and he was not ignorant of Inn and Inn, Passage and Draughts, which are games play'd without the Tables. Moreover, he had great skill at Billiard and Chess; but, above all, his chief game was at Hazard.
Theophilus Lucas, London, 1714

1 Why Gamesters?

The preceding delightful quote from the equally delightfully titled book, *Memoirs of the Lives, Intrigues, and Comical Adventures of the most Famous Gamesters and Celebrated Sharpers of the Reigns of Charles II, James II, William II, and Queen Ann,* by Theophilus Lucas gives some feel of the richness of the territory that game theorists set out to explore. They would have come a long way if they knew how to solve all the games that Lucas lists. Indeed, most of us would feel very erudite if we even knew how to play most of the games. Whist and Brag are familiar as precursors of bridge and poker, which still get played today. Draughts would presumably be checkers if it weren't apparently played without a table. Tick-Tack might perhaps be some form of tic-tac-toe (noughts and crosses). But what could Gleek possibly be?

However, it was not to study such pursuits that game theorists met in Florence in the spring of 1991. Although they use the strategic language of such parlor games, game theorists have their eyes firmly fixed on higher things. In this they follow in the footsteps of Machiavelli—perhaps the most famous gamester of all—who plied his trade in Florence five hundred years ago.

This introduction is intended to explain what gamesters were doing back in Machiavelli's old stamping grounds after so many years. The occasion of their meeting is simple enough. They gathered at the European University Institute in the Tuscan hills above Florence to celebrate the founding of the Interuniversity Center for Game Theory and its Applications by a group of twelve of Italy's distinguished universities.[1] However, to name the common research goals of the gamesters who exchanged ideas at the meeting is by no means easy. The things that excite game theorists are diverse and complicated—so much so that outsiders often notice only the issues that divide them, because these are the issues about which game theorists want to talk. And when they talk, gamesters talk a great deal, since they are a quarrelsome and unruly breed. However, there are good reasons why they do not split into rival clans. Underlying their disputes and differences of approach there is a deeply felt sense of common purpose that holds game theorists together. If this introduction can convey something of this underlying unity of aim, then it will have served some useful purpose. As for the vigor of the subject, the chapters in this volume can be left to speak for themselves.

2   What Are Gamesters For?

The absurdly ambitious ultimate aim of a gamester is imperialistic: to provide a universally applicable theory of conflict and cooperation, both in animal and human societies, and thus to colonize much of the territory now occupied by the social sciences. The gap between this aspiration and what gamesters can actually achieve is enormous. Nevertheless, gamesters are not abashed, because they can see that achieving their ultimate aim would solve at a stroke most of the pressing problems of social science—and they feel that some delay in reaching their final destination is therefore excusable. In the meantime, they press the frontiers of their empire forward wherever progress seems feasible, and avoid those areas which present problems that seem intractable at the moment.

The frontiers of game theory's empire are therefore a general's nightmare. In some areas, the cavalry has broken through and is taking control of the enemy hinterland. In other locations, trench warfare is in progress. Elsewhere, nobody seems yet to have noticed there is supposedly a battle in progress. This introduction will not disperse the fog of war altogether, but it is perhaps feasible to impose some order on current trends in game theory by borrowing von Clausewitz's distinction between strategy and tactics. Gamesters all have the same overall strategic aim, but they pursue this aim using very different techniques and with various degrees of success. To clarify what is going on, some sort of classification of these subsidiary tactical objectives is needed.

Binmore (1990, 22) distinguishes five general tactical purposes for which a game-theoretic model might be designed; namely, prediction, explanation, investigation, description, and prescription. These categories will be used in classifying the chapters of this volume, along with an orthogonal division into applied and theoretical work. The latter will be somewhat narrowly defined as navel gazing—that is, work devoted to developing or criticizing the theory of games itself. Other work will be said to be applied, even though it may have no empirical content at all.

3   Gamesters Looking Out

This section seeks to classify the applied chapters in the volume according to their aims. Such a classification is at best rough and ready, and most of the papers should properly be treated under more than one of the headings below.

3.1   Prediction

Naive positivists see no role for modelling beyond the generation of refutable predictions. Until recently, a naive positivist would therefore have found nothing at all to satisfy him in game theory. However, two comparatively recent developments have changed things dramatically. The first is the discovery that game theory is sometimes capable of predicting biological phenomena with surprising accuracy. How and why game theory should be relevant to the manner in which evolution has shaped the behavior of honeybees and spiders, or even trees and flowers, is outside the scope of this volume.[2] However, the volume contains a fine paper illustrating progress in the second recent line of development: Camerer, Johnson, Rymon, and Sen's "Cognition and Framing in Sequential Bargaining for Gains and Losses."

It seems only yesterday that pioneers in experimental economics were commonly dismissed with contemptuous remarks such as, "Economics is not an experimental science." However, following the successes of Vernon Smith and his school in documenting how well market mechanisms can work under controlled laboratory conditions, it now seems that the whole profession is dabbling with experiments. Game-theoretic experiments with human subjects have been particularly interesting.

As Camerer et al. document, one of the by-products of experimental research into game-theoretic models of bargaining has been the discovery that human subjects do *not* resolve multistage bargaining games with three or more stages of offer and counteroffer using backwards induction. Elaborate theories like Rubinstein's (1982) which depend on the computation of subgame-perfect equilibria in infinite-horizon models, therefore become suspect if used to predict the actual bargaining behavior of real people.

Two schools of thought exist on what this discovery implies. One school argues that game theory is largely irrelevant to the bargaining behavior of real people because they are not motivated by strategic concerns, but by considerations of fairness. A second school holds that the subjects bring with them to the laboratory a menu of fairness norms that actually generate equilibrium behavior in the real-world situations for which they have evolved, but which are not adapted to the situation in the laboratory. Nevertheless, inexperienced subjects continue to use the norms because they do not understand their current predicament. This school therefore advocates that future experiments should simplify the framing of the problems with which subjects are faced, increase the incentives, and provide ample opportunity for learning in order that real-world environments of interest be better simulated.

Camerer et al. have sought to short-circuit the expensive research program proposed by the second school by abandoning the economist's contention that what goes on inside people's heads is something that polite people do not discuss. They therefore provided subjects with a computerized interface for accessing the data of the bargaining problem with which they were confronted. Through this system they were able to keep track of the order in which various pieces of data were consulted, and the time spent studying each item. The idea, of course, is that someone using backwards induction will have a very different data-consultation pattern than someone who, for example, cares only about fairness.

In brief, Camerer and his colleagues confirmed that inexperienced subjects do not have a data-consultation pattern that is consistent with a backwards induction methodology. However, a dramatic change in the patterns followed after instruction in the use of backwards induction was given to subjects. Whatever it is that inexperienced subjects do, it is therefore not invulnerable to alteration. On the other hand, simple repetition of the game against a new opponent each time does not lead to a change towards backwards induction patterns. Camerer et al. speculate, very reasonably, that what is learned depends crucially on the quality of the feedback the subjects receive.

It seems to us that such work as this is vitally important for the progress of game theory as a predictive science. Game theory is mostly about what *rational* people will do under certain highly constrained circumstances. Only experimental work can determine the conditions under which real people will learn to behave as though they were rational.

3.2   Explanation

The urge to explain the world around us does not evaporate when the phenomena that puzzle us are not amenable to direct experimentation or empirical testing. Nor are the explanations advanced under such circumstances somehow unscientific. Archaeology, cosmology, evolution, and meteorology are all counterexamples to such a naively positive assertion. All of these disciplines involve constructing models, either discursive or mathematical, that make no claim at being demonstrably correct. Their purpose is to show only that a particular type of explanation is viable, in the sense that it can be expressed in a logically coherent manner.

It is perhaps in this kind of role that game theory currently finds its major opportunities for application. The manner in which we are accustomed to explain social phenomena to ourselves is often profoundly unsatisfactory. We inherit or invent stories about how and why we do things in which everything that matters is attributed to some *deus ex machina* whose properties are simply to be taken as given. Game theory provides an opportunity for looking inside some of these black boxes.

A particularly successful area in which game theory has contributed much to our understanding in this sort of way is the study of "altruism." We tell ourselves stories about why our sense of moral rectitude leads us sometimes to be nice to each other when we do not obviously reap any advantage other than the tautological one, that it makes us feel better, from the behavior. But morality in such stories is a black box. We need an explanation for *why* we are moral. How did our moral rules evolve? Having evolved, why do they survive?

The theory of repeated games has contributed enormously to our understanding of these questions. If moral rules did not exist, game theorists would have to invent them in order to shift society from equilibria with bad properties to equilibria with good ones. What is more, by studying the evolution of players modeled as computing machines in repeated games, we are beginning to understand how it could be that such moral rules might have emerged spontaneously.

Such explanations are not testable in any real sense. They only provide possible stylized explanations of how things might have come about. One does not therefore believe or disbelieve the supporting models. They show only that a particular way of looking at things, usually one with fewer unexplained entities than the standard viewpoint, is logically coherent. But this can be a valuable insight, since the key to breaking out from the preconceptions that imprison our thoughts is often nothing more than the realization that other ways of thinking are intellectually respectable.

This volume contains no grandiose papers on the nature of morality. But it does contain a paper that seeks to provide a possible explanation for a much more tractable question concerning the behavior of legislators: Austen-Smith's "Explaining the Vote: Constituency Constraints on Sophisticated Voting." Why do legislators sometimes vote sincerely when a strategic vote would better advance what they see as the best interests of their district? One can invent black box explanations without difficulty. For example, they vote sincerely because they think it right to do so. And it may well be that this is how legislators often do explain their behavior to themselves. But such a story does not explain why the behavior survives. Who would continue to vote for a legislator whose moral rectitude prevents his sometimes organizing a little logrolling on behalf of those he represents?

One possible reason why legislators might vote more sincerely than rationality would seem to dictate is that legislators have to explain their past voting behavior to their constituents, and there is a risk that a strategic vote might be misinterpreted as revealing a genuine preference for policies that next year's electorate will not find palatable.

Is it possible to construct a model in which this explanation holds together and everybody is rational? It would not be possible to do so if there were complete information, because the legislator's preferences would then be common knowledge. A suitable model must therefore involve incomplete information about what the legislator's genuine preferences are. His constituents will then need to try to deduce as much as they can about his preferences from how he votes in Washington. They will also have as evidence the explanations that he may offer them for why he voted as he did, but politicians will not be surprised if what they tell their constituents is not always taken at face value.

Austen-Smith constructs a model whose (efficient) equilibria do indeed call for legislators to vote sincerely more often than they would think it appropriate if they had no constituents to mollify. If the explanations that legislators offer for why they voted as they did are to be strategically significant, there needs to be a risk that a legislator who lies will be exposed. The size of the resulting penalty will obviously matter. If it is large, then legislators whose preferences are representative of a majority of their district can afford to vote strategically all the time, because everybody will know that they cannot afford to take the risk of lying about why they did it. But even if the penalty is small, requiring legislators to explain their vote never makes a district worse off. Nor does it hurt a legislator whose views represent the majority of his district.

Austen-Smith's elegant paper is typical of the style of explanation offered within a small but select school of modern political scientists who have seized on the opportunity that game theory offers to put forth a case with the same discipline and concern for logical niceties that economic theorists have long taken for granted. Does the liveliness of their work perhaps signal a revival of the moribund subject of political economy?

Brousseau and Kirman's "The Dynamics of Learning in N-Person Games with the Wrong N" seeks to explain a very different kind of phenomenon. The issue is that of the self-fulfilling prophecy in a market context. Traders need to make forecasts about the future when deciding what to trade and when to trade it. However, such forecasts should not be assigned a purely passive role. Since they determine the behavior of the agents who make them, they help to create the future as well as to predict it. One might say that the manner in which agents learn about their environment is part of the environment about which they have to learn.

Much of modern macroeconomic theory is based on the notion of a rational expectations equilibrium. Only recently has the issue of how agents learn to have the necessary rational expectations for such equilibria been studied seriously. Brousseau and Kirman list a number of well-known papers in which simple learning procedures do indeed result in convergence on a rational expectations equilibrium. Nobody seriously argues that these procedures actually represent the way agents learn in the real world. The examples that use these procedures show only that it is logically coherent to maintain that rational expectations equilibria can be achieved through the use of simple learning rules. These conclusions can be used for rhetorical purposes in defending rational expectations equilibria, but no genuine grounds for complacency exist, since other simple learning procedures can be shown to lead to equilibria in which originally erroneous beliefs about the way things are, are self-fulfilling.

Brousseau and Kirman contribute further to this critical literature. In a simple duopoly context they show that agents may use least-squares learning to make their predictions and mistakenly apply their conclusions to a model that does not correspond to the "true" situation. The particular misrepresentation that they consider is the failure to take an opponent's existence into account. This radical departure from complete knowledge of the game can still lead to agents' forecasts being verified in the long run, and without the agents being required to overlook any inconsistencies between their model and the data they receive. Brousseau and Kirman show further that convergence is not guaranteed in the class of model they consider. Indeed, if limits are imposed on the agents' memories, a sort of cycling can result, recalling an old result of Shapley (1964) and observations by Smale (1980).

Where does this leave game theory insofar as putative applications to macroeconomics are concerned? One possible view is that game theorists would do well to wait before lending what authority they have to possible explanations of stylized facts until the facts are themselves better established.

3.3   Investigation

A mathematician looking into an area for the first time usually has some cloudy notion of what type of theorem might be true. Such notions tend to remain up in the air if the mathematician continues to contemplate the problem in its full generality from a safe distance. A common mathematical research strategy is therefore to abandon the general problem in favor of simple examples that present the problem in a special form, in the hope that their study may crystallize whatever hazy notions the mathematician may be entertaining into a precise conjecture. Once a precise conjecture has been formulated, there comes the question of proof. Again, insight is sought by looking at simpler problems. Particularly important, at this stage, is the search for counterexamples that would prove the conjecture false. If no counterexample is found, the time spent searching for one is seldom wasted, since it typically generates much insight into the structure of the problem.

This brief discussion of how mathematicians often proceed is intended to explain why it can be valuable to look at models in which many layers of realism have been stripped away, leaving an end product that may seem entirely abstract to a layman. Naive positivists see no point in studying such models. For them, all ideas spring into being fully armed, like Athene from the forehead of Zeus. One should, however, compare such abstract models with the laboratory apparatus that research physicists put together when seeking to understand physical phenomena. Such laboratory apparatus will seldom be directly usable as an engineering prototype, but unless it is constructed to investigate the phenomena, nobody will ever know what engineering prototypes are worth building.

Consider, for example, Alpern's "Stationary Equilibrium for Deterministic Graphical Games." Here Alpern is experimenting with a different framework within which to study certain types of games. Traditionally, game theorists describe the rules of a game by using a tree. This is a connected graph with no loops or cycles. Such trees can be very complicated indeed, even when the game they are being used to describe is quite simple. But, for games that can return to a position that they have been in before, such complexity seems redundant. Alpern therefore studies games based on directed graphs that may have loops or cycles. Payoffs are assigned to each node, and an outcome is an infinite path through the graph, starting from a node designated as the first move. Players are assumed to evaluate such an outcome by calculating their long-run average payoff along the path. Alpern calls such an object a "deterministic graph game with time-average payoffs," or a DGA game for short.

An advantage of working with DGA games over traditional games is that one may hope to use backwards induction techniques that are clumsy or difficult when the game is "unfolded" into a traditional tree. Alpern describes how such recursive techniques can be employed and gives some examples. He considers, in particular, a duopoly in which two firms compete over time by altering their prices on alternate days and uses his techniques to find an equilibrium with cycling.

There seems much scope for further research along these lines, especially in the case when there is imperfect information. Cycles in the underlying graph then imply that information sets may be entered more than once on a play when the game is unfolded into a tree (which is outlawed in traditional discussions). It is known that for finite trees in which a play can reenter an information set, Nash equilibria definitely exist, provided that players are allowed to mix over a finite number of behavioral strategies. But what is true in general for DGA games with imperfect information?

Before introducing two further papers, something needs to be said about the current status of cooperative game theory. Half of von Neumann and Morgenstern's *Theory of Games and Economic Behavior* was devoted to this topic, and while noncooperative game theory languished in the doldrums during the fifties and early sixties, it was this strand of their pioneering work that received the lion's share of attention. In more recent years cooperative game theory has been overshadowed by a resurgence of interest in noncooperative games, and it must be admitted that progress in noncooperative game theory has been nothing less than spectacular over the last fifteen years or so. However, now the pendulum seems to be swinging back towards cooperative theory again. Perhaps, in due course, some sort of equilibrium will be achieved. There is certainly no reason why following one approach should be thought to exclude a simultaneous pursuit of the other. Indeed, John Nash advocated precisely such a simultaneous pursuit of the two approaches in a bargaining context. He saw cooperative theory as providing a simple characterization of predicted bargaining outcomes, and the noncooperative modeling of negotiation procedures as providing a means of testing such predictions. That is to say, in the spirit of this section, noncooperative bargaining models were to be seen as representing experiment substitutes for verifying or refuting cooperative bargaining theories.

Greenberg and Weber's "Stable Coalition Structures in Consecutive Games" is a typical example of the revival of interest in cooperative game theory. It updates some of the authors' earlier work on coalition formation that has found some recent applications in the theory of oligopoly.

The problem of coalition formation is one of the knottiest problems for game theory. Although it has been studied continuously since von Neumann and Morgenstern's book appeared in 1944, the theories that survive remain largely speculative. Noncooperative models of coalition formation are particularly thin on the ground. However, certain ideas from cooperative game theory seem fairly certain to be part of whatever theory of coalition formation does eventually emerge, once the dust has settled. This is elaborated by Greenberg and Weber into a notion called the "coalition structure core," which is a generalization of an idea introduced by Aumann and Drèze (1974).

A coalition structure partitions all the players in a game into disjoint coalitions. If the players within each coalition cooperate in their play of the game, each will receive a payoff. One may then ask what n-tuples x of payoffs in an n-person game are compatible with rational play and the existence of a particular coalition structure. A much-studied criterion requires that x be rejected as a possible outcome of the game if some coalition S in the structure can ensure getting more for each of its members than they get with x. The coalition S is then traditionally said to "block" the outcome x. The n-tuple x is said to lie in the coalition structure core if there exists a coalition structure within which no coalition would block it. This differs from the traditional core in that the latter places no restriction on a blocking coalition, but is of course much larger in general. For example, the coalitionproof core of a market game contains all outcomes that are Pareto-efficient and individually rational.

The coalition structure core provides a more realistic assessment of the possible outcomes of a cooperative game than the traditional core for those situations in which it is unrealistic to proceed as though coalitions were protean conglomerations that could get together or disband at the drop of a hat. However, although less exacting as a concept than the traditional core, it can still only be useful in applications for which it does not reduce to the empty set. Greenberg and Weber show that the coalition structure core is never empty for consecutive games.

Consecutive games require that the players be ordered according to some predetermined characteristic. It may be, for example, that they are politicians arranged along some left-right spectrum. A consecutive game then arises if the only coalitions that can form are connected relative to the given ordering. That is to say, the only coalitions that are admitted are those that also contain all players who lie between any two of their members. Consecutive games clearly have many potential applications. The fact that their coalition structure cores are never empty is therefore useful and significant. It would be of interest to know how far Greenberg and Weber's results can be extended to games whose communication structures require a more complex topological description, as, for example, in Myerson (1977) and Kirman, Oddou, and Weber (1986).

Maschler, Potters, and Tijs are also concerned with the core of a cooperative game. However, their "General Nucleolus and the Reduced-Game Property" does not follow Greenberg and Weber in addressing the problem of a core that might be too small; instead, it is interested in selection criteria that apply when the traditional core is too large.

Schmeidler's (1964) concept of the "nucleolus" is a selection criterion that is useful for certain purposes. For example, a community effort may result in benefits to everybody, but how much should each citizen contribute to the cost? Think of any potential attribution of the costs of this effort to the citizens. The members of any group can now evaluate the gain they make from contributing in this way to the collective project rather than undertaking it themselves. The nucleolus is a sort of "fair" cost allocation in that it minimizes the maximum of the gains made by the coalitions.

Essentially the same concept arises at the other end of the game theory spectrum in the theory of two-person zero-sum games. If a player settles for just any maximin strategy in such a game, he sacrifices the opportunity to exploit any mistakes his opponent may make. Are there alternative strategies that allow a player to exploit the foolishness of his opponent in repeated play without risking his getting less than his maximin level? A discussion of Blackwell's approach to this problem appears as an appendix in Luce and Raiffa's *Games and Decisions*, (1950) but Maschler, Potters, and Tijs trace the ideas back to Brown (1950).

These two appearances of the nucleolus in game theory seem widely separated. However, Maschler, Potters, and Tijs show how both applications and others can be tied together under a general scheme that allows an axiomatic characterization of the notion of a nucleolus. This is an intricate paper that requires some mathematical sophistication to appreciate, but it will amply repay careful study.

3.4   Description

One of the things that game theory has to offer the world is an extensive and dispassionate vocabulary within which issues of conflict and cooperation from political, social, or economic contexts can be discussed with a minimum risk of misunderstanding. This service that gamesters provide to the community is not something they think about very much. It emerges as a spin-off from their attempts to come to grips with strategic issues for which our culture provides no adequate paradigms, so that the words available to commentators force them to employ concepts that distort the realities with which they are faced.

Perhaps the major area in which the vocabulary that game theorists are inventing is likely to have a major impact on the language of our culture is in the field of information. Indeed, before von Neumann and Morgenstern's *Theory of Games and Economic Behavior* there was a whole range of informational issues about which even professional economists were unable to think clearly because they lacked the words to formulate the necessary concepts. Consider, for example, the ideas implicit in such terms as *common knowledge, risk-aversion, moral hazard, adverse selection, incentive compatibility,* and *incomplete* as opposed to *imperfect information.*

The paper that fits this category best in the current volume is Forges's "Some Thoughts on Efficiency and Information." Her concern is with the problem of mechanism design, as formulated largely by Myerson. Here a principal has the opportunity to design a game that will be played by one or more agents. The principal will have aims in mind in designing the game that she would have no difficulty in achieving if it were not for the fact that certain information the agents have is not available to her. The principal must therefore consider all the possible pieces of information the agents might have, and for each game she might design, she must predict how each possible piece of information an agent might have would affect the action he would choose to take in that game. A commonly considered case is that of a person with an object to sell who does not know the valuations placed on the object by the potential buyers, but who must design an auctioning mechanism in ignorance of this information.

This literature raises major classification problems. Holmström and Myerson (1983), for example, distinguish six possible meanings for an efficient mechanism. Yet the notion of an efficient mechanism, however construed, may not always be what is required since incentive efficient mechanisms may select outcomes that are ex post inefficient, in that the players may unanimously prefer something else. This raises the question of the extent to which renegotiation-proof mechanisms can be formulated. But what is a renegotiation-proof mechanism? As Forges explains with a minimum of mathematics and some simple examples, the classification problem requires serious attention. Her notion of "outcome renegotiation-proofness" joins other notions such as "durability" and "posterior implementation" in providing some foundations for such a classification.

3.5 Prescription

Just as doctors prescribe courses of treatment with a view to promoting the health of their patients, so social scientists are in the habit of prescribing various courses of action with a view to achieving certain aims in societies, both large and small. Game theorists are particularly well placed to offer advice on two distinct problems. The first is the obvious issue of how best to play a given game. However, the rules of a game cannot always be treated as given, and a second problem for game theorists is therefore to invent rules for the game with a view to ensuring that its play does not lead to socially undesirable outcomes, or, at least, to outcomes undesirable to those who have the power to impose the rules. This second problem, the problem of mechanism design, has already been aired in section 3.4.

Moulin's "On the Fair and Coalition-strategyproof Allocation of Private Goods" represents a different strand of the mechanism design literature. Section 3.3 mentioned the recent revival in cooperative game theory. Part of the reason for this revival is that leading exponents like Moulin are willing to consider less abstract problems than was customary in the past. Instead of confining attention to abstract sets of social states, the new cooperative game theory is often directly concerned with the nature of the goods to be redistributed and the realities of the underlying production processes.

Moulin begins with the classic result of Gibbard (1973) and Satterthwaite (1975) that, apart from certain simple cases, strategyproof mechanisms must necessarily be dictatorial. Strategyproof mechanisms are those in which it is a dominant strategy for a player to report his characteristics truthfully to the referee operating the mechanism. However, this classic result is concerned with the allocation of pure public goods. Matters are not the same with private goods. Fairness (anonymity) of the mechanism is no longer incompatible with strategyproofness but strategyproofness and efficiency are often contradictory. Moulin therefore studies the case when first-best efficiency is replaced by coalitionproofness, which can be thought of as a species of second-best efficiency. There might seem to be some confusion between fairness of the mechanism itself and fairness (envy-freeness) of the allocations it generates. However, Moulin shows that coalitionproof and fair mechanisms yield only fair outcomes, so there is no ambiguity. He gives two elegant examples of allocation problems with a single commodity in which coalitionproofness and anonymity characterize a unique mechanism. This is clearly an area in which much fruitful research is waiting to be done.

4   Gamesters Looking In

The game theory universe is like Lewis Carroll's looking-glass world. It contains phenomena that may seem very strange until one realizes that what is being mirrored is not everything that matters about some real-world phenomenon, but just one crucial aspect of it. This is why gamesters are able to look out from their sometimes crazy world and comment usefully on what is going on in real life.

Now, however, we come to the foundations of game theory in which gamesters comment on their own crazy activities and propose further, apparently bizarre projects for the future. When they get onto this topic, their conversations with each other have a tendency to resemble, not so much the famous interchange between Alice and Humpty Dumpty in which the latter argued that words should mean whatever he found it expedient for them to mean, as the interchange that would have taken place if Alice had been similarly minded. However, confusing though it may be for the layman, developing game theory from the inside is not only a vital task, it is an exciting activity for those lucky enough to be caught up in it.

The chapters in this volume that assess the current state of the art of game theory and where their authors believe it should be going are even harder to classify within the scheme of Section 3 in terms of aims. None of the Authors is sufficiently reckless to predict where game theory is going, and so the first heading will be "explanation."

4.1   Explanation

Some curious sociological divisions have grown up among those who practice game theory. The division between scientifically minded philosophers and political scientists on the one hand and economists on the other fortunately now seems almost defunct. However, it still remains true that operations researchers and economists seldom read each others' game-theoretic papers. It is perhaps more understandable that the same can also be said of mathematicians and economists. Mathematicians have been interested in expanding the areas to which powerful techniques can be applied in solving games, while most economists have been more interested in solving games for which no current techniques exist. However, the meeting in Florence at which the papers in this volume were presented seems to provide evidence that this gap between mathematicians and economists is fast closing.

The existence of such a gap is confirmed by the establishment of a large and well-defended camp of mathematicians who occupied themselves with "dynamic games" (in fact, differential games, which take place in continuous time and are usually treated by the methods of control theory). Progress in this camp over the years among these mathematicians elicited interest only from a small group of macroeconomists concerned with stabilization policies. Other economists stayed well clear of the area, doubtless because progress was for a long time confined to the two-person zero-sum case, where the question of what constitutes a solution to the game is now tolerably well understood. In the meantime, a small and lonely trail was followed by a handful of economists and operations researchers interested in dynamic, often stochastic, but not differential games. Rare excusions were made from one group to the other, such as that of Smale (1980). However, more recently, von Neumann and Morgenstern's idea that the "normal" procedure with an extensive-form game should be to reduce it to a static "strategic form" has become discredited among economists, who now take close account of the sequential structure of a game tree in their analyses. However, they have been careful not to describe their models as "dynamic games," to avoid treading on any mathematical toes.

Haurie's "From Repeated to Differential Games: How Time and Uncertainty Pervade the Theory of Games" is one of numerous signposts that such artificial distinctions have now outlived their usefulness. Mathematicians have begun to take cognizance of the solution concepts developed by economists for games with discrete dynamics. Economists have begun to recognize that they are playing with one hand tied behind their backs when they deny themselves the power of optimal control theory. Haurie explains how the ideas from these different traditions may be interwoven to create a new and more integrated discipline that might perhaps more legitimately be entitled "dynamic game theory" than what has passed under this heading in the past. He points to many difficulties along the way. In particular, he argues that where qualitative results for simplistic repeated games are available, they can often be extended to less trivially dynamic, that is, sequential or market games, although the full passage to stochastic differential games requires care. This passage to genuinely dynamic games is important since, as Haurie observes with gallic panache, "L'histoire ne se répète pas, elle bégaie."[3]

Brams, Kilgour, and Davis's "Unraveling in Games of Sharing and Exchange" also illustrates the breaking down of traditional discipline barriers between game theorists: the first author is a political scientist and his coauthors are mathematicians. The authors' aim is to explain something of what is going on when rational agents find it impossible to "agree to disagree." Economists will be familiar with the result of Milgrom and Stokey (1982), which postulates a world in which it is common knowledge that everyone has the same beliefs about uncertain events, and in which risk-averse agents have traded to a Pareto-efficient outcome. Each agent now receives some private information. Can anyone now exploit their inside information? The answer is no in a rational world, because the mere fact that someone is willing to trade with you reveals enough about what he knows for you to deduce whether the trade is disadvantageous.

Such conclusions retain an air of mystery when they are told as part of an equilibrium story. To dispel the mystery, one needs to do some unpackaging in order to recast the tale as a blow-by-blow account of the process by means of which the agents form their beliefs and make their decisions. Brams, Kilgour, and Davis take their inspiration from mathematician Littlewood's *Mathematical Miscellany* (1953). This includes numerous paradoxes and mind-benders that seem to have found their way into the collective unconscious to surface later in various shapes and forms. (In particular, it includes a sanitized version of the story of the adulterous cannibals said to have prompted Aumann's work on common knowledge.)

Brams, Kilgour, and Davis intend the word "unravelling" to refer to the process by means of which players are able to find their way to conclusions that are often surprising by closely tracing "If-I-think-that-he-thinks-that-I-think- ..." chains of reasoning from some given core of common knowledge. Instead of stating some of their conclusions, which would be like giving away the villain to some about to read a whodunit, they suggest a new poser. In their section 5 they tell us of a situation in which a player can seemingly guarantee getting a payoff that exceeds his Nash equilibrium payoff. How is this to be reconciled with the fact that a player always gets at least his security level in a Nash equilibrium? Here Alice would undoubtedly have been less happy than Humpty Dumpty with the use of the term *Nash equilibrium*.

The final chapter for this section is Samuelson's "Does Evolution Eliminate Dominated Strategies?," which aims to explain to us what we are doing when we delete weakly dominated strategies in a game. Samuelson argues that, some of the time at least, we don't know what we are doing. He begins with an evolutionary model, based on that of Kandori, Mailath, and Rob (1990), in which both selection and mutation appear explicitly. Mutations to all possible strategies occur with a probability that is allowed to become vanishingly small. He shows that, for certain very simple and nonpathological games, the long-run limiting distribution of surviving strategies for one of the players may have support entirely confined to weakly dominated strategies.

If the examples of the type constructed by Samuelson and others are genuinely relevant, then those who hold that the successive deletion of weakly dominated strategies is one of the pillars supporting the enterprise of game theory will have a simple choice. They can deny that their type of game theory is relevant to evolutionary questions. Or they can remove the pillar and see whether the sky falls down. Our own view is that the time has come to abandon the idea that we can get by with just one variety of game theory. Even if one takes an evolutionary line, one cannot expect different evolutionary processes to lead to the same equilibria. Still less can one expect evolution always to mimic the results of rational introspection (see Binmore 1990), especially if combined with some preplay communication between the players. However, there are "money-burning" examples from the signaling literature that cast doubt on the successive deletion of weakly dominated strategies even in the purest of playing environments. There is, therefore, something perhaps to be said for denying that every game-theoretic concept is universally applicable while simultaneously demoting the successive deletion of weakly dominated strategies from its status as one of the pillars of wisdom, even in the branches of the subject where its defenders think their position is strongest.

However, whatever the truth on such deep matters may be, it is plain that game theory is in desperate need of further examples (and experimental evidence) to provide clues about what can happen in simple games when the players do not think things out a priori but find their way to a strategy by some evolutionary process. The set of possible candidates for interesting evolutionary processes, whether biological, social, or economic, is very large. But until we have enough data to pick out some viable processes to serve as canonical objects of study, we seem doomed to flail around in the dark. Perhaps Samuelson's paper and others in the same vein will help to create a much-needed fashion for work in this area.

4.2   Investigation

The keystone concept of noncooperative game theory is that of a Nash equilibrium. However, the notion faces two major difficulties. The first is of a foundational nature. *Why* should rational players restrict their attention to Nash equilibria? Bernheim (1984) and Pearce (1984) suggest that there are no good reasons at all. If all that is given about the players is that it is common knowledge that they are all Bayesian rational, then all that can be said is that the strategies chosen will be "rationalizable."

The second major difficulty with the Nash equilibrium concept, or for that matter with any equilibrium concept including rationalizability, is what to do when the theory does not come up with a unique prescription for rational play. It is perhaps this equilibrium selection problem that is the major stumbling block to further progress in game theory. The volume contains two very different chapters devoted to this question.

The first of the papers on equilibrium selection is Carlsson and van Damme's "Equilibrium Selection in Stag Hunt Games." It is traditional among game theorists to seek to add some luster to their strivings by attributing a certain noncooperative game to the philosopher Jean-Jacques Rousseau. It is doubtful that this game really gets across the message that Rousseau's stag hunt story from the *Inequality of Man* was intended to convey. One can just as plausibly argue that Rousseau was urging us to cooperate in the Prisoner's Dilemma. However, what is important for game theorists is that the game poses the equilibrium selection problem in a particularly acute form.

In the Stag Hunt Game, each of n players may independently act cooperatively or selfishly. The selfish strategy yields a fixed payoff regardless of the choices of the other players. The payoff for the cooperative strategy depends on how many other players choose to cooperate: the return to cooperating is high when the number of cooperators is large and low when the number of cooperators is small. The game has two Nash equilibria in pure strategies. In the first all players act cooperatively. In the second they all act selfishly. The cooperative equilibrium is *payoff-dominant*, that is to say, everyone gets more at the cooperative equilibrium than at the selfish equilibrium. But the cooperative equilibrium is risky because a player who cooperates when others are selfish will get his fingers burned. Indeed, if the selfish payoff is sufficiently large, the selfish equilibrium is *risk-dominant* in the formal sense proposed by Harsanyi and Selten (1988).

Harsanyi and Selten's notion of risk-dominance can be viewed as a generalization of the criterion used by Nash in making a selection from the large set of Nash equilibria that arise in the model of simultaneous unilateral demands that Nash (1950) used as a simple model of bargaining. Both ideas involve maximizing a Nash product. Nash defended his selection criterion by appealing to a perturbed version of the simple Nash demand game, in which players are not entirely certain what payoffs will follow after a given pair of demands has been made. Carlsson and van Damme have adapted Nash's technique to provide an equilibrium selection theory that is applicable to a much wider variety of games—including the Stag Hunt Game. Very roughly, each player knows the payoffs of a game only subject to some noise. Harsanyi's "purification" of mixed Nash equilibria begins with a similar step, but in Carlsson and van Damme, the noise is correlated between the players. The perturbed game generated by the noise is a game of incomplete information whose equilibria converge to equilibria of the original game as the noise is allowed to become negligibly small. However, not all equilibria of the original game are limits of equilibria of the perturbed game. Those which fail to survive Carlsson and van Damme's procedure are then "deselected."

How does Carlsson and van Damme's equilibrium selection criterion compare with various alternatives that have been proposed? It is to answer such a question that Carlsson and van Damme concentrate their attention on the Stag Hunt Game in the current volume. They show that four different equilibrium selection criteria, to which varying degrees of credence have been accorded, all give different answers when applied to the Stag Hunt Game with more than two players. (This allows them to demonstrate in passing that their own theory is not only applicable to games with just two players, although their previous work has been confined to this case.) They do not insist that their own theory is superior to its rivals. Doubtless they are right to regard the equilibrium selection problem as remaining open. Nevertheless, it is striking how much less ad hoc their procedure seems when compared with some of the alternatives.

Bacharach's "Variable Universe Games" is about games of pure coordination. For example, each time we drive to work in the morning, we make a decision about whether to drive on the left or right, as do the various other players in this game. There are two Nash equilibria in pure strategies: one in which we all drive on the left, and one in which we all drive on the right. We know which of the two equilibria to use because the labeling of the strategies has cultural significance for us. In his celebrated *Strategy of Conflict* (1960), Schelling uses the words "salient" and "focal" in discussing this issue, but the precise meaning of these notions is very slippery. If I am a rational person, what exactly is it that I have to know before I can confidently label an equilibrium as focal?

Bacharach's answer goes something like this. Our culture determines the manner in which we perceive a game. That is to say, the features of a society that determine what is or is not salient in that society operate through the manner in which the players frame the gamelike situations in which they find themselves placed. If we model the games as they are perceived by the players, rather than as they are perceived by an outside analyst, then it ceases to be mysterious why one equilibrium is found to be focal. On the contrary, with some simple rationality postulates, Bacharach shows that it is inevitable that the focal equilibrium will be selected.

It is not a reasonable criticism of Bacharach's approach that it reduces the question to sociological and psychological issues. The necessity for such a reduction was apparent from the beginning. If there is to be criticism, it should perhaps be directed at whether the sociopsychological issues are formulated in a manner that makes it possible to conduct worthwhile experimental work using the theory as a basis. And on this topic, the reader must judge for himself.

Hammond's "Aspects of Rationalizable Behavior" discusses Pearce's (1984) notion of "cautious rationalizability" in some detail, but most readers will find their attention captured by Hammond's discussion of the foundational questions raised by the literature on rationalizability.

The idea of rationalizability is very simple. It is taken to be common knowledge that all players in a game are Bayesian-rational. In some games this has the consequence that it becomes common knowledge that certain strategies will not be played. Once these impossible strategies have been deleted, the same procedure can then be carried out with the reduced game that remains. The strategies that survive all iterations of this procedure are said to be "rationalizable." In two-player games an application of von Neumann and Morgenstern's minimax theorem shows that rationalizable strategies are identical with those which survive the iterated deletion of strongly dominated strategies. (Hammond therefore traces the idea back to Farquarhson's Ph.D. dissertation of 1969, but he might as well have gone back to Luce and Raiffa 1950 or before.) In games with more than two players, the considerations become more complex. Should we, for example, allow players to believe that the strategies of their opponents are correlated? Hammond argues that to do this is important when individuals are not forced into the straitjacket of having common expectations. He further argues that the set of all correlated rationalizable strategies can be found by removing all strictly dominated strategies for each player iteratively. The set of all correlated "cautiously rationalizable" strategies can be found by "cautiously" iterating the rule of removing weakly dominated strategies. In particular, when discussing cautiously rationalizable strategies, Hammond shows that these are unconstrained best responses to cautiously rationalizable beliefs.

Section 4.1 mentioned that the current stream of opinion among game theorists has turned aside from the notion that the successive deletion of weakly dominated strategies is always legitimate. Indeed, Samuelson's "Does Evolution Eliminate Dominated Strategies?" casts doubt on the legitimacy of deleting weakly dominated strategies at all. His paper is admittedly not immediately relevant to Hammond's paper, since the former is about evolutive processes that get to equilibrium through some trial-and-error process, while the latter is about eductive processes by which players think their way to a conclusion. Nevertheless, two very different attitudes to game theory are apparent in what these two different authors take for granted.

Perhaps the fundamental point that divides such authors can be found in Hammond's assertion that the common expectations that support equilibria in games are supposed to be determined *endogenously* by the game. One certainly would not want to argue that this must necessarily hold in an evolutive context, but Samuelson would presumably deny such a proposition even in an eductive context. For example, one would not wish to argue that the history of play that led to a subgame H of a game G is necessarily irrelevant to how rational players will behave in the subgame H. So why should one argue that the common culture which players acquire through playing the same "game of life" is irrelevant to how they will play G? It is true that rationalizers like Hammond create a cleaner theory by denying that the players should have any prior information about each other beyond the fact that it is common knowledge that they are Bayesian-rational, but Samuelson would presumably say that this lack of realism is too high a price to pay for a clean theory.

There seems little prospect of closing the gap between those who think like Hammond and those who think like Samuelson. However, Hammond's paper does the community a service in laying bare the philosophy of at least one rationalizer. The discussion of the "money-burning" examples, to which Hammond is led by his need to defend the iterated deletion of weakly dominated strategies, will also be appreciated by those unfamiliar with the controversy. However, readers will need to make up their own minds on whether Hammond is right in thinking that we need not be disturbed by the apparently paradoxical outcomes that emerge in such examples, and indeed, the last word has clearly not been said on the deletion of weakly dominated strategies.

4.3   Description

The chapter in this volume that fits most nearly into this category is Harsanyi's "Normative Validity and Meaning of von Neumann–Morgenstern Utilities." In this chapter Harsanyi sets himself the task of separating a number of commonly made interpretations of von Neumann–Morgenstern utility functions into those which are justified by the axioms and those for which no proper basis exists. Perhaps the most frequently made error that he identifies is the notion that von Neumann–Morgenstern utilities measure how much people like to gamble. This is a view that has been expressed by a number of weighty authorities. But, as Harsanyi points out, if von Neumann–Morgenstern utilities were measuring the pleasure or pain that people may take in the *process* of gambling, then the axiom about compound lotteries would not necessarily be appropriate because people who enjoy the activity of gambling for its own sake would presumably prefer a lottery that is broken up into many small steps. This is one of those observations that is only obvious *after* it has been made.

Harsanyi argues further that, far from the values of a von Neumann–Morgenstern utility function being determined by the decision-maker's attitude to risk, these values are determined by the substitution and complementary relations that hold between the commodity bundles on which the utility function is defined. It is therefore these relations which determine the decision-maker's attitude to risk taking rather than the other way round.

Harsanyi is also instructive on what von Neumann–Morgenstern utility functions have to say about intensities of preference. However, whether his definition of an intensity of preference accords with the standard intuition is something the reader will have to judge for himself.

4.4   Prescription

Only Binmore's "De-Bayesing Game Theory" is rash enough to tell game theorists where they should be going, or rather, where they should not be going. Binmore points out that Savage explicitly denied the validity of some applications of his theory that modern Bayesians take for granted. In particular, Savage (1951) argued that his assumptions make sense only in a "small world" context. Binmore argues that this means, for example, that it is a mistake to identify Bayesian updating with genuine rational learning. Using a version of the halting problem for Turing machines, he argues more generally that the foundations of game theory necessarily require the analyst to work in a "big world." If so, real progress in the foundations of game theory will have to wait on the development of formal techniques for dealing with the vexed problem of scientific induction.

If Binmore is right, much recent work on the foundations of game theory is misconceived. Some of our castles have been built in the air. However, we may take some comfort in the fact that mathematics built castles in the air for thousands of years with great success.

5 Conclusion

In *The Prince* Machiavelli tells us to study power as it is, not as we would have it be. Perhaps there may be those who suspect that the gamesters who met in the Florence of 1991 would have done well to heed the advice of their great predecessor. If so, their attention should be drawn to the words of the world's second great authority on realism. As von Clausewitz ([1832] 1976) explains:

A genuine theorist is like a swimming teacher, who makes his students practice motions on dry land that are meant to be performed in water. To those not thinking of swimming, the motions will appear grotesque and exaggerated. By the same token, theorists who have never swum, or who have not learned to generalise from experience, are impractical and even ridiculous: they teach only what is common knowledge: how to walk.

Gamesters are genuine theorists, and this is why their papers are grotesque and exaggerated. Nevertheless, their influence on how we think about problems of social interaction seems likely to continue in the future at the same exponential rate that we have seen in the recent past. Indeed, it is probably not too much to hope that outsiders will be able to profit from the account of gamesters' activities given in this book to shed new light on the real phenomena that they analyze, for, as Bacon said some 400 years ago, "Lookers on many times see more than gamesters."

Notes

1. The center was founded in 1990 under the directorship of Professor Piero Tani. The address for correspondence is Centro Interuniversitario per la Teoria dei Giochi e le Applicazioni, Dipártimento di Scienze Economiche, Università di Firenze, via Curtatone 1, 50123 Firenze, Italy.

2. See Maynard Smith's *Evolution and the Theory of Games* (1982).

3. History doesn't repeat itself, it stutters.

24   Binmore, Kirman, and Tani

References

Aumann, R. and J. Drèze. 1974. "Cooperative Games with Coalition Structures." *International Journal of Game Theory* 3:217–314.

Bernheim, D. 1984. "Rationalizable Strategic Behavior." *Econometrica* 52:1007–1028.

Binmore, K. G. 1990. *Essays on the Foundations of Game Theory*. Oxford: Basil Blackwell.

Brown, G. 1950. "A Method for Choosing among Optimum Strategies." Rand project.

Gibbard, A. 1973. "Manipulation of Voting Schemes: a General Result." *Econometrica* 41:587–601.

Harsanyi, J., and R. Selten. 1988. *A General Theory of Equilibrium Selection in Games*, Cambridge: M.I.T. Press.

Holmström, B., and R. Myerson. 1983. "Efficient and Durable Decision Rules with Incomplete Information."*Econometrica* 51:1799–1819

Kandori, M., G. Mailath, and R. Rob. 1990. "Learning, Mutation and Long-Run Equilibria in Games." University of Pennsylvania discussion paper.

Kirman, A., C. Oddou, and S. Weber. 1986. "Stochastic Communication and Coalition Formation. *Econometrica*: 54:129–138.

Littlewood J. E. 1953. *Mathematical Miscellany*. London: Cambridge University Press. Edited by B. Bollobas.

Luce, R., and H. Raiffa. 1950. *Games and Decisions*. New York: Wiley.

Maynard Smith, J. 1982. *Evolution and the Theory of Games*. Cambridge: Cambridge University Press.

Milgrom, P., and N. Stokey. 1982. "Information, Trade, and Common Knowledge." *Journal of Economic Theory* 26:17–27.

Myerson, R. B. 1977. "Graphs and Cooperation in Games." *Mathematics of Operations Research* 2:225–229.

Nash, J. 1950. "The Bargaining Problem." *Econometrica* 18:155–162.

Pearce, D. 1984. "Rationalizable Strategic Behavior and the Problem of Perfection." *Econometrica* 52:1029–1050.

Raiffa, H. 1953. "Arbitration Schemes for Generalized Two-Person Games." In H. Kuhn and A. Tucker, eds., *Contributions to the Theory of Games II*. Princeton: Princeton University Press.

Rubinstein, A. 1982. "Perfect Equilibrium in a Bargaining Model." *Econometrica* 50:97–109.

Satterthwaite, M. A. 1975. "Strategy-proofness and Arrow's Conditions: Existence and Correspondence Theorems for Voting Procedures and Social Welfare Functions." *Journal of Economic Theory* 10:198–217.

Savage, L. 1951. *The Foundations of Statistics.* New York: Wiley

Schelling, T. 1960. *The Strategy of Conflict.* Cambridge: Harvard University Press.

Schmeidler, D. 1964. "The Nucleolus of a Characteristic Function Game." *S.I.A.M. Journal of Applied Mathematics* 17:1163–1170.

Shapley, L. 1964. "Some Topics in Two-Person Games." In M. Dresher et al. eds., *Advances in Game Theory.* Princeton: Princeton University Press.

Smale, S. 1980. "The Prisoner's Dilemma and Dynamical Systems Associated to Non-cooperative Games." *Econometrica* 48:1617–1634.

von Clausewitz, C. [1832] 1976. *On War.* Princeton: Princeton University Press.

1 Cognition and Framing in Sequential Bargaining for Gains and Losses

Colin F. Camerer, Eric J. Johnson, Talia Rymon, and Sankar Sen

Introduction

Noncooperative game-theoretic models of sequential bargaining give an underpinning to cooperative solution concepts derived from axioms, and have proved useful in applications (see Osborne and Rubinstein 1990). But experimental studies of sequential bargaining with discounting have generally found systematic deviations between the offers people make and perfect equilibrium offers derived from backward induction (e.g., Ochs and Roth 1989).

We have extended this experimental literature in two ways. First, we used a novel software system to record the information subjects looked at while they bargained. Measuring patterns of information search helped us draw inferences about how people think, testing as directly as possible whether people use backward induction to compute offers. Second, we compared bargaining over gains that shrink over time (because of discounting) to equivalent bargaining over losses that expand over time.

In the games we studied, two players bargain by making a finite number of alternating offers. A unique subgame-perfect equilibrium can be computed by backward induction. The induction begins in the last period and works forward. Our experiments use a three-round game with a pie of $5.00 and a 50-percent discount factor (so the pie shrinks to $2.50 and $1.25 in the second and third rounds). In the perfect equilibrium the first player offers the second player $1.25 and keeps $3.75.[1]

In previous experiments (including ours; see Johnson et al. 1991) subjects actually offer the second player something between the $1.25 equilibrium and $2.50, an equal split of the initial pie. Mean offers are around $2.00. Lower offers, including equilibrium offers of $1.25, are often rejected.

In our expanding-loss experiments subjects began with $5 for each round. Then the players bargained over division of a loss of $5.00 in the first round, a loss of $7.50 in the second round, and a loss of $8.75 in the third round. If they reached no agreement, each lost their $5.00 and the game was over. By adding the $5 stakes to the potential losses at each stage, it is easy to see that the shrinking-gain and expanding-loss games are equivalent if players maximize net wealth. Using backward induction, we derive the same equilibrium as in the shrinking gain game: player 1 offers player 2 a loss of $3.75 (a net gain of $1.25 when the stake is added) and accepts a loss of $1.25.

Comparing behavior in gain-and-loss games tests whether players bargain over final wealth positions, or are instead sensitive to changes in wealth (as suggested by "framing effects" in studies of individual choices, e.g., Kahneman and Tversky 1979). If players "segregate" their $5 stake from the losses they bargain over, and react differently to losses than to gains, then behavior in the two games might be different, even though the games have the same implications for net wealth.

Our work is part of a broader attempt to identify whether there are systematic deviations between actual behavior in games and behavior predicted by solution concepts. The hope is that the study of such deviations might throw light on the basic reasoning processes players use.[2] The presumption is that bounded rationality might cause players to reason differently than theorists do. (Our experiments also shed light on how players learn, if they do not reason game-theoretically.) The two-person alternating-offer bargaining we study is a fruitful setting for searching for deviations because the backward induction that underlies perfect equilibrium calculations is difficult.

We suspect there are three classes of deviations from game-theoretic reasoning: (1) players do not look forward and backward sufficiently; (2) players do not reason sophisticatedly about the choices of others; and (3) players violate expected utility maximization (much as they do in making individual choices). Our experiments test for deviations of the first and third type.

Explaining Observed Anomalies: Fairness vs. Learning

Observed departures from equilibrium bargaining have two possible sources. *Fairness* theories account for the departures by assuming that play is in equilibrium, but players have a preference for fair rules or a utility for fairness (e.g., Bolton 1991). (Rejections of offers above $1.25 among player

2s suggests a *dis*utility for *un*fairness, which might induce an apparent utility for fairness among player 1s.) *Learning* theories account for the observed departures by suggesting that players do not initially understand how the structure of the game conveys bargaining power. Confused, or naive, players resort to conventions of fairness, but experience can teach them how the game's structure creates bargaining power; then they will offer equilibrium divisions (with no concern for fairness).

There is evidence to support both views. In ultimatum games with one round, or dictator games in which player 1 dictates a division player 2 has to accept, players do *not* always offer small sums to others, as perfect equilibrium based on self-interest predicts; many offers are equal splits (e.g., Thaler 1988; Forsythe et al. 1988; but see Hoffman et al. 1991). These data suggest fairness plays some role.

Evidence consistent with the learning hypothesis comes from three experiments on sequential bargaining in which convergence to equilibrium offers occurred with suitable experience. In Binmore, Shaked, and Sutton 1985 experience taught player 2s to make equilibrium offers in a second bargaining trial, when they were placed in the role of player 1. In Harrison and McCabe 1992 offers converged to the perfect equilibrium in several repetitions of a three-stage game, when subjects also played the second-stage subgame between each repetition of the three-stage game. In Neelin, Sonnenschein, and Spiegel 1988 economics students, who probably had some exposure to game theory, chose the perfect equilibrium immediately in a two-stage game.

Our intention is not to resolve the debate over the two interpretations. Instead, we cast the learning hypothesis as an assertion that players do not reason game-theoretically at first, and we test that assertion directly. Our evidence does not resolve the debate because players who do *not* backward induct might be concerned about fairness, too. But if backward induction is a poor description of players' thinking, then any theory which claims the data are *equilibrium* offers, reflecting both fairness and a cognitive understanding based on backward induction, is falsified.

Framing Effects in Sequential Bargaining

An interesting question is whether subjects bargain in the same way over the division of shrinking gains and the division of expanding losses from a stake. Prospect theory (Kahneman and Tversky 1979) accounts for differences between gains and losses which result in the same net wealth, by assuming that people value outcomes compared to a reference point. Then outcomes can be expressed as positive or negative deviations, gains or losses, depending on the "frame" (or reference point) one adopts. Inducing gains and losses by allowing a reference point is different from the orthodox approach, in which people have utility over net wealth, in two ways: (1) people are assumed to have diminishing sensitivity to increasing changes and (2) they are assumed to be more sensitive to losses than to gains (or "loss-averse"). Diminishing sensitivity implies a value function that is concave for gains (corresponding to diminishing marginal utility) and convex for losses (diminishing marginal *dis*utility), reflecting in shape at the origin. Reflection implies that people will take risks when the possible outcomes are all losses.

Many applications of prospect theory have focused on the framing effects of gains and losses. For example, Bazerman (1983) compared the efficiency of bargains achieved by subjects when outcomes were formulated as gains or as losses. His subjects were more likely to disagree when bargaining over losses, consistent with the principle that subjects are more risk-seeking in the domain of losses. Similarly, if our subjects are more risk-seeking in the domain of losses, we expect to see more rejected offers in the expanding-loss game.

Weg and Zwick (1991) studied sequential bargaining over gains and losses when a *fixed* cost is imposed each period (rather than a percentage cost, due to discounting, as in our setup). They found no difference in bargaining over gains and losses. Furthermore, their results, and experiments by Rapoport, Weg, and Felsenthal (1990), suggest that behavior in fixed-cost games is much better predicted by perfect equilibrium than behavior in discounting games is.

Methodology

Subjects were Wharton undergraduates recruited from business or economics classes, or from general sign-up sheets posted around the campus. Ten students met in our lab at a certain time. The methods in the gain-and-loss sessions were the same, except subjects in loss sessions were given $60 at the start, from which losses were later subtracted. The $60 stake represents $5 in each of eight rounds, plus a $20 flat payment. We gave subjects the entire stake at the beginning of the experiment, and encouraged them to put it in their pockets, so they would be more likely to mentally segregate the stake from subsequent losses.

An experimenter read instructions aloud to make them common knowledge. Afterwards, subjects worked through several examples (balanced to avoid biasing their responses) and took a quiz to ensure they understood the instructions.

Each group of ten subjects played eight three-round alternating-offer bargaining games, with a different anonymous opponent each time. This general design helps subjects to learn from "stationary replication" of the game, while avoiding the reputation effects that might arise if two subjects were playing each other repeatedly and knew it.

At the end of the sessions, subjects were paid half of the dollar amounts they actually earned from bargaining, in cash. In the loss sessions, subjects physically paid us back some of their initial stake.

Recording Information Search with MOUSELAB

The novelty of our experiments in this study, and in Johnson et al. 1991, is that we recorded the information search of the players.

Subjects were not told the pie sizes in each of the three stages. Instead, the pie sizes were hidden behind boxes on a computer screen, shown in figure 1.1. The computer screen has six boxes. Behind each box is the amount of the pie in a round (left-hand column boxes) or the role of the subject in a round[3] (right-hand column boxes), for each of the three rounds of the game. To see what is in a box, subjects use a mouse to move a cursor

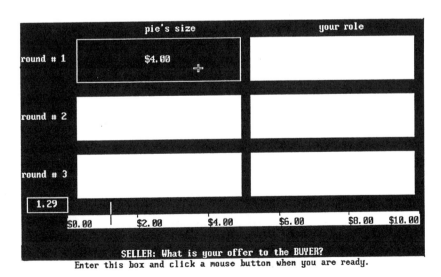

Figure 1.1
The MOUSELAB display of the shrinking-pie game subjects saw

into the box. Once the cursor enters the box, the box automatically opens, revealing the pie size. In figure 1.1, for example, the player opens the first box and sees that the first-round pie is a loss of $4.00.

The computer system we use, called MOUSELAB, records the location of the cursor every 60 milliseconds, giving a fine-grained measure of the time when each box is entered and exited. With these data we can study the order in which boxes were opened, and how long each box was open.

Measuring patterns of information search provides an indirect way of learning about cognitive processes that are not directly observable. Think of the brain as a factory that produces decisions from raw materials (information). If we cannot observe the production process in the factory, the next best thing is to observe the flow of raw materials into it (information into the brain): the order in which materials arrive, how long they are used in the production process, and so forth. A theory about how materials are assembled (or how information is combined to reach a decision) can be tested indirectly by observing the flow of materials.

Results

We conducted three sessions comparable to those reported in Johnson et al. 1991 with 10 subjects and 8 three-round games (or "trials"), for a total of 120 observations.

We will first discuss and compare the offers players made in the gain-and-loss games, and how often offers were rejected. We then will turn to the information search data revealed by MOUSELAB.

Offers, Rejections, and Counteroffers

Three important stylized facts[4] have emerged from alternating-offer bargaining experiments (e.g., Ochs and Roth 1989):

(1) Subjects do not choose equilibrium divisions. The average offer lies somewhere between equal split and equilibrium.

(2) In equilibrium no offers should be rejected, but some are. (About half of the equilibrium offers are rejected in gains, and most of them are rejected in losses.)

(3) *Most* counteroffers (about 80% in gains and 52% in losses) are "disadvantageous": they give less to the person making the offer than he or she previously rejected.

Our first concern is whether these stylized facts are replicated in our experiments. Figures 1.2a and 1.2b, for gains and losses respectively, show histograms of offers made in the first round (pooling across sessions and trials) and plots of rejected first round offers versus resulting second-round counteroffers. (To make the gain data comparable to the loss data, all offered losses were transformed into $5 minus the offer).

In the gain domain the average offer is $2.11. The equal-split point ($2.50) and equilibrium prediction ($1.25) are marked on the figures. Most offers are closer to the equal split than to the equilibrium, but only a few are within a dime of the equal split. The shaded portion of each bar indicates the number of rejected offers. Offers were rejected 10.8 percent of the time in gains, a rate comparable to the rejection rates found in prior experiments. Note that equilibrium offers (between $1.20 and $1.40) are rare, and are rejected about half the time.

In the loss domain the average offer was $2.22 (i.e., player 1 offered player 2 a loss of −$2.78, leaving her with a net gain of $2.22). Offers were rejected 22.5 percent of the time, and low offers were very frequently rejected. For example, gain offers of less than $1.80 were accepted about half the time (see figure 1.2a), but loss offers giving player 2 a net payment less than $1.80 were rejected all but once (see figure 1.2b). Offers were also much more dispersed in the expanding-loss game than in the shrinking-gain game. In the loss domain there are several offers *above* the equal split (indicating player 1's offer to accept more than half the initial loss) and *below* the perfect equilibrium.

First-round rejections result in a second round of play. The right panel of figure 1.2a shows first-round offers rejected by player 2 (vertical axis) plotted against counteroffers player 2 proposed for herself in the second round (horizontal axis). A point above the diagonal line indicates a case where player 2 rejected an offer (e.g., $1.80) then proposed a division of the second-round pie which gave her even less ($1.25). Figure 1.2a shows that 85 percent of second-round offers are disadvantageous, falling above the diagonal line. This striking frequency of disadvantageous counteroffers is close to the fraction observed in earlier studies. However, in the loss domain only 52 percent of the counteroffers are disadvantageous.

Dark circles in figures 1.2a and 1.2b indicate second-round offers which were rejected. In the gain domain 23 percent (3/14) of second-round offers are rejected; in the loss domain, 37 percent (10/27) are rejected. (Two of the three subsequent third-round offers were rejected in the gain domain, and eight of ten in the loss domain.)

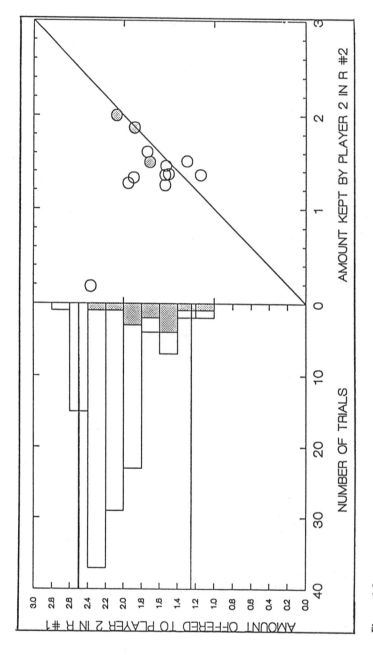

Figure 1.2a
Histogram of first-round offers and scatterplot of offers vs. counteroffers, shrinking-gain game

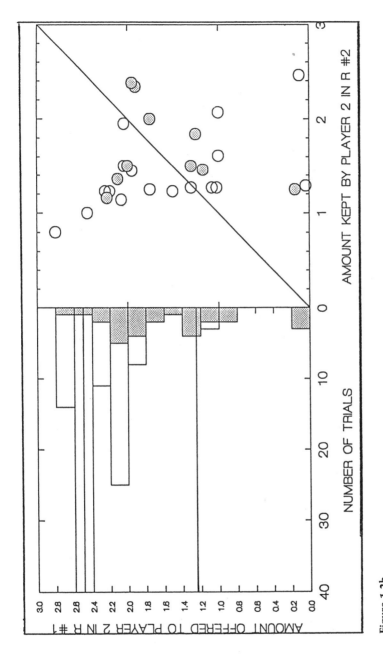

Figure 1.2b
Histogram of first-round offers and scatterplot of offers vs. counteroffers, expanding-loss game

These results roughly replicate the stylized facts discovered in earlier experiments: Mean offers lie between equal split and perfect equilibrium; a substantial minority of offers (10–20%) are rejected; and most counter-offers are disadvantageous. However, in the expanding-loss games offers are more dispersed, more offers are rejected, and fewer counteroffers are disadvantageous.

Information Search: Theory

We examine three measures of information search: (1) *number of acquisitions* per box (number of times each box is opened in a period); (2) *total time examining payoff*, or looking time, per box (amount of clock time each box is open in a period[5]); and (3) *number of transitions* from one specific box to another.

Before presenting data, it is useful to ask: If subjects were using back-ward induction to compute perfect equilibrium offers, what would their pattern of information search look like?

One possible answer is that equilibrium analysis predicts only *outcomes* (equilibrium offers); it says nothing about the *process* by which outcomes are derived. We think this answer is unproductive and wrong[6] If we test only the theory's outcome predictions, it is clearly rejected. We turn to process predictions as a way to see where the theory fails. If we are not allowed to specify the theory as a process and test it with information search data, we are left with a rejected theory and no obvious way of figuring out why it failed.

Players using backward induction to calculate equilibrium offers might search for information as follows:

(1) First look at the third-round payoff, and figure out the equilibrium offer in that round. (This calculation is simplest.)

(2) Then look at the second-round payoff, and figure out the equilibrium offer in that round. This calculation will take more time, and may require subjects to glance back and forth between the second- to the third-round boxes.

(3) Finally, look at the first-round payoff.[7]

Thus, we take equilibrium analysis to predict: transitions from box to box will be predominantly backward transitions, from the nth-round box to the $(n-1)$th-round box; the longest looking time will be in the second box; looking times in the first- and third-round boxes will be shorter.

The reader may object to our characterization of the information search process that is inherent in equilibrium analysis. We are eager to hear alternative characterizations. We also derived an *empirical* characterization of equilibrium information search by training a group of subjects in backward induction (see Johnson et al. 1991) and rewarding them for computing the perfect equilibrium offer. Those subjects looked mostly at the second and third boxes, and moved backward (from future round boxes to current ones) more often than forward.

There is no obvious prediction from game theory about how bargaining over losses and gains will differ, either in offers or in search for information. However, the principle of loss-aversion (losses are more painful than equivalent-sized gains are pleasurable) suggests that people might sacrifice more time and effort—they will work harder—to avoid losses in bargaining than to reap gains. For example, Maule (1989) found that people who were asked to speak aloud while making a choice spoke more when making choices involving losses rather than gains. Similarly, we suspect our subjects might spend more time processing information revealed by boxes, opening boxes, and making transitions between boxes, when bargaining over losses instead of gains.

Information Search before Player 1's First-Round Offer

We start our analysis of information search patterns by studying information search by player 1 subjects in the first round of each game (pooled across all eight trials of all three experimental sessions). Table 1.1 presents these data for the loss domain (for the gain domain data see Johnson et al. 1991).

In both domains most of the looking time (12.91 seconds out of 20.82 total seconds in gains, and 24.17 seconds out of 32.97 total seconds in losses) is spent looking at the first-round pie size. Half as much time in gain, and less than a fourth in loss, is spent looking at the second round. Only 1

Table 1.1
Information search measures, player 1's first-round offer (all trials), expanding-loss game

Round	Number of	Total Time	Transitions		
(loss)	Acquisitions	Examining Payoff	1	2	3
Round 1 ($5.00)	4.10	24.17	—	1.75	0.64
Round 2 ($7.50)	2.85	5.40	1.20	—	1.20
Round 3 ($8.25)	2.25	3.42	0.64	0.68	—

second in gains and 3 seconds in losses are spent looking at the third-round pie size. In fact, in 10 percent of the trial in gain and 14 percent in loss the players did not even open the third-round box (although they opened the first-round box in *every* trial). Without opening each box, players cannot possibly be calculating equilibrium offers by using backward induction.

Notice that each box is opened about 2–4 times each trial in both domains. These data suggest subjects are opening and reopening boxes frequently, rather than memorizing the numbers in the boxes. The pattern of transitions between boxes is shown in the last three columns of table 1.1. Entries show the average number of transitions from the row box to the column box. (For example, players moved from the round 3 box to the round 2 box an average of .68 times per trial.) Contrary to the backward induction prediction, there are always more forward transitions (above the diagonal) than backward ones (below the diagonal).

The pattern of search evident in table 1.1 does not conform to our characterization of equilibrium search. Most looking time is concentrated on the first-round pie, with decreasing attention paid to second- and third-round pies, and subjects make forward transitions rather than backward ones. Figure 1.3 is an icon graph which displays the information processing measures given in table 1.1 (marked LOSS), and corresponding measures for the shrinking-gain game results (marked GAIN) reported in Johnson et al. 1991. Each box corresponds to the approximate position of the three pay-off boxes on the MOUSELAB computer display. The width of each box is proportional to the number of acquisitions of that box (the second column in table 1.1). The height of the shaded area in each box is proportional to the amount of time spent looking at that box (the third column in table 1.1). The shaded areas are standardized so that the box which is open longest (in this case, the first-round payoff in the loss domain) is completely filled. (Horizontal lines show the midpoints of each box to make comparisons easy.)

The arrows represent the number of transitions between boxes (the three right-hand columns in table 1.1). The thickness of each arrow is proportional to its frequency. To simplify the display, we left out arrows marking transitions that occurred less than once a trial, on average.

The icon graphs express visually what table 1.1 shows numerically: in both domains, subjects open the first and second boxes most often, and look at the first box longest. They barely glance at the third box (although in loss they open it more often, for more time, than in gain). They move back and forth between the first and second boxes relatively often, and

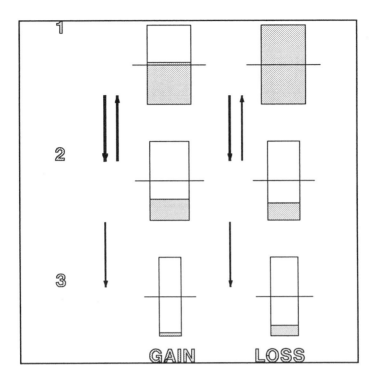

Figure 1.3
Icon graphs of player 1 first-round information search measures

more in gain than in loss. In terms of total looking time and number of box openings, subjects do appear to work harder when bargaining over losses than when bargaining over gains.

The Relation between Information Search and First-Round Offers

Table 1.1 and figure 1.3 show that in both domains, subjects appear to search for information in ways that are inconsistent with backward induction. It is also useful to look for differences in information processing, to see if they are correlated with differences in offers.

Based on first-round offers to player 2s, we divided trials into three groups—"near-perfect" (<$2.01, $n = 23$), middle (between $2.01 and $2.39, $n = 36$), and equal-split ($2.40 or above, $n = 61$). Figure 1.4 shows an icon graph of information processing measures for trials which fall into each of the three groups. Information processing is similar in each of the

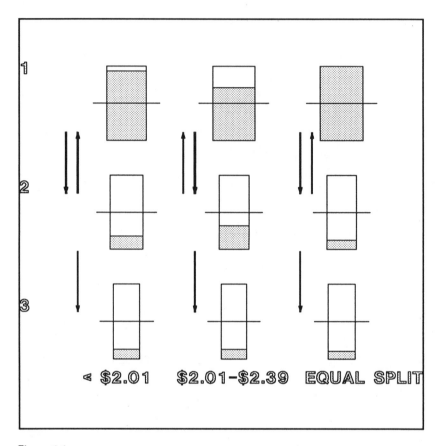

Figure 1.4
Player 1 information search measures classified by first-round offer

three groups. By contrast, in bargaining over gains, subjects who looked further ahead in the game also tended to make lower "near-perfect" offers (see Johnson et al. 1991).

Information Research by Player 2

So far we have concentrated on first-round offers made by player 1. What about information search by player 2s as they consider the offers? (Note that player 2s were not allowed to open boxes until they got a specific offer from player 1.) Figure 1.5 shows icon graphs of information search by player 2s, classified by whether offers were rejected and by the size of offers that were accepted. Generally, search patterns by player 2s look

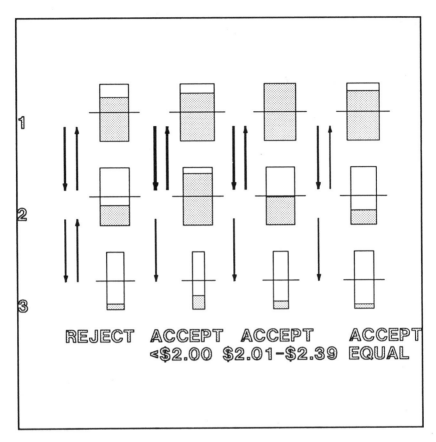

Figure 1.5
Player 2 first-round information search measures classified by rejection or acceptance and first-round offer

much like the patterns for player 1: search is concentrated on the first-round payoff, the third-round box is rarely opened, and transitions tend to be forward (from earlier- to later-round boxes) rather than backward. The most striking difference is between the first column (representing processing by players who reject offers, which tend to be below $2.00) and the second column (players who accept roughly the same offers, below $2.00). Compared to players who reject low offers, players who accept low offers look about twice as long at the second pie size, and make more transitions between the first and second boxes (shown by thicker arrows in the second column). Subjects who accept low offers appear to think through the consequences of rejecting an offer better than rejecting subjects do. A similar difference is evident in bargaining over gains (Johnson et al. 1991).

Learning and Experience

In our experiments each subject participated in eight trials, four as player 1
and four as player 2. Learning might be manifested by changes in information processing over the trials. For example, if subjects learn backward
induction by sheer repetition of bargaining, then there should be a shift in
information processing from round one to future rounds, across trials in an
experiment. Figure 1.6 shows icon graphs of information processing measures over the four trials in which a subject was player 1. There appears to
be no substantial effect of repetition on information processing.

Simply repeating the same game does not seem to teach subjects backward induction. But learning might occur when subjects have an offer

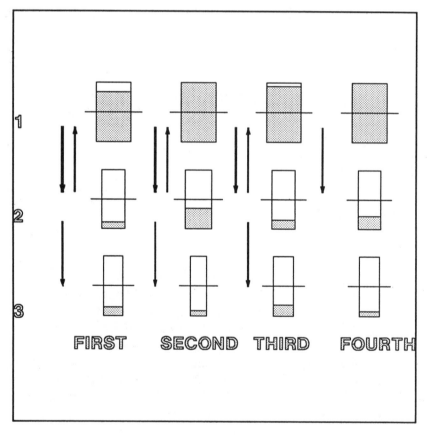

Figure 1.6
Player 1 first-round information search measures across four trials

rejected, and bargaining proceeds to the second round. Then subjects directly experience the consequences of a first-round rejection, which might affect the way they think about their subsequent first-round offer. (Harrison and McCabe's (1992) design mimics this kind of learning by forcing subjects to play subgames between each trial of three-round bargaining.)

To test the effect of a first-round rejection on subsequent play, we compare measures of information processing by a player 1 subject at four points in time: (1) the trial in which a first-round offer was rejected ("1st reject"); (2) the second round of that same trial ("next round"); (3) the "next trial"; and (4) the next trial in which the subject had the role of player 1 again ("next as 1"). Figure 1.7 shows an icon graph comparing information processing measures at these four points. The only striking difference is

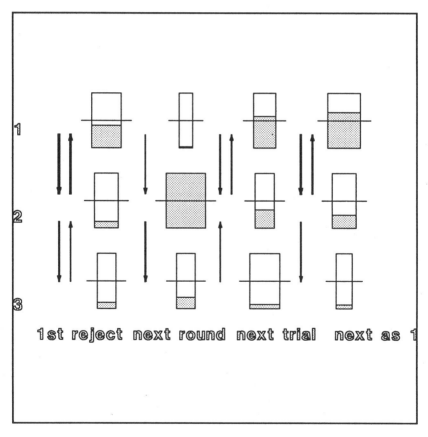

Figure 1.7
Player 1 information search measures classified by four kinds of experience

that in the second round after a first-round rejection (marked "next round"), subjects look much more frequently at the second-round pie size, as one would expect. Experiencing a rejection in the first-round of one trial does *not* cause players to look further ahead in the first-round of the next trial.

Implications and Conclusions

We studied offers and patterns of information search in three-round alternating-offer bargaining over expanding *losses*, and compared the results to a shrinking-*gain* game studied by Johnson et al. (1991). As in most other experiments on bargaining with discounting, offers were scattered between an equal split of the first-round pie and the perfect equilibrium offer (derived from backward induction). About 10 percent of the offers were rejected in gains and 23 percent were rejected in losses.

Patterns of information search showed that most subjects did not look at the pie sizes in the correct order, and for the length of time, necessary for backward induction. Instead, subjects concentrated on the current round when making decisions. In the first round they looked mostly at the first-round pie size and looked only briefly at the third-round pie. Subjects who looked ahead were no more likely to make offers closer to the equilibrium prediction, but they were more likely to accept low offers. Repeating the game, or having a first-round offer rejected, had no discernible impact on information processing.

Since subjects do not appear to be using backward induction to compute offers, it would be helpful to know what they are thinking. We think that subjects try to approximate the profit-maximizing offer, and their attention is guided by (at least) two heuristics: the *size* heuristic directs attention to the largest-sized pies; and the *distance* heuristic directs attention to current-round pies, leading people to ignore distant rounds that are unlikely to occur. A theory that weaves these heuristics into a cognitive account of how subjects choose offers in sequential bargaining would be an extremely useful alternative to the perfect equilibrium theory.

While the gain-and-loss conditions were designed to be identical in terms of subjects' final wealth, there were several notable differences in behavior. In the loss condition subjects opened the boxes more frequently, and looked at the pie sizes about twice as long. Although the average offer was similar for gains and losses, offers were more widely dispersed in the loss condition and were rejected twice as often (see Bazerman 1983).

Recall that two features have been proposed to explain anomalies in sequential bargaining: fairness and learning. Some fairness-based models suggest that people play sophisticatedly but care about their opponent's payoff (e.g., Bolton 1991 in a two-round game). Our information-processing evidence suggests that *any* model that assumes players backward induct is a poor descriptive account of how people think. Such a model might make reasonable predictions, but models that incorporate better representations of human cognition could make even better predictions.

Our data support the initial premise of the learning-based approaches—that players do not begin by reasoning game-theoretically—but we found little evidence that any learning actually occurred. Either learning requires more sheer experience than the eight trials our subjects engaged in, or the experience must be of a different sort. The effect of different amounts and kinds of experience on learning is an important empirical question that our system is well-equipped to answer.

Notes

The financial support of the National Science Foundation to the authors Camerer and Johnson (grants NSF 88-09299 and NSF 90-23531) is gratefully acknowledged. Helpful comments were received from audiences at Harvard, Penn, Cornell, MIT, NYU, Penn State, the Bonn Mathematical Economics Workshop (BoWo IV), and the International Conference on Game Theory (Florence, June 1991).

1. The perfect equilibrium is calculated as follows (assuming players reject offers they are indifferent toward and the smallest unit of currency is \$.01). In the third round, an ultimatum game, player 1 offers \$.01 and keeps \$1.24. Anticipating that, player 2 offers \$1.25 in round 2 and keeps \$1.25. So player 1 offers \$1.26 in round 1 and keeps \$3.74. If players accept offers they are indifferent toward, there are a small band of perfect equilibria from \$1.24–\$1.27. We refer to "the" equilibrium at \$1.25 for simplicity.

2. Our focus on deviations as a source of understanding about typical reasoning is not unusual in science. Researchers often study unusual departures from everyday patterns—the Great Depression, supernovae, volcanic eruptions—in order to learn more about those patterns.

3. In these experiments subjects alternated roles across rounds, but the software was designed to be flexible enough to study nonalternating-offer bargaining, too.

4. Of course, there are many qualifications to the stylized facts. The most important is that learning may create convergence to equilibrium, reducing the number of rejections and disadvantageous counteroffers (as in Binmore, Shaked, and Sutton 1985; and Harrison and McCabe 1992). But the empirical evidence of learning is mixed.

5. To distinguish players actually examining information from those who opened boxes accidentally (usually while moving from one box to another), we filtered out all information acquisitions lasting less than .18 seconds. Psychologists have found

that people do not accurately perceive anything they see that briefly (Card, Moran, and Newell 1983).

6. Data presented in Johnson et al. 1991 show that differences in processing *were* correlated with outcomes in bargaining over gains. Therefore, the idea that offers are independent of information search patterns, so that equilibrium offers could result from any search pattern, is wrong empirically.

7. Of course, to calculate an equilibrium offer to player 2, player 1 does not actually need to look at the first-round payoff at all, as long as she knows the first round pie is bigger (smaller for losses) than the second-round pie.

References

Bazerman, Max H. 1983. "Negotiator Judgment." *American Behavioral Scientist* 27:211–228.

Binmore, Ken, Avner Shaked, and John Sutton. 1985. "Testing Noncooperative Bargaining Theory: A Preliminary Study." *American Economic Review* 75:1178–1180.

Bolton, Gary E. 1991. "A Comparative Model of Bargaining: Theory and Evidence." *American Economic Review* 81:1096–1136.

Card, Stuart K., Thomas P. Moran, and Alan Newell. 1983. *The Psychology of Human-computer Interaction.* Hillsdale, N.J.: Erlbaum.

Forsythe, Robert, Joel Horowitz, N. Savin, and Martin Sefton. 1988. "Replicability, Fairness, and Pay in Experiments with Simple Bargaining Games." Working paper 88-30, University of Iowa.

Harrison, Glenn, and Kevin McCabe. 1992. "Testing Bargaining Theory in Experiments." In R. M. Isaac, ed., *Research in Experimental Economics.* Vol. 5. Greenwich, Conn.: JAI Press.

Hoffman, Elizabeth, Kevin McCabe, Keith Shachat, and Vernon L. Smith. 1991. "Preferences, Property Rights, and Anonymity in Bargaining Games." Working Paper. University of Arizona. Department of Economics.

Johnson, Eric J., Colin Camerer, Sankar Sen, and Talia Rymon. 1991. "Behavior and Cognition in Sequential Bargaining." Working paper, University of Pennsylvania Department of Marketing.

Kahneman, Daniel, and Amos Tversky. 1979. "Prospect Theory: An Analysis of Decision under Risk." *Econometrica* 47:263–291.

Kennan, John, and Robert Wilson. 1990. "Can Strategic Bargaining Models Explain Collective Bargaining Data?" *American Economic Review* 80:405–409.

Maule, A. J. 1989. "Positive and Negative Decision Frames: A Verbal Protocol Analysis of the Asian Disease Problem of Tversky and Kahneman." In H. Montgomery and O. Svenson, eds., *Process and Structure in Human Decision-making.* New York: Wiley.

Neelin, Janet, Hugo Sonnenschein, and Matthew Spiegel. 1988. "A Further Test of Noncooperative Bargaining Theory: Comment." *American Economic Review* 78: 824–836.

Ochs, Jack, and Alvin E. Roth. 1989. "An Experimental Study of Sequential Bargaining." *American Economic Review* 79:355–384.

Osborne, Martin J., and Ariel Rubinstein. 1990. *Bargaining and Markets*. San Diego: Academic Press.

Rapoport, Amnon, Eythan Weg, and Daniel S. Felsenthal. 1990. "Effects of Fixed Costs in Two-person Sequential Bargaining." *Theory and Decision* 28:47–71.

Rubinstein, Ariel. 1982. "Perfect Equilibrium in a Bargaining Model." *Econometrica* 50:97–109.

Spiegel, Matthew, Janet Currie, Hugo Sonnenschein, and A. Sen. 1990. "Fairness and Strategic Behavior in Two-person, Alternating-offer Games: Results From Bargaining Experiments." Working paper, Columbia University.

Stahl, Ingolf. 1972. *Bargaining Theory*. Stockholm: Stockholm School of Economics.

Thaler, Richard H. 1988. "Anomalies: The Ultimatum Game." *Journal of Economic Perspectives* 2:195–206.

Thaler, Richard H., and Eric J. Johnson. 1990. "Gambling with the House Money and Trying to Break Even: The Effect of Prior Outcome on Risky Choice." *Management Science* 36:643–660.

Weg, Eythan, and Rami Zwick. 1991. "On the Robustness of Perfect Equilibrium in Fixed Cost Sequential Bargaining under an Isomorphic Transformation." *Economics Letters* 36:21–24.

Explaining the Vote: Constituency Constraints on Sophisticated Voting

David Austen-Smith

Congressmen are constantly called upon to explain to constituents why they voted as they did. . . . This problem of "explaining the vote," as congressmen call it, has a subtle, but important, effect on their voting behavior.
John Kingdon, *Congressmen's Voting Decisions*

Introduction

Legislators' voting decisions are influenced by the need to justify their Washington behavior to home constituents (Kingdon 1973; Mayhew 1974; and Fenno 1978). An inability to offer a satisfactory explanation for some particular vote is perceived as jeopardizing an incumbent's chances of reelection. This observation has recently been invoked to help explain why some legislators, in some circumstances, vote sincerely when a sophisticated ballot[1] appears prima facie to be instrumentally more appropriate (Denzau, Riker, and Shepsle 1985[2]; Wilkerson 1990). In effect, the claim is that the need to explain the vote induces legislators to vote sincerely when, other things being equal, a sophisticated vote would better promote their districts' interests.

Most models of legislators' voting decisions assume complete information. In this case there can be no role for explanation. Outcome-oriented constituents can perfectly monitor whether the legislator voted in their interests at any stage of a decision-making sequence. Should a legislator behave otherwise, say by voting sincerely when a sophisticated ballot was appropriate, constituents can elect some challenger at the next opportunity: explanations can add nothing. For explanation to matter, therefore, there must be some informational asymmetry between representatives and their constituents.

In their purely decision-theoretic model Denzau, Riker, and Shepsle (1985) assume the constituents and the legislator share identical preferences over policy outcomes, and that this is common knowledge. Further, constituents are also assumed to prefer that the legislator vote sincerely, conditional on the outcome being unaffected by the vote. That is, if the legislator's vote is pivotal, the legislator should vote sophisticatedly, but otherwise the legislator should vote sincerely. The possibility of having to explain a given vote then arises because constituents are unsure whether or not a legislator cast a pivotal or a nonpivotal vote. But it is not clear that there is any problem of explanation here if constituents are rational. Specifically, for there to be such a problem, rational constituents must be unsure as to their representative's preferences over policy outcomes. Were this not the case, then, ceteris paribus, a legislator could always justify legislative behavior as being in the interests of the district: the legislator has no incentive to lie, and this is common knowledge. However, in the presence of such informational asymmetry, rational outcome-oriented constituents will use their legislator's voting record to make inferences about the legislator's preferences, *independent* of any subsequent explanations the legislator might volunteer for his actions. Indeed, by focusing on specific aspects of an incumbent's voting history, challengers for a legislative office explicitly encourage an electorate to make inferences of this sort.

The observations above motivate the two main questions addressed in this chapter. First: How does the signaling role of voting behavior per se affect the vote decisions of legislators interested in reelection? And second: What further effects, if any, can explanation add to the signaling properties of a given voting record?

In what follows I offer a simple game-theoretic model of legislative voting and constituency explanation in which representatives and constituents care only about policy outcomes. Insofar as legislators seek reelection, therefore, it is to further their desired policy outcomes. Of course representatives are rarely so single-minded; for example, the pecuniary benefits of holding office per se are of concern to many. But since the empirical motivation here concerns the role of constituency constraints on legislative voting behavior, it is appropriate initially to abstract from issues other than policy outcomes. Should it turn out that such an abstraction is inconsistent with the findings of Kingdon, Fenno, and others, then the model points to the importance of things other than policy outcomes for understanding the relationship between constituency and legislative decision-making.[3]

However, despite the framework being one in which there is considerable incentive for legislators to vote sophisticatedly, the signaling role of voting per se does yield sincere voting in circumstances where sophisticated behavior is warranted. Moreover, if constituents can demand an explanation for a legislator's behavior, then (subject to one technical qualification) it turns out that constituents and some types of legislator are on average better off than with no requirement to explain.

The next three sections contain the formal model and a discussion of the principal results. A concluding section draws the threads together, and considers some implications of the argument for the theory of representation.

Model

Figure 2.1 summarizes the sequence of events, individual preferences, and informational assumptions described in detail below.

Agents and Decisions

Consider a given electoral district in which there is a well-defined pivotal voter. Because, by definition, the pivotal voter's electoral choices determine the district's electoral decisions, I shall refer throughout to "the district" rather than to "the pivotal voter in the district." There is an incumbent legislator l, who is one of two types (defined later): l is either a "representative" type ($l = R$), or an "independent" type ($l = I$).

There are two legislative periods. In the first the legislature must select an alternative from a given set of options, $\{x, y, z\}$. The decision-making process is majority voting over an amendment agenda in which x is first put against y, the winner against z. The surviving alternative constitutes the final outcome. Once this outcome is realized, the legislature dissolves and l returns to the district to seek reelection. At this stage I consider two cases: first, l is offered no opportunity to explain l's first-period voting record and the district simply chooses whether to reelect l to office; and second, l is required to explain l's voting record, following which the district reelects or rejects l as before. In the event the district rejects l and elects a challenger, this new official is similarly an R-type or an I-type.

In a more general framework with many legislators and districts, whether or not any given legislator such as l is pivotal at any vote would be derived endogenously. Here this complication is ignored and it is assumed common knowledge (correctly) that l is pivotal in the vote between x and y in the first period. Additionally, there is no abstention. Under some circumstances these are strong assumptions. The justification for making them is purely methodological: the more unequivocally the environment is structured to give legislators incentives to vote sophisticatedly, the more

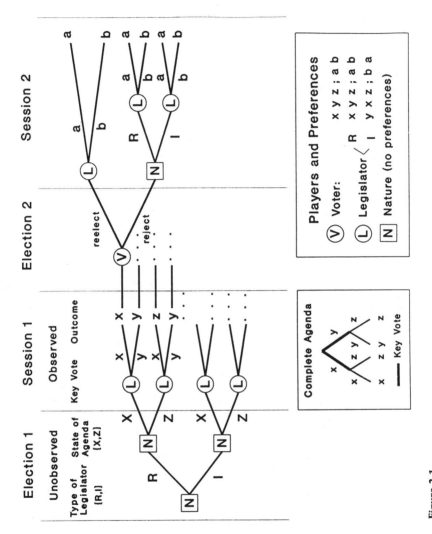

Figure 2.1
The decision sequence

confidence we can have in results that generate sincere voting as rational behavior due to the signaling role of voting per se.

The consequences of having one type of legislator rather than the other in office during the second legislative session will, in general, depend on the policy issues that arise, the votes that have to be taken, and so on. Rather than derive these consequences explicitly, I simply assume that the second-period legislator can choose some course of legislative action that leads deterministically to one of two end-of-period outcomes, a or b. This abstraction is a reduced form summarizing the presumption that the type of legislator elected to second-period office is consequential for the district. Were the choice not consequential, there would be no reason why constituents should care about who they elect to office. After the actions are taken, the outcome is realized and the legislature dissolves.

Preferences

As discussed in the introduction, all agents in the model are assumed purely outcome-oriented. The district and the R-type legislator l share identical preferences with normalized von Neumann–Morgenstern utility representation:

$$u(x) = 1 > u(y) = v > u(z) = 0; \quad \text{and} \quad u(a) - u(b) = B > 0.$$

The I-type legislator, however, has preferences similarly described by:

$$\tilde{u}(y) = 1 > \tilde{u}(x) = v > \tilde{u}(z) = 0; \quad \text{and} \quad \tilde{u}(b) - \tilde{u}(a) = B > 0.$$

Thus while an R-type has the same preferences as the district, an I-type legislator, unlike the district, prefers y to x in the first period and prefers b to a in the second period (both types think z is the worst alternative available in the first period). Additionally, preferences are assumed to be quantitatively symmetric: the measure of the importance either type of legislator places on the intermediate alternative from $\{x, y, z\}$, the value v, is the same. So legislator types differ only in their ordinal rankings of $\{x, y\}$ and of $\{a, b\}$.

Given legislator's preferences and the details of legislator selection for the second period, the value of reelection to the incumbent is

$$u(a) - [qu(a) + (1 - q)u(b)] = (1 - q)B, \quad \text{if } l = R;$$

$$\tilde{u}(b) - [q\tilde{u}(a) + (1 - q)\tilde{u}(b)] = qB, \quad \text{if } l = I.$$

Thus, as asserted earlier, legislators are concerned with reelection solely for policy-outcome reasons. If reelected, l can ensure the outcome she most favors; but if a challenger is elected in her place, there is a risk that this agent will not share the same preferences over $\{a, b\}$.

Information

Only the incumbent legislator l knows her own type. The district's common knowledge belief is that $l = R$ with probability $q \in (0, 1)$, and that $l = I$ with probability $1 - q$. Similarly, if the district chooses to elect a challenger to office for the second legislative period, the district believes the challenger's type is R with probability q and I with probability $1 - q$. (Letting the challenger be an R-type with probability different from that of the incumbent adds nothing but notational complexity; so long as the probabilities are not degenerate, the qualitative results continue to hold.)

Legislators are inherently more informed about the daily workings of Congress than are their constituents. And as indicated in the introduction, it is the combination of constituents being unsure both of legislator preferences and of the decision-making environments in which legislators operate, that generate a rationale for demanding explanations of behavior. If constituents knew that their representative would always act in their interest, then it is irrelevant that they understand the legislative environment; and if the details of strategic decision making are common knowledge, then constituents can directly observe whether their representative acts in their interests, irrespective of knowledge of the representative's own preferences over outcomes.

To capture the idea that the district is unsure not only about the incumbent's type, but also about the legislative decision-making environment, assume that the district does not know whether sophisticated or sincere voting over the agenda for $\{x, y, z\}$ is in the district's interests. Specifically, assume that the "sophisticated equivalent" (McKelvey and Niemi 1978) of x winning the vote against y is known at the time of the first vote only by l. That is, given x succeeds against y at the first ballot, the alternative that will prevail at the second stage, x or z, is not known ex ante by the district, but is known by l. The idea here is that there is some feature of the first-period legislative decision-making environment observable only by legislators themselves; for example, the distribution of preferences across the legislature as a whole at the time of the vote. Let $S \in \{X, Y\}$ denote which of two possible legislative environments (states) prevails. State Z occurs with common knowledge prior probability p, and state X with complementary probability $1 - p$. In state Z the sophisticated equivalent of x is z; and in state X the sophisticated equivalent of x is x. The legislator is assumed to observe which state, X or Z, is realized prior to casting her vote over (x, y), but the state is not directly observable by the district. In both states the sophisticated equivalent of voting for y is y itself, and this is common knowledge.[4]

In sum, there are two sources of informational asymmetry in the model: only the incumbent knows the incumbent's preferences over outcomes, and only the incumbent knows exactly what the first-period policy outcome will be from voting for x over y.

The above description completes the specification of the model. Before proceeding to the results, it is useful to summarize the strategic tensions captured in the model. First, note that, if the incumbent (first-period legislator) is an R-type, then in state Z she "should" vote sophisticatedly for y over x, and in state X she "should" vote sincerely for x. In other words, if there is no uncertainty about the incumbent's type, or if the incumbent is wholly insensitive to any reelection concerns, then canonic sophisticated voting theory predicts an R-type will cast a sophisticated vote in state Z and a sincere vote in state X; these actions uniquely maximize such a legislator's payoffs from the first period. Similarly, under such circumstances an I-type legislator best promotes the I-type's immediate interests by voting for y over x in both states of the world. Both types will vote identically at the final stage (against z), whatever the state of the world.

When the district is uncertain about the incumbent's preferences and the legislative decision-making environment, and when the incumbent is concerned to be relected, then the first-period voting decision is more complex. To see this, consider an R-type legislator in state Z. The best decision for the legislator and the district here is to vote sophisticatedly for, and obtain, outcome y. But this is also the best decision for an I-type legislator. So if the R-type does choose to vote for y, the R-type risks being misidentified by the district as an I-type and subsequently not reelected to office. The value to the R-type of obtaining y rather than z in the first period must be set against the likelihood of being misidentified and not elected to the second legislature. This suggests that R-types will sometimes sacrifice y to z by voting sincerely for x in the first period, to try and signal their type to the district. Whether or not such a type can do this credibly, however, is not immediate; I-type incumbents might value second-period office sufficiently highly that they, too, are willing to try to convince the district that they are R-types by voting for x in state Z. Thus the interaction between legislative and electoral objectives induces a conflict between voting-to-signal-type and voting-to-promote-outcomes. Exactly how this conflict balances out and what difference, if any, it makes to allow legislators to explain their first-period voting record are the subjects of the following sections.

Signaling Constraints on Sophisticated Voting

This section addresses the first question posed in the introduction. Suppose the legislator l has no opportunity to explain l's first-period voting record prior to the district's decision on whether or not to reelect l's. Then the issue is l's voting behavior, given that the district will use l's first-period record when making the reelection decision.

Given the amendment agenda described above for the legislative decision over $\{x, y, z\}$, and given preferences $u(\cdot)$ and $\tilde{u}(\cdot)$, it is evident that both l-types will vote identically at the final vote, whatever the state of the world, Z or X. So when there is no chance to explain the vote, the legislator's effective strategy is a map associating with her type and the state of the world a probability of voting for x:

$$\sigma: \{R, I\} \times \{Z, X\} \to [0, 1].$$

Thus $\sigma(R, Z)$ is the probability that l of type R in state Z votes for x at the first ballot, and so on. Similarly, the district's strategy is a map associating with any observed vote and outcome a probability of reelection:

$$\delta: \{x, y\} \times \{x, y, z\} \to [0, 1].$$

So $\delta(x, z)$ is the probability that the district, having observed l vote for x at the first ballot and generate an outcome z, reelects l. If the legislator in the second legislative period is an R-type (resp. I-type), then the legislator has a dominant strategy to act to generate outcome a (resp. b). Therefore, without loss of generality, the specification of second-period strategies can be left implicit hereafter.

The basic solution concept on which the results below are based is sequential equilibrium. Such equilibria have the property that at every decision, the relevant decision maker chooses an action to maximize his or her expected final payoff from the process, given the actions of other decision-makers. Further, beliefs at every stage are required to be consistent with Bayes's rule, where this is defined. However, as with most signaling games, sequential equilibrium is too weak a concept. By specifying beliefs appropriately in those circumstances where Bayes's rule is not defined, it is generally possible to support prima facie implausible strategies in equilibrium. There is exactly one circumstance where this is possible in the current model. Hence the notion of sequential equilibrium used here is refined somewhat. In effect, the refinement requires that an R-type legislator, when choosing how to vote in state X, always puts positive weight on voting for x. Since such a legislator and the district both strictly prefer x to alternatives y and z, the requirement is that with positive probability, l votes sincerely to generate l's and the district's most favored outcome. This seems innocuous.

The first result gives some properties of the full equilibrium set (throughout, starred values of σ, etc., denote equilibrium choices).[5]

PROPOSITION 1

(i) $\forall l, S, \sigma^*(l, S) \in \{0, 1\}$ almost always;

(ii) $\forall (q, p, v, B), \sigma^*(R, X) = 1$ in all equilibria; and, $\forall (q, p, v, B)$, there exists an equilibrium such that $(\sigma^*(R, Z), \sigma^*(R, X)) = (0, 1)$;

(iii) $\delta(y, y) = 0$ is always a best response; and $\delta(x, x) = 0$ is never a best response.

Proposition 1(i) is technical. It claims that, to all intents and purposes, it is legitimate to ignore equilibria in which legislators use mixed strategies.

Propositions 1(ii) and 1(iii) are substantive. The first part of proposition 1(ii) states, as one would expect, that an R-type legislator always votes sincerely for x over y when this leads to x, the most-preferred alternative of R-types and the district. The second part of proposition 1(ii) is somewhat less expected. It claims that, whatever the given parameter values (e.g., the probability q of an electoral challenger being an R-type, or the relative value v of the intermediate alternative), there exists an equilibrium in which R-type legislators vote as predicted by canonic sophisticated voting theory, irrespective of subsequent electoral concerns; that is, R-types vote x in X, and vote y in Z. This result will be considered further, following the statement of a corollary to proposition 2 below.

In proposition 1(iii) the intuition behind the district always having "reject the incumbent" as best response after observing l vote for y, is that the district cannot infer either which state, Z or X, obtained or, given the l-type's preferences, any additional information about l's true type. Hence, rejecting the first-period incumbent for a challenger cannot make the district any worse off (expectationally). Clearly, in view of this property of the district's strategy, R-type incumbents might be deterred from voting sophisticatedly in state Z.

Say that an equilibrium is *efficient* if, given the legislator knows her preferences before the state of the world $S \in \{Z, X\}$ is revealed, there is no other feasible equilibrium in which any l-type or the district receives a higher expected payoff and no agent receives a lower payoff. Then the following is true.

PROPOSITION 2   All possible efficient equilibria are described in figures 2.2a, 2.2b, and 2.2c below.

The three figures of proposition 2 are essentially the same, with a unique efficient equilibrium in each of three intervals for q, the probability that l is an R-type. Fix the relative value, $v \in (0, 1)$, of the second-ranked alternative (i.e., y for R-types and the district, and x for I-types). For low values of q the efficient equilibrium is fully separating, with R-types not voting sophisticatedly; for intermediate values of q the efficient equilibrium is partially separating, with the district capable of distinguishing R-types from I-types in state Z (resp. X) when $B > 1$ (resp. < 1); and for higher values of q, the efficient equilibrium is pooling, with both types voting for y in state Z and for x in state X. When $B = 1$, the intermediate range vanishes.

It is worth observing here that the larger is q, the more likely it is that the legislator, whatever the legislator's type, will vote "correctly" to promote the interests of the district with respect to $\{x, y, z\}$ (if l was originally elected by some competitive majoritarian process, then we would expect $q > 1/2$). Separation occurs when the prior belief about the legislator's preferences favors $l = I$. The intuition is straightforward. Suppose the probability q of an R-type challenger for second-period office is high. Then the probability that a will be the second-period outcome is also high. Consequently, since l is outcome-oriented, it becomes worth voting sophisticatedly for y in state Z. Conversely, an I-type legislator is willing to sacrifice y to x in state X to ensure being in office for the second period. For if such a legislator is rejected, the probability that a will be subsequently chosen is large. The intuition behind separation occurring for low q is symmetric.

COROLLARY 1

(i)   No equilibrium in which some legislator uses a mixed voting strategy is efficient;

(ii) Not all equilibria in which R-type legislators use canonic sophisticated voting strategies are efficient;

(iii) There is a unique efficient limit equilibrium as B goes to infinity and as B goes to zero.

In both cases R-type legislators vote exactly as predicted by canonic sophisticated voting theory; in the first case ($B \rightarrow \infty$) I-type legislators vote identically to R-types; and in the second case ($B \rightarrow 0$) I-type legislators vote for y surely in both states, Z and X.

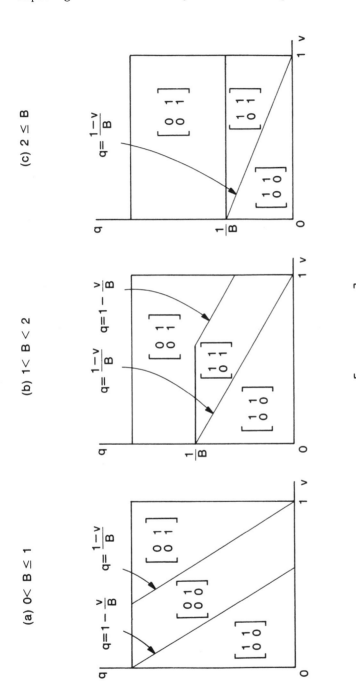

Figure 2.2
Efficient equilibria with no explanation

The first two parts of corollary 1 follow directly from comparing, respectively, propositions 1(i) and 1(ii) with proposition 2. Corollary 1(i) implies that, whenever an equilibrium in which some legislator uses a mixed voting strategy exists, there is always a distinct equilibrium in which the legislator uses a pure strategy and at least one agent is strictly better off, and no agent is worse off, than in the mixed strategy equilibrium. More importantly from a substantive perspective, corollary 1(ii) implies that if attention is confined exclusively to efficient equilibria, if the district uses the incumbent's voting record to make inferences about the latter's type, and if this signaling role is recognized by the incumbent, then these facts are sufficient to explain why outcome-oriented legislators might vote sincerely when a sophisticated vote is prima facie warranted (i.e., R-types in state Z).

Finally, consider corollary 1(iii). This result follows from inspection of figure 2.2: letting B go to infinity in figure 2.2c leaves only the pooling equilibrium; and letting B go to zero in figure 2.2a rules out both the separating equilibrium and the pooling equilibrium. Given $q \in (0, 1)$, the result claims that as the value of second-period office goes either to zero or to infinity, then the only efficient equilibrium is such that R-type legislators vote sophisticatedly where appropriate. I-type legislators, on the other hand, always vote for y when the state of the world is Z (and are thus indistinguishable from R-type legislators from the district's perspective); but when the state of the world is X and B goes to infinity (resp. zero), I-types vote for x (resp. y). So for R-type legislators to choose not to vote sophisticatedly sometimes, it is necessary for the value of office to be nonnegligible, but not extreme.

The result when B goes to zero is not surprising. As B gets small, the importance of staying in office for the second period is diminished. In the limit the current incumbent has negligible interest in being reelected. Therefore I will choose to maximize payoffs from the first-period decision alone. For R-types, this means securing y in state Z and x in state X; and for I-types, this means voting for and getting y in both states. The intuition behind the result when B goes to infinity is more subtle. In this case the value of being reelected is extremely large, and so the current incumbent has every incentive to ensure reelection. However, if the district could infer I's type by observing her voting record over $\{x, y, z\}$, then I would surely be rejected when $I = I$. Recognizing this, an I-type incumbent will mimic the first-period voting choices of an R-type to conceal her preferences. And, therefore, because there is no credible way for $I = R$ to signal I's type to the district through the voting record, I can do no better in the first period than vote to maximize I's short-term gains.

The results above provide considerable intuition about how allowing legislators to explain their vote might improve on R-types' and the district's overall payoffs. In particular, there is a suggestion that being able to explain the vote will permit R-types to vote sophisticatedly more often, yet still get reelected to promote district interests surely in the second legislative session. Although it turns out that this is true under some circumstances, in other situations the need to explain votes improves payoffs by *reducing* the amount of sophisticated voting by R-types.

Explaining the Vote

Kingdon (1973) and Fenno (1978) emphasize the importance of legislators being capable of explaining their voting behavior, should they be called upon to do so. In what follows I assume that legislators will surely be required to justify their voting choices.

The structure of the game is just as for the previous section, save for the addition of an "explanation" stage immediately following the policy decision from $\{x, y, z\}$ and prior to the district's reelection decision. Consequently, the legislator's voting strategy σ over $\{x, y\}$ is exactly as defined above. But now it is necessary to define an "explanation" strategy and, for the district, a reelection strategy that takes account of any explanation that is offered. Let us consider each of these in turn.

An explanation strategy for the legislator is a map associating with the legislator's type, her vote over $\{x, y\}$, and the policy decision realized a probability that l declares she is an R-type. Define

$$\mu : \{R, I\} \times \{x, y\} \times \{x, y, z\} \to [0, 1].$$

So, for instance, $\mu(I, x, z)$ is the probability that legislator l of type I, having voted for x over y at the first period to yield an outcome z, announces that l is of type R. This model of explanation requires some justification.

Recall that the only facts the district does not necessarily know for sure once the policy decision over $\{x, y, z\}$ is realized, are the legislator's type (R or I) and the state of the world prevailing at the time of the vote over $\{x, y\}$ (Z or X). In particular, the district knows the legislator's vote over $\{x, y\}$, the final policy decision, and that l is a rational policy-oriented individual. Therefore, whatever the rhetoric of the speech, an explanation of voting behavior in this environment can only involve l giving the district information about either l's type, or which state of the world prevailed, or both. However, there is only one vote/outcome pair that can leave the district unsure of the state of the world after the pair is observed; namely, (y, y).

Furthermore, the only fact of value to the district for its reelection decision is whether or not the incumbent legislator is an R-type (so will promote a if reelected), or an I-type (so will promote b if reelected). All else is irrelevant. Hence, the only information of concern in a legislative explanation is the legislator's type.[6] And this is exactly what is captured in the specification of the explanation strategy, μ. Observe that "no information" is possible here; suppose both I-types give the same speech for all vote/outcome pairs $(\mu(R, \cdot, \cdot) \equiv (\mu(I, \cdot, \cdot))$. Then the district can infer nothing from the explanation that it could not deduce from the vote/outcome pair itself.

Let $m \in \{R, I\}$ denote the realization of the explanation strategy μ. Then the district's reelection strategy is a straightforward extension of the strategy δ. Specifically,

$$\hat{\delta} : \{x, y\} \times \{x, y, z\} \times \{R, I\} \to [0, 1].$$

So $\hat{\delta}(r, w, m)$ is the probability the district reelects l, given l voted r, produced outcome w, and explained that she is an m-type.

Let $c \geq 0$ be a penalty imposed on any legislator who is discovered to have lied to the district in her explanation. For example, if l claims $l = R$ and subsequently takes actions to yield b over a, then the district can infer $l = I$ and the penalty is imposed. (Although I assume that the penalty is surely imposed when l is discovered to have lied, this is not essential: one can interpret c more generally as an expected cost of lying.) Substantively, c can be thought of in terms of l's credibility loss among peers, or future employers. In a more general framework such a cost would be modeled explicitly; here, however, it is convenient to treat it parametrically. Assume throughout that $B \geq c$; penalties cannot be disproportionate (loosely speaking) to the value of office.[7]

Again the solution concept is sequential equilibrium subject to a mild refinement to exclude absurd predictions of the sort discussed in the previous section.

PROPOSITION 3   For all vote/outcome pairs (r, w):

(i) $\mu^*(R, r, w) = 1$;

(ii) Given that the vote record alone fails to identify the incumbent's type, $\mu^*(I, r, w) < 1 \Rightarrow c \geq qB$.

Proposition 3(ii) says that conditional on their type not being revealed by their first-period voting behavior, I-type legislators will invariably lie about their type unless the penalty for being discovered dissembling is sufficiently high. In particular, if this penalty is less than the expected value of second-period office to an *I*-type, then the district learns *no* additional information from hearing an explanatory speech by the incumbent. However, requiring explanations can still lead to the district and *R*-type incumbents being better off overall. Before making this claim precise, it is useful to identify efficient equilibrium voting behavior when explanations are required of first-period incumbents.

PROPOSITION 4

(i) Suppose $c < qB$. Then the incumbent's voting behavior in all possible efficient equilibria when there is an explanation stage is described in figures 2.3a, 2.3b and 2.3c below;

(ii) Suppose $c \geq qB$. Then the unique efficient equilibrium involves *R*-types voting exactly as canonic sophisticated voting theory predicts; and *I*-types vote for *y* in both states, *Z* and *X*.

Comparison of figures 2.2 and 2.3 yields two results for $c < qB$. First, if the penalty for lying is zero ($c = 0$), then there is no difference between the situation without an explanation and with one. And second, for any strictly positive penalty ($c > 0$), *R*-types vote sincerely in state *Z* more often, and *I*-types mimic the voting record of *R*-types less often, when there is an explanation stage than when there is not (subject to $c < qB$). In view of proposition 3(ii), therefore, despite there being no information regarding the incumbent's preferences given in any explanation of first-period voting behavior, the mere fact that an explanation is required, coupled with some penalty for being caught dissembling, leads to a change in first-period voting patterns relative to the no-explanation case. Specifically, for $0 < c < qB$, being required to justify legislative behavior leads *R*-type legislators to vote sincerely more often than they otherwise would.

When the penalty for being caught lying in explanation is sufficiently high ($c \geq qB$), proposition 4(ii) asserts that the only efficient equilibrium is one in which all incumbent types vote to maximize their payoffs from the first-period decision. In this case *R*-type legislators can credibly justify any sophisticated voting behavior to the district ex post, while *I*-types cannot. Hence, *I*-type legislators simply vote for *y* in both states, and get rejected by the district for sure.

Comparing expected equilibrium payoffs across regimes in the no-explanation and the explanation scenarios yields the main result of this chapter.

PROPOSITION 5   Suppose only efficient equilibria are played. Then for all parametrization (q, p, v, B) and for all penalties c, the expected equilibrium

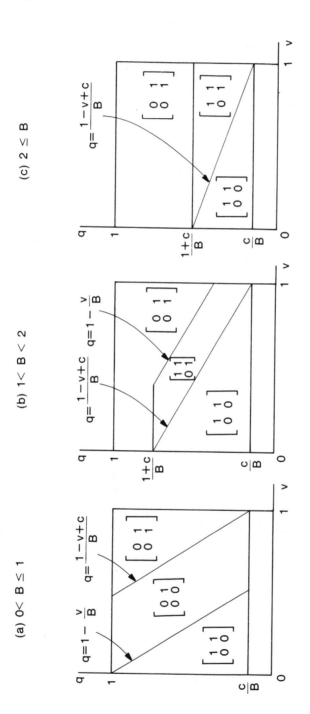

Figure 2.3
Efficient equilibria with explanation, $c < qB$

payoff of the district and of the R-type incumbent is always at least as great when legislators must explain their vote as when there is no opportunity for explanation; and for some (q, p, v, B) and all $c > 0$, these expected equilibrium payoffs are strictly greater.

The qualification concerning efficient equilibria in proposition 5 is to rule out exactly one case. If $c < qB$, $B > 1$, $qB \geq (1 - v) + \varepsilon$ for sufficiently small $\varepsilon \geq 0$, and an inefficient equilibrium is played rather than the efficient (in this instance, separating) equilibrium, then the district and R-type incumbent can be made worse off by requiring explanations. Since these circumstances are negligible in the parameter space (if not strictly speaking of measure zero), and since they involve inefficient equilibria, this qualification to the proposition is arguably of technical interest only.

As remarked in the introduction, the improvement in payoffs when $c > 0$ comes about in two distinct ways, depending on the value of c relative to qB.

When $c < qB$, explanation per se adds nothing to the district's information set. However, legislators' voting decisions will be influenced in ways that allow the district to screen out independents more frequently than when explanation is not required. In particular, "representative" legislators will vote sincerely when they "should" vote sophisticatedly more often to signal their type. Similarly, although "independent" legislators are still willing to dissemble in explanation if necessary, they are less willing to risk being put in a position of having to do this. By voting in such a way as to signal their type directly to the district, the explanation becomes irrelevant, and the I-type can simply reveal I-type's preferences honestly at no cost (save not being reelected). The improvement in welfare therefore comes about by the gain in screening efficiency—I-types can be rejected relatively more frequently—dominating the loss in first-period payoffs due to R-types voting sophisticatedly less often in state Z.

On the other hand, when $c \geq qB$, explanations do add information. The only efficient equilibrium here involves legislator types completely separating at the explanation stage (i.e., both types honestly reveal themselves in explanation) but not at the voting stage: R-types now vote sophisticatedly when necessary (state Z) and are thus indistinguishable in their choice from I-types in state Z. It is the ability of R-types to justify a vote for y over x credibly that permits sophisticated voting and unambiguously improves the district's overall payoff.

So explanation can matter and affect voting behavior when all actors are instrumentally rational and policy-oriented.

Table 2.1
Equilibria to the no-explanation game

$\sigma(l,Z)$ / $\sigma(l,X)$	$\sigma(R,Z)=1$	$\sigma(R,X)=1$ / $\sigma(R,Z)\in(0,1)$	$\sigma(R,Z)=0$	Row
1 / 1	$\delta(xz) - \delta(yy) \geq \max\{1/H, v/H'\}$ $\delta(xx) - \delta(yy) \geq (1-v)/H$ $\delta(yy) \in [0,1)$ $1 - (v/B) \geq q \geq 1/B$	none	none	1
$\varepsilon(0,1)$ / 1	$\delta(xz) = 1 = 1/H; \delta(yy) = 0$ $\delta(xx) \geq (1-v)/H$ $1/(1+v) \geq q = 1/B$	$\delta(xz) - \delta(yy) = 1/H = v/H'$ $\delta(xx) - \delta(yy) \geq (1-v)/H$ $\delta(yy) \in [0,1)$ $1 - (v/B) \geq q = 1/(1+v) > 1/B$	none	2
0 / 1	$\delta(xz) = 1; \delta(yy) = 0$ $\delta(xx) \geq (1-v)/H$ $\min\{1/B, 1 - (v/B)\} \geq q$ $\geq (1-v)/B$	$\delta(xz) = 1; \delta(yy) = 0$ $\delta(xx) \geq (1-v)/H$ $1/(1+v) \geq q = 1 - (v/B)$ $\geq (1-v)/B$	$\delta(xz) - \delta(yy) \leq \min\{1/H, v/H'\}$ $\delta(xx) - \delta(yy) \geq (1-v)/H$ $\delta(yy) \in [0,1)$ $q \geq (1-v)/B$	3
0 / $\varepsilon(0,1)$	$\delta(xz) = 1; \delta(yy) = 0$ $\delta(xx) = 1$ $\min\{1/B, 1 - (v/B)\}$ $\geq q = (1-v)/B$	$\delta(xz) = 1; \delta(yy) = 0$ $\delta(xx) = (1-v)/H$ $1/(1+v) \geq q = 1 - (v/B)$ $= (1-v)/B$	$\delta(xz) \leq \min\{1/H, v/H'\}$ $\delta(yy) = 0; \delta(xx) = 1$ $q = (1-v)/B$	4
0 / 0	$\delta(xz) = 1; \delta(yy) = 0$ $\delta(xx) = 1$ $\min\{(1-v)/B, 1 - (v/B)\} \geq q$	$\delta(xz) = 1; \delta(yy) = 0$ $\delta(xx) = 1$ $\max\{1/(1+v) \cdot (1-v)/B\}$ $\geq q = 1 - (v/B)$	$\delta(xz) \leq \min\{1/H, v/H'\}$ $\delta(yy) = 0; \delta(xx) = 1$ $q < (1-v)/B$	5
Col.	1	2	3	

Notes: $H = qB$; $H' = (1 - q)B$. Boldface statements give necessary and sufficient conditions for the specified equilibria to exist. There exist no equilibria in which both $\sigma(l,Z) > 0$ and $\sigma(l,X) < 1$.

Conclusion

This chapter has been concerned with two closely related issues in regard to legislators' voting behavior. The first issue concerns the effect on such behavior of incumbents recognizing that their respective districts will use the voting record to help make reelection decisions; and the second issue concerns the additional role, if any, played by legislators having the opportunity to explain their voting record to the district.

There are three main conclusions. First, if only efficient equilibria are observed, then under some circumstances legislators will vote sincerely when they "should" (i.e., according to canonic sophisticated voting theory) vote sophisticatedly. Second, given that only efficient equilibria are observed, requiring incumbents to explain their voting records leads to relatively more sincere voting decisions. And third, so long as the penalty for being detected dissembling in explanation is positive, requiring explanations never makes the district or the "representative"-type legislators worse off relative to the no-explanation case, and sometimes makes them strictly better off. Moreover, subject to one essentially negligible exception, this last result does not depend on selecting only efficient equilibria.

Although the focus of analysis has been on understanding two observed features of legislative behavior (that legislators periodically vote sincerely when they "should" vote sophisticatedly; and that the need to explain legislative decisions to constituents influences such behavior), the results have implications for the theory of representation. An important theme in the literature concerns the ability of citizens to control the behavior of elected officials once they have taken office (Pitkin 1967). The problem arises because electoral accountability is circumscribed, first, because many legislative actions are unobservable and, second, because the connection between such actions and final outcomes is uncertain. In this context the problem is one of moral hazard and the extent to which the threat of losing office is sufficient to induce legislators to act in constituents' interests is moot (e.g., Ferejohn 1986). In the current chapter, however, the problem is one of adverse selection. Actions are fully observable, as are their consequences, but the decision-making environment is not. Consequently, the set of outcomes that the legislator could have generated is uncertain to constituents, and it is therefore unclear whether the legislator acted to promote the district's preferences (R-types) or the legislator's preferences (I-types).

Subject to mild qualification, the results imply that for the incumbent's voting record fully to reveal the incumbent's type, so that there is no adverse selection problem for the second legislative session, the "correct" (R-type) incumbent will vote sincerely when sophisticated voting best promotes the district's preferences. Furthermore, when R-type legislators do vote appropriately to promote the district's immediate preferences in all circumstances, then the adverse selection problem is most acute; the voting record alone is insufficient for the district to be able to distinguish legislator types. If, in addition to voting, incumbents have the opportunity to explain their behavior, then the situation improves overall in welfare terms. That is, the district can distinguish legislator types more frequently with than without explanation. However, this can occur at the expense of having first-period policy outcomes be the best available from the district's perspective. On balance, the district is better off resolving the adverse selection problem than having maximal short-run payoffs at the risk of electing the "incorrect" (I-type) legislator to second-period office.

The model from which the results above are derived is sparse. In particular, the class of explanations that might be offered is very narrow, amounting simply to an argument about whether the incumbent will vote for one alternative over another in the subsequent legislative period. From the descriptions provided by Fenno (1978, chap. 5) inter alia, it is clear that although explanations involve the incumbent's attempting to reassure constituents that the incumbent's voting decisions in Washington are consistent with at least the long-run interests of the district, these explanations frequently focus on more than simply a statement of how the incumbent would behave if reelected. For example, if subsequent periods' legislative environments are subject to some uncertainty and correlated with the realized state in the current period, then constituents will have an interest in both the legislator's "type" and the legislative state in which he or she made voting decisions. Further, with a richer class of legislator types, it is not evident in this extended specification of the model that the district unambiguously prefers one type over all others in all possible states of the world.

To develop a fuller understanding of homestyle explanation, therefore, a more complicated model than the one explored is necessary. However, as remarked elsewhere in the text, the framework here is set up to focus specifically on how the signaling properties of a given voting record influence development of that record, and to explore how and why explanation might matter. By introducing nonpolicy motivations, multiple types, and so on, the link between voting-to-signal type and voting-to-promote outcomes is considerably attenuated.

Notes

This is an abbreviated version of a paper originally published in the *American Journal of Political Science*, vol. 36, no. 1, February 1992, pp. 68–95. The author is grateful to the University of Texas Press for permission to publish this version.

1. Throughout, I use terms *sophisticated ballot, sophisticated voting,* and so on in the sense of Farquharson 1969 and McKelvey and Niemi 1978.

2. See also Krehbiel and Rivers 1990 on the Powell amendment case. In contrast to Denzau, Riker, and Shepsle (1985), these authors argue that in fact there was considerably less opportunity for sophisticated voting here than is often claimed.

3. Conversely, if nonpolicy issues turn out to be unnecessary for generating the relevant phenomena, this does not imply that they are irrelevant in general. For examples of models where nonpolicy-outcome issues are important to constituent/legislator interactions, see Barro 1973; Ferejohn 1986; and Austen-Smith and Banks 1989.

4. Strictly speaking, therefore, there are four (game-theoretic) "types" in the model, given by the pairs (l, S). Abuse of the technical concept here is justified by the natural substantive interpretation of legislator type in the model.

5. In the interests of space I have excluded all formal definitions of equilibrium and proofs for the propositions (and for the most part these are routine). The interested reader can find the formal arguments supporting the results to follow in the complete version of this paper; see the *American Journal of Political Science* 36(1): February 1992.

6. Evidently, some important aspects of explanation are precluded in this framework. The issue is considered further in the concluding section of this chapter.

7. As will become apparent momentarily, this assumption is without loss of generality. It is invoked here simply to avoid additional technical notation when proving the results to follow.

References

Austen-Smith, David, and Jeffrey Banks. 1989. "Electoral Accountability and Incumbency." In Peter Ordeshook, ed., *Models of Strategic Choice in Politics.* Ann Arbor: University of Michigan Press.

Barro, Robert. 1973. "The Control of Politicians." *Public Choice* 14:19–42.

Denzau, Arthur, William H. Riker, and Kenneth Shepsle. 1985. "Farquharson and Fenno: Sophisticated Voting and Homestyle." *American Political Science Review* 79: 1117–1134.

Farquharson, Robin. 1969. *Theory of Voting.* New Haven: Yale University Press.

Fenno, Richard. 1978. *Homestyle.* Boston: Little, Brown.

Ferejohn, John. 1986. "Incumbent Performance and Electoral Control." *Public Choice* 50:5–25.

Kingdon, John. 1973. *Congressmen's Voting Decisions.* New York: Harper & Row.

Krehbiel, Keith, and Doug Rivers. 1990. "Sophisticated Voting in Congress: A Reconsideration." *Journal of Politics* 52:548–578.

Mayhew, David. 1974. *Congress: The Electoral Connection.* New Haven: Yale University Press.

McKelvey, Richard, and Richard Niemi. 1978. "A Multistage Game Representation of Sophisticated Voting for Binary procedures." *Journal of Economic Theory* 18:1–22.

Pitkin, Hannah. 1967. *The Concept of Representation.* Berkeley: University of California Press.

Wilkerson, John. 1990. "Reelection and Representation in Conflict: The Case of Agenda Manipulation." *Legislative Studies Quarterly* 15:263–282.

3

The Dynamics of Learning in N-Person Games with the Wrong N

Vincent Brousseau and Alan P. Kirman

The way in which people learn in game-theoretic contexts has recently attracted some attention (see, for example, Crawford and Haller 1990; Marcet and Sargent 1989, Kalai and Lehrer 1990; and Jordan 1990). The individuals concerned may be trying to learn about the strategies used by their opponents (see, for example, Fudenberg and Kreps 1990; Milgrom and Roberts 1991; and Shapley 1964), or more generally about the structure of the game in which they are involved. In the latter case, for example, they may try, as Bayesians or through some other learning mechanism, to estimate the parameters of the payoff function (see, for example, Jordan 1991; Kiefer and Nyarko 1989). A more general problem would be that of establishing not just the parameter of a particular model but also criteria for rejecting that model. If the space of parameters is made general enough, this general problem reduces to the simpler one. What we do in this chapter is to consider the case in which the agents start out by having an erroneous idea about the n of the n-person game that they are playing. We then examine the ways in which, by learning, they might realize their mistake, or alternatively might converge to a situation in which their beliefs are confirmed by their observations (see Nyarko 1990). Such self-fulfilling expectations are of course related to those in the "sunspots" literature (see, for example, Woodford 1990). Indeed, in our example, the agents will leave out of consideration the actions of their opponents, that is, they will play as if n were smaller than it really is, whereas one can think of the sunspots equilibrium as adding an additional, but a priori irrelevant, player who controls the sunspot variable but whose payoff is unrelated to that of the other n players. Thus sunspots equilibria and those that we are studying can be considered as examples of symmetric errors, resulting from agents considering n to be too large or too small.

It might seem strange to think of players not being aware of the number of their opponents and thus not taking into account the actions of some of them. However, in economic applications this is very plausible. What general equilibrium teaches us is that everything depends on everything else in the economy. In principle, at least in a finite economy where everybody has positive weight, an agent should therefore take into account the actions of all the other actors in the economy. This is clearly unrealistic, although it is possible to treat the full-market problem as a game and to examine its Nash equilibrium. However, even in much more circumscribed situations such as that of an oligopoly, who the players are is far from clear. If products are differentiated, how different do they have to be from one's own before their producers can reasonably be ignored? How far does one supermarket have to be from another for it not to be considered as a rival? These are natural questions for the economist applying game theory to his problems, and they make it worth considering what happens when a player fails to take into account the actions of some of his opponents.

The essential problem with learning in these situations is that the action of the individual who is trying to learn influences the outcomes that he is trying to learn from. He is unable, when looking at his payoffs, to distinguish the consequences of his own behavior from those of the other players, or indeed from the consequences of nature's actions. This poses a very difficult theoretical question. In the case where the other player is observed, one may treat him as behaving according to some prespecified but unknown choice, and therefore one simply observes the frequency with which he takes various actions. Alternatively one may, if one observes his payoffs, attribute some more sophisticated reasoning to his behavior. However, as one learns, one is trying to improve one's payoff and there is an implicit contradiction between this goal in the short run and learning more for the long run (see Green 1983; Aghion, Espinosa, and Julien 1990). This involves a problem of optimal experimental design. How much should I be prepared to sacrifice in profit today to have better information, and thus to do better in the future? Even in the monopoly case with a two-unknown-parameter linear demand curve (see Balvers and Cosimano 1990; Easley and Kiefer 1988; and Kiefer and Nyarko 1989), this problem seems to be rather intractable, and we will do no more than attribute rather simple learning behavior to our individuals.

We will consider a particularly simple example developed by one of us (Kirman 1975, 1983), in which each of the two players of a duopoly game fails to take into account the other's existence and tries to maximize what he believes to be his short-term monopoly profit.

We discuss briefly a series of results which show that a whole class of self-sustaining equilibria can be attained from particular starting conditions if the agents use least-squares learning. Whereas it was conjectured earlier (Kirman 1983) that the learning process would converge in general, we show, developing results in Brousseau and Kirman 1991, that this apparent convergence is due to the slowing down of the process by the weight of the memory. This evokes the decelerating cyclical behavior found by Shapley (1964). As in his case, truncating the memory changes the behavior radically. We examine in some detail the consequences of this for price dynamics. We also show that reducing the weight in earlier observations and making a continuous-time approximation shows that the process is, in general, unstable.

We find regions of stability, and also complicated dynamics in the short memory game that evoke the idea of a chaotic process. Thus, even with a very simple example, rather complicated phenomena may arise as individuals try to learn about an environment that they themselves influence. Learning about the wrong game may lead, by chance, to self-fulfilling expectations but may also lead to a complicated evolution of the payoffs to the participants, particularly if they do not have very long memories.

As we have explained, the complexity of the dynamics of this simple example is due to the feedback from the players' own strategy and the unobserved strategy of his opponent into the variable that he observes. However, in the short-memory game, where dependence on initial conditions becomes very indirect, price dynamics although complex are not completely unpredictable. The price are captured by a "pseudo-limit" but then move away from it. Thus there is, as in the case of full memory, apparent convergence. However, in the short-term memory case, the convergence to a certain region cannot be attributed to a slowing down of the process. Indeed the "convergence" in the five-period memory case, although slower than in the two-period case, is stronger in the sense that deviations from the "pseudo limit" are smaller. Finally, this limit itself depends on the length of the memory.

Thus we will see that the convergence of the learning process in the simple game that we are studying is heavily dependent on the behavior of omitted players. This observation is of particular interest to those who wish to apply game-theoretic reasoning to empirical economics.

A Simple Duopoly Game

Consider a symmetric duopoly in which the demand functions for firms 1 and 2 are given by the "true model":

$$d_1[p_1(t), p_2(t)] = \alpha - \beta p_1(t) + \gamma p_2(t); \tag{1}$$

$$d_2[p_1(t), p_2(t)] = \alpha - \beta p_2(t) + \gamma p_1(t), \tag{2}$$

where $p_i(t)$ is the price set by firm i at time t. Assume, in the tradition of Cournot, that production is costless. The payoff to each firm is then given by

$$M_i(p_1(t), p_2(t)) = p_i(t)d_i(p_1(t), p_2(t)).$$

Now assume, as in Kirman 1983, that the two firms, through ignorance or inertia, are unaware that their demand depends on each other's actions. As we have suggested, in a duopoly situation, such an assumption is implausible, but it is more realistic in a several-firm situation in which each firm feels unable to take into explicit account the behavior of all the opponents, and hence focuses on the "own-price" demand curve or on a demand curve involving only some of the prices of its opponents and adds a random term to take into account the, to the firm unpredictable, behavior of the other firms. All our results can be generalized to an n-firm model, such as that developed by Gates, Rickard, and Wilson (1977, 1978).

The two firms will thus have the following "perceived model":

$$d_1[p_1(t)] = \alpha_1 - b_1 p_1(t) + \varepsilon_1(t); \tag{3}$$

$$d_2[p_2(t)] = \alpha_2 - b_2 p_2(t) + \varepsilon_2(t). \tag{4}$$

We shall make no specific assumptions about the distribution of the error terms, although to be rigorous our agents should make specific assumptions if they adopt the learning procedure suggested.

We shall now look at how the players should learn about the parameters of their model with two questions in mind:

(i) Does the learning process converge?

(ii) If so, does the limit correspond to a solution of the true game?

If ignorance is only partial, in the sense that players believe with certainty that $b_i = \beta$ (the "slope of the true demand curve") and try to learn about a_i, then it is easily shown using a fictitious play argument (Kirman 1975) that prices will converge to the Cournot-Nash solution

$$p_i^* = \frac{\alpha}{2\beta - \gamma}. \tag{5}$$

Now consider the case where neither of the parameters a_i or b_i is assumed to be fixed. If players maximize one-period payoffs,[1] and if they believe that $E(\varepsilon_i(t)) = 0$, then the optional price or strategy is given by

$$p_i(t) = \frac{\hat{a}_i(t)}{2\hat{b}_i(t)}, \tag{6}$$

where $\hat{a}_i(i)$ and $\hat{b}_i(i)$ are the estimates at time t of the two parameters, given the quantities and prices observed up to that point.

So, at each period, given its estimates, each firm will charge a price, and the demand realized as a result of these prices will, of course, be given by the true model specified by equations 1 and 2. This new observation of a price-quantity pair will lead to a revision of the estimates of the parameters and, in turn, to new prices and so forth.

It is now standard practice in the case where there is ignorance of both the parameters to assume that each firm tries to fit the observed data by means of least squares. This can be justified from the Bayesian viewpoint (see Zellner 1971) or as a special case of general updating processes (see Aoki 1976). The model we consider is a special case of that developed by Gates, Rickard, and Wilson (1977), in which the authors allow for n firms and variable weights for preceding observations. They were obliged, however, to confine their attention to particular cases to obtain analytic results.

In our particular model, the ordinary least-square estimates for a_i and b_i are given by

$$\hat{b}_i(t) = -\frac{\sum_{k=1}^{t-1} [d_i(k) - \bar{d}_i(t)][p_i(k) - \bar{p}_i(t)]}{\sum_{k=1}^{t-1} [p_i(k) - \bar{p}_i(t)]^2}; \tag{7}$$

and

$$\hat{a}_i(t) = \bar{d}_i(t) + \hat{b}_i(t)\bar{p}_i(t) \quad (i = 1, 2), \tag{8}$$

where

$$\bar{d}_i(t) = \frac{\sum_{k=1}^{t-1} d_i(k)}{t - 1} \quad \text{and} \quad \bar{p}_i(t) = \frac{\sum_{k=1}^{t-1} p_i(k)}{t - 1}.$$

Observe that (7) can be rewritten for firm 1 as

$$\hat{b}_i(t) = \beta - \gamma \frac{\sum_{k=1}^{t-1} [p_i(k) - \bar{p}_i(t)][p_2(k) - \bar{p}_2(t)]}{\sum_{k=1}^{t-1} [p_1(k) - \bar{p}_1(t)]^2}, \tag{9}$$

and similarly for firm 2.

Given this, it is easy to see why estimates of the parameters of the perceived model are influenced by the behavior of the opponent. The second term in (9) is the covariance of the prices or the bias due to the omission of a variable correlated with one of the included variables. Indeed, it is precisely the fact that the prices are interrelated in this way that generates problems in the evolution of the system.

The whole system is clearly recursive. Hence, from the equation for the true demand (3.1), we have for firm 1,

$$p_1(t) = \frac{[(\alpha + \gamma \bar{p}_2(t))] \sum_{k=1}^{t-1} [p_1(k) - \bar{p}_1(t)]^2 - \gamma \bar{p}_1(t) \sum_{k=1}^{t-1} [p_1(k) - \bar{p}_1(t)][p_2(k) - \bar{p}_2(t)]}{2(\beta \sum_{k=1}^{t-1} [p_1(k) - \bar{p}_1(t)]^2 - \gamma \sum_{k=1}^{t-1} [p_1(k) - \bar{p}_1(t)][p_2(k) - \bar{p}_2(t)])},$$

$$(10)$$

and similarly for firm 2.

This recurrence relation is a special case of that given by Gates, Rickard, and Wilson (1977). It is apparent that even in this form it is not a trivial matter to establish whether convergence does or does not occur.

Can Equilibria be Self-Sustaining?

In a model such as that which we have just described, a natural question arises. Can the game get "stuck" in an equilibrium in which the observations made by players confirm their mistaken beliefs about the model, and hence where their own optimizing behavior leads that equilibrium to persist? The answer to this question is yes, and can be given in two parts. First, for any positive prices p_1 and p_2 there are estimates of the parameters a_i and b_i such that, were the individuals to make these estimates, they would never move from those prices. For given p_1^* and p_2^* these are given by

$$b_1^* = -\beta + \frac{\alpha + \gamma p_2^*}{p_1^*};$$

$$b_2^* = -\beta + \frac{\alpha + \gamma p_1^*}{p_2^*};$$

and

$$a_1^* = 2(\alpha - \beta p_1^* + \gamma p_2^*);$$

$$a_2^* = 2(\alpha - \beta p_2^* + \gamma p_1^*).$$

Clearly, if at some $\bar{t}$ it is the case that

$$\hat{a}_i(\bar{t}) = a_i^* \quad \text{and} \quad \hat{b}_i(\bar{t}) = b_i^*,$$

then $p_i(t) = p_i^*$ for $i = 1, 2$ and all $t \geq \bar{t}$.

The second part of the answer is that we can actually find initial conditions such that the least-squares learning procedure will subsequently converge to values of the parameters, in the set defined above.

This is shown by the following

THEOREM 1 (KIRMAN 1983)   If for p_1^* and p_2^*, the parameters a_1^*, a_2^*, b_1^* and b_2^* defined in (1) and (2) satisfy

$$\gamma^2 \geq (\beta - b_1^*)(\beta - b_2^*) \geq 0,$$

then there exist $p_1(1)$, $p_1(2)$, $p_1(3)$ and $p_2(1)$, $p_2(2)$, $p_2(3)$ such that

$$\tilde{a}_1(4) = a_1^* \qquad \text{and} \qquad \hat{b}_1(4) = b_1^*;$$

$$\hat{a}_2(4) = a_2^* \qquad \text{and} \qquad \hat{b}_2(4) = b_2^*.$$

Hence $p_1(t) = p_1^*$ and $p_2(t) = p_2^*$ for all $t \geq 4$.

Thus there is a large set of self-sustained equilibria which can be attained through least-squares learning and which of them is attained clearly depends on initial conditions.

This result is not fully satisfactory, since the sudden collapse of the error terms to zero for the fourth period onwards might disturb the agents. However, it is possible to show that a continuum of equilibria can be attained in two steps. Thus there is no error in the perceived demand curve; the first two price-demand conditions determine it, and the optimal price demand choice remains on that curve. This can be summarized as

THEOREM 2   Consider any $p^* = (p_1^*, p_2^*)$ in $\mathbb{R}_{++}^2$ such that $\alpha + \gamma p_2^* \neq \beta p_2^*$ and $\alpha + \gamma p_2^* \neq \beta p_1^*$, and assume $\beta \neq \gamma$, then there is a line $\Delta(p^*)$ through p^* with positive slope with the following property: if $p_1(1) = p_1^*$ and $p_2(1) = p_2^*$ and $(p_1(2), p_2(2))$ lies on $\Delta(p^*)$, then

$$\left(\frac{\hat{a}_1(3)}{2\hat{b}_1(3)}, \frac{\hat{a}_2(3)}{2\hat{b}_2(3)} \right)$$

also lies on $\Delta(p^*)$.[2]

Thus if the initial conditions, that is, the first two price pairs, are aligned in a particular way, they will generate optimal prices and resultant quantities that will lie on the demand curves generated by these initial conditions. Let us call an equilibrium generated in this way a *perfectly self-sustaining equilibrium*.

Given this definition, the natural question is what is the nature of the set of such equilibria? The answer is provided by

THEOREM 3   Assume $\beta \neq \gamma$, then the set E of points $\left(\frac{a_1}{2b_1}, \frac{a_2}{2b_2} \right)$, where a_1, a_2, b_1, b_2 are strictly positive, that are perfect self-sustaining equilibria is a continuum of dimension 1 in $\mathbb{R}^2_{++}$ and satisfies the equation $2\beta(\gamma(x^2 + y^2) - 2\beta xy) - \alpha(\gamma - 2\beta)(x + y) - \alpha^2 = 0$.

If we are to consider only positive a_i and b_i then the relevant part of this hyperbola is that from A to A' in figure 3.1. This continuum of equilibria constitutes part of the boundary of the region of self-sustaining equilibria given by the first results cited.

An interesting feature of this type of equilibrium is that it contains the cooperative joint monopoly solution, but not the Cournot-Nash equilibrium. The joint monopoly solution is achieved if in the first two periods

$$p_1(t) = p_2(t) \qquad t = 1, 2,$$

then for all $t \geq 3$

$$p_1(t) = p_2(t) = \frac{\alpha}{2(\beta - \gamma)}.$$

Thus, curiously, in this example unconscious imitation leads to a cooperative solution. This adds another example to the discussion in the literature

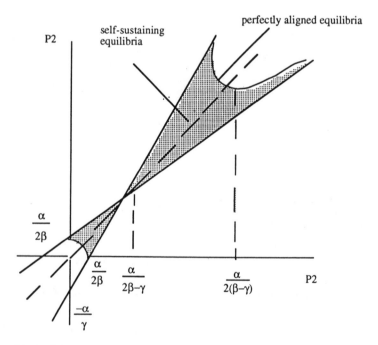

Figure 3.1

as to how players can coordinate on a Pareto-superior equilibrium, although in general the discussion involves coordinating as one of several Nash equilibria.

The General Dynamics of Least-Squares Learning

In Kirman 1983 it was conjectured that starting from any initial conditions the least-squares learning process employed by both agents would lead to the convergence of prices. Repeated simulations showed apparent convergence. The easiest way to look at this convergence is to examine the variance-covariance matrix of the observed price series. In cases analogous to the one described in theorem 1, namely, where there are initial observations that do not lie on the limit demand curves, the empirical variance-covariance matrix, itself, converges. In the case described in theorem 2, that of perfectly aligned equilibria, this matrix only changes in modulus. Although we cannot, and we will see later why, establish the general convergence of the process, we do have the following characterization of the limits of these sequences that do converge. Somewhat imprecisely stated, we have

THEOREM 4   If the least-squares learning procedure converges to stationary values of p_1 and p_2, then these must be those which can be attained from the initial conditions constructed in theorems 1 and 2.

In order to understand theorem 4, it is useful to introduce some notation.

$$x(t_0) = \frac{1}{t} \sum_{t=1}^{t_0-1} p_1(t) \qquad y(t_0) = \frac{1}{t} \sum_{t=1}^{t_0-1} p_2(t) \qquad u(t_0) = \frac{1}{t} \sum_{t=1}^{t_0-1} p_1^2(t)$$

$$v(t_0) = \frac{1}{t} \sum_{t=1}^{t_0-1} p_1(t)p_2(t) \qquad w(t_0) = \frac{1}{t} \sum_{t=1}^{t_0-1} p_2^2(t); \tag{11}$$

$$U(t_0) = u - x^2 \qquad V(t_0) = v - xy \qquad W(t_0) = w - y^2. \tag{12}$$

Now we can rewrite the recursive price process as

$$p_1(t_0) = \frac{1}{2} \frac{\alpha(u - x^2) + \gamma(yu - xv)}{\beta(u - x^2) - \gamma(v - xy)} = \frac{1}{2} \frac{\alpha U + \gamma(yU - xV)}{\beta U - \gamma V}; \tag{13}$$

$$p_2(t_0) = \frac{1}{2} \frac{\alpha(w - xy) + \gamma(xw - yv)}{\beta(w - y^2) - \gamma(v - xy)} = \frac{1}{2} \frac{\alpha W + \gamma(xW - yV)}{\beta W - \gamma V}. \tag{14}$$

We add two further definitions:

$$g_1(t_0) = p_1(t_0) - x = \frac{1}{2}\frac{(\alpha - 2\beta x)(u - x^2) + \gamma(yu + xv + 2x^2y)}{\beta(u - x^2) - \gamma(v - xy)}$$

$$= \frac{1}{2}\frac{(\alpha + \gamma y - 2\beta x)U + \gamma xV}{\beta U - \gamma V};\tag{15}$$

$$g_2(t_0) = p_2(t_0) - y = \frac{1}{2}\frac{(\alpha - 2\beta y)(w - y^2) + \gamma(yv + xw + 2xy^2)}{\beta(w - y^2) - \gamma(v - xy)}$$

$$= \frac{1}{2}\frac{(\alpha + \gamma x - 2\beta y)W + \gamma yV}{\beta W - \gamma V}.\tag{16}$$

In all of the above we drop the argument to the right-hand side to make the notation more manageable. Now the dynamics of the system are completely described by those of the five variables x, y, U, V and W. The five vector at time $t + 1$ is determined by its values at time t. We have

$$\begin{bmatrix} x \\ y \\ U \\ V \\ W \end{bmatrix}(t + 1) = \begin{bmatrix} x \\ y \\ U \\ V \\ W \end{bmatrix}(t) + \frac{1}{t + 1}\begin{bmatrix} g_1 \\ g_2 \\ g_1^2 - U \\ g_1 g_2 - V \\ g_2^2 - W \end{bmatrix}(t).\tag{17}$$

Clearly there are two classes of equilibria, those for which the right-hand vector is zero and those which are attained as this vector changes in such a way that the variance-covariance matrix changes promptly over time. In one case both prices and the associated statistics are unchanged over time; in the other, prices do not change, but the associated statistics do. In the cases we have examined, the "perfectly aligned" equilibria have a matrix of price statistics that changes over time, whereas in those which are attained after three periods the variance-covariance matrix is unmodified over time.

Now recall that the variance-covariance matrix is given by

$$T = \begin{bmatrix} U & V \\ V & W \end{bmatrix},\tag{18}$$

and that

$$T(t + 1) - T(t) = \frac{1}{t + 1}G^TG;\tag{19}$$

then we have an equilibrium either when

$$T(t + 1) = T(t) \quad \text{or when} \quad \frac{1}{t + 1} G^Y G = \lambda T(t).$$

Taking these cases one at a time, we have in the first $G = 0$. But then solving these equations gives

$$(\alpha + \gamma y - 2\beta x)U + \gamma x V = 0; \tag{20}$$

$$(\alpha + \gamma x - 2\beta y)W + \gamma y V = 0. \tag{21}$$

These are nothing other than the conditions already mentioned and found in Kirman 1983. In this case, the matrix T does not degenerate.

If we consider the second case, we must solve

$$G^T G = \lambda T(t).$$

If we replace U, V and W by g_1^2, g_1, g_2, g_2^2, then the solution to the above corresponds to

$$g_1 = \lambda \frac{(\alpha + \gamma y - 2\beta x)g_1 + \gamma x g_2}{2(\beta g_1 - \gamma g_2)}; \tag{22}$$

$$g_2 = \lambda \frac{(\alpha + \gamma x - 2\beta y)g_2 + \gamma y g_1}{2(\beta g_2 - \gamma g_1)}. \tag{23}$$

In this case we need the determinant of the matrix below to be zero

$$\begin{vmatrix} 2g_1(\beta g_1 - \gamma g_2) & (\alpha + \gamma y - 2\beta x)g_1 + \gamma x g_2 \\ 2g_2(\beta g_2 - \gamma g_1) & (\alpha + \gamma x - 2\beta y)g_2 + \gamma y g_1 \end{vmatrix}. \tag{24}$$

But this amounts to the following

$$\beta \gamma y g_1^3 + (\beta \alpha - \beta \gamma x - 2\beta^2 y + \gamma \alpha)g_1^2 g_2$$

$$+ (\beta \gamma y - \gamma \alpha - \beta \alpha + 2\beta^2 x)g_1 g_2^2 + (-\beta \gamma x)g_2^3 = 0, \tag{25}$$

which is of course the polynomial that corresponds to the "perfectly aligned" equilibria.

This shows how theorem 4 is proved.[3]

Out of Equilibrium Dynamics

Having established the nature of the equilibria, we can now look at how the system evolves out of equilibrium. Examination of equation 17 shows clearly where the apparent convergence of earlier simulations, already mentioned, come from. The term $1/(t + 1)$ shows down the whole process. This is because all previous observations in the case of least-squares estimation are given the same weight. Thus, as the process evolves over time, if memory is unbounded, each successive observation has less impact than the previous one. Thus, even if the time path itself does not converge, progress along that path becomes slower. This is reminiscent of an old observation of Shapley (1964), who studied a simple matrix game in which players tried to learn about the mixed strategies of their opponents by observing the empirical frequencies with which the pure strategies were played. If memory was unbounded, Shapley showed that the game would cycle from one equilibrium to another, but more and more slowly.

We can examine the dynamics of our process by reducing the weight attributed to earlier observations. We will proceed in two steps. First, we will approximate our system by a continuous-line process and will examine its stability. The natural question is, if the initial conditions that lead to one equilibrium are perturbed, will the same equilibrium be attained? The answer is given by the following result.

THEOREM 5   The equilibria of the discrete system are all unstable with respect to its continuous-time approximation.

To see this, consider the following differential equation system

$$\frac{d}{dt} \begin{bmatrix} x \\ y \\ U \\ V \\ W \end{bmatrix} = \begin{bmatrix} g_1 \\ g_2 \\ g_1^2 - U \\ g_1 g_2 - V \\ g_2^2 - W \end{bmatrix}. \tag{26}$$

Solving this is equivalent to replacing t by $\log t$ in the original system, and solving by numerical integration.

The idea of the proof of instability as given in full in Brousseau and Kirman 1991 is simple. When the direction of the trajectory of the process is studied at any of the equilibria other than those on the boundary of the set of figure 3.1, it turns out to be a straight line through that point. Thus the motion of the system will always carry it through any such point to the boundary. However, since the boundary is a continuum, any perturbation of the initial conditions will carry the process to another of these equilibria.

Dynamics with Truncated Memory

A reasonable solution to the difficulties involved with the unlimited memory least-squares learning, or the continuous-time approximation, is simply to truncate individuals' memories. Since this removes the direct influence of the initial conditions, one might hope that this would increase the possibility of obtaining stability of equilibria. However, Shapley's (1964) example, mentioned previously, would seem to suggest the opposite. The idea of limiting the number of previous observations taken into account is not new, and Gates, Rickard, and Wilson (1977), working in a similar context to ours, considered the case in which agents used only two previous observations. However, curiously they assumed that, at period *t*, agents used the (− 1)th and first observation. When convergence occurs in this case, the limit clearly depends on the initial conditions. Smale (1980) emphasized the role of bounded memory and suggested that agents could only keep some summary statistics for the past. However, as we have seen, this alone is not enough.

A first remark is in order. Supposing the process were to converge after a finite number of periods, as in the earlier theorems, if the agents were to have only finite memories, the process would no longer be defined. The optimal response of agents is to set prices as follows.

$$p_i(t) = \frac{\hat{a}_i(t)}{2\hat{b}_i(t)},$$

but if over the length of the memory the price were to be constant, and the corresponding depends also, then the estimates $\hat{a}_i$ and $\hat{b}_i$ would no longer be defined. The matrix of statistics of the price process

$$\begin{bmatrix} u & v \\ v & w \end{bmatrix}$$

would suddenly become zero, and the subsequent steps of the process would be impossible to calculate.

When we simulate the process with memories of differing but finite lengths, we observe behavior suggesting convergence in the sense that the process fluctuates close to certain values and then moves away, sometimes fairly far before again returning to the values in question. Thus, when the process does not cycle, it exhibits erratic behavior, but around a well-defined point.

To see this in the simplest case, consider individuals whose memory is limited to two observations. Thus at each point in time they have a perfectly fitting demand curve. In this case the recursive relation defining the price process reduces to

$$p_i(t) = \frac{\alpha(p_i(t-2) - p_i(t-1)) + \gamma(p_i(t-2)p_j(t-1) - p_j(t-2)p_i(t-1))}{\beta(p_i(t-2) - p_i(t-1)) - \gamma(p_j(t-2) - p_j(t-1))}$$

$$i = 1, 2 \quad i \neq j. \tag{27}$$

In this case the process oscillates around the values

$$p_1^* = p_2^* = \frac{\alpha}{2\beta}.$$

Thus it might seem that this solution would correspond to that in which the players knew the values of the parameters affecting their variable and simply attributed zero weight to the strategy of the opponent. However, unfortunately, this is not correct. In order to sustain the prices p_1^* the values of the estimates $\hat{a}_i$ and $\hat{b}_i$ must be given by

$$\hat{a}_i = \alpha + \frac{\alpha\gamma}{\beta}; \tag{28}$$

$$\hat{b}_i = \beta + \gamma. \tag{29}$$

Thus the role of the interference of the other player becomes very clear; indeed, as γ diminishes, we obviously return to the monopoly case.

In figures 3.2a and 3.2b the time path of the process is shown. It should be observed that, although the process seems to settle down after the first few periods, it does not in fact remain there; the movements that can be seen around period 230 recur if the simulation is continued. It is not therefore, as has been remarked already, possible to argue that the process converges to

$$\left(\frac{\alpha}{2\beta}, \frac{\alpha}{2\beta}\right),$$

but one could think of this as an accumulation point of the attractor of the process. In figure 3.2c another example is shown where the oscillations clearly restart after period 270.

In some simulations the process briefly oscillated wildly, even attaining negative prices. However, for some special cases it is possible to show that there are "stable regimes" in the sense that the process will not leave that region once it has attained a point within it.

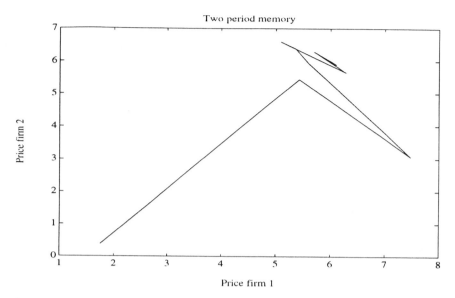

Figure 3.2a

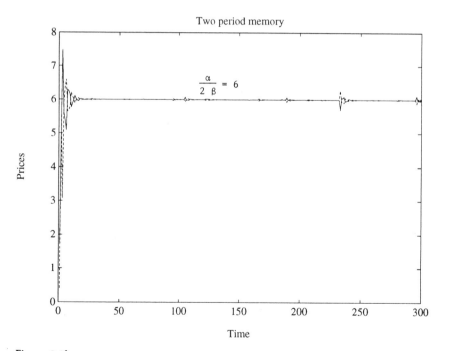

Figure 3.2b

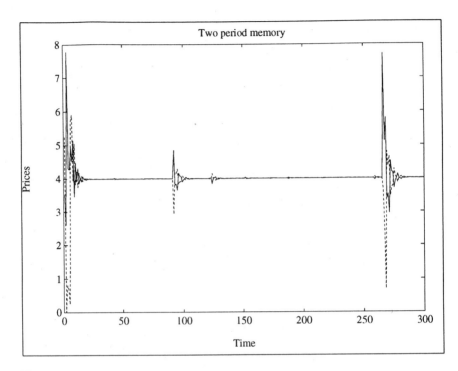

Figure 3.2c

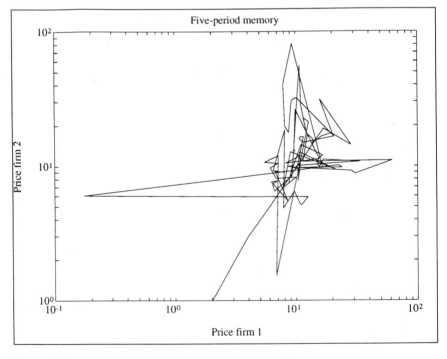

Figure 3.2d

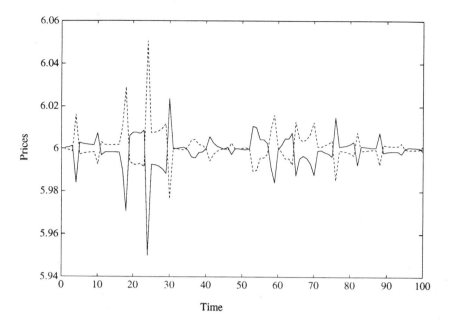

Figure 3.2e

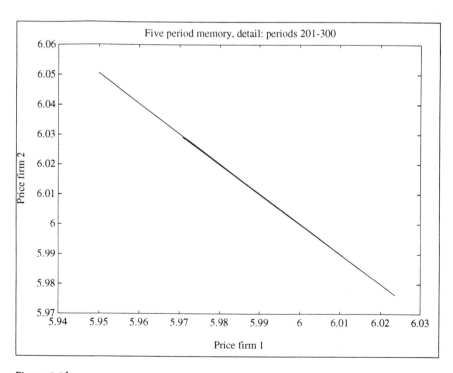

Figure 3.2f

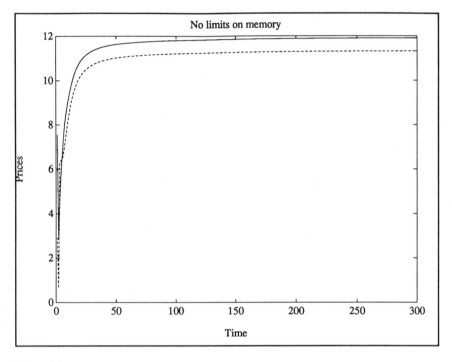

Figure 3.2g

Next we tried increasing the length of memory to five periods, as shown in figures 3.2d, e, and f. Here the process went close to a point given by

$$\frac{\alpha}{2\beta - \gamma}.$$

Although once again the two prices given by the dotted and solid lines seem to converge, in fact sufficiently long simulations caused movements away from these points again. This is due of course to the particular estimation procedure being used, and it is an open question as to whether this would happen with other types of learning. As a simple comparison, we show an example with no limits on memory, and here we can see a clear apparent convergence of prices, but in this case, however, to an asymmetric solution (figure 3.2g). Here we found that the simulations often had a new "pseudo-limit," which was no longer

$$\frac{\alpha}{2\beta}, \frac{\alpha}{2\beta}$$

but rather

$$\left(\frac{\alpha}{2\beta - \gamma}, \frac{\alpha}{2\beta - \gamma}\right),$$

the Nash equilibrium. This is of particular interest since it provides a theoretical explanation for results found in experiments where players in an oligopoly, who were ignorant of each others' strategies and payoffs converged rapidly to the Nash equilibrium. Whether this observation, which is discussed in Kirman 1993, was due to the participants using least-squares learning is of course a different issue.

One final observation concerning the simple example studied here is that the periodic divergence of the process may be due to the lack of movement of prices near the "pseudo limit," and hence to the extreme sensitivity of the parameter estimates of any small changes in the observations. This could be overcome if small "trembles" were added to the game so that individuals would always have dispersed points from which to estimate their parameters. Simulations with white noise added to the true payoff functions simply produced larger fluctuations around the "pseudo limit." Thus this noise did not affect the basic characteristics of the underlying process.

A Related Example

Finally, in order to relate our discussion of the evolution of our process in misperceived models to the other literature on misperception, that on "sunspots," we look at another simple example. Consider the following rather strange demand function

$$d_i(t) = 0 \qquad p_i(t) > 2$$

$$d_i(t) = \max(1/2, \min(2p_j(t) - p_i(t), 2p_j(t) - 1)) \qquad i = 1, 2 \quad i \neq j. \quad (30)$$

This in illustrated in figure 3.3. Now assume that the players play the game normally, taking their opponents' actions into account.

LEMMA d_i is nonnegative and decreasing. Furthermore, the subspace of strategies $[1, 2] \times [1, 2]$ is stable with respect to the best response functions, and there is a continuum of Nash equilibria $p_1 = p_2$ $1 \leq p_1 \leq 2$.

Proof   The function is clearly positive for $p_i \leq 2$ since there is the constant term $1/2$ in the max and zero for all $p_i > 2$. The function is decreasing since $2p_j - p_i$ is decreasing in p_i, $2p_j - 1$ is constant, therefore the min is decreasing. $1/2$ is constant; therefore the max is decreasing in p_i.

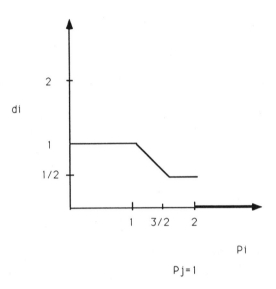

Figure 3.3

To see the stability of the best response, let $\bar{p}_j \in [1, 2]$ and consider the problem

$$\max_{p_i} p_i d_i.$$

This can be rewritten

$$\max_{p_i \in [0, 2]} \left[\max \left[\frac{p_i}{2}, [p_i \times \min(2\bar{p}_j - p_i, 2\bar{p}_j - 1)] \right] \right].$$

The function $(p_i \times \min(2\bar{p}_j - p_i, 2\bar{p}_j - 1))$ is concave C^1 on $[0, 2]$. The maximum cannot occur for $p_i < 1$ since $2\bar{p}_j - 1 > 0$ for $\bar{p}_j \in [1, 2]$. For $p_i \in [1, 2]$ the function is

$$2\bar{p}_j p_i - p_i^2,$$

and is maximized at $p_i = \bar{p}_j$.

The problem can now be rewritten

$$\text{Max}_{p_i \in [0, 2]} \left[\max \left(\frac{p_i}{2}, \bar{p}_j^2 \right) \right].$$

Since $\bar{p}_j^2 \geq 1$ the maximum value is always given by $\bar{p}_j^2$, therefore $p_i = \bar{p}_j$ is the solution and the Nash equilibria for the strategy subspace $[1, 2] \times [1, 2]$ are $p_1 = p_2 \in [1, 2]$.   □

This solution corresponds to the solution of the special case of our original example with

$$\alpha = 0 \quad \beta = 1 \quad \gamma = 2,$$

but economists would have found this objectionable for obvious reasons, although as an abstract game it is well defined.

This example has multiple Nash equilibria and they are Pareto-ordered. It is easy to create a trivial sunspot equilibrium that selects one of the Nash equilibria. Consider an irrelevant player k who always sets a fixed price $\bar{p}_k \in [1, 2]$. Suppose, in addition, that both players in our example mistakenly believe that they are playing against k and not against each other. They will both clearly choose $p_i = p_j = \bar{p}_k$ after two observations, and this is a perfect-foresight Nash equilibrium, which will be sustained from $t = 3$ onwards. Of course, if player k is for other reasons doing something more complicated, the price process of the duopoly game will also be more complicated, as the players try to learn. Nevertheless, in this rather trivial example mistaking the identity of the players, that is, basing one's own strategy on the behavior of an irrelevant "sunspot" player, allows a selection among the multiple equilibria.

Conclusion

We have examined, in the context of a simple example, the consequences of individuals failing to take into account the behavior of their opponents. If agents use full-blown unbounded memory least-squares learning to estimate the parameters of their "false" models, they can get stuck in a large class of self-fulfilling equilibria. However, the apparent general convergence observed in simulations of this process is due to the slowing down of the process, as each successive observation carries less and less weight. Approximating this process by one in continuous time shows that only "perfectly aligned" equilibria can be equilibria. Thus in this case the set of candidates for limit points of the process is greatly reduced. When we looked at a modified version of the process in which the agents' memories were bounded, we found strange dynamics and recognizable accumulation points; in particular, when the length of memory was extended somewhat, the system oscillated around the Nash equilibrium. Thus, once the system was no longer restricted by the weight of its long memory, learning in the "false" game led to fluctuations about the noncooperative equilibrium of the true game.

Notes

The authors would like to thank Ed Hopkins for his valuable comments and suggestions, and in particular for producing the figures.

1. This assumption avoids the experimental design problem mentioned previously.

2. For full details and the proofs of theorems 1–3 see Brousseau and Kirman 1991.

3. For the complete proof see Brousseau and Kirman 1991.

References

Aghion, P., M. P. Espinoza, and B. Jullien. 1990. "Dynamic Duopoly with Learning through Market Experimentation." Groupe HEC, Jouy-en-Josas, France. Mimeo.

Aoki, M. 1976. *Optimal Control and System Theory in Dynamic Economic Analysis.* New York; Elsevier.

Balvers, R. J., and T. F. Cosimano. 1990. "Actively Learning about Demand and the Dynamics of Price Adjustment." *Economic Journal* 100:882–898.

Brousseau, V., and A. Kirman. 1991, "The Dynamics of Learning in Mis-specified Models" European University Institute, Working paper ECO 91/40, Firenze (Italy).

Crawford, V. P., and H. Haller. 1990. "Learning How to Cooperate: Optimal Play in Repeated Coordination Games." *Econometrica* 58:571–595.

Easley, D., and N. M. Kiefer. 1988. "Controlling a Stochastic Process with Unknown Parameters." *Econometrica* 56:1045–1064.

Fudenberg, D., and D. Kreps. 1990, "Learning and Experimentation in Games." Manuscript, M.I.T.

Gates, D. J., J. A. Rickard, and D. J. Wilson. 1977. "A Convergent Adjustment Process for Firms in Competition." *Econometrica* 45:1349–1364.

Gates, D. J., J. A. Rickard, and D. J. Wilson. 1978. "Convergence of a Market-Related Game Strategy." *Journal of Mathematical Economics* 5:97–110.

Green J. 1983. "Comment on: 'Mistaken Beliefs and Resultant Equilibria' (by A. Kirman.)" In *Individual Forecasting and Aggregate Outcomes*, ed. R. Frydman and E. S. Phelps, Cambridge: Cambridge University Press, 166–168.

Jordan, J. S. 1990. "Convergence to Rational Expectations in a Stationary Linear Game." Center for Economic Research Discussion Paper no. 258, University of Minnesota.

Jordan, J. S. 1991. "Bayesian Learning in Normal Form Games." *Games and Economic Behavior* 3(1):60–81.

Kalai, E., and E. Lehrer. 1990. "Rational Learning Leads to Nash Equilibrium." Discussion paper no. 858, Northwestern University.

Kiefer, N. M., and Y. Nyarko. 1989. "Optimal Control of an Unknown Linear Process with Learning." *International Economic Review* 30(3):571–586.

Kirman A. P. 1975. "Learning by Firms about Demand Conditions." In *Adaptive Economic Models*, ed. R. H. Day and T. Groves, 137–156. New York: Academic Press.

Kirman, A. P. 1983. "On Mistaken Beliefs and Resultant Equilibria." In *Individual Forecasting and Aggregate Outcomes*, ed. R. Frydman and E. Phelps, 147–166. Cambridge: Cambridge University Press.

Kirman, A. P. 1993. "Theory and Experimental Evidence on Learning in Misspecified models." Forthcoming in *Learning and Rationality in Economics*, ed. A Kirman and M. Salmon, London: Blackwell.

Marcet, A., and T. Sargent. 1989. "Convergence of Least-Squares Learning Mechanisms in Self-Referential Linear Stochastic Models. *Journal of Economic Theory* 48: 337–368.

Milgrom, P., and J. Roberts. 1991. "Adaptive and Sophisticated Learning in Normal Form Games." *Games and Economic Behavior* 3:82–100.

Nyarko, Y. 1990. "Learning in Mis-Specified Models and the Possibility of Cycles." Economic research report no. 90-01, C. V. Starr Center for Applied Economics, New York

Shapley, L. 1964. "Some Topics in Two-Person Games." In *Advances in Game Theory*. Annals of Mathematical Studies 5:1–28. Princeton: Princeton University Press.

Smale, S. 1980. "The Prisoner's Dilemma and Dynamical Systems Associated to Noncooperative Games." *Econometrica* 48(7):1617–1634.

Woodford, M. 1990. "Learning to Believe in Sunspots." *Econometrica* 58:277–307.

Zellner, A. 1971. *An Introduction to Bayesian Inference in Econometrics*. New York: Wiley.

4

Stationary Equilibria for Deterministic Graphical Games

Steve Alpern

Introduction

Deterministic graphical (DG) games were introduced by Washburn (1990) as directed graph analogues of perfect-information finite tree games. Instead of a position moving along the nodes of an (implicitly directed) tree, an arbitrary directed graph is allowed. The only difference is that the position may cycle, and consequently the play of the game may be unending. A simple example of such a game is chess without any artificial stop rules (only checkmate or stalemate). Two types of payoffs have been suggested for such games. Washburn considered given payoffs at terminal nodes (as in tree games), with all unending plays having zero payoff for all players. We will call these "DGT games," or "deterministic graphical games with terminal payoff." Such games can also be analyzed with discounting. A more general payoff structure was defined by the author (Alpern 1991): the limiting average of local payoff vectors encountered along played arcs. We call these "DGA games," or "deterministic graphical games with (time) average payoff." Games of both types can be found in economics, and we shall give DG versions of Rubinstein (1982) bargaining and duopoly pricing.

Since the games described above are generalizations of finite games of perfect information, it is natural to ask to what extent the Zermelo–Kuhn theory on pure strategy equilibria can be maintained. In the zero-sum case this theory (Zermelo 1913) asserts the existence of a value and optimal pure strategies; more generally (Kuhn 1957), the existence of a subgame perfect pure strategy Nash equilibrium profile. In considering such questions in the DG context, it is necessary to distinguish between pure strategies that depend only on the current node (called "stationary") and those which remember the history of the play. (In a rooted tree, each node has unique history, so the notions coincide.) As we shall see, for DGT and DGA games the Zermelo (zero-sum) theory can be maintained within the class of stationary strategies, and for DGA games the Kuhn (nonzero-sum) theory can only be maintained by allowing history-remembering strategies.

DG Dynamics

A deterministic graphical game has the following (DG) dynamics: A finite directed graph G is given, together with an assignment of a player from the set $\{1, \ldots, n\}$ to each nonterminal node of G. (A terminal node is one with no arc out of it.) Beginning at a given start node of G, the player assigned to the current node selects one of the successor nodes (or, equivalently, one of the arcs out of the current node). Play proceeds in this manner either forever or until a terminal node is reached.

The reader should observe that the traditional extensive form of such a game (really pregame, since payoffs have not yet been defined) is an infinite tree whose nodes correspond to finite paths from the start node of G. Notions such as subgame perfectness will always refer to this extensive form. At this point it is also useful to observe that games with DG dynamics may be special cases of recursive games or stochastic games, depending on the payoff type. However, as we will see below, stronger theoretical or algorithmic results can sometimes be obtained within the classes of DG games than in the more general settings.

DG Strategies

In this section we define various classes of strategies that may be used in DG games. We restrict our attention to pure strategies, since the main thrust of this chapter is to determine to what extent Zermelo's theorem for finite trees can be extended to DG games.

A pure strategy for player i assigns to every path from the start node to a player i node one of the arcs leaving that node. This definition agrees with the usual notion of pure strategy on the extensive form infinite tree associated with G. A *stationary strategy* for player i is a history-independent pure strategy; it assigns to every player i node a unique out arc, which will be played whenever that node is reached. An *m-automated strategy* is a pure strategy that can be implemented by a finite automaton with m internal states. It may, however, have to remember (encode) parts of the path of play that occurred arbitrarily far in the past.

We conclude this section with a brief review of game-theoretic equilibrium concepts, intended for any graph theorists who may find these unfamiliar. An n-tuple of strategies (one for each player) is called a "strategy profile." Every such profile determines a unique path in G. All of the payoff types discussed below will assign a real n-tuple (payoff) to every such path, and by extension, to every such profile. A strategy profile such that no player can increase his payoff by unilateral deviation is called a "Nash equilibrium." A stationary Nash equilibrium profile is subgame-perfect. This means that it induces a Nash equilibrium at every node of the associated infinite extensive-form game tree, or equivalently, after every partial history (path) in G.

DGT Games

The most natural way to define the payoff for DG games is by analogy with finite tree games. That is, a payoff n-tuple is assigned to every terminal node of G. Every play of the game ending at a given terminal node is associated with this payoff, regardless of the path taken. This leaves open the question of the payoff associated with unending play, but this is dealt with by assigning the zero-payoff n-tuple to all such plays.

Games of this type, in the two-person zero-sum setting, were first considered as a class by Washburn (1990), who called them "deterministic graphical games." We prefer to use this name for all the game types considered in this chapter and we rename Washburn's games "zero-sum two-person DGT games." For such games, Washburn exhibited an algorithm for finding a pair of stationary optimal pure strategies (and hence the value) in polynomial time with respect to the number of nodes of G. It should be noted that the *existence* of the value follows from the theory of recursive games (Everette 1957). An improved algorithm for finding optimal strategies was given by Baston and Bostock (1990). They have also shown (Baston and Bostock 1993) that a two-person zero-sum DGT game on a graph with countably many nodes has a value and ε-optimal pure strategies.

An example of a DGT game is chess without any stop rules (the game ends only if a king is checkmated or stalemate occurs). Infinite play is considered a draw. The algorithms just mentioned will in principle find a winning strategy for one of the players, or a drawing strategy for each, extending Zermelo's results for finite chess.

Discounted and Supercounted DGT Games

In a DGT game the payoff upon reaching a terminal node depends only on that node and not how it was reached. A more general approach is to multiply the payoff assigned to that node by δ^t if the node was reached by a path of length t in G. If the given number δ satisfies $0 < \delta < 1$, we call the resulting game a "discounted DGT game," and if $\delta > 1$, a "super-counted DGT game." Discounted DGT games were introduced by Washburn, whose algorithm gives stationary optimal strategies and a value for the zero-sum two-person forms of these games as well. Note that in this case the existence of a value doesn't follow from the theory of recursive games, since the payoff is history-dependent. However, the theory of stochastic games would give the existence result. For the supercounted case ($\delta > 1$) even the theory of stochastic games will not give the existence of a value. However, an algorithm of Baston and Bostock (1990) establishes the existence of a value here, if it is understood that a value of $\pm\infty$ is allowed. In the supercounted case, history-remembering or behavioral strategies may be needed to postpone arrival at a desired terminal node. It should be noted that the games in this section have been defined in the n-person nonzero-sum setting, but all the quoted results are only for the two-person zero-sum case.

Example 1 (Bargaining)   The well-known alternating-offer bargaining model of Rubinstein (1982), in a discrete version, is a DGT game. Let $S = \{s^1, \ldots, s^k\}$ be a finite set of probability pairs ($s_1^i + s_2^i = 1$), considered as proposed divisions of a homogeneous good (pie). Starting with player 1 at $t = 1$, the players alternate in making a move that consists either in naming a demand $d_t \in S$ or in accepting the last demand of the other. An infinite sequence of demands $d_1, d_2, \ldots$ has payoff $(0, 0)$, while an accepted demand of $s = d_{t-1}$ on the tth move results in a payoff vector of $\delta^t s$, where $\delta < 1$ is a given discount factor common to both players. This game can be modeled as a discounted DGT game on a directed graph G_R described as follows, and drawn in Figure 4.1 for $k = 2$. The nodes of G_R consist of a start node $*$ and four groups of $k = \#(S)$ nodes each. The k far-left nodes, indexed by S, represent terminal nodes, where player 1 has accepted player 2's demand. The k left nodes represent the decision of player 1 after player 2 has demanded s_i, $i = 1, \ldots, k$. Each of these nodes has a directed arc to the left, accepting s_i, and an arc to each of the right k nodes. These in turn represent player 2's decision after player 1 has demanded s_i and have arcs

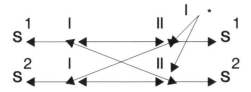

Figure 4.1

to the k left nodes and an arc to the far right, accepting s_i. The start node of player 1 has arcs to the k right nodes. The payoffs of the (accepting) far-left and right nodes are simply the demand that has been accepted.

DGA Games

One limitation of the DGT payoff structure is that the players must be indifferent to all unending plays. A more general payoff structure was introduced by the author (Alpern 1991) under the name DGA games, short for "deterministic graphical games with (time) average payoff." In these games the directed graph G is assumed to have no terminal nodes. (This is no restriction, since games modeled with some terminal nodes can also be modeled with a loop at those nodes.) Thus all plays are infinite. A local payoff vector is assigned to every arc. The total payoff associated with a play of the game is defined to be the long-term (Césaro) average of the local payoffs earned during the play. If this limit doesn't exist, we can take the lim inf or lim sup. Note that if a "terminal" vertex is reached (i.e., one with just a loop leaving it), then the total payoff converges to the local payoff on that loop. Hence every DGT game is equivalent to the DGA game obtained by putting loops at terminal vertices, and setting the local payoff vector equal to the zero vector at all arcs except for terminal loops, where it is set equal to the terminal payoff from the DGT game. Thus the theory of DGA games subsumes that of DGT games. However, some of Washburn's results for DGT games do not hold for DGA games. In particular, the author (Alpern 1989) has given an example of a DGA game possessing no stationary Nash equilibrium, as pictured in Figure 4.2.

The graph G has four nodes labeled 0, 1, 2, 3, and six arcs a, b, x, y, c, d. Player 1 decides at 0 (the start node), player 2 at node 3, and nodes 1 and 2 are transit nodes with a single leaving arc (irrelevant who "decides"). The local reward vectors are indicated next to the name of each arc. As each player has only two stationary strategies, the possible stationary equilibria

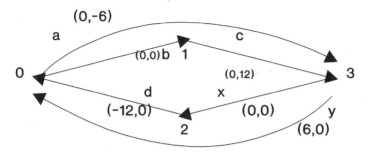

Figure 4.2

are those corresponding to the matrix below:

$$
\begin{array}{c}
 & x & & y \\
a & \left[\begin{array}{ccc} (-4,-2) & \leftarrow & (3,-3) \\ \downarrow & & \uparrow \\ b & (-3,3) & \rightarrow & (2,4) \end{array}\right].
\end{array}
$$

The total payoff corresponding to strategies a and x is the average payoff over the cycle axd, which is $(-4,-2)$, and the other entries are calculated similarly. The arrows leaving each entry show which player would prefer to leave the strategy pair, if the other is fixed, so none of the four is a Nash equilibrium. A similar example cannot be given for zero-sum DGA games, as follows from the appropriate interpretation of a result of Ehrenfeucht and Mycielski (1979), which would say that all such games have stationary Nash equilibria. This zero-sum result can also be obtained from the theory of stochastic games (Gillette 1957; Liggett and Lippman 1969).

Returning to the general (nonzero-sum) DGA game, it can be shown that pure-strategy history-remembering Nash equilibria always exist. The author (Alpern 1991) gave a recursive algorithm which produces a particular pure strategy Nash equilibrium profile called (in Alpern 1989) the Z-solution. The Z stands for Zermelo, since this profile is the DGA analog of the traditional backwards recursion solution of Zermelo, von Neumann, and Kuhn. In general, there may be many pure-strategy equilibria, but when there is only one (the generic situation for the zero-sum case), it is this Z-solution. Associated with the generically unique Z-solution is a cycle C of the graph G, called the "equilibrium cycle." If all players play the Z-solution, the cycle C is eventually repeated indefinitely, and the payoff vector is the average of the local payoffs along C. (At this equilibrium the

Césaro limit exists.) If a single player deviates, then no cycle that occurs in the play has an average payoff for this player that exceeds his payoff from C. This strong property of the Z-solution is made precise in (Alpern 1991), where it is also demonstrated that it is m-automated, where m is the factorial of the number of nodes of G.

Example 2 (Duopoly Pricing)   Suppose that two competing firms supplying a similar good set their prices on alternate days. On days $t = 1, 3, \ldots$, firm 1 chooses a price from a finite price set P_1, and firm 2 chooses from P_2 on even days. On any day when firm 1's price is i and firm 2's price is j the two firms' profits are given by the 2-vector $\pi(i, j)$. The game where both players seek to maximize the discounted sum of their profits was considered by Maskin and Tirole (1988). However, if the firms seek to maximize their long-term average profit, the game may be simply modeled as a "complete bipartite graph on P_1 and P_2." This is the directed graph with nodes $P_1 \cup P_2$ and arcs from every node in one of these sets to every node in the other, and no arcs within either P_1 or P_2. Every node i in P_1 is a player 2 node corresponding to the situation in which player 2 must set a price after player 1 has just set price $i \in P_1$. Similarly, the player 1 nodes are those in P_2. For any pair $(i, j) \in P_1 \times P_2$, the local payoff on the arc from i to j and also on the arc from j to i, is $\pi(i, j)$. The start node (if $t = 1$ is the first day) can be any node in P_2.

References

Alpern, S. 1989. "A Zermelo Algorithm Solving Deterministic Graph Games with Average Payoff." *I.E.E.E. Proceedings*, 2445–2448. 28th C.D.C., Tampa, Fla.

Alpern, S. 1991. "Cycles in Extensive Form Perfect Information Games." *Journal of Mathematical Analysis & Applications* 159:1–17.

Baston, V., and F. Bostock. 1990. "On Washburn's Deterministic Graphical Games." *Proceedings of the Fourth International Symposium on Differential Games and Applications*. Helsinki.

Baston, V., and F. Bostock. 1993. "Infinite Deterministic Graphical Games." *SIAM Journal of Control and Optimization* (forthcoming).

Everett, H. 1957. "Recursive Games." In *Contributions to the Theory of Games III*, ed. M. Dresher. A. W. Tucker, and P. Wolfe. Annals of Mathematical Studies 39:47–78. Princeton: Princeton University Press.

Ehrenfeucht, A., and J. Mycielski. 1979. "Positional Strategies for Mean Payoff Games." *International Journal of Game Theory* 8:109–113.

Gillette, D. 1957. "Stochastic Games with Zero Stop Probability." In *Contributions to the Theory of Games III*, ed. M. Dresher, A. W. Tucker, and P. Wolfe. Annals of Mathematical Studies 39:179–188. Princeton: Princeton University Press.

Kuhn, H. 1957. "Extensive Games and the Problem of Information." In *Contributions to the Theory of Games II*, ed. H. Kuhn and A. Tucker. Annals of Mathematical Studies 28:189–200. Princeton: Princeton University Press.

Liggett T., and S. Lippman. 1969. "Stochastic Games with Perfect Information and Time Average Payoff." *S.I.A.M. Review* 2:604–607.

Maskin, E., and J. Tirole. 1988. "A Theory of Dynamic Oligopoly I, II: Price Competition, Kinked Demand Curves, and Edgeworth Cycles." *Econometrica* 56: 549–599.

Rubinstein, A. 1982. "Perfect Equilibrium in a Bargaining Model." *Econometrica* 53: 97–109.

Washburn, A. 1990. "Deterministic Graphical Games." *Journal of Mathematical Analysis & Applications* 153:84–96.

Zermelo, E. 1913. "Über eine Anwendung der Mengenlehre auf die Theorie des Schachspiels." Proceedings of the Fifth International Congress of Mathematicians, vol. II. Cambridge: Cambridge University Press, 501–504.

5 Stable Coalition Structures in Consecutive Games

Joseph Greenberg and Shlomo Weber

1   Introduction and Motivation

In many social and economic situations individuals carry out activities in subgroups of the entire society. Examples of such situations are provided by: segregation due to racial, religious, or national differences; local public goods—which due to congestion either in production or in consumption are best provided by local communities; production being carried out in more than "one large firm"; the existence of social and sports clubs; labor unions, political parties, etc. However, in contrast to this widespread phenomenon, where individuals sort themselves into groups ("clubs," "teams"), relatively little formal analysis of such situations has so far been made. (For reasons for this lacuna see the recent survey on coalition formation in Greenberg 1993).

Cooperative games with coalition structures provide a natural framework for the formal analysis of these situations. One of the most interesting and fruitful solution concepts within this framework is the "coalition structure core":[1] Individuals are partitioned into a number of coalitions in such a way that there exists no group of individuals that can do better on their own. (See definition 2). In Greenberg and Weber 1986 we introduced a class of games, which we called "consecutive games," and established that they admit a nonempty coalition structure core. The main characteristic of a consecutive game is that a coalition S can form if and only if it is "connected," ("convex" or "without holes") in the sense that if two individuals i, k are members of S then the "in between" individuals (i.e., all $j, i < j < k$) also belong to S.

The purpose of this chapter is fourfold. First, we offer a simple proof that the coalition structure core of every consecutive game is nonempty. This result was proved in Greenberg and Weber 1986 by showing that the superadditive cover of a consecutive game is Scarf (1967) balanced. In contrast, the proof offered here is elementary, using induction arguments instead of variants of fixed point theorems. (However, according to Kaneko and Wooders 1982, our inductive proof implies that consecutive games are balanced.) Second, our proof is constructive, thus providing a partial characterization both of the payoffs as well as of the stable coalition structures. (The average overall permutations of the individuals of the stable payoffs that we construct happen to yield the Shapley value in superadditive games with side payments.) Third, we extend the analysis to games with an infinite (countable and a continuum) number of players. We show that the coalition structure core of such consecutive games is nonempty whenever the set of admissible coalitions is finite, thus generalizing the result for the finite case. We also demonstrate that this restriction on the set of admissible coalitons cannot, in general, be dropped. The fourth purpose of this paper, encouraged by some recent works, is to suggest that our results on consecutive games can be useful in a rather wide range of economic environments. For example, Demange and Henriet (1991) applied the techniques of this paper to the theory of oligopoly. (See also Le Breton, Owen, and Weber 1990; and Demange 1990.) It is for this reason that we decided to publish now this "old" paper (most of the results of which were already written in 1986). Other models where consecutive games are likely to prove useful include:

Hierarchical games   Consider a society (e.g., an army) where each individual has a "rank," and in order for rank i to communicate with a higher rank k, all ranks between i and k must be involved.

Location games   Let the n players be located along the line and assume that the "value of a coalition" depends on the profits generated by transporting some commodities between the locations of its members. If individuals have property rights over the location in which they reside, then without the consent of all individuals who own property between locations i and k, no transportation between these two locations can be carried out. (In medieval times, crossing the river Rhine involved toll payments to all the landlords along the way. The many different castles along the Rhine testify to this effect.)

Political games   In his book Axelrod (1970) studies the configuration of multiparty coalitions in parliamentary democracies. He considers a one-dimensional policy space over which parties have single-peaked (or, convex) preferences, and contends that only consecutive (or, in Axelrod's terminology, *connected*) coalitions will actually form, since "a coalition consisting of adjacent parties tends to have relatively low dispersion and thus low conflict of interest. ..." (p. 169). This hypothesis, which is very similar to that of Leiserson's (1966), is strongly supported by De Swann's (1973), as well as others', empirical data. It is for this reason that Gardner (1985) restricted the set of winning coalitions (parties) to consist only of consecutive coalitions (ordered according to the ideologies of the parties).

Local public goods   Conventional wisdom suggests that due to incentive constraints and lack of information the first-best solution to producing public goods and financing them by means of lump-sum taxes is, in general, not attainable. A second-best solution typically involves proportional or equally shared taxes. In this case the induced game is often subadditive, resulting in the public goods being provided by local jurisdictions. These induced second-best taxation games might well have the property that the coalition structure core of the consecutive game coincides with the coalition structure core of the game itself. (A class of such games, where, in addition, the core constitutes the set of strong Tiebout equilibria, was identified in Greenberg and Weber 1986.)

The next section of this chapter includes our model and our formal definitions. In section 3 we prove the nonemptiness of the coalition structure core for an arbitrary finite consecutive game (theorem 1). Sections 4 and 5 extend our result to games with an infinite (countable many and continuum) number of players, when the set of admissible coalitions is finite. We show that, in general, this finiteness restriction cannot be dropped.

2   Notations and Definitions

The following definitions, some of which are not novel, are given here for the sake of completensss. *Notation* Let $x \in \mathbb{R}^N$, where N is a finite set given by $N = \{1, 2, \ldots, n\}$ and $\mathbb{R}^N$ denotes the Euclidean space of dimension n. A nonempty set $S \subset N$ denotes a *coalition*. For $\mathbf{x} \in \mathbb{R}^N$ and $S \subset N$, x^S denotes the projection of $\mathbf{x}$ on S, i.e., $x^C \in \mathbb{R}^S$ with $(\mathbf{x}^S)^i = x^i$ for $i \in S$. Similarly, for a set $A \subset \mathbb{R}^N A^S$ denotes the projection of A on S. For $\mathbf{x}, \mathbf{y} \in \mathbb{R}^N$ we write $\mathbf{x}^S \geq \mathbf{y}^S$ ($\mathbf{x}^S > \mathbf{y}^S$) if $x^i \geq y^i$ ($x^i > y^i$) for all $i \in S$. The cardinality of S is denoted by $|S|$.

DEFINITION 1   The pair (N, V) is called a "game" (in characteristic function form), where N is the set of players and V is a correspondence that assigns to every $S \subset N$ a subset $V(S)$ of $\mathbb{R}^N$ which satisfies the following requirements:

(D.1.1) *Closedness:* Each $V(S)^S$ is a closed subset of $\mathbb{R}^S$ that contains the origin;

(D.1.2) *Boundedness:* There exists a real number λ such that for any $S \subset N$ and any $\mathbf{x} \in V(S)$, $x^i \leq \lambda$ for all $i \in S$;

(D.1.3) *Comprehensiveness:* For all $S \subset N$ and any $\mathbf{x} \in V(S)$, $\mathbf{y} \in \mathbb{R}^N$ and $\mathbf{x}^S \geq \mathbf{y}^S$ imply $\mathbf{y} \in V(S)$.

DEFINITION 2   Let $S \subset N$. A collection $P = \{S_1, S_2, \ldots, S_H\}$ of pairwise disjoint subsets of S is called a "coalition structure" or a "partition" of S if

$$\bigcup_{h=1}^{H} S_h = N.$$

The set of all coalition structures of S is denoted by $\mathscr{P}_S$ and $\mathscr{P}$ will stand for $\mathscr{P}_N$.

DEFINITION 3   Let $\mathbf{x} \in \mathbb{R}^N$. A coalition S *blocks* $\mathbf{x}$ if there exists $\mathbf{y} \in V(S)$ such that $\mathbf{y}^S > \mathbf{x}^S$. For $P \in \mathscr{P}$ the *P-coalition structure core* is defined and given by

$$C_P(V) := \left\{ \mathbf{x} \in \bigcap_{S \in P} V(S) \,\middle|\, \nexists T \subset N \text{ which blocks } \mathbf{x} \right\}.$$

The $\{N\}$-coalition structure core is called the "core" of (N, V) and is denoted by $C(V)$. The *coalition structure core* is $\bigcup_{P \in \mathscr{P}} C_P(V)$, that is, the game (N, V) has a nonempty coalition structure core if there exists a partition $P \in \mathscr{P}$ for which $C_P(V) \neq \varnothing$.

DEFINITION 4   A coalition S is called "consecutive" if for any three players i, j, k with $i < j < k$, if $i, k \in S$, then $j \in S$.

DEFINITION 5   The consecutive structure of S, denoted $P^c(S)$, is the (unique) partition S to consecutive coalitions that are maximal with respect to the set inclusion. Equivalently, it is the (unique) partition of S to consecutive coalitions that contains the minimal number of coalitions. (Note that $P^c(S) = S$ if and only if S is consecutive.)

DEFINITION 6   Let (N, V) be a game. The *consecutive game* (N, V_c) generated by (N, V) is given by

$$V_c(S) = \bigcap_{T \in P^c(S)} V(T),$$

that is, the vector $\mathbf{x} \in \mathbb{R}^N$ belongs to $V_c(S)$ for every coalition $T \in P^c(S)$.

3   The Theorem and Its Proof

The first result of this paper is

THEOREM 1   Let (N, V) be a game. Then the consecutive game (N, V_c) has a nonempty coalition structure core. Moreover, there exists a payoff $\mathbf{x}$ in the coalition structure core of (N, V_c) such that for every $T = \{1, 2, \ldots, t\}$, $t \leq n$, $\mathbf{x}^T$ belongs to the coalition structure core of the game (N, V_c^T) where, for all $S \subset T$, $V_c^T(S)$ is the projection of $V_c(S)$ on $\mathbb{R}^T$.

Remark 1   Given a game (N, V) define the game (N, V^c) as follows:

$$\tilde{V}^c(S) = \begin{cases} V(S) & \text{if } S \text{ is consecutive} \\ \{\mathbf{x} \in \mathbb{R}^N | \mathbf{x}^S \leq 0\} & \text{otherwise.} \end{cases}$$

(Recall that $0 \in V(S)$ for all S.) It is easy to verify that while the two games $(N, \tilde{V}^c)$ and (N, V^c) do not, in general, coincide, their coalition structure cores are identical. This trivial remark allows us to analyze the simpler game $(N, \tilde{V}^c)$ rather than (N, V^c).

Proof of Theorem 1   For any $i \in N$ define $v_i = \max\{x^i | \mathbf{x} \in V(\{i\})\}$. By (D.1.1) and (D.1.2), each v_i is well defined. Put $\alpha_1 = v_1$ and assume that α_1, $\alpha_2, \ldots, \alpha_{k-1}$, $k \leq n$, have already been derived. Define for each t, $1 \leq t \leq k$,

$$V^\alpha(\{t, \ldots, k\}) = \{\mathbf{x} \in V(\{t, \ldots, k\}) | x^i \geq \alpha_i \; \forall i = t, \ldots, k - 1\}$$

and for each k, $2 \leq k \leq n$,

$$\alpha_k \equiv \max\left\{x^k \middle| \mathbf{x} \in \bigcup_{t=1}^{k} V^\alpha(\{t, \ldots, k\})\right\}.$$

By (D.1.1) and (D.1.2), the maximum is well defined and by choosing $t = k$ we have $\alpha_k \geq v_k$. We claim that the vector $\alpha = (\alpha_1, \ldots, \alpha_k)$ belongs to the coalition structure core of the game (N, V^c), that is, there exists a partition $P^\alpha = \{S_1, \ldots, S_J\}$ such that

$$\alpha \in V^c(S_j) \; \forall j = 1, \ldots, J; \text{ and } \not\exists S \subset N \text{ and } \mathbf{x} \in V^c(S) \text{ s.t. } \mathbf{x} > \alpha.$$

Let us first construct P^α. By the definition of α_n and (D.1.3), there is a consecutive coalition, say, S_1 such that $n \in S_1$ and $\alpha \in V(S_1)$. If $S_1 = N$, let $P^\alpha = \{S_1\}$. Otherwise, $S_1 = \{i_1 + 1, \ldots, n\}$ where $i_1 \geq 1$. By the definition of vector α and (D.1.3), there is a consecutive coalition $S_2 = \{i_2 + 1, \ldots, i_1\}$ with $\alpha \in V(S_2)$. Again, if $S_2 = N \backslash S_1$, let $P^\alpha = \{S_1, S_2\}$. Otherwise,

$N \backslash (S_1 \cup S_2) = \{1, \ldots, i_2\}$ where $i_2 \geq 1$. Since $\alpha \in V(1)$, continuing in the same manner at most n times, generates the partition $P^\alpha = \{S_1, \ldots, S_j\}$. Clearly, by the construction of P^α, $\alpha \in \bigcap_{S \in P^\alpha} V(S)$, that is, α is a feasible payoff for the coalition structure P^α. It remains to be shown that α is not blocked by any coalition. Assume, in negation, that there is a coalition S that blocks α. Without loss of generality, let S be a consecutive coalition, that is, $S = \{k, k+1, \ldots, l\}$. But then there exists $\mathbf{y} \in V(S)$ such that $y^i > \alpha_i$ for all $i \in S$, in particular, $y^l > \alpha_l$, contradicting the choice of α_l.   □

Remark 2   Let (N, V) be a superadditive game with side payments. If there is a stable structure for this game, then the grand coalition $\{N\}$ is also a stable coalition structure. Moreover, for a superadditive game, the payoff α that we constructed above is given by

$$\alpha_1 = V(1);$$

$$\alpha_i = V(\{1, \ldots, i\}) - V(\{1, \ldots, i-1\}) \quad \text{for } i \geq 2.$$

Let Π be any ordering (permutation) of the individuals. Each Π generates α^Π in an obvious way:

$$\alpha_{\Pi(1)} = V(\Pi(1));$$

$$\alpha_{\Pi(i)} = V(\{\Pi(1), \ldots, \Pi(i)\}) - V(\{\Pi(1), \ldots, \Pi(i-1)\}) \quad \text{for } i \geq 2.$$

It might be of interest to know that the Shapley value $\phi(V)$ for the game (N, V) is the center of gravity of the vectors α^Π, that is,

$$\phi(V) = \frac{1}{n!} \sum_\Pi \alpha^\Pi.$$

4   Countable Many Players

In this section we shall define and analyze consecutive games with a countable set of players. The existence of the coalition structure core is proved under the assumption that the set of admissible blocking coalitions is finite. The examples provided below show that without this additional assumption the coalition structure core of a consecutive game with a countable number of players might be empty.

Let $\mathcal{N} = \{1, 2, \ldots\}$ be the set of countable many players. For any nonempty coalition $\mathbf{S} \subset \mathcal{N}$ let l_S^∞ be the space of all bounded sequences on S. l_S^∞ is endowed with the usual norm, that is, for all $\mathbf{x} \in l_S^\infty$, $\|\mathbf{x}\| \equiv \sup\{x^i | i \in S\}$. This norm generates the norm topology on l_S^∞. We denote

$$l^\infty \equiv l_{\mathcal{N}}^\infty \quad \text{and} \quad (l_S^\infty)_- \equiv \{x \in l^\infty | x^i \leq 0 \ \forall i \in S\}.$$

DEFINITION 7   The pair $(\mathcal{N}, V)$ is called a "game" (in characteristic function form with countable many players) where V is a correspondence which assigns to every $S \subset \mathcal{N}$ a subset $V(S)$ of l^∞ which satisfies conditions D.1.1–D.1.3 of definition 1 above with l^∞ replacing $\mathbb{R}^N$.

Similarly, definitions 2–4 and remark 1 remain the same when l^∞ substitutes $\mathbb{R}^N$. We can now state the main result of this section.

THEOREM 2   Let $(\mathcal{N}, V)$ be an arbitrary game and let $\mathcal{D}$ be a finite set of consecutive coalitions. Then there exists a partition P of $\mathcal{N}$, $P = \{S_1, \ldots, S_J\}$ and $\mathbf{x} \in \bigcap_{T \in P} V(T)$ such that no $S \in \mathcal{D}$ blocks $\mathbf{x}$.

Proof   In view of remark 1, it suffices to show that the coalition structure core of the game $(\mathcal{N}, V^{\mathcal{D}})$ is nonempty where

$$V^{\mathcal{D}}(S) = \begin{cases} V(S) & \text{if } S \in \mathcal{D} \\ (l_S^\infty)_- & \text{if } S \notin \mathcal{D}. \end{cases}$$

We shall construct a finite game (K, W) whose coalition structure core will generate a payoff in the coalition structure core of $(\mathcal{N}, V^{\mathcal{D}})$. Let $K \equiv \{1, 2, \ldots, k\} \subset \mathcal{N}$ be such that

$S \subset K$ whenever $S \in \mathcal{D}$ and S is finite;
$S \cap K \neq \varnothing$ whenever $S \in \mathcal{D}$ and S is infinite;
$S \cap K \neq T \cap K$ whenever $S, T \in \mathcal{D}, S \neq T$.

Since $\mathcal{D}$ consists of a finite set of coalitions, such a k exists. Define the game (K, W) by truncating $(\mathcal{N}, V^{\mathcal{D}})$ with the set K. That is, for any $Q \subset K$

$$W(Q) = \begin{cases} V^{\mathcal{D}}(S)^K & \text{if } \exists S \in \mathcal{D} \text{ s.t. } Q = S \cap K \\ \{\mathbf{x} \in \mathbb{R}^K | x^i \leq 0 \ \forall i \in S\} & \text{otherwise.} \end{cases}$$

In order to verify that (K, W) is indeed a game, note that, by (D.1.1)–(D.1.3), whenever $S \in \mathcal{D}$, the projection $V(S)$ on S is closed, bounded and comprehensive, and thus the same is true for projections of $W(Q)$ on K, $Q \subset K$. Since all $S \in \mathcal{D}$ and K are consecutive, all $S \cap K$ are also consecutive and, therefore, the induced consecutive game (K, W_c) coincides with (K, W). Hence, by theorem 1, the coalition structure core of (K, W) is nonempty. That is, there exists a partition P of K into consecutive coalitions, $P = \{Q_1, \ldots, Q_H\}$, and a vector $\mathbf{z} \in \bigcap_{Q \in P} W(Q)$, such that no $Q \subset$

K blocks $\mathbf{z}$ in (K, W). Without loss of generality, let $k \in Q_H$. Define $\mathbf{y} \in l^\infty$ by

$$y^t = \begin{cases} z^t & \text{if } t \in K \\ 0 & \text{if } t \notin K. \end{cases}$$

By (D.1.3) and the definition of the game (K, W), $\mathbf{y}$ is feasible for the partition (of $\mathcal{N}$), $\tilde{P} = \{Q_1, \ldots, Q_{H-1}, \mathcal{N} \setminus \bigcup_{h=1}^{H-1} Q_h\}$, that is, $\mathbf{y} \in \bigcap_{S \in \tilde{P}} V^{\mathscr{D}}(S)$. Moreover, there is no $\bar{S} \in \mathscr{D}$ that blocks $\mathbf{y}$ since otherwise $\bar{Q} = \bar{S} \cap K$ would block z in (K, W). Thus, $\mathbf{y}$ belongs to the coalition structure core of $(\mathcal{N}, V^{\mathscr{D}})$.   □

The assumption that $\mathscr{D}$ consists of a finite number of coalitions is, no doubt, restrictive. However, it is obvious the restriction on a coalition structure to consist of a finite number of coalitions might well be compatible with stability for subadditive games with an infinite number of players. Indeed, consider the following game:

Example 1   Let $(\mathcal{N}, V)$ be a game, where

$$V(S) = \begin{cases} \{\mathbf{x} \in l^\infty \mid x^i \leq 1\} & \text{if } S = \{i\} \\ \{\mathbf{x} \in l^\infty \mid x^j \leq \frac{1}{2} \, \forall j \in S\} & \text{if } |S| \geq 2. \end{cases}$$

Individual rationality implies that each player receives at least 1, an outcome which is realizable only by the singleton partition $\{\{1\}, \{2\}, \ldots\}$.

One might nevertheless wonder whether allowing coalition structures to consist of an infinite number of coalitions will rescue Theorem 2 (without the restriction that $\mathscr{D}$ consists of a finite number of coalitions). The following example shows that there is a more serious reason for the emptiness of a coalition structure for infinite games than the one captured by the previous example.

Example 2   For $n = 1, 2, \ldots$, denote $T_n = \{n, n+1, \ldots\}$ and let $\mathscr{D} \equiv \{\{T_n\}_{n=1}^\infty\}$. Note that all coalitions in $\mathscr{D}$ are consecutive. Define the game $(\mathcal{N}, V^{\mathscr{D}})$ by

$$V^{\mathscr{D}}(S) = \begin{cases} \left\{\mathbf{x} \in l^\infty \,\middle|\, x^i \leq \dfrac{n}{n+1}, i \geq n\right\} & \text{if } S = T_n \in \mathscr{D} \\ (l_S^\infty)_- & \text{otherwise.} \end{cases}$$

Clearly, the game $(\mathcal{N}, V^{\mathscr{D}})$ satisfies (D.1.1)–(D.1.3) and it is also superadditive. Moreover, the coalition structure core of $(\mathcal{N}, V_c^{\mathscr{D}})$ is empty. Otherwise, there exists a partition P with, possibly, infinite number of coalitions and $\mathbf{x} \in \bigcap_{S \in P} V(S)$ such that no coalition $T \subset \mathcal{N}$ blocks it. Now, if P does not contain some coalition of the form T_n (implying $\mathbf{x} \leq 0$), then every T_n blocks $\mathbf{x}$. But on the other hand, every $\mathbf{x} \in V^{\mathcal{D}}(T_n)$ is blocked by some $\mathbf{y} \in V^{\mathcal{D}}(T_{n+1})$, thus, P cannot not contain any coalition of the form T_n. Hence, the coalition structure core of $(\mathcal{N}, V^{\mathcal{D}})$ is empty.

5   Continuum of Players

We conclude the chapter by considering games with a continuum set of players. The model and, in particular, the proofs for this case are somewhat more involved than those in the two previous sections. Specifically, some elementary definitions and results from measure theory (e.g., Fatou's lemma) are used to derive the continuum analogues of the previous sections.

Let $(M, \mathcal{M}, \mu)$ be a probability measure space where M is the interval $[0, 1]$, μ is the probability (Lebesgue) measure on M and $\mathcal{M}$ is the set of all μ-measurable subsets of M. In the standard interpretation, M is the set of players and a coalition is a measurable subset of M with a positive measure. Let $\mathcal{M}_+ \equiv \{S \in \mathcal{M} | \mu(S) > 0\}$. As usual, we do not distinguish between two coalitions if their symmetric difference is a μ-null set. More precisely, two coalitions, $S, T \in \mathcal{M}_+$ are called "equivalent" $(S \sim T)$ if $\mu(S \Delta T) = \mu(S \setminus T) + \mu(T \setminus S) = 0$.

Denote by L^∞ the space of all almost everywhere (a.e.) bounded scalar functions on M. The topology on L^∞ will be that induced by the norm where $\|\mathbf{x}\| \equiv \inf\{d | \mu\{t | x^t > d\} > 0\}$ for all $\mathbf{x} \in L^\infty$. Let

$$L^\infty \equiv L^\infty_M \quad \text{and} \quad (L^\infty_S)_- \equiv \{x \in L^\infty | x^t \leq 0 \text{ a.e. on } S.\}$$

All notations of section 2 remain the same with only L^∞ replacing $\mathfrak{R}^n$, and every inequality should be interpreted to hold almost everywhere. In order to avoid any possible ambiguity, we explicitly modify definitions 1–4.

DEFINITION 8 $(M, \mathcal{M}, \mu, V)$ is a *game* (in characteristic function form with a continuum of players) where V is a correspondence that assigns to each coalition $S \subset \mathcal{M}_+$ a subset $V(S)$ of L^∞ which satisfies the following requirements:

(D.8.1) *Closedness:* Each $V(S)^S$ is a closed subset of L^∞_S containing the origin;

(D.8.2) *Boundedness:* There exists a real number λ, such that for any $S \subset \mathcal{M}_+$ and any $\mathbf{x} \in V(S)$, $x^t \leq \lambda$ a.e. on S;

(D.8.3) *Comprehensiveness:* For any $S \subset \mathcal{M}_+$ and any $\mathbf{x} \in V(S)$, $\mathbf{y} \in L^\infty$ and $\mathbf{x}^S \geq \mathbf{y}^S$ imply $\mathbf{y} \in V(S)$.

DEFINITION 9 $P = \{S_1, S_2, \ldots, S_H\}$ where $S_h \in \mathcal{M}_+$, $h = 1, \ldots, H$, is called a "coalition structure" or a "partition" of M if

(D.9.1) $\mu(M \setminus \bigcup_{h=1}^{H} S_h) = 0$;

(D.9.2) $\mu(S_i \cap S_j) = 0$ for all $S_i, S_j \in P$, $i \neq j$.

The set of all coalition structures of M is denoted by $\mathcal{P}$.

DEFINITION 10   Let $\mathbf{x} \in L^\infty$. A coalition S *blocks* $\mathbf{x}$ if there exists $\mathbf{y} \in V(S)$ such that $\mathbf{y} > \mathbf{x}$ almost everywhere on M.

For $P \in \mathcal{P}$ the *P-coalition structure core* is defined and given by

$$C_P(V) := \left\{ \mathbf{x} \in \bigcap_{S \in P} V(S) \;\middle|\; \nexists T \subset \mathcal{M}_+ \text{ which blocks } \mathbf{x} \right\}.$$

We say that the game $(M, \mathcal{M}, \mu, V)$ has a nonempty coalition structure core if there exists a partition $P \in \mathcal{P}$ for which $C_P(V) \neq \varnothing$.

DEFINITION 11   A coalition S is called "consecutive" if there exists a closed interval $T \in [0, 1]$ which is equivalent to S. Thus, without loss of generality, each consecutive coalition is a closed interval.

Now we are able to state the main result of this section:

THEOREM 3   Let $(M, \mathcal{M}, \mu, V)$ be an arbitrary game, and let $\mathcal{D}$ be a finite set of consecutive coalitions. Then there exists a partition $P = \{S_1, \ldots, S_J\}$ and $\mathbf{x} \in \bigcap_{T \in P} V(T)$ such that no $S \in \mathcal{D}$ blocks $\mathbf{x}$.

Proof   In view of remark 1, it suffices to show that the coalition structure core of $(M, \mathcal{M}, \mu, V)$ is nonempty where

$$V^{\mathcal{D}}(S) = \begin{cases} V(S) & \text{if } S \in \mathcal{D} \\ (L_S^\infty)_- & \text{if } S \notin \mathcal{D}. \end{cases}$$

For all closed intervals $S \in \mathcal{D}$ define $l(S) \equiv \min\{t | t \in S\}$ and $r(S) \equiv \max\{t | t \in S\}$. Denote $A \equiv \{l(S), r(S)\}_{S \in \mathcal{D}}$. Let $t_1 < t_2 < \cdots < t_{k+1}$ be such that $A = \{t_i\}_{i=1,2,\ldots,k+1}$. For all $i = 1, 2, \ldots, k$ denote by F_i the interval $[t_i, t_{i+1}]$. We shall construct a finite game (K, W) with k players, whose coalition structure core will generate a payoff in the coalition structure core of $(M, \mathcal{M}, \mu, V)$. Let $K = \{1, 2, \ldots, k\}$ be a set of k players, where player i "represents" interval F_i, $i = 1, 2, \ldots, k$. For a coalition $Q \subset K$ define the set

$$Q^{\mathcal{D}} = \begin{cases} \bigcup_{i \in Q} F_i & \text{if } \bigcup_{i \in Q} F_i \in \mathcal{D} \\ \varnothing & \text{otherwise.} \end{cases}$$

Then the characteristic function W for nonempty subsets Q of K is defined as follows:

$$W(Q) = \begin{cases} \{z \in \mathbb{R}^K | \exists y \in V^{\mathscr{D}}(Q^{\mathscr{D}}) \text{ s.t. } z^j \leq \int_{F_j} y \, d\mu, \forall j \in Q\} & \text{if } Q^{\mathscr{D}} \neq \varnothing \\ \{z \in \mathbb{R}^K | z^j \leq 0\} & \text{otherwise.} \end{cases}$$

Since by (D.8.2), $\int_S y \, d\mu$ is uniformly bounded for all $S \in \mathscr{D}$ and all $y \in V^{\mathscr{D}}(S)$, it follows that for all $Q \subset K$ the projection of $W(Q)$ on $\mathbb{R}^Q$, $W(Q)^Q$, is bounded. Comprehensiveness of $W(Q)$ follows immediately from (D.8.3). To conclude that (K, W) is indeed, a game (see definition 1), we have to show that $W(Q)^Q$ is closed for all $Q \subset K$. The statement is trivial if $Q^{\mathscr{D}} = \varnothing$. Assume, therefore, that $Q^{\mathscr{D}} \neq \varnothing$ and let $z_n \in W(Q)$ be a sequence such that $\lim_{n \to \infty} z_n^j = z_0^j$ for all $j \in Q$. We have to show that $z_0 \in W(Q)$. By the definition of the game (K, W), for each z_n there exists a corresponding sequence $y_n \in V^{\mathscr{D}}(Q^{\mathscr{D}})$ where $z_n^j \leq \int_{F_j} y_n \, d\mu$ for all $n = 1, 2, \ldots$, and all $j \in Q$. By Fatou's lemma (see, for example, Hildenbrand 1974) and (D.8.1), there exist $y_0 \in V^{\mathscr{D}}(Q^{\mathscr{D}})$ and a subsequence $\{y_{n_m}\}$ of $\{y_n\}$ such that $\lim_{m \to \infty} \int_{F_j} y_{n_m} \, d\mu = \int_{F_j} y_0 \, d\mu$ for all $j \in Q$. Thus, $z_0^j \leq \int_{F_j} y_0 \, d\mu$ for all $j \in Q$, that is, $W(Q)^Q$ is a closed subset of $\mathbb{R}^Q$.

Since $\mathscr{D}$ consists of consecutive coalitions (in fact, of closed intervals), it follows that the consecutive game (K, W_c) coincides with (K, W). Therefore, by theorem 1, the coalition structure core of (K, W) is nonempty. That is, there exists a partition P of K, $P = \{Q_1, \ldots, Q_H\}$, and $z \in \bigcap_{T \in P} W(Q)$ such that no $Q \subset K$ blocks x in (K, W). Denote $S_h \equiv Q_h^{\mathscr{D}}$, $h = 1, \ldots, H$, and $S_0 = M \backslash \bigcup_{h=0}^H S_h$. Since $z \in W(Q_h)$ for all $h = 1, \ldots, H$, we have that for each h there exists y_h, such that $z^j \leq \int_{F_j} y_h \, d\mu$ for all $j \in Q_h$, $h = 1, 2, \ldots, H$. Define $y \in L^\infty$:

$$y^t = \begin{cases} y_h^t & \text{for } t \in Q_h^{\mathscr{D}} \\ 0 & \text{otherwise.} \end{cases}$$

Clearly, y is feasible for the partition $\{S_0, S_1, \ldots, S_H\}$, that is, $y \in \bigcap_{h=0}^H V(S_h)$. Moreover, y cannot be blocked by any $S \in \mathscr{D}$ since, otherwise, the coalition Q (recall that $Q^{\mathscr{D}} = \bigcup_{j \in Q} F_j$) would block z in (K, W). It follows, therefore, that y belongs to the coalition structure core of $(M, \mathscr{M}, \mu, V)$. $\square$

As in the previous section, we shall now demonstrate that theorem 3 is not valid without the restriction that $\mathscr{D}$ consists of only a finite number of coalitions. Again, one reason is that the above restriction is, in general, incompatible with stability for subadditive games with a continuum of players. Indeed,

Example 3   Consider the game $(M, \mathcal{M}, \mu, V)$ where for any coalition S:

$V(S) = \{\mathbf{x} \in L^{\infty} | x^t \leq 1 - \mu(S) \text{ a.e. on } S\}$.

Individual rationality implies that each player will receive, at least, 1. But this means that only null coalitions will form and the partition must consist of a continuum of coalitions. Demange and Henriet (1991) avoided the problem raised in example 3 by assuming that "small" coalitions do not block, that is, there exists a number $r > 0$ such that the set $\mathcal{D}$ consists of coalitions whose measure exceeds r. The following example shows that, without this restriction, even allowing for partitions to consist of an infinite number of coalitions will not rescue theorem 3 for an infinite set $\mathcal{D}$:

Example 4   Consider the game $(M, \mathcal{M}, \mu, V)$. For a coaliton S denote by $m_-(S)(m_+(S))$ the "essential" leftmost (rightmost) point of the set S, that is, $m_-(S) \equiv \sup\{t | \mu([0, t] \cap S) = 0\}$ and $m_+(S)$ inf $\sup\{t | \mu([t, 1] \cap S) = 0\}$. For each coalition S define

$$V(S) = \begin{cases} \{\mathbf{x} \in L^{\infty} | x^t \leq m_-(S) + 1 \text{ a.e. on } S\} & \text{if } S \sim [m_-(S), m_+(S)] \\ (L_S^{\infty})_- & \text{otherwise.} \end{cases}$$

Suppose, in negation, that there exists a partition P and $\mathbf{x} \in \bigcap_{T \in P} V(T)$ such that no $S \in \mathcal{M}_+$ blocks it. If P does not contain any consecutive coalition (implying $\mathbf{x} \leq 0$), then $\mathbf{x}$ is blocked by the interval $[1/2, 1]$. If P contains an interval $[a, b]$ with $0 \leq a < b \leq 1$, then $\mathbf{x}$ is blocked by the interval $[(a + b)/2, b]$. Hence, regardless of the number of coalitions that P may contain, the coalition structure core of $(M, \mathcal{M}, \mu, V)$ is empty.

Notes

The authors wish to thank Herbert Scarf for his helpful suggestions.

1. This concept was originally introduced (for the cooperative games with side payments) in Aumann and Drèze 1974.

References

Aumann, R. J., and J. Drèze. 1974. "Cooperative Games with Coalition Structures." *International Journal of Game Theory* 3 : 217–237.

Axelrod, R. (1970). *Conflict of Interest*. Chicago: Markham.

Demange, G. 1990. "Intermediate Preferences and Stable Coalition Structures." Discussion paper, DELTA EHESS, Paris.

Demange, G., and D. Henriet. 1991. "Sustainable Oligopolies." *Journal of Economic Theory* 54 : 417–428.

DeSwaan, A. 1973. *Coalition Theories and Cabinet Formation*. New York: Elsevier, North Holland.

Gardner, R. 1985. "Non-Transferable Utility Voting Games." Discussion paper A-18, SFB 303, University of Bonn.

Greenberg, J. 1993. "Coalition Structures." In *Handbook of Game Theory with Economic Applications*, ed. R. J. Aumann and S. Hart. New York: Elsevier North Holland.

Greenberg, J., and S. Weber. 1986. "Strong Tiebout Equilibrium under Restricted Preferences Domain." *Journal of Economic Theory* 38:101–117.

Hildenbrand, W. 1974. *Core and Equilibrium of a Large Economy*. Princeton: Princeton University Press.

Kaneko, M., and M. H. Wooders. 1982. "Cores of Partitioning Games." *Mathematical Social Sciences* 3:313–327.

Le Breton, M., G. Owen, and S. Weber. 1990. "Strongly Balanced Games." Discussion paper, SFB 303, University of Bonn.

Leiserson, M. 1966. "Coalitions in Politics." Ph.D. diss., Yale University.

Scarf, H. 1967. "The Core of an N-Person Game." *Econometrica* 35:50–69.

6

The General Nucleolus and the Reduced-Game Property

Michael Maschler, Jos Potters, and Stef Tijs

1 Introduction

The *nucleolus* of a cooperative game with side payments (TU-game) was introduced in Schmeidler 1969. It quickly gained popularity and was applied in several areas.[1] Perhaps the most attractive property of the nucleolus is that it is a unique point in the *core* of the game, whenever the core is not empty. Thus, it may be a good candidate for situations in which it is desirable to have a rule which selects one outcome in the core of the game.[2]

The nucleolus is also a unique point in every nonempty ε-*core* (Schmeidler 1969). This, and other nice properties of the nucleolus induced Shubik (1983, 340) to say that "the nucleolus represents as nearly as any single imputation can the location of the core of the game ... its effective center," and "if the core is empty, the nucleolus represents its 'latent' position."

However, the nucleolus is not the only rule to choose a unique core point. One can think of others—the center of gravity of the core, for example. Why should one prefer the nucleolus? One reason might be the attractiveness of its definition as an outcome of a lexicographic minimization procedure. Other reasons are, perhaps, nice properties of the nucleolus that may be relevant to particular applications. But these criteria are hard to grasp. What one needs is an *axiomatic* characterization of the nucleolus. If one can characterize the nucleolus by means of *intuitively acceptable and simple axioms*, one can check each application to see whether these axioms are relevant to the needs. If they are, then the logical choice must be the nucleolus; but—and this is equally important—if for some applications the axioms do not make sense, then the nucleolus should be rejected for them. Such a system of axioms was given for the *prenucleolus*—a related solution concept—in the intriguing paper Sobolev 1975.[3] Sobolev's axioms are intuitive indeed. The essential one among them is the requirement that the solution concept be *consistent*, or equivalently, satisfy a *reduced-game property*. Heuristically, it requires that at the solution point every nonempty subset of the players, who look at their payments and at the same time examine their "own game" (the reduced game on them), will not want to move away, because they will find that their payments constitute the solution also for the reduced game.[4]

The idea of lexicographically minimizing (maximizing) a vector of objective functions need not be applied only to TU-games. Indeed, it was applied in several other conflict situations. Already in the forties, game theorists at Rand recommended a lexicographic maximization[5] for player 1 and a lexicographic minimization for player 2 who participate in a zero-sum two-person game. The idea was to exploit an opponent's mistakes without sacrificing one's own safety levels.[6] This recommendation is described in Brown 1950. Eventually it was published in Dresher 1961. We shall call the set of recommended strategies the *nucleolus of the game* (for player 1/2). These nucleoli were encountered again more recently when van Damme proved that they constitute precisely the *set of proper equilibria* for the game (see van Damme 1983).

In a somewhat different setup Potters and Tijs (1992) introduced a *general nucleolus*,[7] by means of which they were able to confront the nucleolus of TU-games with the nucleolus of matrix games. They found interesting correspondences between the two concepts and were able to establish for matrix-nucleoli an analogue of Kohlberg's characterization of the TU-nucleolus in terms of balanced sets (see Kohlberg 1971).

This paper is concerned with the general nucleolus of Potters and Tijs and with further generalizations as well as applications. Specifically, we consider *classes* of pairs (II, F), where the II's are topological spaces and the F's are finite vectors whose components are real and continuous functions defined on II. The nucleolus for such a class is defined in section 2. The class itself will be called the "domain of the nucleolus." The main task of this paper is to characterize the nucleolus concept axiomatically. It will turn out that the required axioms depend heavily on the domain. Different domains require different sets of axioms.

This is an interesting phenomenon. The characterization of the nucleolus by means of a lexicographic minimization (section 2), does not depend on the domain of the nucleolus: lexicographic minimization characterizes the nucleolus of each individual pair (II, F), regardless of the class to which it belongs. Characterization by axioms as done in sections 3–6, depends forcefully on the intended applications; namely, on the class of the pairs that we consider as the domain of the nucleolus. Thus, the axioms can be regarded as "social norms" that apply to various potential circumstances. Different sets of circumstances require different norms.

2 The General Nucleolus

Our object of study is a class Ω of pairs (II, F). In each pair, II is a topological space and $F := \{F_j\}_{j \in M}$ is a finite set of real continuous functions on II. This setup has many applications. We give here two examples which should be sufficient for motivation:

Example 2.1 Ω is derived from the class of all TU-games $(N; v)$ on finite sets of players. For each game, II is the *set of preimputations* of the game and $F = \{F_S\}_{S \subseteq N}$, where the various F_S's are the *excess functions*, $F_S(x) := v(S) - x(S)$.

Example 2.2 Ω is a class of potential "decision spaces." In each particular case a decision maker has to make a decision x which is a point in a "decision space" II. Any such choice may affect a set of cities M. The effect can be measured in monetary terms. $F_j(x)$ is the damage caused to city j if the decision x is taken.

The central concepts in this paper are the *least core*[8] and the *nucleolus* defined by[9]

$$\mathscr{LC}(\text{II}, F) := \left\{x \in \text{II}: \bigvee_{j \in M} F_j(x) \le \bigvee_{j \in M} F_j(y) \text{ for all } y \in \text{II}\right\}; \tag{2.1}$$

$$\mathscr{N}(\text{II}, F) := \{x \in \text{II}: \Theta \circ F(x) \precsim_{lex} \Theta \circ F(y) \text{ for all } y \in \text{II}\}. \tag{2.2}$$

Here $\Theta : \mathbb{R}^M \to \mathbb{R}^m$ is the *coordinate* ordering map[10] and "lex" is the lexicographic ordering[11] on $\mathbb{R}^m$, $m = |M|$. For the special case $M = \varnothing$ we define

$$\mathscr{LC}(\text{II}, F) = \mathscr{N}(\text{II}, F) = \text{II}. \tag{2.3}$$

It should be noted that both the nucleolus and the least core may be empty sets. In view of possible applications in section 6, we refrain from adding conditions that guarantee nonemptiness.

We shall now state a few properties that a *solution concept*[12] Φ, defined on a class Ω, might have. We shall then show that the nucleolus possesses these properties. In subsequent sections some of these properties will serve as axioms.

$(\mathbf{P_0})$ *Restricted nonemptiness:* $\Phi(\text{II}, F) \neq \varnothing$ if II is a nonempty compact set;

(P_1) *Nondiscrimination:* $\Phi(\text{II}, F) = \text{II}$ if $M = \varnothing$ (in the absence of objective functions, every choice is equally good under Φ);

(P_2) *Redundancy:* $\Phi(\text{II}, F) = \Phi(\text{II}, F_{-j})$ if F_j is constant on II (if one of the functions makes no distinction between the points of II, it has no influence on the outcomes under Φ);

(P_3) *Inclusion in the least core:* $\Phi(\text{II}, F) \subseteq \mathscr{LC}(\text{II}, F)$ (if the largest value among the $F_j(x)$'s exceeds the largest value among the $F_j(y)$'s for some y, then x will not be chosen under Φ);

(P_4) *Restriction to the least core:* $\Phi(\text{II}, F) = \Phi(\mathscr{LC}(\text{II}, F), F)$ (points outside the least core do not affect the choices under Φ);

(P_5) *Invariance with respect to rearrangement:* If (II, F) and $(\text{II}, \tilde{F})$ are elements of Ω and $\{F_j(x) : j \in M\} = \{\tilde{F}_j(x) : j \in M\}$ for each x in II, then $\Phi(\text{II}, F) = \Phi(\text{II}, \tilde{F})$ (here = means equality of sets with counting multiplicities,[13] the solution concept considers only what and how often values of F occur and does not care which functions take them);

(P_6) *Invariance with respect to max/min:* $\Phi(\text{II}, F) = \Phi(\text{II}, F_i \vee F_j, F_i \wedge F_j, F_{-ij})$ for every $i, j \in M$, $i \neq j$ (the outcomes under Φ do not change if we replace an F_i and F_j by their maximum and their minimum and leave the other members of F unchanged);

(P_7) *Independence of irrelevant alternatives:* If II$'$ is a subset of II, with $(\text{II}', F) \in \Omega$, and $\varnothing \neq \Phi(\text{II}, F) \subseteq \text{II}'$, then $\Phi(\text{II}, F) = \Phi(\text{II}', F)$ (this is the well-known IIA property formulated for set-valued solution concepts;

(P_8) *Strong IIA property:* If II$'$ is a subset of II, with $(\text{II}', F) \in \Omega$ and if $\Phi(\text{II}, F) \cap \text{II}' \neq \varnothing$ then $\Phi(\text{II}', F) = \Phi(\text{II}, F) \cap \text{II}'$ (this time one only requires that $\Phi(\text{II}, F)$ intersects II$'$);

(P_9) *Contravariance:* If $\Lambda : \text{II}' \to \text{II}$ is a continuous map and $\Lambda^{-1}\Phi(\text{II}, F) \neq \varnothing$ then $\Phi(\text{II}', F \circ \Lambda) = \Lambda^{-1}\Phi(\text{II}, F)$ (this is an even stronger version of IIA;

(P_{10}) *Closedness:* $\Phi(\text{II}, F)$ is a closed set for all pairs (II, F) in Ω.

In the following we shall prove that the nucleolus $\mathscr{N}$ has the above properties whenever the appropriate statement is meaningful.[14]

THEOREM 2.3 The nucleolus $\mathscr{N}$, defined on an arbitrary class Ω, satisfies P_0-P_{10}, whenever the appropriate statement is meaningful.

ALGORITHM 2.4 In order to determine the nucleolus for a pair (II, F) in Ω:

(Step 1) Remove all functions from F which are constant on II.

(Step 2) If $M = \emptyset$ then $\mathcal{N}(\text{II}, F) = \text{II}$. Go to step 6.

(Step 3) If $M \neq \emptyset$ compute $\mathcal{LC}(\text{II}, F)$. If $\mathcal{LC}(\text{II}, F) = \emptyset$, then $\mathcal{N}(\text{II}, F) = \emptyset$. Go to step 6.

(Step 4) If $m \geq 2$, replace $F = (F_1, \ldots, F_m)$ by $\tilde{F} = (\tilde{F}_1, \ldots, \tilde{F}_m)$, where $\tilde{F}_p = \bigvee_{j \leq p} F_j \wedge F_{p+1}$ for $p = 1, \ldots, m-1$ and $\tilde{F}_m = \bigvee_{j \leq m} F_j$.

(Step 5) Replace II with $\mathcal{LC}(\text{II}, F)$. Go to step 1.

(Step 6) Stop. You have reached the general nucleolus.

3 Axioms for the General Nucleolus

In this section we shall characterize the nucleolus for every class that is "rich enough" in the sense that it satisfies the following properties:
For each (II, F) in Ω,

(α) $(\mathcal{LC}(\text{II}, F), F) \in \Omega$;

(β) $(\text{II}, F_{-j}) \in \Omega$ whenever $j \in M$ and F_j is constant on II;

(γ) For all pairs i, j in M, $i \neq j$, $(\text{II}, \tilde{F})$ is also in Ω. Here, $\tilde{F} = (\tilde{F}_1, \ldots, \tilde{F}_m)$, where $\tilde{F}_k = F_k$ for $k \in M \backslash \{i, j\}$, $\tilde{F}_i = F_i \wedge F_j$, $\tilde{F}_j = F_i \vee F_j$.

THEOREM 3.1 Let Ω be a class of pairs (II, F) satisfying (α)–(γ) above. Let Φ be a solution concept satisfying $\mathbf{P}_1$ (nondiscrimination), $\mathbf{P}_2$ (redundancy), $\mathbf{P}_4$ (restriction to the least core), and $\mathbf{P}_5$ (invariance with respect to rearrangement). Under these conditions, $\Phi(\text{II}, F) = \mathcal{N}(\text{II}, F)$.

Discussion To judge if these axioms make sense on intuitive grounds let us check them in the case of example 2.2. Similar checks should be performed for other applications. For this example, a decision maker should choose the nucleolus if he accepts the following norms.

($\mathbf{P}_1$) This axiom follows if we want a choice to be governed *solely* by the damages. In the absence of reported damages, every choice is equally good.

($\mathbf{P}_2$) If damage to a city does not depend on your actual choice, ignore the city. (Anyway, you cannot help the city.)

($\mathbf{P}_4$) This is perhaps the strongest norm. It says in this context that if the highest damage under a choice x can be reduced by another choice, not only x should not be taken,[15] but it should not influence the actual decision.[16] In many social situations involving value judgment, lowering highest damages as much as possible is an acceptable desire. In other applications one has a different goal: to lower damage to as many cities as possible. In such cases one may, for example, prefer to keep, or even slightly worsen, a highest damage, if that greatly improves many (even some) cities. If one has such a goal, then one should look at so-called compromises between conflicting desires. In such cases the nucleolus should be rejected, or modified.

(P_5) This axiom says again that the decision should be governed solely by the package of damages (sets with multiplicities) and not influenced, for example, by questions such as which city suffers what damage. Again, that might not be appropriate: some cities may have many inhabitants, so that the damage (assumed additive) for each member is small. In other cases the opposite is true: although financially the damage per person is small, the decision maker may anger many people, thus risking reelection. In all such cases the nucleolus is a bad choice and should either be modified or abandoned.

THEOREM 3.2   The axioms P_1, P_2, P_4, P_5 are logically independent; that is, there are solutions which fail to satisfy exactly any one of them.

4   The General Nucleolus in the Convex Case

We start this section by stating an unfortunate fact and a fortunate one. The unfortunate fact is that in the game-theoretic applications of the nucleolus, the classes involved do *not* satisfy condition γ of section 3. For instance, the maximum and the minimum of two excess functions in example 2.1 are *not* themselves excess functions. The fortunate fact is that in these applications the F_j's are *convex*—even linear. We shall see that in this case condition γ is *not needed*. Accordingly, we shall speak in this section about classes Ω_1 satisfying the following requirements: For each (II, F) in Ω_1,

(α) $(\mathscr{LC}(II, F), F) \in \Omega_1$;

(β) $(II, F_{-j}) \in \Omega_1$ whenever $j \in M$ and F_j is constant on II;

(δ) II is a *convex* and closed set in a topological vector space and each F_j is a real, continuous, convex function whose domain is II.

THEOREM 4.1   Let Ω_1 be a class of pairs (II, F) satisfying (α), (β), (δ) above, then the nucleolus on Ω_1 is characterized by P_1 (nondiscrimination), P_2 (redundancy), and P_4 (restriction to the least core).

Algorithm 2.4 can be adapted to an algorithmic scheme to compute the nucleolus in a class Ω_1. Step 4 is not needed to obtain a constant function and can be skipped. The relevant examples in theorem 3.2 all satisfy (α), (β), and (δ) and therefore show that each of the axioms of theorem 4.1 does not follow from the others.

For use later on, we state and prove two additional properties of the general nucleolus defined on a class Ω_1 satisfying (α), (β), and (δ) (they are not true in other classes):

($\mathbf{P}_{11}$) *Deletion of the smaller of two functions with constant difference:* If $(II, F) \in \Omega_1$ and $F_i = F_j + \lambda$ for some i and j, $i \neq j$, with $\lambda \in \mathbb{R}_+$, then $\Psi(II, F) = \Psi(II, F_{-j})$;

($\mathbf{P}_{12}$) *Indifference:* F is constant on $\Psi(II, F)$.

THEOREM 4.2   The nucleolus of a class Ω_1 satisfying (α), (β) and (δ) satisfies $\mathbf{P}_{11}$ and $\mathbf{P}_{12}$.

5 The Nucleolus of Matrix Games

Let A be a $m \times n$-matrix zero-sum game. We can associate with it a pair (II, F), where $II := \Delta_{II}(A)$ (the set of mixed strategies for player 2), and $F_i(q) = \mathbf{e}_i A q$ for all q in $\Delta_{II}(A)$. Here $M := \{1, \dots, m\}$. Thus, $F_i(q)$ is the payment to player 1 if he takes row i and player 2 takes q. Our class Ω_2 will consist in this section of all such pairs, for all matrix games.

As in Potters and Tijs 1992 (see also Dresher 1961; Brown 1950; and section 1) the *nucleolus of the game* for player 2 was defined by

$$\mathcal{N}_{II}(A) := \mathcal{N}(\Delta_{II}(A), \{F_i\}_{i \in M}). \tag{5.1}$$

It is easy to see that $\mathcal{LC}(\Delta_{II}(A), F) = O_{II}(A)$, the set of optimal strategies of player 2 in the matrix game A.

In this section we are going to axiomatize the nucleolus of A. We face two tasks. On the one hand to formalize the axioms in game-theoretic terminology, and on the other hand to overcome the fact that our class Ω_2 does not satisfy condition α of section 4. There are two ways to circumvent the last difficulty. We can extend the theory of matrix games to zero-sum games defined on polytopes. We can then apply theorem 4.2 to this class. We can, however, adopt a different approach. Consider player 2's set of optimal strategies. It is a polytope $\mathcal{P} := \text{conv}\{q_1, q_2, \dots, q_k\}$. We can therefore *identify* the game in which player 2's strategies are restricted to $\mathcal{P}$ with a classical matrix game B, with m rows and k columns, with $b_{ij} = \mathbf{e}_i A q_j$, $i \in M, j \in K := \{1, 2, \dots, k\}$, and remain within the class of the classical games. Formally, that means that we replace axiom $\mathbf{P}_4$ by $\mathbf{P}_0$, $\mathbf{P}_3$, and $\mathbf{P}_9$ (contravariance). With these remarks we can now formulate

THEOREM 5.1   The nucleolus for player 2 for the class of matrix games is characterized by the following axioms:

(P_0) $\Phi(A) \neq \varnothing$ for all matrix games A;

(P_1) $\Phi(A) = \Delta_{II}(A)$ if the entries in each row are constant;

(P_2) $\Phi(A) = \Phi(A_{-i})$ if the i-th row has constant entries and[17] $|M| \geq 2$;

(P_3) $\Phi(A) \subseteq O_{II}(A)$;

(P_9) If $\Lambda : \Delta \to \Delta_{II}(A)$ is a linear map, where Δ is an arbitrary simplex, and if $\Lambda^{-1}\Phi(A) \neq \varnothing$ then $\Phi(A \circ \Lambda) = \Lambda^{-1}\Phi(A)$. Here, $A \circ \Lambda =: B$ is a matrix game with m rows and k columns, $b_{ij} = \mathbf{e}_i A q_j$, $i \in \{1, \ldots, m\}$, $j \in \{1, 2, \ldots, k\}$, where q_j is the image under Λ of the jth extreme point of Δ.

Remark   It can be proved that the axioms of theorem 5.1 are logically independent.

6   The Nucleolus of a TU-Game with Permissible Coalitions and Permissible Imputations

Schmeidler's (1969) classical nucleolus is obtained from a TU-game $(N; v)$ if we take II to be the set of imputations[18] (for a given coalition structure, usually $\{N\}$),[19] and $F = \{F_S\}_{S \subseteq N}$, where F is the excess function of the coalition S, namely, $F_S(x) = e(S, x) = v(S) - x(S)$. The class of these nucleoli does not satisfy (α) and (β) of section 5, because the least core is usually not a set of imputations and because $\{F_S\}$ has to be the set of *all* excess functions of a given game. In order to be able to use the setup and results of the previous section we shall *extend the class of games*

(i) by allowing games in which certain coalitions are *not permissible*;

(ii) by allowing games in which the set of imputations is *restricted a priori to a given polyhedral set*.[20]

The games restricted in this way will be called "truncated games," or more informatively,"TU-games with permissible coalitions and permissible imputations." Formally, a truncated game will be a quadruplet $(N, \mathscr{S}, v, \text{II})$, where $N = \{1, 2, \ldots, n\}$ is the *set of players*, $\mathscr{S}$ is a subset of $2^N \setminus \{\varnothing, N\}$, called the "set of permissible coalitions."[21] $v : \mathscr{S} \to \mathbb{R}$ is the characteristic function and II—the *set of permissible imputations*—is a set of the form

$$\text{II} = \{x \in \mathbb{R}^N : x(N) = v(N), x(U) \geq a_U, \text{ for all } U \in \mathscr{U}\}. \tag{6.1}$$

Here $\mathscr{U}$ is a, possibly empty, collection of coalitions and the numbers a_U, $U \in \mathscr{U}$ are given numbers.[22]

Remarks Ordinary TU-games are, of course, truncated games. They are obtained by taking $\mathscr{S} = 2^N \setminus \{\emptyset, N\}$, $\mathscr{U} = \{\{i\} : i \in N$ and $a_{\{i\}} = v(\{i\})\}$.

Discussion It is easy to interpret $\mathscr{S}$. As suggested by its name, we extend the scope of the cooperative games to situations in which the formation of some coalitions is out of the question. The members of such coalitions are not on speaking terms with each other, or an antitrust law prevails, or communication barriers exist, or simply, people do not wish to be bothered; these are among the many good examples which may be found. It is more difficult to interpret II. To do so, we have to go back to the idea of the core, remembering at the same time that we constantly discuss a cooperation of all the players towards forming the grand coalition. A requirement for being in the core means that the players will not cooperate unless each coalition gets at least its worth. Implicit in II is a generalization of this concept. The players will not consent to cooperate in forming N unless it is guaranteed that *certain coalitions*[23] (members of $\mathscr{U}$) receive at least certain amounts (the amounts a_U). Such a priori restrictions may occur in real life. Actually,[24] we can regard II as a generalization of the (strong) ε-core. An outcome x belongs to the (strong) ε-core if the excess of each coalition (other that $\emptyset$ and N) is not larger than ε. Here, we require various coalitions to have excesses not larger than certain numbers—not necessarily the same for all. For coalitions not in $\mathscr{U}$ we lay no a priori restrictions on their excesses. This way of looking at II stresses again the fact that the nucleolus is tied to the core concept; namely, it is a rule that selects outcomes which reside in any nonempty "generalized" core.

Note that in ordinary TU-games $v(N)$ and $v(\{i\})$, $i \in N$, have a double connotation. On the one hand they provide a monetary expression of the *worth* of each coalition, and in this capacity they resemble any other $v(S)$. On the other hand they serve to form a priori reduction of the space of imputations to those which are both individually rational and efficient. Here the two roles are extended to other coalitions.

For truncated TU-games we define the least core and the nucleolus by

$$\mathscr{LC}(N, \mathscr{S}, v, \mathrm{II}) := \mathscr{LC}(\mathrm{II}, \{e(S, \cdot)\} \, s \in \mathscr{d}); \tag{6.2}$$

$$\mathscr{N}(N, \mathscr{S}, v, \mathrm{II}) := \mathscr{N}(\mathrm{II}, \{e(S, \cdot)\} \, s \in \mathscr{d}). \tag{6.3}$$

Note that the classical nucleolus and the classical prenucleolus of a game are particular nucleoli of this type. Note, however, that if II is not bounded and if some coalitions are missing from $\mathscr{S}$, both the nucleolus and the least core may be empty.[25]

Let Ω_3 be a class of truncated games satisfying (α) and (β) of section 4.[26] Then, by theorem 4.2, the nucleolus for this class is characterized by axioms $\mathbf{P_1}$, $\mathbf{P_2}$, and $\mathbf{P_4}$, which make perfect sense within the framework of truncated games. The purpose of this section is to provide a *different axiomatic characterization*, using the concept of a "reduced game." However, contrary to classical reduced games, in which one discards sets of players, here we shall discard *sets of coalitions*.

DEFINITION 6.1   Let $(N, \mathscr{S}, v, \mathrm{II})$ be a truncated game, and let $\mathscr{T}$ be a subset of $\mathscr{S}$. Let x be a point in II. The *reduced game* of $(N, \mathscr{S}, v, \mathrm{II})$ on $\mathscr{T}$ at x is the truncated game $(N, \mathscr{T}, v|\mathscr{T}, \mathrm{II}^x_{\mathscr{S} \to \mathscr{T}})$, where

$$\mathrm{II}^x_{\mathscr{S} \to \mathscr{T}} := \mathrm{II} \cap \{y \in \mathbb{R}^N : y(S) = x(S) \text{ for all } S \in \mathscr{S} \setminus \mathscr{T}\}. \tag{6.4}$$

Here, $v|\mathscr{T}$ is the restriction of the domain of v to $\mathscr{T}$. Thus, in the reduced game, the set of permissible coalitions is restricted to $\mathscr{T}$, and II is also reduced to those imputations that have the same excess at x for coalitions of $\mathscr{S}$ outside $\mathscr{T}$.

Comment   The original Davis-Maschler (1965) reduced game is nevertheless closely related to this one. Remember that a classical reduced game on a subset of players T, at a preimputation x, is given by

$$v_T^x(S) = \begin{cases} \max\{v(S \cup Q) - x(Q) : Q \subseteq N \setminus T\} & \text{if } \varnothing \neq S \subseteq T \\ x(S) & \text{if } S \in \{T, \varnothing\}. \end{cases} \tag{6.5}$$

Compare this formula with the one obtained by reducing $(N, 2^N \setminus \{N, \varnothing\}, v, \mathrm{II})$ at x on $\mathscr{T} := 2^N \setminus (\{N, \varnothing\} \cup \{\{i\} : i \in N \setminus T\})$. In this reduced game we freeze the payments to the members of $N \setminus T$ at $x^{N \setminus T}$; thus, in effect, only the players in T are playing. For them the space of preimputation is the same as that of $(T; v_T^x)$ and every nonempty proper[27] subsets of T can ensure $v_T^x(S)$, and no more, by choosing proper partners Q from $N \setminus T$, paying them the fixed rate $x(Q)$. Now, formally, there are more options in the reduced game of this section. Several coalitions of the type $S \cup Q$ are permitted, for Q's being subsets of $N \setminus T$ and a fixed S, $S \subseteq T$. If $S = \varnothing$, the excesses of these coalitions in the reduced game are constant and they can be omitted for the purpose of computing the nucleolus (axiom $\mathbf{P_2}$). If $S \neq \varnothing$ then the difference of the excesses in the reduced game, $\hat{e}(S \cup Q_1, y) - \hat{e}(S \cup Q_2, y) = [v(S \cup Q_1) - y(S) - x(Q_1)] - [v(S \cup Q_2) -$

$y(S) - x(Q_2)]$ is constant in y, for every y in $\mathrm{II}^x_{\mathscr{S} \to \mathscr{T}}$; so, by $\mathbf{P}_{11}$, only the Q's for which $v(S \cup Q) - x(Q)$ is maximal need to be considered for the purpose of looking for the nucleolus. Thus, for a society that believes in the nucleolus, the two reduced games are equivalent.

DEFINITION 6.2 We say that a solution concept Φ, defined on a class of truncated games, *satisfies the reduced-game property*, or *is consistent*, if it satisfies

($\mathbf{P}_{13}$) *Reduced-game property:* $x \in \Phi(N, \mathscr{S}, v, \mathrm{II})$ implies
  $x \in \Phi(N, \mathscr{T}, v | \mathscr{T}, \mathrm{II}^x_{\mathscr{S} \to \mathscr{T}}$, whenever $(N, \mathscr{T}, v | \mathscr{T}, \mathrm{II}^x_{\mathscr{S} \to \mathscr{T}}$
  belongs to the domain of Φ.

LEMMA 6.3 The nucleolus defined on an arbitrary class of truncated games satisfies the reduced-game property.

Discussion One interpretation of the reduced-game property runs as follows. Suppose x in a solution Φ is being proposed, then someone may improve its payment by manipulation. He approaches members of a coalition S (or several coalitions) and tells them: "Please make your coalition unavailable ($=$ nonpermissible). In return I shall give you $x(S)$ (or slightly more)." If this manipulation were beneficial, then Φ could be critized for being *unstable*, or *inconsistent*. Satisfying the reduced-game property means that this manipulation cannot benefit any player.

Although the reduced-game property is essentially a special case of the strong IIA property, we can use it to axiomatize the nucleolus.

THEOREM 6.4 Let Ω_N be the class of all[28] truncated games on a fixed set of players N. Let Φ be a solution concept for this class that satisfies the following axioms:

($\mathbf{P}_1$) (Nondiscrimination) $\Phi(N, \mathscr{S}, v, \mathrm{II}) = \mathrm{II}$ if $\mathscr{S} = \varnothing$;

($\mathbf{P}_2$) (Redundancy) $\Phi(N, \mathscr{S}, v, \mathrm{II}) = \Phi(N, \mathscr{S} \backslash \{S\}, v, \mathrm{II})$, if $e(S, \cdot)$ is constant on II;

($\mathbf{P}_3$) $\Phi(N, \mathscr{S}, v, \mathrm{II}) \subseteq \mathscr{LC}(N, \mathscr{S}, v, \mathrm{II})$;

($\mathbf{P}_{13}$) Φ satisfies the reduced-game property.

Under these conditions, $\Phi(N, \mathscr{S}, v, \mathrm{II}) \subseteq \mathscr{N}(N, \mathscr{S}, v, \mathrm{II})$ for every truncated game in Ω_N.

COROLLARY 6.5 The nucleolus of the class Ω_N is the largest solution concept satisfying $\mathbf{P}_1$, $\mathbf{P}_2$, $\mathbf{P}_3$, and $\mathbf{P}_{13}$.

Comparison between Our Axioms and the Axioms of Sobolev (1975)   Sobolev's class of games is richer in the sense that it requires that the domain of the nucleolus consists of *all* n-person TU-games,[29] whereas we can stay with the class of all truncated games on a *fixed* set of players N. Our class is richer in the sense that it contains *truncated games*—not only ordinary TU-games. Sobolev's axioms characterize only the prenucleolus. Our characterize simultaneously the nucleolus, the prenucleolus, and many other nucleoli.

However, Sobolev's result is deeper, and his proof is quite ingenious, whereas our proofs are much simpler. This is because we require the solution to be in the least core—an axiom that is not needed in Sobolev's theory. We feel that this is an important axiom because it points out what the nucleolus is all about: a desire to minimize maximum excess as a primary goal. This makes it a core-motivated solution; namely, a solution concept that "points" to the location of the core, and if it is empty—to its latent image (Shubik 1983; see also section 1).

7   Characterization of the Nucleolus of a Truncated Game by Balanced Collections

Let x be an imputation in a TU-game $(N; v)$. Define

$$\mathscr{B}_t(x) := \{S : e(S, x) \geq t\}; \tag{7.1}$$

$$\mathscr{C}(x) := \{\{i\} : x_i = v(\{i\})\}. \tag{7.2}$$

Kohlberg (1971) proved that a necessary and sufficient condition that x is the *nucleolus* of the game is that whenever $\mathscr{B}_t(x) \neq \varnothing$, $\mathscr{B}_t(x) \cup \mathscr{C}(x)$ is weakly balanced[30] with positive coefficients for the coalitions of $\mathscr{B}_t(x)$. Sobolev (1975) showed that a similar condition for the *prenucleolus* holds, if one replaces $\mathscr{C}(x)$ by the empty set. Related theorems for other nucleoli appear in Owen 1977; Wallmeier 1983; and Potters and Tijs 1992. Note the special role of the single-person coalitions. These are the coalitions responsible for the determination of the space of imputations. This suggests that a similar characterization holds for the nucleolus of truncated games.

DEFINITION 7.1   Let $\mathscr{B}$ and $\mathscr{C}$ be two collections of coalitions. We shall say that $\mathscr{B}$ is *balanced with the help of C*, if positive λ_S's exist for each S in $\mathscr{B}$ and nonnegative μ_U's exist for every U in $\mathscr{C}$ such that

$$\sum_{S \in \mathscr{B}} \lambda_S \mathbf{e}_S + \sum_{U \in \mathscr{C}} \mu_U \mathbf{e}_U = \mathbf{e}_N. \tag{7.3}$$

Here $\mathbf{e}_T$ is an n-tuple consisting of zeros and ones, whose i-th coordinate, $i \in N$, is 1 if $i \in T$ (i.e., $\mathbf{e}_T$ is the *characteristic vector* of T).

For an imputation x in a truncated game $(N, \mathscr{S}, v, \mathrm{II})$ we now define

$$\mathscr{B}_t(x) := \{S \in \mathscr{S} : e(S, x) \geq t\}, \tag{7.4}$$

$$\mathscr{C}(x) := \{U \in \mathscr{U} : x(U) = a_U\}, \tag{7.5}$$

(see equation 6.1). We can prove

THEOREM 7.2   An imputation x in II is a nucleolus point of a truncated TU-game $(N, \mathscr{S}, v, \mathrm{II})$ if and only if $\mathscr{B}_t(x)$ is balanced with the help of $\mathscr{C}(x)$, whenever $\mathscr{B}_t(x) \neq \varnothing$.

Notes

A paper entitled "The General Nucleolus and the Reduced-Game Property" appeared in 1992 in the *International Journal of Game Theory* 21:85–106. The reader can find there the proofs of the results presented here, as well as other results.

1. We refer the reader to the survey (Maschler 1991), where several properties of the nucleolus, as well as its applications are summarized and discussed.

2. This desire is natural, for example, in problems of *cost allocation*. It is hard to imagine parties who are willing to share costs in a way in which they are asked to pay more than they would had they themselves bought the same benefits.

3. Following Sobolev, axiom systems were introduced in Potters 1991 and in Snijders, 1991 to axiomatize the nucleolus itself.

4. Consistency is a natural requirement. What is not so obvious is how to define the reduced game. Different definitions lead to different solution concepts (see, for example, Hart and Mas-Colell 1989).

5. Precise definitions will be given in section 5.

6. We are indebted to Lloyd S. Shapley, who briefed us about the history of these discoveries.

7. This is the one defined in section 2.

8. In example 2.1 this is the smallest ε-*core* (Shapley and Shubik 1966) that is not empty (Maschler, Peleg, and Shapley 1979).

9. In this paper, $\bigvee$ and $\bigwedge$ are the max and min operators.

10. That is, $\Theta \circ F(x)$ is an m-vector, $m = |M|$, with the same components as in $F(x)$, but ordered in a weakly decreasing order.

11. An m-vector a is lexicographically smaller than an m-vector b if, in the first coordinate where they differ, the coordinate of a is smaller than the coordinate of b.

12. A rule Φ that assigns to each element (II, F) of Ω a subset $\Phi(II, F)$ of II.

13. That is, every value occurs among the $F_j(x)$'s and among the $\tilde{F}_j(x)$'s the same number of times.

14. For example, property $\mathbf{P}_2$ would be meaningless if (II, F_{-j}) had not been a member of Ω.

15. That alone would be requirement $\mathbf{P}_3$.

16. This incorporates an IIA-type property, in fact, we could replace $\mathbf{P}_4$ by $\mathbf{P}_3$ and $\mathbf{P}_7$. We could then prove that if Φ satisfies $\mathbf{P}_1$, $\mathbf{P}_2$, $\mathbf{P}_3$, $\mathbf{P}_5$, and $\mathbf{P}_7$, then Φ is the nucleolus for all pairs in which it is not empty. (Nonemptiness is needed; indeed, let Ω be such that all the II's of its pairs are connected. Then, $\Phi = $ II, whenever F is constant, and otherwise $\Phi = 0$ satisfies all of these five axioms; and in general it differs from the nucleolus.)

17. We do wish to include matrix games with an empty matrix, therefore we required $|M| \geq 2$ and added $\mathbf{P}_0$.

18. Preimputations, if we consider the prenucleolus.

19. Note, however, that Schmeidler's original definition took II to be an arbitrary closed set in $\mathbb{R}^N$.

20. One could deal with richer classes, but we wish to restrict the classes to a reasonable minimum for our purpose.

21. Not allowing N in $\mathscr{S}$ is a technical convention. Actually, we *are* discussing the nucleolus for the grand coalition, so that N *will* form. The convention has been created because the excesses of N and $\varnothing$ are constant.

22. Other classes can be defined; for example, permissible imputations for coalition-structures other than $\{N\}$.

23. This can be the situation even if these coalitions are not permissible. A permissible coalition can threaten to form (in order to improve the payments to its members). In contrast, a coalition can simply refuse to cooperate to form N (for the same purpose) even if it is not allowed to form.

24. We are indebted to R. J. Aumann for this remark.

25. Precisely because of this feature we included the possibility of an empty nucleolus in the axiomatization of sections 3 and 4.

26. Clearly, (δ) is also satisfied.

27. Note the special role of T: even if $\max v(\{(T \cup Q) - x(Q) : Q \subseteq N \backslash T\})$ is greater than $x(T)$, this fact plays no role in determining the space of preimputations of both reduced games. Similarly, $\varnothing$ has no effect.

28. Actually, the theorem is true for every class of truncated games that, with each (N, S, v, Π), contains all the other truncated games mentioned in the theorem and in the proof.

29. For example, if the domain is the class of all TU-games on four players, or less, take as a solution any nonnucleolus kernel point for some four-person games, together with the nucleoli points for all other games. This "solution" satisfies all Sobolev's axioms, but is is not the nucleolus (B. Peleg, oral communication).

30. That is, the balancing coefficients are allowed to be zeros.

References

Brown, G. W. 1950. "A Method for Choosing among Optimum Strategies." RM-376, Rand Project, May 2.

Davis, M., and M. Maschler. 1965. "The Kernel of a Cooperative Game." *Naval Research Logistics Quarterly* 12:223−246.

Dresher, M. 1961. *Games of Strategy*. Englewood Cliffs, N.J.: Prentice Hall.

Hart, S., and A. Mas-Colell. 1989. "Potential, Value and Consistency." *Econometrica* 57:589−614.

Justman, M. 1977. "Iterative Processes with 'Nucleolar Restrictions.'" *International Journal of Game Theory* 6:189−212.

Kohlberg, E. 1971. "On the Nucleolus of a Characteristic Function Game." *SIAM Journal of Applied Mathematics* 20:62−66.

Maschler, M. 1992. "The Bargaining Set, Kernel and Nucleolus." In *Handbook of Game Theory with Economic Applications*, vol. I, ed. R. J. Aumann and S. Hart. New York: Elsevier, North Holland.

Maschler, M., and B. Peleg. "Stable Sets and Stable Points of Set-Valued Dynamic Systems with Applications to Game Theory." *SIAM Journal of Control and Optimization* 14:985−995.

Maschler, M., B. Peleg, and L. S. Shapley. 1979. "Geometric Properties of the Kernel, Nucleolus, and Related Solution Concepts." *Mathematics of Operations Research* 4:303−338.

Owen, G. 1977. "A Generalization of the Kohlberg Criterion." *International Journal of Game Theory* 6:249−255.

Potters, J. A. M. 1991. "An Axiomatization of the Nucleolus." *International Journal of Game Theory* 19:365−373.

Potters, J. A. M., and S. H. Tijs. 1992. "The Nucleolus of Matrix Games and Other Nucleoli." *Mathematics of Operations Research:* 17:164−174.

Schmeidler, D. 1969. "The Nucleolus of a Characteristic Function Game." *SIAM Journal of Applied Mathematics* 17:1163−1170.

Shapley, L. S., and M. Shubik. 1966. "Quasi-Cores in a Monetary Economy with Non-Convex Preferences." *Econometrica* 34:805–827.

Shubik, M. 1983 *Game Theory in the Social Sciences: Concepts and Solutions*. Cambridge: MIT Press.

Snijders, C. 1991. "Axiomatization of the Nucleolus." RM, Part of a Master's thesis, Department of Mathematics, University of Utrecht, May 15.

Sobolev, A. I., 1975. "The Characterization of Optimality Principles in Cooperative Games by Functional Equations" (in Russian, English Summary). In *Mathematicheskie Metody v Sotsial'nykh Naukakh*, ed. N. N. Vorobjev, 94–151. Proceedings of the seminar, Institute of Physics and Mathematics, Academy of Sciences of the Lithuanian SSR, Vilnius.

van Damme, E. E. C. 1983. *Refinements of the Nash Equilibrium Concept*. Berlin: Springer Verlag.

Wallmeier, E. 1983. "Der *f*-Nukleolus und ein Dynamisches Verhandlungsmodell als Lösungskonzepte für Kooperative n-Personenspiele." Ph.D. diss. Skripten zur Mathematischen Statistik, Nr. 5, Westfälischen Wilhelm-Universität Münster, Institut für Mathematische Statistik.

7   Some Thoughts on Efficiency and Information

Françoise Forges

1 Introduction

The study of collective decision problems with incomplete information has shown that several definitions of Pareto efficiency were conceivable in this framework. Wilson (1978) introduced the concepts of "coarse" and "fine" efficiency, and Holmström and Myerson (1983), fixed the terminology in the context of Bayesian mechanism design (see also Myerson 1991, chap. 10). Holmström and Myerson distinguish six classes of efficient mechanisms according to the circumstances in which collective decisions can be improved; improvements may or may not be made conditional on incentive constraints; they may be envisaged at various times relative to the revelation of information (ex ante, interim, ex post). In this literature, the term *ex post* means "given the state of nature." It should be noted that the definition of a Bayesian collective choice problem does not usually entail public knowledge of the state of nature at some stage. Two criteria are widely used. The first one is *classical* efficiency; this can be defined as efficiency at every state of nature. In the taxonomy of Holmström and Myerson, it corresponds to "ex post stage" and "no incentive constraints." The second criterion is *incentive* efficiency; it is useful to compare incentive compatible mechanisms in terms of the interim expected welfare of the agents.

Holmström and Myerson, followed by many authors (see, for example, Wilson 1985), have argued that classical efficiency was not an appropriate criterion even combined with incentive compatibility (stated as an autonomous property). They claim that it does not reflect the effective strategic possibilities in collective decision problems with incomplete information.

A standard formulation is that the agents must choose a decision rule or *mechanism* at the *interim* stage. Such a mechanism must satisfy incentive constraints in order to be feasible. It is (incentive) efficient if there is no other feasible (in particular, incentive compatible) mechanism which makes all agents better off (in terms of their interim expected utility).

The previous approach is successful in modeling the efficiency of *mechanisms*. However, incentive efficient mechanisms may select inefficient *outcomes*; ex post, the agents may unanimously prefer another solution. One may fear that outcomes selected in this way will not be stable and that a phase of renegotiation will ensue. This does not seem compatible with efficiency, at least if this property is understood from a positive point of view, in the spirit of the Coase theorem (1960). This suggests that ex post efficiency, as considered, for instance, by d'Aspremont and Gérard-Varet (1979), is far from being meaningless and might be worth investigating again.

In this chapter we first formulate an ex post efficiency criterion that coincides with the classical one in the case of private values (i.e, when the value of a decision for an agent cannot vary with the information of other agents). Here the information conveyed by the mechanism on the types of other agents is not relevant and one may act as if these types were revealed ex post. When values are not private, the information revealed by the mechanism to every agent is crucial for the evaluation of the decision. Our concept assumes implicitly that the final decision is the only output of the (direct) mechanism. No assumption of private values is made in Holmström and Myerson 1983 either. The relevance of such models is more and more recognized (see, for example, Johnson, Pratt, and Zeckhauser 1990). Our concept of efficiency does not enter any of the six classes determined by Holmström and Myerson (except for the particular case mentioned above). In general, it does not imply, nor is it implied by, classical efficiency, as the examples below will show.

It is well known that there exists a classically efficient incentive compatible mechanism for any Bayesian collective choice problem with private values, and that this is not true without private values (see example 3.1). If our definition of efficiency is adopted, a general existence property holds. The proof is a mere generalization of the well-known argument in the private values case. This suggests that our criterion is the accurate formulation of ex post efficiency in the general case.

In spite of this positive result, the inefficiencies identified by the criterion of this chapter may not be relevant; indeed, they are associated with a specific state of nature, although the agents evaluate their welfare as a function of their ex post information and may thus be uncertain about the state. This difficulty is apparent in example 3.2. In a subsequent study (Forges 1991) we depart from the classical definition of ex post efficiency and consider as equivalent all the states of nature that are compatible with a given decision. In other words, improvements are only made conditional on the outcome of the mechanism. Another concept emerges from this approach: *posterior* efficiency. The criterion developed in the present chapter is useful from a didactic point of view since it captures the properties of ex post efficiency in collective choice problems without private values.

As a second purpose of this chapter, we would like to point out that the conjunction of incentive compatibility on the one hand and of ex post efficiency on the other is not a satisfactory property because it does not capture the descriptive aspect of Pareto optimality, namely, *outcome renegotiation-proofness*. The combination of the two previous requirements, which results from an axiomatic approach to mechanism design, is meaningful from a normative point of view but is only a *necessary condition* to renegotiation-proofness.

More precisely, let us fix a *classically efficient incentive compatible* mechanism in a given Bayesian collective choice problem, say with private values (so that there is no ambiguity over the ex post efficiency criterion). Let us model an explicit approval phase after the selection of an outcome by the mechanism. Let us propose an alternative decision to the agents, which will be implemented if they unanimously agree on it. A truthful report of the type followed by rational approval of the outcome selected by the mechanism may *not* be a Nash equilibrium. Typically, the possibility of ex post renegotiation could modify the incentive constraints. This is illustrated in example 3.3. Thus, in models of incomplete information, efficiency can definitely not be investigated independently of incentive compatibility. But, at the ex post stage, the problem is hard to formulate as the choice of an incentive compatible mechanism for the original collective choice problem (observe that such a formulation is nevertheless proposed implicitly, for taxonomy purposes, in Holmström and Myerson 1983).

This leads us to introduce the notion of "outcome renegotiation-proofness" for mechanisms, which strengthens both incentive compatibility and efficiency. We only hope to suggest that a positive interpretation of outcome efficiency requires that a precise scenario be added to the mechanism, including revelation of information as well as renegotiation possibilities. We propose such a scenario and associate a notion of renegotiation-proofness with it; these requirements are somewhat arbitrary and are mainly chosen for their simplicity. The procedure should depend on the environment in which the mechanism must be applied.

The model is described in section 2. Section 3 is devoted to our variant of ex post efficiency and to renegotiation-proofness. Concluding remarks (in section 4) include a comparison between our concept and "durability," which was introduced in Holmström and Myerson 1983 and further studied by Crawford (1985). The latter property relates to the renegotiation of *mechanisms* as it can be envisaged at the *interim* stage, while we are interested in the *ex post* stage. From this point of view, the present chapter has common features with an article of Green and Laffont (1987), which was motivated by ex post considerations, too. The notion of "posterior implementation" developed there also requires us to care about the information revealed by mechanisms. But the purpose is not Pareto improvement. An important literature has grown recently over the theme of renegotiation. We will not even try to survey it. Let us just mention that most of these studies pertain to contract theory and are thus elaborated for particular economic and institutional circumstances (see, for example, Dewatripont 1989). The notion of renegotiation-proofness used in Palfrey and Srivastava 1989 is formally similar to ours, but applies to the interim stage as do the ones mentioned before.

2   Model

Our basic framework is a *Bayesian collective choice problem* (see Myerson 1985, 1991); n agents (indexed by $i = 1, \ldots, n$) must jointly choose a decision in a simplex D, which is typically interpreted as the set of probability distributions over a finite set of primitive decisions. Each agent i has private information (in a finite set T_i) that is relevant to the value of decisions; a state of information $t_i \in T_i$ is called a *type* of agent i ($i = 1, \ldots, n$). The preferences of agent i are described by a utility function, $u_i : T \times D \to \mathbb{R}$, ($i = 1, \ldots, n$), with $T = \prod_{i=1}^{n} T_i$. Notice that the preferences of the different agents are not related to each other but that the information of one agent can influence the preferences of another. With the interpretation above, the u_i's correspond to expected utilities, so that $u_i(t, d)$ is linear in $d \in D$, for every $t \in T$. The model is completed by a probability distribution p over T, which describes the beliefs of the agents about each other.[1]

We shall use the expression "private values" to refer to the particular case where the utility function u_i of each agent i depends only on his own type (i.e., $u_i(t, \ldots, t_i, \ldots, t_n) = u_i(t_i, d)$ for every $d \in D$, $t_i \in T_i$, $i = 1, \ldots, n$).

A joint strategy of the agents, namely, a mapping $\mu : T \to D$, is called a "mechanism." We will formulate and discuss some desirable properties of mechanisms. The first one is *incentive compatibility*. In order to make this notion precise, let us fix a mechanism μ. Let $G_0(\mu)$ be the following game, played with the help of a planner:

(0) At a virtual preliminary stage, $t = (t_1, \ldots, t_n)$ is chosen in T according to p; player i is only informed of t_i;

(1) Every agent i $(i = 1, \ldots, n)$ sends a message $m_i \in T_i$ to the planner;

(2) Given $m = (m_1, \ldots, m_n)$, the planner makes the decision $\mu(m)$ for the agents.

μ is *incentive compatible* if the truthful strategies (where each agent i reveals his type t_i) form a Nash equilibrium of $G_0(\mu)$. In other words, μ satisfies the following linear inequality:

$$\sum_{t_{-i}} p(t_{-i}|t_i) u_i(t_i, t_{-i}, \mu(t_i, t_{-i})) \geq \sum_{t_{-i}} p(t_{-i}|t_i) u_i(t_i, t_{-i}, \mu(t_i', t_{-i})) \tag{2.1}$$

for all $i = 1, \ldots, n$, $t_i, t_i' \in T_i$ (with the usual convention $t_{-i} = (t_1, \ldots, t_{i-1}, t_{i+1}, \ldots, t_n)$). The left-hand side is the equilibrium expected payoff of agent i of type t_i and will be denoted as $U_i(\mu|t_i)$.

Let $\mathcal{I}$ be the set $(\subseteq D^T)$ of all incentive compatible mechanisms. By the revelation principle (see Myerson 1991), any Nash equilibrium of any game of the form above (even with arbitrary sets of messages at stage 1) reduces to an incentive compatible mechanism. $\mathcal{I}$ can thus be viewed as the set of *feasible* solutions to the Bayesian collective choice problem, and an *efficient* solution can be defined as an element μ of $\mathcal{I}$ such that no element of $\mathcal{I}$ is unanimously preferred to μ (i.e., there is no v in $\mathcal{I}$ such that $\forall i = 1, \ldots, n$, $\forall t_i \in T_i$, $U_i(v|t_i) > U_i(\mu|t_i)$.[3]

As recalled in the introduction, this approach has been followed by Holmström and Myerson and seems more appropriate to study the efficiency of mechanisms (in D^T) than the efficiency of outcomes (in D). We observed that this latter notion is not meaningless, and its precise formulation should be a first step toward the characterization of mechanisms μ that are resistant to outcome renegotiation after stage 2 of $G_0(\mu)$.

Obviously, the assumptions on the agents' information at that moment matter in a crucial way. The classical approach is sometimes justified by the interpretation that the vector of types t is revealed to all agents at the same time as the decision $\mu(t)$. Recall that μ is *classically outcome efficient* if for every $t \in T$, $\mu(t)$ is efficient in D, in the usual sense (i.e., there is no $d \in D$ such that $\forall i = 1, \ldots, n$, $u_i(t, d) > u_i(t, \mu(t))$). Ex post symmetric information makes sense in many economic applications but is usually not assumed in Bayesian collective choice problems. Ex post complete information may seem achievable in the game $G_0(\mu)$ generated by an incentive compatible mechanism μ since the planner knows all types and can reveal them to the agents. However, it should not be forgotten that the simple scenario of $G_0(\mu)$ and the restriction to truthful strategies in $G_0(\mu)$ result from the

revelation principle. This yields a convenient canonical representation but
should otherwise not be taken too seriously. Consider, for instance, a constant mechanism μ selecting a given decision d_0 in D ($\mu(t) = d_0$ for all
$t \in T$.) We may obviously apply the revelation principle and imagine that
the agents report their types to a planner who does not listen to them and
decides d_0 in any case. But why should we assume that the agents know
more about each other when the decision d_0 is made, if this outcome does
not depend on their types? The fact is that an analogue of the revelation
principle would not hold at a renegotiation phase carried on by the original
agents, because their happiness may depend on their information (see examples 3.1, 3.2). If one wants to restrict oneself to direct mechanisms as a
consequence of the revelation principle, it seems sensible to assume that the
joint decision process described by $G_0(\mu)$ will convey the agents minimal
information over each other's types, namely, that only $\mu(t)$ (not t) will be
observed by the agents.

This discussion motivates the following description of the *information
conveyed by a given mechanism* $\mu \in \mathscr{I}$. Agent i of type t_i assigns a prior
probability $p(t_{-i}|t_i)$ to the vector of types t_{-i} of the others. Suppose he
observes a decision $d \in Im \, \mu$; his posterior beliefs are defined as

$$P_\mu(t_{-i}|t_i, d) = \frac{p(t_{-i}|t_i)I(\mu(t_i, t_{-i}) = d)}{\sum_{s_{-i}} p(s_{-i}|t_i)I(\mu(t_i, s_{-i}) = d)}, \tag{2.2}$$

where I is the indicator function. This corresponds to usual Bayesian updating, with respect to the probability distribution induced by p and the
truthful strategies.[4] As a simple example, the posterior beliefs associated
with the constant mechanism above ($Im \, \mu = \{d_0\}$) coincide with the prior

$$P_\mu(t_{-i}|t_i, d_0) = p(t_{-i}|t_i).$$

To take another extreme case, if μ is one-to-one,

$$P_\mu(t_{-i}|t_i, d) = I(\mu(t_i, t_{-i}) = d)$$

for every $d \in Im \, \mu$. In the first example the mechanism is nonrevealing; in
the second one it is completely revealing. Hybrid mechanisms are obviously conceivable.

3   An Efficiency Criterion

We start in a naive (but usual) way and investigate outcome efficiency
without insisting on incentive constraints. We propose a variant of the
classical approach by defining the outcome efficiency of a mechanism, giv-
en the minimal information that it conveys.

Let us fix $\mu \in \mathscr{I}$. We will say that μ is *not efficient* if

$$\exists t \in T \; \exists d \in D \qquad \forall i = 1, \ldots, n$$

$$\sum_{s_{-i}} P_\mu(s_{-i}|t_i, \mu(t))[u_i(t_i, s_{-i}, d) - u_i(t_i, s_{-i}, \mu(t))] > 0, \tag{3.1}$$

where P_μ is defined by (2.2). With posteriors evaluated in this way, the definition would not be meaningful for a mechanism μ that is not incentive compatible.

At this point, our efficiency criterion is best interpreted as a *no-regret* condition, without any implication about the behavior of the agents. Suppose that μ is efficient; then, given the decision selected by μ, all agents cannot prefer that another decision be made. To deduce from this that the decision selected by μ would be resistant to renegotiation is a more complicated matter, as we shall show.

In the particular case of *private values*, (3.1) reduces to

$$\exists t \in T \; \exists d \in D \qquad \forall i = 1, \ldots, n$$

$$u_i(t_i, d) - u_i(t_i, \mu(t)) > 0, \tag{3.2}$$

and we just recover *classical* outcome efficiency. Indeed, as we recalled in section 2, μ is not classically (outcome) efficient if

$$\exists t \in T \; \exists d \in D \qquad \forall i = 1, \ldots, n$$

$$u_i(t, d) - u_i(t, \mu(t)) > 0. \tag{3.3}$$

This criterion implicitly assumes that t is revealed at the same time as $\mu(t)$. In the case of private values this has no consequence, and our efficiency criterion coincides with the classical one. (3.1) and (3.3) are also identical when μ is completely revealing. But in general, (3.1) only uses the information revealed by $\mu(t)$; if $\mu(t)$ is the decision resulting from the mechanism, agent i's beliefs are $P_\mu(s_{-i}|t_i, \mu(t))$, and he evaluates other decisions d accordingly.

As a further illustration, the constant mechanism $\mu(t) = d_0$ for all t's is not efficient if

$$\exists t \in T \; \exists d \in D \qquad \forall i = 1, \ldots, n$$

$$\sum_{s_{-i}} p(s_{-i}|t_i)[u_i(t_i, s_{-i}, d) - u_i(t_i, s_{-i}, d_0)] > 0.$$

There are two variants of the definition one can think of. According to the standard terminology, (3.1) underlies a weak efficiency criterion. This could be modified by requiring only that one inequality be strict. Although

meaningful, such an approach would be less appropriate in view of renegotiation. For the other variant, recall that D is the set of probability distributions over a finite set of basic decisions (say, D_0) so that mechanisms
can be interpreted as random (i.e., as systems of probability distributions
$\mu(\cdot|t)$ over D_0, given $t \in T$). One may thus consider as outcomes associated with a mechanism μ the elements of D_0 selected by $\mu(t)$ (rather than
the lottery $\mu(t)$ itself). This generates the following definition: μ is not
efficient if

$$\exists d_0 \in D_0, \ \exists t \in T : (p \times \mu)(t, d_0) > 0,$$

$$\exists d \in D_0, \qquad \forall i = 1, \ldots, n \tag{3.4}$$

$$\sum_{s_{-i}} (p \times \mu)((s_{-i}|t_i, d_0)[u_i(t_i, s_{-i}, d) - u_i(t_i, s_{-i}, d_0)] > 0,$$

where $p \times \mu$ is the probability distribution over $T \times D_0$ generated by p
and μ. In the complete information case (or more generally, if values are
private) such an interpretation of the ex post stage as the very end enlarges
the set of efficient mechanisms and does not seem usual. In general, the
comparison between (3.1) and (3.4) may be delicate, due to information
effects. In Forges 1991 we formulate efficiency criteria for random mechanisms and further discuss the differences between random and deterministic
mechanisms.

Let $\mathscr{E}$ be the set $(\subseteq D^T)$ of efficient mechanisms (in the sense of (3.2)).
Similarly, let $\mathscr{E}_c$ be the set of classically efficient mechanisms (defined by
(3.3)). In the private values case, $\mathscr{E} = \mathscr{E}_c$. A standard approach would lead
us to investigate the set $\mathscr{I} \cap \mathscr{E}$ (see d'Aspremont and Gérard-Varet 1979;
and Holmström and Myerson 1983). From a normative point of view, it is
reasonable to require that a mechanism be incentive compatible and efficient at the same time. However, even in the private values case, where our
concepts coincide with the usual one, the combination of incentive compatibility and efficiency may not be relevant in a descriptive perspective. This
will be shown in example 3.3. Before that, we illustrate some differences
between our criterion and classical efficiency. The first example is borrowed
from Holmström and Myerson.

Example 3.1 Let

$$n = 2, \qquad T_1 = \{t_1, t_1'\}, \qquad T_2 = \{t_2, t_2'\}, \qquad D_0 = \{d_1, d_2\},$$

$$p(t) = \tfrac{1}{4} \qquad \forall t \in T = T_1 \times T_2;$$

the utility functions can computed from

	(t_1, t_2)	(t_1, t_2')	(t_1', t_2)	(t_1', t_2')
d_1	6, 0	0, 0	2, 2	0, 0
d_2	0, 6	2, 2	0, 0	2, 2

One of the features of this Bayesian collective choice problem is that $\mathscr{I} \cap \mathscr{E}_c = \varnothing$. Indeed, $\mu \in \mathscr{E}_c$ implies $\mu(t_1', t_2) = d_1$, $\mu(t_1, t_2') = \mu(t_1', t_2') = d_2$. Agent 1 of type t_1 can thus get an expected payoff of 4 by pretending that his type is t_1'. Hence, we must have $\mu(t_1, t_2) = d_1$ to prevent agent 1 from cheating. But this mechanism μ is not incentive compatible: agent 2 of type t_2 gets an expected payoff of 1 if he tells the truth, of 3 if he lies.

Nevertheless, the constant mechanism $\mu(t) = d_2$ for all t's is in $\mathscr{I} \cap \mathscr{E}$. It is trivially incentive compatible, and agent 2 get always the best payoff he can expect (given his belief over T_1, which never moves from the prior).

This first example illustrates that $\mathscr{E}$ is not included in $\mathscr{E}_c$. We will show that unlike $\mathscr{I} \cap \mathscr{E}_c$, $\mathscr{I} \cap \mathscr{E}$ is never empty. In the second example, $\mathscr{E}_c$ is not included in $\mathscr{E}$.

Example 3.2   The setup is exactly the same as in example 3.1, except for the payoffs, which are now

	(t_1, t_2)	(t_1, t_2')	(t_1', t_2)	(t_1', t_2')
d_1	$-2, -2$	$4, -4$	$-4, 4$	0, 0
d_2	0, 0	0, 0	0, 0	0, 0

The constant mechanism $\mu(t) = d_2$ for all t's is clearly in $\mathscr{I} \cap \mathscr{E}_c$. Agent 1 of type t_1 and agent 2 of type t_2 both get an expected utility of 0. Let us show that $\mu \notin \mathscr{E}$. μ does not yield any information on the agents' types. Hence, the (ex post) expected payoff associated with d_1 is $1 > 0$ for both agents, who thus prefer d_1 to $\mu(t_1, t_2)$ when they are of type t_1 and t_2, respectively.

The mechanism μ is incentive efficient. Another incentive efficient mechanism is the one which selects d_1 (resp. d_2) when agent 1 announces t_1 (resp. t_1'), independently of agent 2's message. This mechanism is in $\mathscr{I} \cap \mathscr{E}$.

We turn to the question of existence of incentive compatible efficient mechanisms. It is known that $\mathscr{I} \cap \mathscr{E}_c$ is never empty in the private values case and that without this assumption, the property is no longer guaranteed (see example 3.1). The argument proving the existence of classical efficient incentive compatible mechanisms in the private values case can be extended to show that $\mathscr{I} \cap \mathscr{E}$ is never empty. This suggests that our efficiency criterion is the proper formulation of classical (ex post) efficiency when values are not private.

PROPERTY $\mathscr{I} \cap \mathscr{E} \neq \emptyset$.

Proof   The way in which we construct an incentive compatible efficient mechanism is standard. It consists of choosing one agent (say agent 1) as leader. Let, for every $t_1, t_2, \ldots, t_n$, $\mu(t_1, t_2, \ldots, t_n) = \mu(t_1)$ be a decision d_1 in D that maximizes agents 1's expected utility (with respect to his prior belief), that is,

$$\sum_{s_{-1}} p(s_{-1}|t_1)\mu_1(t_1, s_{-1}, d_1).$$

Such a decision rule can be called "1-mechanism." μ is such that agent 1 cannot learn anything new about the other agents' types. Hence, $\mu(t_1)$ remains an optimal decision for player 1 ex post (since communication can only be performed through μ).

The next example illustrates that incentive compatible mechanisms need not be renegotiation-proof; values are private in this example so that $\mathscr{E} = \mathscr{E}_c$.

Example 3.3   Let

$$n = 2, \qquad T_1 = \{t, t_1'\}, \qquad T_2 = \{t_2\}, \qquad D_0 = \{d_1, d_1', d\},$$

$$p(t_1) = p(t_1') = \tfrac{1}{2};$$

where payoffs are

	t_1	t_1'
d_1	0, 1	0, 1
d_1'	$-1, -1$	1, -1
d	1, 0	$-1, 0$.

The following mechanism, $\mu : \mu(t_1) = d_1, \mu(t_1') = d_1'$, belongs to $\mathscr{I} \cap \mathscr{E}$. Nevertheless, μ would not resist ex post renegotiation. Suppose that the decision resulting from μ is submitted to approval after stage 2 of $G_0(\mu)$; let d be the alternative decision, implemented if both agents say so. Agent 2 would certainly reject d_1' in favor of d, since he strictly prefers d to d_1'. Such a behavior can be expected whatever agent 2's beliefs: his preferences do not depend on any state of information. But if there is a further approval stage, agent 1 of type t_1 should pretend that his type is t_1' so that d_1' be selected by μ; agent 1 would then reject d_1' in favor of d, which would become the final decision as a result of a unanimous agreement.

The problem is easy to understand. The incentive compatibility of the mechanism μ, as expressed by conditions 2.1, guarantees that agent 1 will reveal his type if the planner decides on $\mu(m)$ at stage 2 of $G_0(\mu)$. But these conditions become meaningless in the more complex game where the players have to approve the decision $\mu(m)$. However, studying such a game seems unavoidable to relate ex post efficiency with procedures of ex post approval. This motivates our next definition.

Let us fix a mechanism $\mu \in D^T$ and let us associate with it a collection of multistage games $G(\mu, d)$, indexed by $d \in D$. Stage 0 and stage 1 of $G(\mu, d)$ are as in $G_0(\mu)$ (see section 2). Stage 2 is modified as follows:

(2) Given $m = (m_1, \ldots, m_n)$, the planner suggests $\mu(m)$ to the agents.

Two further stages are added:

(3) Every agent accepts $\mu(m)$ or rejects it in favor of d (formally, agent i reports 1 for acceptance of $\mu(m)$ and 0 for refusal);

(4) The final decision is d if the agents unanimously reject $\mu(m)$ in favor of d (i.e., if all agents choose 0 at stage 3), $\mu(m)$ otherwise.

A (pure) *strategy* for agent i in $G(\mu, d)$ is a pair of mappings (σ_i, τ_i) for stage 1 and stage 3, respectively:

$$\sigma_i : T_i \to T_i$$

$$\tau_i : T_i \times Im\,\mu \to \{0, 1\}.$$

The *truthful* strategy of agent i consists of revealing his type at stage 1; that is, σ_i is the identity mapping, and his preference at stage 3, given his beliefs about the others' types at that stage. More precisely, if the truthful strategies are used at stage 1, player i computes his posterior probability distribution as in (2.2) and $\tau_i(t_i, \mu(m)) = 0$ if and only if

$$\sum_{s_{-i}} P_\mu(s_{-i}|t_i, \mu(m))[u_i(t_i, s_{-i}, d) - u_i(t_i, s_{-i}, \mu(m))] > 0.$$

We can introduce the following:

DEFINITION μ is (outcome) *renegotiation-proof* if for every $d \in D$, the truthful strategies form an equilibrium of $G(\mu, d)$ and implement μ, that is, for every t, the final decision is $\mu(t)$.

There are two aspects: first, specific strategies must form an equilibrium; second, the outcome must be $\mu(t)$ for every t (see examples 3.4 and 3.5). Observe that requiring that strategies be "truthful" at stage 3 after having been truthful at stage 1 introduces a substantial restriction. Indeed, for every incentive compatible mechanism μ (thus satisfying (2.1)) and for every $d \in D$, $G(\mu, d)$ has a trivial equilibrium which implements μ: it suffices to take the identity mapping for σ_i and the constant mapping 1 for τ_i ($i = 1, \ldots, n$). But this cannot necessarily be turned into a truthful equilibrium (recall example 3.3).

The previous refinement is a simple way of getting rid of the trivial Nash equilibrium. When values are not private, the way in which beliefs are evaluated at stage 3 may obviously matter. We consider the effective posterior probability distribution, given $\mu(m)$, which agent i computes at stage 3. One may argue that agent i should only worry about the consequences of his vote when all the other agents choose the alternative d and that he should evaluate his preferences according to the associated beliefs. Such an approach to posterior durability has been followed by Rovesti (1991). The idea of anticipating the fact that the other agents would vote for the alternative in the evaluation of beliefs was already present in Holmström and Myerson 1983. However, the condition looks more natural there because beliefs are formed at an intermediary stage, namely, after voting but before participating to the mechanism that has won the vote. In fact, the way in which beliefs are evaluated may not be essential. The important condition concerns the agents' preferences that are independent of their knowledge of others' types (see example 3.4).

The definition of renegotiation-proofness given above is a convenient way of reconciling incentive compatibility and ex post efficiency. Many other definitions can be obtained by varying the scenario of the games $G(\mu, d)$. The fact that a collection of games $G(\mu, d)$ indexed by d is considered may be puzzling. No procedure for selecting d, for pointing it out to the agents, has been made explicit. Our definition should be interpreted in the tradition of Pareto-optimality, which already has the above drawback in models of complete information. (Obviously, in this case, the task is simplified by the fact that all agents fully know the decision problem; however, the selection of a Pareto improvement may be an issue; see, in this regard, Crawford 1985) Once again, our modest goal is to formulate a definition of ex post efficiency that takes account of the incentive constraints, while capturing the resistance to renegotiation in a single dynamic setup.

Notice that a single game $G(\mu)$ could be considered. At stage 3 of $G(\mu)$, the agents would be asked whether they would reject $\mu(m)$ in favor of d, for every $d \in D$. (τ_i would become a mapping with values in $\{0, 1\}^D$). Stage 4 would also have to be modified so that the final decision could always be determined unambiguously. The mechanism μ could then be interpreted as a way of choosing a disagreement point as a function of the types.

Let $\mathcal{R}$ be the set ($\subseteq D^T$) of renegotiation-proof mechanisms. The following property establishes that incentive compatibility and efficiency are necessary to renegotiation-proofness.

PROPERTY $\quad \mathcal{R} \subseteq \mathcal{I} \cap \mathcal{E}$.

Proof Let $\mu \in \mathcal{R}$. For every $d \in D$, the agents reveal their types t at stage 1 of $G(\mu, d)$ and $\mu(t)$ is then implemented. The agents would, a fortiori, reveal their types in the simplified game $G_0(\mu)$. Hence, $\mu \in \mathcal{I}$.

Next, let us assume that $\mu \notin \mathcal{E}$ and let us show that $\mu \notin \mathcal{R}$ (we assume that $\mu \in \mathcal{I}$ so that our definition of efficiency makes sense). From (3.1), $\exists t \in T$, $\exists d \in D$ such that $\forall i = 1, \dots, n$, $\tau_i(t_i, \mu(t)) = 0$, where τ_i is agent i's truthful strategy at stage 3 of $G(\mu, d)$. Hence, the truthful strategies could not implement μ. $\qquad\qquad\square$

As shown by example 3.3, $\mathcal{R}$ may be *strictly* included in $\mathcal{I} \cap \mathcal{E}$. The mechanism considered there is in $\mathcal{I} \cap \mathcal{E}$, but the truthful strategies do not form an equilibrium of $G(\mu, d)$; in this game, agent 1 of type t_1 can gain by reporting that his type is t_1'.

The next example shows that "j-mechanisms" for some agent j (as constructed to prove that $\mathcal{I} \cap \mathcal{E} \neq \varnothing$) may not be renegotiation-proof.

EXAMPLE 3.4 Let

$$n = 2, \qquad T_1 = \{t_1\}, \qquad T_2 = \{t_2, t_2'\}, \qquad D = \{d, d', d_1\},$$

$$p(t_2) = p(t_2') = \tfrac{1}{2};$$

where both agents have the same payoffs described by

	t_2	t_2'
d	2	-2
d'	-2	2
d_1	1	1

The 1-mechanism μ consists of deciding d_1 whatsoever. Consider the game $G(\mu, d)$. The truthful strategy of agent 1 prescribes to vote for d_1 at stage 3. This is not a best reply to the truthful strategy of agent 2 at stage 3. The latter strategy does not depend on any belief of agent 2 (since he is the only informed player) and consists of voting for d on t_2 and for d_1 on t_2'. The best reply of agent 1 is obviously to vote for d, so that d (resp. d_1) be implemented on t_2 (resp. t_2').

In example 3.3 the renegotiation-proofness breaks down at stage 1, because of the incentive constraints. In example 3.4 the truthful strategies are not in equilibrium at stage 3. It may also happen that the truthful strategies form an equilibrium but do not implement μ. Take a problem with the same structure as example 3.2, where $u_i(t, d_1) > u_i(t, d_2)$ for $i = 1, 2$ and all t's, and consider the constant mechanism μ choosing d_2 at all states of nature.

We have just seen that j-mechanisms may not belong to $\mathcal{R}$, although they are always in $\mathcal{I} \cap \mathcal{E}$. We shall say that agent j is "informationally autonomous" in a given collective choice problem if $u_j(t, d) = u_j(t_j, d)$ for every (t, d). For instance, if only one agent has private information, this agent is informationally autonomous. If values are private, all agents are informationally autonomous. It is easily checked that

PROPERTY   If agent j is informationally autonomous, every j-mechanism belongs to $\mathcal{R}$.

4   Concluding Remarks

We end this chapter with some comments on *durability* and *individual rationality*.

The first concept has been introduced in Holmström and Myerson 1983. This seminal study of efficiency in collective decision problems with incomplete information has much oriented the present one. Although the motivations for introducing durability are close to the ones detailed above, there is an important difference between Holmström and Myerson's approach and ours: they focused on the problem of choosing a mechanism at the *interim* stage; we were concerned with the ex post stability of decisions suggested by a mechanism. In particular, we had to worry about the information (about agents' types) that can be conveyed by the application of a mechanism. Holmström and Myerson had to take account of the information that the agents could reveal while negotiating over the mechanism to be used. Apart from the stage where it takes place, the approval procedure described above is very similar to the one proposed in Holmström and Myerson 1983.

As one may expect, durability does not imply outcome renegotiation-proofness. In example 3.3 only one agent has private information. The mechanism μ is interim incentive efficient and thus also durable (by theorem 3 of Holmström and Myerson). However, as we have argued, μ is not renegotiation-proof. Let us also mention that Holmström and Myerson suggested a concept of "posterior" durability in their concluding comments. As pointed out above, such a notion was studied by Rovesti (1991).

In the analysis above, we have concentrated on two properties of mechanism: incentive compatibility and efficiency. We did not investigate *individual rationality*. Strictly speaking, this property is not relevant to Bayesian collective choice problems, as opposed to Bayesian bargaining problems (see Myerson 1991, chap. 10). The latter differ from the former by the specification of a disagreement decision d to be made if the agents do not agree on a mechanism. In this framework, μ is said to be (interim) individually rational[5] if

$$U_i(\mu|t_i) \geq \sum_{t_{-i}} p(t_{-i}|t_i)u_i(t_i, t_{-i}, d),$$

where $U_i(\mu|t_i)$ is defined as in section 2. In other words, all agents would accept to participate to $G_0(\mu)$ if they were asked so after stage 0.

In the context of a Bayesian collective choice problem, the agents cannot choose whether or not to participate. However, the solutions considered above are individually rational in the game-theoretic sense. More precisely, each agent gets at least his minmax level in the games $G_0(\mu)$ and $G(\mu, d)$ (see Crawford 1985 for a similar treatment of individual rationality together with the incentive constraints).

As one may expect, our analysis does not help to circumvent the dramatically negative results on ex post efficiency in Bayesian bargaining problems (see Myerson 1991, ex. 10.3; Myerson and Satterthwaite 1983; Osborne and Rubinstein 1990, sect. 5.6). Our approach is valid as long as participation constraints are formulated on decisions (i.e., on D) independently on the types, but the construction should be reconsidered if further constraints are imposed on the mechanisms.

Notes

This chapter was drafted while visiting Duke, Northwestern, and Stanford. The author specially thanks H. Moulin, R. Myerson, and R. Wilson for their hospitality. Discussions with C. d'Aspremont were very helpful.

1. The framework is exactly as in Holmström and Myerson 1983. The concepts introduced below would make sense in more general contexts, but the existence results might not extend. For instance, our analysis cannot be applied directly to the model of d'Aspremont and Gérard-Varet (1979) or bargaining problems (see section 5).

2. With the previous interpretation of D, we can restrict ourselves to deterministic mechanisms, as in Holmström and Myerson 1983. Mechanisms may also be de-

fined as transition probabilities; as far as Holmström and Myerson's efficiency concepts are concerned, deterministic and random mechanisms are equivalent. This is not necessarily true for efficiency concepts which require the evaluation of the posterior expected welfare of the agents (see Forges 1991).

3. This defines *interim* (incentive) efficiency because the expected payoffs are evaluated at the interim stage (between stage 0 and stage 1 of $G_0(\mu)$), that is, as $U_i(\mu|t_i)$. Ex ante and ex post incentive efficiency are also conceivable but less meaningful (see Holmström and Myerson 1983).

4. Another formulation consists of defining mechanisms as transition probabilities so that Bayesian updating can be realized conditionally on the final outcome (in the set of primitive decisions). Recall note 2 and see the comments preceding (3.4).

5. Ex ante and ex post individual rationality can be defined in a similar way. When values are not private, the same problem arises with ex post individual rationality as with ex post efficiency. The concept depends on the information available to the agents after the effect of the mechanism (see Forges 1990).

References

Coase, R. H. 1960. "The Problem of Social Cost." *Journal of Law and Economics* 3:1–44.

Crawford, V. 1985. "Efficient and Durable Decision Rules: A Reformulation." *Econometrica* 53(4):817–835.

d'Aspremont, C., and L.-A. Gérard-Varet. 1979. "Incentives and Incomplete Information." *Journal of Public Economics* 11:25–45.

Dewatripont, M. 1989. "Renegotiation and Information Revelation over Time: The Case of Optimal Labor Contracts." *Quarterly Journal of Economics* 104:589–619.

Forges, F. 1990. "Trading Games with Asymmetric Information." Discussion paper 880, Center for Mathematical Studies in Economics and Management Science, Northwestern University.

Forges, F. 1991. "Posterior Efficiency." CORE discussion paper 9145. Forthcoming in *Games and Economic Behavior*.

Green, J., and J.-J. Laffont. 1987. "Posterior Implementability in a Two-Person Decision Problem." *Econometrica* 55:69–94.

Holmström, B., and R. Myerson. 1983. "Efficient and Durable Decision Rules with Incomplete Information." *Econometrica* 51:1799–1819.

Johnson, S., J. Pratt, and R. Zeckhauser. 1990. "Efficiency despite Mutually Payoff-Relevant Private Information: The Finite Case." *Econometrica* 58:873–900.

Myerson, R. 1985. "Bayesian Equilibrium and Incentive Compatibility." In *Social Goals and Social Organization*, ed. L. Hurwicz, D. Schmeidler, and H. Sonneschein, 229–259. Cambridge: Cambridge University Press.

Myerson, R. 1991. *Game Theory: Analysis of Conflict*. Cambridge: Harvard University Press.

Myerson, R., and M. Satterthwaite. 1983. "Efficient Mechanisms for Bilateral Trading." *Journal of Economic Theory* 29:265−281.

Osborne, M., and A. Rubinstein. 1990. *Bargaining and Markets*. New York: Academic Press.

Palfrey, T., and S. Srivastava. 1989. "Revised ... Efficient Trading Mechanisms with Pre-Play Communications." California Institute of Technology. Mimeo.

Rovesti, C. 1991. "Mechanism Design: Efficiency and Durability of a Decision Rule." CORE discussion paper 9147.

Wilson, R. 1978. "Information, Efficiency and the Core of an Economy." *Econometrica* 46:807−816.

Wilson, R. 1985. "Incentive Efficiency of Double Auctions." *Econometrica* 53: 1101−1115.

8

On the Fair and Coalitions-Strategyproof Allocation of Private Goods

Hervé Moulin

1 Introduction

We consider resource allocation mechanisms where only the domain of individual preferences (types) and the number of participating agents are known at the time the mechanism is chosen. The designer, in particular, cannot use any statistical information about the distribution of agents' types (Bayesian mechanisms are ruled out). In order to decentralize the decision making, the mechanism must be direct (each agent reporting only some—or all—information about his own preferences). If communication among individual agents is not feasible, the incentive compatibility constraint takes the familiar form of *strategyproofness*: truthful report of one's type is a dominant strategy. If, on the other hand, agents can form coalitions and manipulate the mechanism by jointly misreporting their types, then the incentive compatibility must be strengthened into *coalition-strategyproofness*: if a joint misreport by a coalition strictly benefits one member of the coalition, it must strictly hurt at least one (other) member (see definition 1).[1]

We address in this paper the problem of designing coalition-strategyproof mechanisms to allocate private goods. Recall that most of the literature on strategyproofness (starting with the seminal papers Gibbard 1973 and Satterthwaite 1975) studies the allocation of pure public goods; its central finding is that a strategyproof mechanism must be grossly unfair; namely, dictatorial, unless it confines a priori the feasible outcomes within a narrow subset, for example, a binary choice in the voting context or a one-dimensional line in the continuous case (Zhou 1990). This fundamental dilemma between the normative requirement of equity and the positive constraint of strategyproofness is robust to a number of simple restrictions on preferences, such as continuity (Barbera and Peleg 1990), or convexity (Barbera and Jackson 1991, or convexity and monotonicity (Zhou 1990).

To eliminate the dilemma, we must work in a severely restricted domain, such as that of single-peaked preferences over the real line—or over a tree—(Moulin 1980; Demange 1982), or that of Euclidian preferences with spherical indifference contours and a bliss point (Laffond 1980; Border and Jordan 1983; and Peters, Van der Stel, and Storcken 1990), or perhaps that of additively decomposable preferences over a product set (Moreno and Walker 1991; Barbera, Sonnenschein, and Zhou 1991).

A different song comes from the small literature on the allocation of private goods. This time, a strategyproof mechanism can be fair (e.g., in Fair Division, divide the pie in equal shares no matter what), but then it is inefficient; or if it is efficient (Pareto-optimal), then it must be dictatorial. In other words, among strategyproof mechanisms, there appears to be a trade-off between efficiency and equity. One must be careful here because very few general theorems are available: the cleanest result to date (due to Zhou 1991; and strengthening Hurwicz 1972) says that in the Fair Division problem with any number of goods among *two* agents with convex, monotonic preferences, the only strategyproof and efficient mechanisms are those where one agent eats the whole pie. Zhou conjectures that among three agents or more, a strategyproof and efficient mechanism will necessarily deny any share of the cake to at least one agent (but it will not necessarily give all the cake to someone).

Other results with the same flavor have been obtained under less palatable assumptions on individual preferences. For instance, Hurwicz and Walker (1990) work in the much-studied context of quasi-linear preferences (where all utilities are linear in some good called money, and where endowments of money are essentially unbounded); they show that strategyproofness and efficiency are generally incompatible. The same conclusion is obtained by Dasgupta, Hammond, and Maskin (1979), in a much more general context, but in a repugnant preference domain allowing for discontinuous preferences.

These results, however incomplete, suggest strongly that if we are serious about the strategyproofness requirement, we must abandon first-best efficiency and content ourselves with the second-best efficiency allowed by coalition-strategyproofness. I submit, however, that a fruitful object of research is the class of coalition-strategyproof and fair mechanisms where fairness is given its simplest meaning of anonymity (one man—one vote). Section 2 shows, in particular, that every mechanism in this class must select envy-free allocations (lemma 1). Hence the interpretation of fairness is unambiguous in this class of incentive compatible mechanisms.

Moreover, we know of several simple allocation problems where the properties of coalition-strategyproofness and anonymity characterize a unique mechanism (sections 3 and 4). We will argue that these mechanisms deserve our attention, and discuss possible generalizations of these findings to more complicated allocation problems.

2   Coalition-Strategyproofness and Anonymity Imply No-Envy

Consider an allocation problem among n agents who all have the same consumption set Z, a convex subset of some Euclidian space, and the same domain $\mathcal{D}$ of individual preferences. Each preference in $\mathcal{D}$ is assumed to be convex, continuous, and nonlocally satiated (that is, if the upper contour set of z contains z' as an interior point, then z' is strictly preferred to z); moreover, each preference in $\mathcal{D}$ is monotonic with respect to a proper cone of the Euclidian space (this cone may reduce to $\{0\}$, in which case there are no monotonicity restrictions). For convenience, preferences are represented by utility functions u_i, where i runs over the set of agents.

A *mechanism* associates to every preference profile $(u_1, \ldots, u_n)$ in $\mathcal{D}^n$ an allocation $(z_1, \ldots, z_n)$ in Z^n. Note that the feasibility constraints on allocations (e.g., in a fair division problem, $\sum_i z_i$ exhausts the whole cake) need not be made explicit for the purpose of lemma 1.

We denote a mechanism by F and write $z_i = F_i(u_1, \ldots, u_n) = F_i(u)$.

DEFINITION 1

(i) F is *anonymous* if for all profile u and for all agents $i, j, u_i = u_j$ implies $u_i(F_i(u)) = u_j(F_j(u))$;

(ii) F is *envy-free* if for all profile u and for all i, j we have $u_i(F_i(u)) \geq u_i(F_j(u))$;

(iii) F is *coalition-strategyproof* if for all coalition T in $\{1, \ldots, n\}$, all profile u and all joint message v_T in $\mathcal{D}^T$ we have

$$\{u_i(z_i') > u_i(z_i) \text{ for some } i \in T\} \Rightarrow \{u_j(z_j') < u_j(z_j) \text{ for some } j \in T\},$$

where $z_i = F_i(u)$ and $z_i' = F_i(v_T, u_{N \setminus T})$.

LEMMA 1   If a mechanism is anonymous and coalition-strategyproof, then it is envy-free as well.

Proof   For a pair v, z in $\mathcal{D} \times Z$ we denote by $C_+(v, z)$ and $C_-(v, z)$, respectively, the upper contour and lower contour sets of v at z (e.g., $C_+(v, z) = \{y \mid v(y) \geq v(z)\}$).

Let F be an anonymous and coalition-strategyproof mechanism. Assume that at some profile $(u_1, u_2, \ldots, u_n)$, agent 1 envies agent 2; then

$$u_1(z_1) < u_1(z_2), \quad \text{where } z_i = F_i(u). \tag{1}$$

We choose an element u_0 of $\mathscr{D}$ such that

$$C_+(u_0, z_1) = C_+(u_1, z_1)$$

and   (2)

$$C_+(u_0, z_2) \cap C_-(u_2, z_2) = \{z_2\}.$$

We let the reader check that such an element can always be found in $\mathscr{D}$. This is essentially the property of monotonic closedness of the domain $\mathscr{D}$ (see Maskin 1985). Note that lemma 1 holds true on any domain where a utility u_0 satisfying (2) exists whenever (1) is true.

In view of the nonlocal satiation assumption, if the upper contours of u_1 and u_0 coincide at z_1, then so do their indifference contours and lower contours (because the indifference contour is the topological boundary of the upper contour). Therefore, assumption (2) implies:

for all z such that $u_1(z) = u_1(z_1)$, we have $C_\varepsilon(u_0, z) = C_\varepsilon(u_1, z)$,

$$\varepsilon = +, -. \tag{3}$$

We now derive a contradiction from (1), (2).

Set $z_i' = F_i(u_1, u_0)$ for $i = 1, 2$ (we drop $u_3, \ldots, u_n$ for simplicity, as they remain constant throughout). By strategyproofness z_2' is in $C_+(u_0, z_2)$ and in $C_-(u_2, z_2)$, hence by (2) we get $z_2' = z_2$. It follows that if $u_1(z_1') > u_1(z_1)$, coalition $\{1, 2\}$ can manipulate at (u_1, u_2) by reporting (u_1, u_0); and if $u_1(z_1) > u_1(z_1')$, then $\{1, 2\}$ manipulates at (u_1, u_0) by reporting (u_1, u_2). Thus

$$z_2' = z_2 \quad \text{and} \quad u_1(z_1') = u_1(z_1).$$

Now consider $z_i'' = F_i(u_0, u_0)$ for $i = 1, 2$. By strategyproofness for agent 1 we have

$$u_0(z_1'') \geq u_0(z_1') \quad \text{and} \quad u_1(z_1'') \leq u_1(z_1').$$

In view of property (3) this implies $u_0(z_1'') = u_0(z_1')$. Next, if we have $u_0(z_2'') < u_0(z_2)$, then $\{1, 2\}$ manipulates at (u_0, u_0) by (u_1, u_0). Thus by coalition-strategyproofness we must have $u_0(z_2'') \geq u_0(z_2)$. Now assumption (1) and property (3) imply $u_0(z_2) > u_0(z_1) = u_0(z_1'')$. So we deduce $u_0(z_2'') > u_0(z_1'')$ in contradiction of anonymity. $\square$

Remark 1 Lemma 1 is reminiscent of the well-known equivalence between anonymity and no-envy in exchange economies with an atomless set of agents (see Hammond 1979; and Mas-Colell 1985, chap. 7).

Remark 2 By a very similar proof technique, it can be shown that an anonymous mechanism satisfying Maskin's monotonicity (see Maskin 1985) is envy-free.[2] However, Maskin's monotonicity is not implied by coalition-strategyproofness. Notice also that ordinary strategyproofness (a consequence of Maskin's monotonicity given our assumptions on $\mathscr{D}$) does not seem to be enough, in combination with anonymity, to rule out envy, although I have not been able to find a counterexample.

3 Uniform Rationing and Fair Division

One of the simplest problems of fair division is that of allocating one unit of a single commodity among n agents who have single-peaked preferences over the quantity of the commodity they consume (free disposal is not allowed). Here an element u_i of $\mathscr{D}$ is a strictly quasi-concave function on $[0, 1]$ with a unique peak denoted a_i.

The uniform rationing mechanism works as follows. Each agent reports his peak a_i. If $\sum_i a_i = 1$, each receives precisely this amount, and this is the best of all worlds. If $\sum_i a_i > 1$ (excess demand), a uniform cap λ on individual consumption is computed as the unique solution of

$$\sum_i \min\{a_i, \lambda\} = 1.$$

Agent i's final consumption is then $\min\{a_i, \lambda\}$. Finally, if $\sum_i a_i < 1$ (excess supply), a floor λ on individual consumption is computed by

$$\sum_i \max\{a_i, \lambda\} = 1.$$

Agent i's final consumption is then $\max\{a_i, \lambda\}$.

From the positive angle, the mechanism is coalition-strategyproof, and even first best efficient. From the normative angle, besides anonymity and no-envy, uniform rationing possesses many appealing properties (such as resource monotonicity and consistency; see Thomson 1991a, 1991b). For the sake of our argument, its most remarkable feature is the following result:

THEOREM 1 (Sprumont 1991) The uniform rationing mechanism is the *only* mechanism that is anonymous, coalition-strategyproof and unanimous (i.e., if $\sum_i a_i = 1$, agent i receives a_i for all i).

The proof technique is instructive. First one checks that a coalition-strategyproof mechanism must satisfy the "peak only" property; namely, individual messages convey only the information about their peak (equivalently, the outcome is unaffected if an agent reports a different utility with the same peak). The central role of this property in the case of voting has been uncovered by Barbera and Peleg (1990) (see also Zhou 1990; Barbera and Jackson 1991).

Given the "peak only" property, it is easy to characterize all strategyproof mechanisms with one agent. They take the form

$$F(u_i) = \text{med}\{\alpha, \beta, a_i\},$$

where α and β are two constant numbers, $0 \leq \alpha \leq \beta \leq 1$, a_i is the peak of u_i and "med" is the median operator.

Therefore, with n agents, an anonymous "peak only" mechanism takes the form

$$F_i(u_1, \ldots, u_n) = \text{med}\{\alpha(a_{-i}), \beta(a_{-i}), a_i\},$$

where $\alpha(\cdot)$ and $\beta(\cdot)$ are two functions defined over $[0, 1]^{n-1}$ and such that $0 \leq \alpha(\cdot) \leq \beta(\cdot) \leq 1$. The problem now reduces to solve the following functional equation in $\alpha(\cdot)$, $\beta(\cdot)$:

$$\sum_{i=1}^{n} \text{med}\{\alpha(a_{-i}), \beta(a_{-i}), a_i\} = 1 \quad \text{for all } a_1, \ldots, a_n \text{ in } [0, 1]. \tag{4}$$

In turn, one checks that this equation has a unique solution, where $\alpha(a_{-i})$ is precisely agent i's uniform rationing share when his own peak is zero, and $\beta(a_{-i})$ is his uniform rationing share when his own peak is one. Interestingly, the determination of all coalition-strategyproof solutions (whether anonymous or not) leads to a functional equation analogous to (4), yet much harder to solve.

Consider now a Fair Division problem where n agents divide a vector $\omega = (\omega_a, \omega_b)$ consisting of two goods A and B. To construct an anonymous and coalition-strategyproof mechanism fix an arbitrary positive price (p_a, p_b), and then play the uniform rationing mechanism along this price from the equal-split initial endowments. In other words, given the (reported) utilities $(u_1, \ldots, u_n)$, compute agent i's demand along the budget line

$$p_a x_a + p_b x_b = (p_a \omega_a + p_b \omega_b)/n. \tag{5}$$

Let x_a^i be agent i's demand. If $\sum_i x_a^i = \omega$, then everyone receives precisely his demand. If $\sum_i x_a^i > \omega$, then good A is in excess demand, hence rationed:

agent i receives $\min\{x_a^i, \lambda\}$, where λ solves

$$\sum_i \min\{x_a^i, \lambda\} = \omega,$$

and the corresponding consumptions of good B are determined by the budget balance equation 5. If, on the other hand, $\sum_i x_a^i > \omega$, then good B is in excess demand: $\sum_i x_b^i > \omega$, and the above rationing rule is now applied to good B.

The analogy with the uniform rationing rule is clear, and checking coalition-strategyproofness is straightforward. Under additional regularity assumptions, there is hope to show a converse property: in a Fair Division problem, with two goods, the only anonymous and coalition-strategyproof mechanisms are the fixed-price rationing mechanisms just described.

4   Serial Cost Sharing

The simplest model of cooperative production has a one input–one output technology, utilized jointly by a given set of agents. Let $x = C(y)$ denote the cost x of producing the amount y of output; we assume decreasing returns to scale: more precisely, C is strictly convex and increasing, with $C(0) = 0$.

Agent i's utility $u_i(x_i, y_i)$ is decreasing in his input contribution x_i, increasing in his output share y_i, and quasi-concave in (x_i, y_i). The problem is to determine an equitable and incentive compatible production plan $(x_1, \ldots, x_n : y_1, \ldots, y_n) \in \mathcal{R}_+^{2n}$ under the feasibility constraint $\sum_i x_i = C(\sum_i y_i)$. For interpretations and examples of this problem, see Moulin 1987, 1990; Roemer and Silvestre 1988; and Moulin and Shenker 1992.

The serial (direct) mechanism is defined as follows. Given a profile $(u_1, \ldots, u_n)$, compute first every agent's demand (x_i^1, y_i^1) over the set of allocations defined by

$$x^1 = \frac{C(ny^1)}{n}. \tag{6}$$

In other words, (x_i^1, y_i^1) maximizes u_i over the set of allocations defined by (6). Note that the strict convexity of C and the convexity of preferences guarantee that the maximization has a unique solution.

Pick an agent with the lowest demand and assume, without loss, that this agent is agent 1. Set (x_1^1, y_1^1) to be agent 1's final consumption. Next, compute for every agent $i = 2, \ldots, n$ the (unique) allocation (x_i^2, y_i^2) maximizing u_i over the set of allocations (x^2, y^2), defined by

$$y^2 \geq y_1^1 \qquad \text{and} \qquad x^2 = \frac{C((n-1)y^2 + y_1^1) - x_1^1)}{n-1}.$$

Say, without loss, that the lowest demand (x_i^2, y_i^2) is agent 2's. That agent's final consumption is thus (x_2^2, y_2^2). And so on. After (x_j^j, y_j^j) have been determined for $j = 1, \ldots, i$, we compute (x_k^{i+1}, y_k^{i+1}) as agent k's demand $(k = i + 1, \ldots, n)$ over the allocations (x^{i+1}, y^{i+1}) such that

$$y^{i+1} \geq y_i^i \qquad \text{and}$$

$$x^{i+1} = \frac{C((n-i)y^{i+1} + y_i^i + \cdots + y_1^1) - (x_i^i + \cdots + x_1^1)}{n-i}. \tag{7}$$

We call $(i + 1)$ an agent with the lowest such demand and we make $(x_{i+1}^{i+1}, y_{i+1}^{i+1})$ that agent's final consumption.

Just like uniform rationing, the serial cost-sharing mechanism has a number of normatively appealing features. Besides anonymity and no-envy (as implied by theorem 2 below and lemma 1), the mechanism also sets tight bounds on the utility levels of a given agent: at most, his stand-alone utility (achieved by using the technology all by himself) and at least his unanimity utility (achieved by the best egalitarian allocation $x_i = x_j$, $y_i = y_j$ all i, j). See Moulin 1992 for further discussion of these bounds.

THEOREM 2 (Moulin and Shenker 1991a) The serial mechanism is anonymous and coalition-strategyproof.

The easiest proof of theorem 2 is to consider another, simpler, mechanism where agent i's message is simply the quantity q_i of output he requests and where the cost shares x_i are then computed by formulas (6), (7), once the agents are labeled by increasing demands $y_1 \leq \cdots \leq y_n$. Note that the formulas follow from the combination of anonymity and the fact that an agent's cost share is unaffected by demands bigger than his own. It turns out that this mechanism has a unique Nash equilibrium at all profiles in $\mathscr{D}^n$, and the equilibrium allocation is precisely the allocation of the serial direct mechanism described above. Thus the serial direct mechanism is exactly implementable in Nash equilibrium. Over a monotonically closed domain of preferences, this property always implies coalition-strategyproofness (Dasgupta, Hammond, and Maskin 1979).

Remarkably, a converse of theorem 2 holds when we restrict attention to direct mechanisms satisfying a nonimposition condition (agent i's output share is not restricted by a given set of messages for the other agents) and some smoothness assumptions. Those assumptions are almost as demanding as continuous differentability of the mapping from $\mathscr{D}^n$ into $\mathscr{R}^{2n}$, when $\mathscr{D}$ is endowed with the appropriate topology.

THEOREM 3   (Moulin and Shenker 1991)   The serial mechanism is the only anonymous and coalition-strategyproof mechanism satisfying non-imposition and some smoothness assumptions.

Without specifying the smoothness assumptions in detail, we will outline in the next section the main step in the proof of theorem 3, which could well be the key to the analysis of coalition-strategyproof mechanisms in more general contexts.

We note that the serial cost-sharing idea can be applied, mutatis mutandis, to other cooperative production problems such as the provision of a public good, where an analogue of theorem 3 is a very plausible conjecture (see Moulin 1991).

5   The Case of Differentiable Mechanisms

Consider an abstract mechanism F defined over a domain $\mathscr{D}$ of utility functions that is an open subset of the space of continuously differentiable functions (e.g., the set of strictly convex and differentiable utility functions). We suppose that F is differentiable in every direction, and we denote by $D(v_i)$ the derivation operator in the direction v_i.

At a given utility profile $(u_1, \ldots, u_n)$ in $\mathscr{D}^n$, we now define the *pattern of influence* between agents as follows:

$\delta_{ij} = 1$ (agent i influences agent j) if and only if $D_{(v_i)} u_j(F_j(u)) \neq 0$
          for some v_i in $\mathscr{D}$;

$\delta_{ij} = 0$ (agent i does not influence agent j) otherwise.

LEMMA 2   If the mechanism F is coalition-strategyproof at $(u_1, \ldots, u_n)$, then the matrix of influences $[\delta_{ij}]$ is acyclic.

Proof   Note that ordinary strategyproofness implies $\delta_{ii} = 0$, and so the matrix of influence does not have a cycle of length one. Now consider a shortest cycle $\{1, \ldots, L\}$ of this matrix. This means that for $1 \leq i, j \leq L$, $\delta_{ij} = 1$ is true if and only if $j = i + 1$ or $i = L$ and $j = 1$. For each $i = 1, \ldots, L$ pick a direction v_i such that

$$D_{(v_i)} u_{i+1}(F(u)) > 0 \quad \text{(with the convention } L + 1 = 1\text{)}.$$

By construction we have also

$D_{(v_i)}u_j(F(u)) = 0$ for all $j \neq i + 1$.

Moving along the path u^ε in $\mathscr{D}^n$ given by

$u_i^\varepsilon = u_i + \varepsilon v_i$ for $i = 1, \dots, L$

$\quad\;\; = u_i$ for $i = L + 1, \dots, n,$

we have

$\dfrac{d}{d\varepsilon} u_i(F(u^\varepsilon)) > 0$ for all $i = 1, \dots, L$

in contradiction of coalition-strategyproofness.   □

Lemma 2 was originally obtained by Satterthwaite and Sonneschein (1981) under different assumptions (namely strategyproofness and the ad hoc assumption of *nonbossiness*). It implies under appropriate regularity assumptions (those that were deliberately left vague in the statement of theorem 3), that in any profile where F is coalition-strategyproof, the agents can be ordered, say as $1, 2, \dots, n$, in such a way that

agent 1 is influenced by no one in the sense that

$D_{(v_j)}F_1(u) = 0$ for all $j \geq 2$ and all v_j;

agent 2 is not influenced by agents $3, \dots, n$ in the sense that

$D_{(v_j)}F_2(u) = 0$ for all $j \geq 3$ and all $v_j, \dots,$

. . .

agent $(n - 1)$ is not influenced by agent n.

In the simple cost-sharing problem of section 5, these conditions, together with the feasibility constraint $(\sum_i x_i = C(\sum_i y_i))$, in effect determine the derivatives of F, once we know the "ordering of influence." Given anonymity, they can be integrated back and deliver precisely the serial formula (see Moulin and Shenker 1991).

Thus the differential techniques pioneered by Satterthwaite and Sonnenschein (1981) can in some cases uncover some truly interesting mechanisms. Whether or not those techniques can be applied in other contexts with similar successes is a challenging question to which, hopefully, an answer will sooner or later be given. In any event, the existing results amply support the argument that much is to be learned from a systematic study of fair and coalition-strategyproof mechanisms.

Notes

1. This concept supposes that cooperation within the coalitions is essentially free of the incentive constraints that we face for the coalition as a whole when we design a mechanism: in other words, we give maximal manipulative power to coalitions. For weaker assumptions on the cooperative options open to coalitions in the context of mechanism design, see Cremer 1989. For a critique of the strong equilibrium concept in the context of the general strategic games, see Bernheim, Peleg, and Whinston 1987.

2. Geanakoplos and Nalebuff (1988) prove a similar result under the additional assumption of efficiency and for two-agent problems only.

References

Barbera, S., and M. Jackson. 1991. "A Characterization of Strategyproof Social Choice Functions for Economies with Pure Public Goods." Northwestern University. Mimeo.

Barbera, S., and B. Peleg. 1990. "Strategyproof Voting Schemes with Continuous Preferences." *Social Choice and Welfare* 7(1):31–38.

Barbera, S., H. Sonnenschein, and L. Zhou. 1991. "Voting by Committees." *Econometrica* 59(3):595–610.

Bernheim, D., B. Peleg, and M. Whinston. 1987. "Coalition-Proof Nash Equilibrium I." *Journal of Economic Theory* 42:1–12.

Border, K., and J. Jordan. 1983. "Straightforward Elections, Unanimity, and Phantom Voters." *Review of Economic Studies* 50:153–170.

Cremer, J. 1989. "Manipulations by Coalitions under Asymmetric Information: The Case of Groves Mechanisms." Virginia Polytechnic Institute and State University, Blacksburg. Mimeo.

Dasgupta, P., P. Hammond, and E. Maskin. 1979. "The Implementation of Social Choice Rule." *Review of Economic Studies* 46:185–216.

Demange, G. 1982. "Single-Peaked Orders on a Tree." *Mathematical Social Sciences* 3(4):389–396.

Geanakoplos, J., and B. Nalebuff. 1988. "On a Fundamental Conflict, between Equity and Efficiency." Princeton University. Mimeo.

Gibbard, A. 1973. "Manipulation of Voting Schemes: A General Result." *Econometrica* 45:665–681.

Hammond, P. 1979. "Straightforward Individual Incentive Compatibility in Large Economies." *Review of Economic Studies* 46(2):262–282.

Hurwicz, L. 1972. "On Informationally Decentralized Systems." In *Decision and Organization*, ed. B. McGuire and R. Radner. Amsterdam: North Holland.

Hurwicz, L. and M. Walker. 1990. "On the Generic Non-Optimality of Dominant-Strategy Allocation Mechanisms: A General Theorem That Includes Pure Exchange Economies." *Econometrica* 58:683–704.

Laffond, G. 1980. "Révélation des Préférences et Utilités Unimodales." Ph.D. diss., Université Dauphine Paris.

Mas-Colell, A. 1985. *The Theory of General Economic Equilibrium*. Cambridge: Cambridge University Press.

Maskin, E. 1985. "The Theory of Implementation in Nash Equilibrium: A Survey." In *Social Goals and Social Organization*, ed. L. Hurwicz, D. Schmeidler, and H. Sonnenschein. Cambridge: Cambridge University Press.

Moreno, D., and M. Walker. 1991. "Non-Manipulable Voting Schemes When Participants' Interests Are Partially Decomposable." *Social Choice and Welfare* 8(3):221–234.

Moulin, H. 1980. "On Strategy-Proofness and Single-Peakedness." *Public Choice* 35:437–455.

Moulin, H. 1987. "A Core Selection for Pricing a Single-Output Monopoly." *The Rand Journal of Economics* 18(3):395–407.

Moulin, H. 1990. "Joint Ownership of a Convex Technology: Comparison of Three Solutions." *Review of Economic Studies* 57:439–452.

Moulin, H. 1991. "Excludable Public Goods and the Free Rider Problem." Duke University. Mimeo.

Moulin, H. 1992. "Welfare Bounds in the Cooperative Production Problem." In *Games and Economic Behavior* 4:373–401.

Moulin, H., and S. Shenker. 1991. "Strategyproof Cost Sharing under Decreasing Returns."

Moulin, H., and S. Shenker. 1992. "Serial Cost Sharing." *Econometrica* 60:1009–1037.

Peters, H., H. van der Stel, and T. Storcken. 1990. "Pareto Optimality, Anonymity, and Strategyproofness in Location Problems." University of Limburg, Maastricht. Mimeo.

Roemer, J., and J. Silvestre. 1988. "Public Ownership: Three Proposals for Resource Allocation." University of California at Davis. Mimeo.

Satterthwaite, M. 1975. "Strategy-Proofness and Arrow's Conditions: Existence and Correspondence Theorems for Voting Procedures and Social Choice Functions." *Journal of Economic Theory* 10:187–217.

Satterthwaite, M. and H. Sonnenschein. 1981. "Strategy-Proof Allocation Mechanisms at Differentiable Points." *Review of Economic Studies* 48:587–597.

Sprumont, Y. 1991. "The Division Problem with Single-Peaked Preferences: A Characterization of the Uniform Allocation Rule." *Econometrica* 59(2):509–520.

Thomson, W. 1991a. "A Consistent Solution to the Problem of Fair Division When Preferences are Single-Peaked." University of Rochester. Mimeo.

Thomson, W. 1991b. "Monotonic Solutions to the Problem of Fair Division When Preferences are Single-Peaked." University of Rochester. Mimeo.

Zhou, L. 1990. "Impossibility of Strategy-Proof Mechanisms in Economies with Pure Public Good." *Review of Economic Studies*

Zhou, L. 1991. "Inefficiency of Strategy-Proof Allocation Mechanisms in Pure Exchange Economies." *Social Choice and Welfare* 8:247–254.

9 From Repeated to Differential Games: How Time and Uncertainty Pervade the Theory of Games

Alain Haurie

L'histoire ne se répète pas, elle bégaie.

1 Introduction

Our aim in this paper is to exhibit the links that can be established between the *stochastic differential games* formalism, which is directly inspired from optimal control theory, and some of the stochastic models recently considered in the realm of the *classical theory of games*, which are inspired from economic theory. The two threads through which these different game structures are related consist of the explicit representation of time dependency and of randomness. Time dependency forces players to adapt their decisions to a changing context; it also permits them to recall past information and to modify their commitments if they perceive a breach of a possible cooperative agreement. Randomness places the decision-making process in an environment of imperfect information.

In section 2 we propose a generic stochastic differential game, called a "stochastic diffusion game with random modal changes," which includes several interesting features such as an hybrid state variable and two time scales for its dynamics. The fast dynamic corresponds to a stochastic diffusion whereas the slow dynamic is described as a jump process affecting the operational mode of the system. The two dynamics are controlled by several players. This generic model will then be put in relation to a set of concepts defined in the realm of the "classical" theory of games. We review in section 3 the extensive form of a game and recall the basic definitions concerning the information structure. In section 4 we consider the paradigm of *repeated games*, for which we consider in particular the equilibria obtained when one allows the use of memory strategies. In section 5 the general formalism of *Markov games* is presented. These games provide an interesting operational way to study the interactions between time and randomness in strategic decision making. In particular, they permit the modeling of *cooperative equilibria* for stochastic games with imperfect information. In section 6 we show how the formalism of the stochastic diffusion game with random modal changes initially introduced in section 2 can be related to this class of models where "memory" strategies incorporate threats. In section 7 we propose a numerical approach for the solution of this class of games. This approach, initially introduced in the realm of stochastic control theory, is based on the solution of a sequence of simple Markov games. We are then in almost unchartered territories, and so we content ourselves to list some important open problems. Finally, in conclusion, we try to derive from this perspective on game theory some indications concerning the operational value of these paradigms.

2   A Diffusion Game with Random Modal Jumps

In this section we introduce a many-player *stochastic differential game* that has several features permitting one to model complex interactions among several agents who control the same system. This game involves a dynamical system having two dynamics, a fast one corresponding to a continuous state variable that evolves according to a controlled diffusion process (Ito equations) and a slow one corresponding to a discrete state variable that evolves according to a controlled jump process.

2.1   Game Dynamics

2.1.1   *State Equations*
Let $M = \{1, \ldots, m\}$ be a set of players. We consider a system with the dynamic given by the stochastic evolution equations

$$dx(t) = f^{\xi(t)}(x(t), \mathbf{u}(t)) \, dt + \sigma^{\xi(t)}(x(t)) \, d\varepsilon(t), \tag{1}$$

where $x \in \mathbb{R}^n$ is a continuous state variable, $\xi \in E = \{1, \ldots, e\}$ is a discrete state variable, and $\mathbf{u} = \{u_j\}_{j \in M}$ is a composite control variable obtained from the controls $u_j \in \mathbb{R}^{m_j}$, $j \in M$ of the m players who drive the system.

In equation 1, $\{\varepsilon(t) : t \geq 0\}$ is a Brownian motion and $\{\xi(t) : t \geq 0\}$ is a random jump process defined over a probability space $(\Omega, \mathcal{F}, P)$. We assume that there exist jump rates $q_{kl}(x, \mathbf{u})$ such that for $k, l \in E$

$$P[\xi(t + dt) = l | \xi(t) = k, x(t) = x, \mathbf{u}(t) = \mathbf{u}] = q_{kl}(x, \mathbf{u}) \, dt + o(dt), \tag{2}$$

where $\dfrac{o(dt)}{dt} \to 0$ uniformly in $(x, \mathbf{u})$ when $dt \to 0$. As usual we denote

$$q_{kk}(\cdot, \cdot) = -\sum_{l \neq k} q_{kl}(\cdot, \cdot).$$

Remark 1 The *game dynamic* is thus defined as a controlled stochastic process. The requirement that the ξ-variable be discrete is not essential. The important feature of this model is the combination of fast (diffusion) and slow (jumps) dynamics.

2.1.2 Control Structure
Let $\{\mathcal{F}_t\}_{t \geq 0}$ be a filtration generated by the history $\{(x(t), \xi(t)) : t \geq 0\}$ of the processes. An *admissible control* for the system is an $\mathcal{F}_t$-adapted process in $\mathbb{R}^m$ such that

$$\mathbf{u}(t) \in \prod_{j \in M} U_j^{\xi(t)}(x(t)), \tag{3}$$

where, for each $j \in M$ and $k \in E$, $U_j^k(\cdot)$ is a measurable set-valued mapping from $\mathbb{R}^n$ into $\mathbb{R}^{m_j}$, $(\sum_{j \in M} m_j = \underline{m})$.

Remark 2 The game-theoretic information structure (further discussed in section 3) implied by this definition of controls corresponds to the so-called complete and imperfect information (simultaneous actions) with perfect recall.

With an initial hybrid state $s^0 = (x^0, \xi^0)$ and an admissible control $\mathbf{u}(\cdot)$ is associated a response of the dynamic system that is the stochastic process $(x(\cdot), \xi(\cdot))$, solution of equations 1, 2, 3.

2.1.3 Rewards
For each player $j \in M$ a reward is defined as

$$J_j(s^0, \mathbf{u}(\cdot)) = E_\mathbf{u}\left[\int_0^\infty e^{-\rho t} g_j^{\xi(t)}(x(t), \mathbf{u}(t)) \, dt \,|\, s^0 \right], \tag{4}$$

where $g_j^k(\cdot, \cdot) : \mathbb{R}^n \times \mathbb{R}^m \mapsto \mathbb{R}$, $j \in M$, $k \in E$ are continuous functions, and $\rho > 0$ is a given discount rate. The expectation is taken with respect to the probability measure induced by the control $\mathbf{u}(\cdot)$.

2.2 Nash Equilibrium

Let $\mathbf{u}^*(\cdot)$ be a given composite control. We denote $\mathbf{u}^{*(j)}(\cdot)$ a control obtained when only player j departs unilaterally from the u_j^*-control and uses a control $u_j(\cdot)$.

DEFINITION 1 The control $\mathbf{u}^*(\cdot)$ is an equilibrium at $s^0 = (x^0, \xi^0)$ if, for each $j \in M$ and any admissible control $\mathbf{u}^{*(j)}(\cdot)$, the following holds

$$J_j(s^0, \mathbf{u}^*(\cdot)) \geq J_j(s^0, \mathbf{u}^{*(j)}(\cdot)). \tag{5}$$

Remark 3   As usual in an equilibrium solution, each control u_j^* represents the best reply of player j to the choice of $u_{j'}^*$-controls by all the other players $j' \in M - \{j\}$.

2.3   Feedback Equilibria and Dynamic Programming Equations

Among the admissible controls we shall consider the particular class of stationary *feedback* or *memoryless* controls defined as mappings $\tilde{u}_j(\cdot) : s = (x, \xi) \mapsto U_j^\xi(x)$ from the state space into the control spaces.

THEOREM 1   Consider the set of coupled Hamilton-Jacobi-Bellman (HJB) equations, $\forall j \in M$, $k \in E$ and $x \in \mathbb{R}^n$,

$$\rho V_j(x, k) = \frac{1}{2} \sum_{i,i'=1}^n a_{i,i'}^k(x) \frac{\partial^2 V_j(x, k)}{\partial x_i \partial x_{i'}} + \max_{u_j \in U_j^k(x)} \{g_j(x, [\mathbf{u}^{*(-j)}(x, k), u_j])$$

$$+ f^k(x, \mathbf{u}^{*(j)}(x, k))' \frac{\partial V_j(x, k)}{\partial x} + \sum_{l \in E} q_{kl}(x, [\mathbf{u}^{*(-j)}(x, k), u_j]) V_j(x, l)\},$$

$$\tag{6}$$

with

$$\frac{1}{2} \sum_{i,i'=1}^n a_{i,i'}^k(x) \frac{\partial^2 V_j(x, k)}{\partial x_i \partial x_{i'}} = \frac{1}{2} \text{trace} \left[\sigma^k(x) \sigma^k(x)^T) \frac{\partial^2 V_j(x, k)}{\partial x^2} \right],$$

and where $[\mathbf{u}^{*(-j)}(x, k), u_j]$ is the control obtained when all the players use the $\mathbf{u}^*$ control except for player j who uses his control u_j. A solution to these equations defines a feedback Nash equilibrium $\{\tilde{u}_j^*\}_{j \in M}$ with expected rewards $J_j(s, \mathbf{u}^*) = V_j(x, k)$, $j \in M$ from any initial state $s = (x, k) \in \mathbb{R}^n \times E$.

3   Games in Extensive and Strategic Form

In this section we recall the fundamental description of a game in its extensive form and we show the relation that exists with the differential game formalism of section 2.

3.1   Decision and Chance Nodes

A game is described as a sequence of moves. If there are two players, then the game is represented as a tree with four types of nodes:

(1) Nodes where player 1 moves;

(2) Nodes where player 2 moves;

(3) Nodes where nature moves;

(4) Terminal nodes where payoffs (rewards) are obtained by the two players.

In figure 9.1 the fundamental structure of the game tree is shown. An arc in the game tree represents a move by one of the players, that is, a choice of a particular action in a prescribed set. Nature always moves by choosing an arc at random, according to a prespecified probability distribution. The sequence of moves by the players and nature makes the *state* of the game to evolve over a sequence of *stages*.

One can establish a correspondence between a game tree and the state equations 1. In a differential game setting the nature moves are represented by the random perturbations in the state equations 1. The players' moves correspond to the choice of a control value at each instant of time $t \geq 0$.

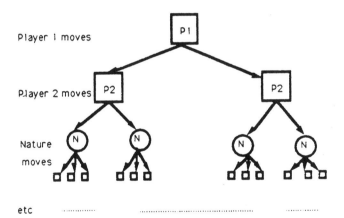

Figure 9.1
Game tree

3.2   Information Structure

When a player selects an arc (i.e., an action), he has some information. At the finest level of information the player knows the precise node representing the position of the game. At coarser levels of information he only knows that the position of the game is in a given subset of the set of nodes.

In figure 9.2 we have represented, for a two-player game, the information structure corresponding to the so-called *simultaneous action* case. Here the two players select their actions in a sequential and symmetric way, knowing only the current state of the game, but not knowing what the other player has selected at the present stage. This information structure is the one implicitly assumed in differential games. The state of the dynamic system denoted $s = (x, \xi)$, is controlled by the actions chosen by the players (including nature, which is a random disturbance). Usually in a differential game one assumes that the players observe the state but don't observe directly the actions undertaken by their opponents. The players

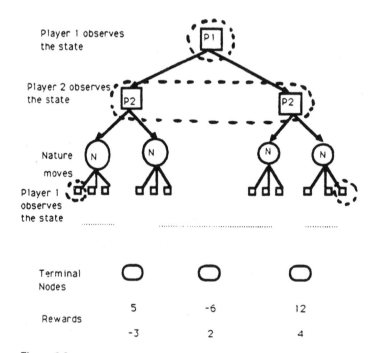

Figure 9.2
Simultaneous action information structure

are also assumed to have *perfect recall*, that is, they can remember all past information.

In figure 9.3 we have represented the information structure corresponding to the so-called *sequential Stackelberg* case, with player 1 as the *leader*. Here player 1 selects his actions in a sequential way knowing only the state of the system, while player 2 selects his action knowing not only the state of the system but also what player 1 has selected at the present stage. This sequential Stackelberg information structure has been discussed in Simaan and Cruz 1973; Başar and Haurie 1984 where it has been introduced under the name of "feedback Stackelberg information structure" in the setting of discrete and continuous time differential games.

Remark 4   A differential game can be interpreted as a "limit" of a game in extensive form when the set of stages (i.e., periods when one player moves) tends to infinity and is dense in the real line. In Friedman 1971; Krassovski and Subbotin 1977 this approach has been used to give a precise formal

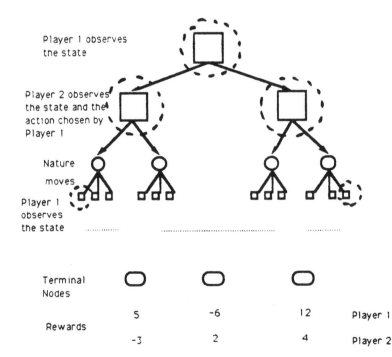

Figure 9.3
Sequential Stackelberg information structure

definition of a deterministic zero-sum differential game. Similar approaches have been used in Başar and Haurie 1984; Tolwinski, Haurie, and Leitman 1986 in the context of nonzero-sum differential games.

3.3   Strategic Form of a Game

3.3.1   *The Normal Form of a Game*
Once the information structure is specified, the game may be described in a *strategic form* also called the "normal form" of the game. A *strategy* is a mapping that associates an action, for the player who has to move, with the information retained by this player. So a strategy specifies a complete course of action for each player.

When each player $j \in M$ has selected his strategy γ_j in his admissible strategy set Γ_j, a strategy vector $\gamma_M \in \Gamma_M = \prod_{j \in M} \Gamma_j$ has been defined and the game has an outcome where each player $j \in M$ obtains a payoff $V_j(\gamma_M)$; this defines the payoff vector $V_M(\gamma_M)$.

The normal form of the game is precisely this mapping $V_M : \Gamma_M \mapsto \mathbb{R}^m$.

The differential game of section 2 has a normal form defined by the control laws (3) and the payoff functionals (4).

3.3.2   *Matrix Games*
When the strategy sets are finite and M reduces to two players, the game in normal form can be described by a payoff matrix. In table 9.1 such a matrix game is described. Each line and each column corresponds to a choice of a *pure strategy* by one of the two players. By allowing the players to use *mixed strategies*, that is, probability distributions over their respective pure strategy sets one "convexifies" the normal form of this game. Matrix games do not seem, at first sight, to be much related to differential games; however, they are used in *repeated* and *Markov games*, which are themselves quite close structurally to differential games.

Table 9.1
Matrix game

P2 P1	I	II	III
a	6, 10	4, 4	3, 2
b	6, 10	14, 15	8, 20
c	4, 10	8, 20	12, 25

3.3.3 Cournot Oligopoly Game

The imperfect competition model introduced by Cournot (1838) is a good example of a game in normal form with a continuum of pure strategies. This oligopoly game will be the basic example in the development of a dynamic theory of games, so we recall below its fundamental structure.

Consider a market for a homogeneous good produced by m firms. Let q_j be the quantity produced by firm j and let $Q = q_1 + \cdots + q_m$ be the total quantity supplied on the market. The market is described by the (inverse) demand law $P = D[Q]$ where P is the clearing price for the good and $D[\cdot]$ is a downward sloping function. The game in normal form is defined by the payoffs corresponding to the profits of each player (firm)

$$V_j(q_M) = D[Q]q_j - C_j(q_j),$$

where $C_j(q_j)$ is the production cost of firm j.

Remark 5 This is the "static" Cournot game where each firm is supposed to consider only what happens during a single time period. Of course it is very natural to consider "dynamic" versions of this model, where the firms have either to repeat their decisions over a sequence of time periods or to control, for example, through their investment schedule, the evolution over time of their production capacity. These extensions uhich lead to a dynamic setting will be discussed shortly.

3.4 Equilibria

Once a game has been described in its normal form one can define the *equilibrium* optimality concept. In an equilibrium each player has chosen a strategy that is the best reply to the strategies of the other players. Therefore no player has any incentive or temptation to change unilaterally his (her) strategic choice.

DEFINITION 2 A strategy vector γ_M^* is an equilibrium if

$$V_j(\gamma_M^*) \geq V_j(\gamma_M^{*(j)}), \qquad \forall \gamma_M^{*(j)} \in \Gamma_M,$$

where $\gamma_M^{*(j)}$ is the strategy defined when onl·· of the γ^* strategy.

There is a list of issues related to the e⟨ we may highlight the following three:

(1) Existence of equilibria (see Nash 1951 for . for Cournot oligopoly games; and Rosen ɪ

(2) Uniqueness of equilibria (See Rosen 1965 for concave games);

(3) Computational methods (see Lemke and Howson 1964 for matrix games; Rosen 1965 for concave games).

3.5 Time Consistency and Subgame Perfectness

The equilibrium solution concept uses the *normal-form* description of a game, that is, the mapping $V_M : \gamma_M \mapsto \mathbb{R}^m$, which associates a vector of payoffs $V_M(\gamma_M)$ with any admissible strategy vector γ_M. As indicated in section 3.3 this normal form description of the game "collapses" the time dimension of the game. If the players are not bound to use, over the whole course of the game, the strategy chosen at the start of the game, then two phenomena can appear:

(1) At any intermediate point, in the evolution of the game, the players can call for a "reopening" of the game and consider the new game, which is defined from this intermediate point on;

(2) some players may not play "correctly" over some periods and thus the *state* of the game may end up in a position that was not supposed to be visited if all the players had used the equilibrium strategies; from such an intermediate point the game can be replayed.

The two requirements of *time consistency* and *subgame-perfectness* place a restriction on the normal form solutions (e.g., equilibria) in order to get a *stability* of the solution concept with respect to these two possibilities of "reopening" a game during the course of its play.

3.5.1 *Time Consistency Requirement*

A solution concept is *time consistent* if it is stable with respect to any restart of the game at any intermediate point of the evolution of the play. In deterministic differential games the *open-loop* equilibrium concept is time consistent, since, from any intermediate state of the equilibrium trajectory, a reopening of the game would yield to the same continuation of the equilibrium controls. Actually, time consistency is closely related, in this case, to the possibility of establishing a "maximum principle" for the characterization of the equilibrium. For this same class of games the *Nash bargaining solution* (Nash 1950) is not time consistent (see Haurie neither is the *open-loop Stackelberg* solution (see Başar and Olsder

3.5.2 Subgame-Perfectness Requirement

An equilibrium is *subgame-perfect* if the same strategy is again an equilibrium at any point reached by the game, even after a temporary breach of equilibrium by one or several players. This requirement has been introduced by Selten (1975) as a condition for credibility of threats. As we shall discuss shortly, there is a possibility to define equilibria that incorporate a threat of retaliation if one notices that a player is not implementing an "agreement." These threats are *credible* according to Selten, only if the use of the threat is still the best reply of the player who uses it. Therefore one sees the need for subgame-perfectness: in an equilibrium supported by a set of credible threats there is an agreement to play according to some cooperative strategy; there should be no temptation, for a player who plays "correctly," to deviate unilaterally from this agreement due to the existence of threats that would be used as a punishment as soon as the other players notice a deviation. If a player does not play according to the agreement, he does not play "correctly"; however, it could take time before this deviation is detected, and the game will have an unexpected evolution. Once the deviation has been detected, the threats will be used, and if these threats are in equilibrium, each player, playing "correctly," will still have no temptations to deviate.

3.5.3 Stochastic Games and Dynamic Programming

In a stochastic game there is a player (nature) who always plays in an unpredictable way. The randomness in the evolution of the game is taken into account if the players use *feedback strategies*, as described in section 2.3, that is, if they base their actions on an observation of the state of the game. The dynamic programming equations characterize *feedback equilibria*. These equilibria are time consistent and subgame-perfect. The dynamic programming approach is, in our opinion, the only practical way to implement subgame-perfectness. We shall illustrate this in section 6.3, where we show how to build an equilibrium, based on an agreement supported by a set of credible threats, through the use of an appropriately defined dynamic programming equation.

4 Repeated Games

A *repeated game* is a "supergame" in which the same (static) game is played several times and possibly an infinity of times. As said by Friedman (1986), such a structure corresponds to a game in a *semiextensive form* where the move structure is not totally obscured. In this section we quickly review

the main feature of these repeated games, namely, the possibility to construct equilibria based on the use of memory strategies. When the actions
of players are not totally observable, due to random disturbances, the
definition of equilibria with memory strategies becomes more delicate, and
one has to use the concept of "Markov" or "sequential game." This will be
addressed in the next section.

4.1 Repeated Games and the Use of Memory Strategies

4.1.1 A Deterministic Repeated Cournot Game

For our presentation of repeated games we consider the Cournot oligopoly
game defined in section 3. Let $t = 1, \ldots, \infty$ be the sequence of time
periods. Let $\mathbf{q}^t \in \mathbb{R}^m$ be the production vector chosen by the m firms at
period t and $V_j(\mathbf{q}^t)$ the payoff to player j at period t. Over the infinite time
horizon the rewards of the players are defined as

$$\tilde{V}_j(\mathbf{q}^1, \ldots, \mathbf{q}^t, \ldots) = \sum_{n=0}^{\infty} \beta_j^t V_j(\mathbf{q}^t),$$

where $\beta_j \in [0, 1)$ is a discount factor used by player j.

We assume that at each period t all players have the same information
$\mathscr{I}_t$, which is the history of passed productions $\mathscr{I}_t = (\mathbf{q}^0, \mathbf{q}^1, \ldots, \mathbf{q}^{t-1})$.

A symmetric Cournot equilibrium is defined by playing repeatedly the
production levels q_j^c, $j = 1, 2$. The dominating Pareto outcome is defined
by playing repeatedly the production levels q_j^*, $j = 1, 2$. Let us define

$$\Phi_j(\mathbf{q}^*) = \max_{q_j} V_j(\mathbf{q}^{*(j)}).$$

It has been shown by Friedman (1971) that it is possible to construct a
subgame-perfect equilibrium for the supergame corresponding to this repeated Cournot game if the following inequality holds:

$$\beta_j > \frac{\Phi_j(\mathbf{q}^*) - V_j(\mathbf{q}^*)}{\Phi_j(\mathbf{q}^*) - V_j(\mathbf{q}^c)}.$$

This equilibrium is reached through the use of a so-called *trigger strategy*
defined as follows:

If $(\mathbf{q}^0, \mathbf{q}^1, \ldots, \mathbf{q}^{t-1}) = (\mathbf{q}^*, \mathbf{q}^*, \ldots, \mathbf{q}^*)$, then $q_j^t = q_j^*$;

otherwise, $q_j^t = q_j^{*c}$.

Remark 6 According to this strategy the $\mathbf{q}^*$ production levels correspond
to a cooperative mood of play, while the $\mathbf{q}^c$ correspond to a *punitive* mood
of play. The punitive mood is a *threat*. As the punitive mood of play

consists to play the Cournot solution, which is indeed an equilibrium, it is a credible threat. Therefore the players will always choose to play in accordance with the Pareto solution $\mathbf{q}^*$, and thus the equilibrium defines a non-dominated outcome and is also subgame-perfect.

"Trigger strategy" have been studied by Radner (1980, 1981, 1985) and by Friedman (1971, 1977, 1986). When the horizon is finite but long; namely, when the number of repeated Cournot games is large, the approach permits only the construction of ε-equilibria, that is, approximate equilibria (Radner 1980).

4.1.2   A Stochastic Repeated Cournot Game with Partial Information
In Porter 1985 and in Green and Porter 1984, the authors have considered the case of an infinitely repeated Cournot game with a stochastic (inverse) demand law $P = D[Q, \xi]$, where ξ is a random perturbation. It is assumed that the players (firms) observe only the price P but are not able to observe the production decisions of their opponents. The authors have constructed dominating equilibria based on the use of trigger strategies.

This equilibrium is not Pareto-optimal; however, it dominates the repeated static Cournot equilibrium. For this construction of a dominating equilibrium Green and Porter had to use the concept of Markov games. Actually the whole approach can be adapted to the class of sequential (Markov) games as shown in Haurie and Tolwinski 1990. This is the topic discussed in the next section.

5   Markov Games

In order to introduce the concept of a "Markov game" first given by Shapley (1953) in the context of zero-sum games, we first consider a simple uncontrolled Markov chain $\{\xi(n) : t \in \mathbb{N}\}$ described by the diagram in figure 9.4. There are two states ($s \in \{1, 2\}$). The parameters q_{ij} associated with the arcs are the transition probabilities of the Markov chain $\xi(\cdot)$ satisfy

$$\Pr[\xi(t + 1) = j | \xi(t) = i] = q_{ij},$$

where

$$q_{ij} \geq 0, \quad \sum_{j=1}^{2} q_{ij} = 1.$$

Now, with each possible state s, we associate a matrix game. For simplicity we have chosen two 3×3 matrix games and we have called $u \in$

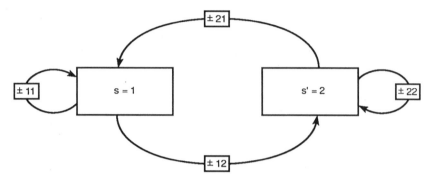

Figure 9.4
A two-state Markov chain

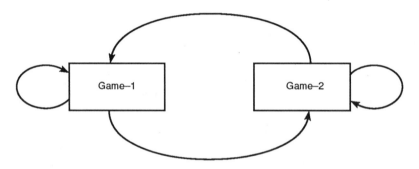

Figure 9.5
A two-state Markov game

$\{a, b, c\}$ the action available to player 1 and $v \in \{I, II, III\}$ the action available to player 2, respectively. Assume that the transition rates of the Markov chain depend on the choice of actions by the two players. They are now denoted $q_{ij}(u, v)$ and defined as

$$\Pr[\xi(t + 1) = j | \xi(t) = i, u, v] = q_{ij}(u, v), \qquad i, j \in \{1, 2\},$$

where

$$q_{ij}(u, v) \geq 0, \qquad \sum_{j=1}^{2} q_{ij}(u, v) = 1.$$

This dynamical game structure is represented in figure 9.5, where the two matrix games called game 1 and game 2, respectively, are represented in tables 9.2–9.3.

Table 9.2
Game 1

P2 P1	I	II	III
a	−2, 13	−4, 4	3, −2
b	16, −10	4, 5	−8, 20
c	4, −10	−8, 20	−12, 25

Table 9.3
Game 2

P2 P1	I	II	III
a	6, 10	4, 4	3, 2
b	6, 10	14, 15	8, 20
c	4, 10	8, 20	12, 25

We say that the game is in state $s = 1$ if game 1 is played; in state $s = 2$, if game 2 is played. The transitions from one state to the other are random and described by transition probabilities that depend on the actions chosen by the players when they play game 1 or game 2. We call the sequence $\mathscr{I}_t = \{s_0, s_1, \ldots, s_t\}$ of states visited up to time t, the "history" of the game at time t. A strategy for player 1 is a sequence $\gamma_1 = \{\gamma_1^t\}_{t \in \mathbb{N}}$ of mappings $\gamma_1^t : \mathscr{I}_t \mapsto \{a, b\}$. We define similarly a stategy γ_2 for player 2. Then we associate with an initial state s_0 and a strategy choice $\gamma = (\gamma_1, \gamma_2)$ by the two players a pair of payoffs

$$V_j(s_0, \gamma) = E_\gamma \left[\sum_{t=0}^{\infty} \beta_j^t G_j(s_t, u_t, v_t) | s_0 \right], \qquad j = 1, 2, \tag{7}$$

where $G_j(s_t, u_t, v_t)$ is called the "transition reward" for player j and $\beta_j \in (0, 1)$ is a discount factor for player j. E_γ is the expectation taken with respect to the probability measure generated by the strategy vector γ, which also determines the stochastic processes (s_t, u_t, v_t), $t = 1, \ldots, \infty$.

Equation 7, for a given initial state s_0, defines a game in normal form, and we can consider equilibria for this class of games.

5.1 The Dynamic Programming Operators

In a more general setting let S be a finite state space and $A_j(s)$ the finite set of actions available to player j, $j \in M$, when the game is in state s. Let $p_{ss'}(\mathbf{a})$

be the transition probability from state s to s' when the action vector $\mathbf{a}$ has been chosen by the players. Let $G_j(s, \mathbf{a})$ be the transition reward to player j and $\beta_j \in (0, 1)$ his (her) discount factor. We introduce the so-called *local reward functions*

$$h_j(s, \mathbf{a}; v_j(\cdot)) = G_j(s, \mathbf{a}) + \beta \sum_{s' \in S} p_{ss'}(\mathbf{a}) v_j(s'), \quad j \in M, \tag{8}$$

where the functions $v_j(\cdot) : S \mapsto \mathbb{R}$ are given *reward-to-go* functionals (in this case they are vectors of dimension $v = \text{card}(S)$) defined for each player j. The local reward (8) is the sum of the transition reward for player j and the discounted expected reward-to-go from the new state reached after the transition. Notice that, for a given s and a given set of reward-to-go functionals $v_j(\cdot)$, $j \in M$, the local rewards (8) define a matrix game over the pure strategy sets $A_j(s)$, $j \in M$. We call a mapping γ_j that associates to any state s a probability distribution $\{\alpha(a_j) \geq 0, \sum_{a_j \in A_j(s)} \alpha(a_j) = 1\}$ over the actions in the admissible set $A_j(s)$, a "Markov policy" for player j. We assume independence of the probability distributions associated with different states and/or players.

We now define, for any given Markov policy vector $\gamma = \{\gamma_j\}_{j \in M}$, an operator H_γ, acting on the space of reward-to-go functionals, (i.e., v-dimensional vectors) and defined as

$$(H_\gamma \mathbf{v}(\cdot))(s) = \{\mathrm{E}_{\gamma(s)}[h_j(s, \tilde{\mathbf{a}}; v_j(\cdot))]\}_{j \in M}. \tag{9}$$

We also introduce the operator F_γ defined as

$$(F_\gamma \mathbf{v}(\cdot))(s) = \left\{ \sup_{\gamma_j} \mathrm{E}_{\gamma^{(j)}(s)}[h_j(s, \tilde{\mathbf{a}}; v_j(\cdot))] \right\}_{j \in M}, \tag{10}$$

where $\tilde{\mathbf{a}}$ is the random action vector and $\gamma^{(j)}$ is the Markov policy obtained when only player j adjusts his policy, while the other players keep their γ-policies fixed.

The dynamic programming formalism initially developed by Denardo (1967) for the Markov decision process and extended by Whitt (1980) to more general Markov (or sequential) games with continuous state and action spaces, leads to the following powerful results:

THEOREM 2   Consider the sequential game defined above, then

(1) The expected payoff vector associated with a stationary Markov policy γ is given by the unique fixed point $\mathbf{v}_\gamma(\cdot)$ of the contracting operator H_γ.

(2) The operator F_γ is also contracting, and thus admits a unique fixed-point $\mathbf{f}^\gamma(\cdot)$.

(3) The stationary Markov policy γ^* is an equilibrium strategy if and only if

$$\mathbf{f}^{\gamma^*}(s) = \mathbf{v}_{\gamma^*}(s), \qquad \forall s \in S. \tag{11}$$

(4) There exists an equilibrium defined by a stationary Markov policy.

5.2   Trigger Strategy Equilibrium in Stochastic Sequential Game

The *sequential game* formalism can be extended to continuous state and action spaces. Consider the stochastic duopoly model defined by the following linear demand equation

$$x(t + 1) = \alpha - \rho[u_1(t) + u_2(t)] + \varepsilon(t),$$

which determines the price $x(t + 1)$ of a good at period $t + 1$, given the total supply $u_1(t) + u_2(t)$ decided at the end of period t by players 1 and 2. Assume a unit production cost equal to γ. The profits at the end of period t by both players (firms) are then determined as

$$\pi_j(t) = (x(t + 1) - \gamma)u_j(t).$$

Assume that the two firms have the same discount rate β, then over an infinite time horizon, the payoff to player j will be given by

$$V_j = \sum_{t=0}^{\infty} \beta^t \pi(t).$$

This game is repeated, therefore an obvious equilibrium solution consists to play repeatedly the (static) Cournot solution

$$u_j^c(t) = \frac{\alpha - \delta}{3\rho}, \qquad j = 1, 2, \tag{12}$$

which generates the payoffs

$$V_j^c = \frac{(\alpha - \rho)^2}{9\rho(1 - \beta)} \qquad j = 1, 2. \tag{13}$$

A symmetric Pareto (nondominated) solution is given by the repeated actions

$$u_j^P(t) = \frac{\alpha - \delta}{4\rho}, \qquad j = 1, 2,$$

and the associated payoffs

$$V_j^p = \frac{(\alpha - \delta)}{8\rho(1 - \beta)} \qquad j = 1, 2,$$

where $\delta = \alpha - \gamma$.

The Pareto outcome dominates the Cournot equilibrium but it does not represent an equilibrium. The question arises: *Is it possible to construct a pair of memory strategies which would define an equilibrium with an outcome dominating the repeated Cournot strategy outcome and which would be as close as possible to the Pareto nondominated solution?*

The random perturbations affecting the price mechanism do not permit a direct extension of the approach described in the deterministic context. Since it is assumed that the actions of players are not directly observable, there is a need to proceed to some filtering of the sequence of observed states in order to *monitor* the possible breaches of agreement.

Green and Porter (1984) have constructed a dominating memory strategy equilibrium, based on a *one-step memory* scheme. We propose below another approach, using a *multistep memory scheme*, that yields an outcome closer to the Pareto solution.

The basic idea consists of extending the state space by introducing a new state variable, denoted v, used to monitor a *cooperative policy* that all players have agreed to play and that is defined as $\phi : v \mapsto u_j = \phi(v)$. The state equation governing the evolution of this state variable is designed as follows:

$$v(t + 1) = \max\{-K, v(t) + x^e - x(t + 1)\}, \tag{14}$$

where x^e is the expected outcome if both players use the cooperative policy; namely,

$$x^e = \alpha - 2\rho\phi(v).$$

It should be clear that the new state variable v provides a cumulative measure of the positive discrepancies between the expected prices x^e and the realized ones $x(t)$. The parameter $-K$ defines a lower bound for v. This is introduced to prevent a compensation of positive discrepancies by negative ones. A positive discrepancy could be an indication of *oversupply*, that is, an indication that at least one player is not respecting the agreement and is maybe trying to take advantage of the other player.

If these discrepancies accumulate too fast, the evidence of *cheating* is mounting, and thus some retaliation should be expected. To model the retaliation process, we introduce another state variable, denoted y, which is a *binary* variable; namely, $y \in \{0, 1\}$. This new state variable will be an indicator of the prevailing mood of play. If $y = 1$ then the game is played cooperatively; if $y = 0$, then the game is played in a noncooperative manner, interpreted as a *punitive* or *retaliatory* mood of play.

This state variable is assumed to evolve according to the following state equation:

$$y(t + 1) = \begin{cases} 1 & \text{if } y(t) = 1 \quad \text{and} \quad v(t + 1) < \theta(v(t)), \\ 0 & \text{otherwise,} \end{cases} \qquad (15)$$

where the positive valued function $\theta : v \mapsto \theta(v)$ is a *design parameter* of this monitoring scheme.

According to this state equation, the cooperative mood of play will be maintained, provided the cumulative positive discrepancies do not increase too fast from one period to the next. Also, this state equation tells us that, once $y(t) = 0$, then $y(t') \equiv 0$ for all periods $t' > t$; a punitive mood of play will last forever. In the models discussed later on we shall relax this assumption of everlasting punishment.

When the *mood of play* is *non*cooperative ($y = 0$), both players use as a *punishment* (or retaliation) the static Cournot solution forever. This generates the expected payoffs $V_j^c, j = 1, 2$ defined in equation 13. Since the two players are identical, we shall not use the subscript j anymore.

When the mood of play is cooperative ($y = 1$), both players use an agreed-upon policy that determines their respective controls as a function of the state variable v. This agreement policy is defined by the function $\phi(v)$. The expected payoff is then a function $W(v)$ of this state variable v.

For this agreement to be stable, that is, not to provide a temptation to cheat to any player, it must be an equilibrium. Note that the game is now a *sequential Markov game* with a continuous state space. The dynamic programming equation characterizing an equilibrium is given below:

$$W(v) = \max_u \{[\alpha - \delta - \rho(\phi(v) + u)]u$$

$$+ \beta P[v' \geq \theta(v)]V^c$$

$$+ \beta P[v' < \theta(v)]E[W(v')|v' < \theta(v)]\}, \qquad (16)$$

where we have denoted

$$v' = \max\{-K, v + \rho(u - \phi(v)) - \varepsilon\}$$

the random value of the state variable v after the transition generated by the controls $(u, \phi(v))$.

In equation 16 we recognize the immediate reward $[\alpha - \delta - \rho(\phi(v) + u)]u$ of player 1 when he (she) plays u while the opponent sticks to $\phi(v)$. This is added to the conditional expected payoffs after the transition to either the *punishment mood of play*, corresponding to the values $y = 0$, or the *cooperative mood of play*, corresponding to $y = 1$.

A solution of these *DP* equations can be found by solving an associated fixed-point problem, as indicated in Haurie and Tolwinski 1990. To summarize the approach, we introduce the operator

$$(T_\phi W)(v, u) = [\alpha - \delta - \rho(u + \phi(v))]u + \beta(\alpha - \delta)^2 \frac{F(s - \theta(v))}{9\rho(1 - \beta)}$$

$$+ \beta W(-K)[1 - F(s - K)] + \beta \int_{-K}^{\theta(v)} W(\tau) f(s - \tau) \, d\tau,$$

$$(17)$$

where $F(\cdot)$ and $f(\cdot)$ are the cumulative distribution function and the density probability function, respectively, of the random disturbance ε. We have also used the following notation:

$$s = v + \rho(u - \phi(v)).$$

An equilibrium solution is a pair of functions $(w(\cdot), \phi(\cdot))$ such that

$$W(v) = \max_u T_\phi(W)(v, u) \tag{18}$$

$$W(v) = (T_\phi W)(v, \phi(v)). \tag{19}$$

Haurie and Tolwinski (1990) show that one can compute the solution of this sort of fixed-point problem by adapting the Howard *policy improvement algorithm* (Howard 1960). Their numerical experiments, using a quadratic function $\theta(\cdot)$ and a Gaussian distribution law for ε, show that one can define by this approach a subgame-perfect equilibrium that dominates the repeated Cournot solution.

Porter (1983) has studied this problem in the case where the (inverse) demand law is subject to a multiplicative noise. He has obtained a qualitative result that proves the existence of a dominating equilibrium based on a simple *one-step memory* scheme, where the variable v satisfies the following equation:

$$v(t + 1) = \frac{x^e - x(t + 1)}{x(t)}.$$

This is the case where one does not monitor the cooperative policy through the use of a cumulated discrepancy function, but rather on the basis of repeated identical tests. Also in Porter's approach the punishment period is finite.

In Haurie and Tolwinski 1990 it is shown that the approach could be extended to a full-fledged Markov game, that is, a sequential game rather than a repeated game. A simple model of fisheries management was used in that work to illustrate this type of sequential game *cooperative* equilibrium.

An easy extension of the method would lead to random transitions between the two moods of play, with transition probabilities depending on the monitoring statistic v. Also a punishment of random duration is possible in this model. In the next section we illustrate these features when we propose a differential game model with *random moods of play*.

Remark 7   The use of memory strategies for the definition of a larger class of equilibria has been considered, in a different setting, by several authors in the "dynamic game—differential game" literature. We refer the reader to Başar and Olsder 1982 for a complete list of references. In our approach, by extending the state space description (i.e., introducing the new variables v and y), we retained a Markov game formalism for an extended game and this has permitted us to use dynamic programming for the characterization of subgame-perfect equilibria.

6   A Stochastic Differential Game with Cooperative Equilibria

In this section we return to the stochastic differential game formalism introduced in section 2, and we show how this formalism can be used to define *cooperative equilibria* based on the use of threats supporting an agreement. This model extends the approach described in section 5.2 in the realm of Markov games. The approach has already been discussed in Haurie 1991, and we only repeat a part of those developments herein.

6.1   A Stochastic Diffusion Game

We consider a dynamical system described by the Ito state equation

$$dx(t) = f(x(t), \mathbf{u}(t)) \, dt + \sigma \, d\varepsilon(t),$$

where $x \in \mathbb{R}$ is the state variable (e.g., the biomass for a given species of fish) and $\mathbf{u} = (u_j)_{j \in M} \in \mathbb{R}^m$ is the composite control (e.g., the fishing efforts) of the m players in M (e.g., the different fisheries that exploit on the same ground). For more details about modeling fisheries exploitation as control or differential game problems we refer to Clark 1980; Hamalainen, Haurie, and Kaitala 1985; and Munro 1979. Associated with a feedback strategy $\gamma : x(t) \mapsto \mathbf{u}(t)$ we define the m payoff functionals

$$V_j(x, \gamma) = \mathrm{E}\left[\int_0^\infty e^{-\rho t} g_j(x(t), \mathbf{u}(t))\, dt \,|\, x(0) = x\right]. \qquad j \in M.$$

A feedback equilibrium is obtained as a solution to the m-coupled H.J.B. equations

$$\rho V_j^*(x) = \max_{u_j \in U_j(x)} \left[g_j(x, [\gamma^{*(j)}, u_j]) + f(x, [\gamma^{*(j)}, u_j]) \frac{\partial}{\partial x} V_j^*(x) \right]$$

$$+ \frac{1}{2}\left(\sigma^2 \frac{\partial^2}{\partial x^2} V_j^*(x) \right) \quad j = 1, \ldots, m, \tag{20}$$

where $[\gamma^{*(j)}, u_j]$ is the control obtained when all players use the equilibrium policy and player j uses the control u_j. The question we want to address is, How can we construct a subgame-perfect equilibrium that dominates the Nash feedback equilibrium γ^*?

For this construction we shall follow an approach similar to the one used in section 5.2; namely, we shall build a monitoring and retaliation scheme and look for an equilibrium supported by these threats. This is detailed in the following subsection.

6.2   A Monitoring and Retaliation Scheme

We introduce again two additional state variables $y \in \{0, 1\}$ and $z \in \mathbb{R}$, which are an *indicator of the mood of play* and a *monitoring* variable, respectively.

$y = 0$ means that the game is played noncooperatively

$y = 1$ means that the game is played in a cooperative mood.

When the game is played cooperatively the *collusive* policy is defined as the function $\tilde{\gamma}^1(x, z)$. The monitoring variable z obeys a state equation designed as follows:

$$dz(t) = dx(t) - f(x(t), \tilde{\gamma}^1(x, z(t)))\, dt, \tag{21}$$

$$z(\tau) = 0, \qquad t \geq \tau. \tag{22}$$

Thus the variable z measures the cumulated discrepancies, from time τ on, between the state $x(t)$ and its conditional expected value when all players use the collusive policy $\tilde{\gamma}^1(x, z)$.

When the game is played noncooperatively, the *punishment* policy is given by the function $\tilde{\gamma}^0(x)$. Notice that this policy does not use the information given by z. Of course there is nothing to monitor in the non-cooperative mood of play.

The switches between the two possible moods of play are determined by a Markov jump process $\xi(t)$, $t \geq 0$, with values in $\{0, 1\}$ and jump rates

$$P[\xi(t + dt) = 0 | \xi(t) = 1, z(t)] = q_{10}(z(t))\, dt + o(dt) \tag{23}$$

$$P[\xi(t + dt) = 1 | \xi(t) = 0] = q_{01}\, dt + o(dt) \tag{24}$$

The Markov process $\xi(\cdot)$ describes the evolution of the state variable y. The elementary probability of switching from a cooperative ($y = 1$) to a noncooperative ($y = 0$) mood depends on the value of the monitoring variable z. When the punishment is in force ($y = 0$), the elementary probability of switching back to a cooperative mood of play is constant. This means that the length of the *punishment period* is an exponential random variable with expected value $\dfrac{1}{q_{01}}$.

These jump rates, defining the Markov process that drives the moods of play, are design parameters of the cooperative equilibrium scheme. By changing these functions, one obtains different equilibria. Also, at a jump time τ from noncooperative ($\xi(\tau^-) = 0$) to cooperative ($\xi(\tau^+) = 1$) mood of play, the monitoring variable is reset to a 0 value, that is, $z(\tau^+) = 0$.

6.3 Characterization of Equilibria through Dynamic Programming

The extended state $((x, z), y)$ is hybrid (continuous and discrete). The discrete state variable evolves according to a random jump Markov process, while x and z obey Ito equations. We are thus in the realm of the *piecewise diffusion game* introduced in section 2. A new feedback equilibrium can be determined in this extended formulation.

Such an equilibrium is characterized by the following coupled HJB dynamic programming equations

$$\rho \tilde{V}_j^*(1, (x, z))$$

$$= \frac{1}{2}\sigma^2 \left\{ \frac{\partial^2}{\partial x^2} \tilde{V}_j^*(1, (x, z)) + \frac{\partial^2}{\partial z^2} \tilde{V}_j^*(1, (x, z)) + 2 \frac{\partial^2}{\partial x \partial z} \tilde{V}_j^*(1, (x, z)) \right\}$$

$$+ q_{10}(z)(\tilde{V}_j^*(0, x) - \tilde{V}_j^*(1, (x, z)))$$

$$+ \max_{u_j} \left[g_j(x, [\tilde{\gamma}^{1(-j)}(x, z), u_j]) + f(x, [\tilde{\gamma}^{1(-j)}(x, z), u_j]) \frac{\partial}{\partial x} \tilde{V}_j^*(1, (x, z)) \right.$$

$$\left. + [f(x, [\tilde{\gamma}^{1(-j)}(x, z), u_j]) - f(x, \tilde{\gamma}^1(x, z)] \frac{\partial}{\partial z} \tilde{V}_j^*(1, (x, z)) \right] \tag{25}$$

$$\rho \tilde{V}_j^*(0, x) = \frac{1}{2}\sigma^2 \frac{\partial^2}{\partial x^2} \tilde{V}_j^*(0, x) + q_{01}(\tilde{V}_j^*(1, (x, 0)) - \tilde{V}_j^*(0, x))$$

$$+ \max_{u_j} \left[g_j(x, [\tilde{\gamma}^{0(-j)}(x), u_j]) + f(x, [\tilde{\gamma}^{0(-j)}(x), u_j]) \frac{\partial}{\partial x} \tilde{V}_j^*(0, x) \right],$$

$$(26)$$

where $[\tilde{\gamma}^{1(-j)}(x, z), u_j]$ is the control obtained when all the players use the cooperative policy $\tilde{\gamma}^1(x, z)$, while player j uses his control u_j. Similarly $[\tilde{\gamma}^{0(-j)}(x), u_j]$ is the control obtained when all other players use the punishment policy $\tilde{\gamma}^0$ and player j uses his control u_j.

If one can solve these equations and if the monitoring and switching schemes are well designed, it may be possible to define an equilibrium that will dominate the Nash feedback equilibrium of the original game. Only a numerical approach can be attempted to check this statement. This is the object of the next section. Notice that in the numerical approach we deal with *approximate* or *ε-equilibria* and not anymore with *strict equilibria*.

7   Numerical Approximation of the Equilibrium in a Stochastic Differential Game

In this section we address the problem of how to compute feedback equilibria for the class of differential games described in section 2. We propose to adapt the Kushner (1977) method, which Kushner successfully applied to stochastic control problems.

Recall we want to solve

$$\rho V_j(x, k) = \frac{1}{2} \sum_{i,i'=1}^{n} a_{i,i'}^k(x) \frac{\partial^2 V_j(x, k)}{\partial x_i \partial x_{i'}} + \max_{u_j \in U_j^k(x)} \left\{ g_j(x, [\mathbf{u}^{*(-j)}(x, k), u_j]) \right.$$

$$\left. + f^k(x, \mathbf{u}^{*(j)}(x, k))' \frac{\partial V_j(x, k)}{\partial x} + \sum_{l \in E} q_{kl}(x, [\mathbf{u}^{*(-j)}(x, k), u_j]) V_j(x, l) \right\},$$

$$(27)$$

7.1   Kushner's Discretization and the Associated Markov Game

Let $\mathbb{R}_h^n$ denote the h grid on $\mathbb{R}^n$ defined by

$$\mathbb{R}_h^n = \left\{ x : x = \sum_{i=1}^{n} r_i e_i h, \ r_i \text{ integers} \right\},$$

where e_i denotes the unit vector in the ith direction.

According to the approximation method developed by Kushner (1977), we use the following rules for approximating partial derivatives:

$v_{x_i}(x) \rightarrow [v(x + e_i h) - v(x)]/h$ if $f_i^k(x, \mathbf{u}) \geq 0$

$v_{x_i}(x) \rightarrow [v(x) - v(x - e_i h)]/h$ if $f_i^k(x, \mathbf{u}) < 0$

$v_{x_i x_i}(x) \rightarrow [v(x + e_i h) + v(x - e_i h) - 2v(x)]/h^2.$

For $i \neq j$ and $a_{ij}^k(x) \geq 0$,

$$v_{x_i x_j}(x) \rightarrow [2v(x) + v(x + e_i h + e_j h) + v(x - e_i h - e_j h)]/2h^2$$
$$- [v(x + e_i h) + v(x - e_i h) + v(x + e_j h) + v(x - e_j h)]/2h^2.$$

For $i \neq j$ and $a_{ij}^k(x) < 0$,

$$v_{x_i x_j}(x) \rightarrow - [2v(x) + v(x + e_i h - e_j h) + v(x - e_i h + e_j h)]/2h^2$$
$$+ [v(x + e_i h) + v(x - e_i h) + v(x + e_j h) + v(x - e_j h)]/2h^2.$$

Then we define the interpolation interval

$$\Delta t^h(x, \mathbf{u}) = h^2/Q_h^k(x, \mathbf{u}),$$

where

$$Q_h^k(x, \mathbf{u}) = -q_{kk}(x, \mathbf{u})h^2 + \sum_{i=1}^n a_{ii}^k(x) - \sum_{j \neq i} \frac{|a_{ij}^k(x)|}{2} + h \sum_{i=1}^n |f_i^k(x, \mathbf{u})|.$$

Now we define the transition probabilities

$$p^h((x, k), (x \pm e_i h, k)|\mathbf{u}) = \left[\frac{a_{ii}^k(x)}{2} - \sum_{j \neq i} \frac{|a_{ij}^k(x)|}{2} + hf_i^{k\pm}(x, \mathbf{u}) \right] \bigg/ Q_h^k(x, \mathbf{u})$$

$$p^h((x, k), (x + e_i h + e_j h, k)|\mathbf{u}) = p^h((x, k), (x - e_i h - e_j h, k)|\mathbf{u})$$
$$= a_{ij}^{k+}(x)/2Q_h^k(x, \mathbf{u})$$

$$p^h((x, k), (x + e_i h - e_j h, k)|\mathbf{u}) = p^h((x, k), (x - e_i h + e_j h, k)|\mathbf{u})$$
$$= a_{ij}^{k-}(x)/2Q_h^k(x, \mathbf{u})$$

$$p^h((x, k), (x, l)|\mathbf{u}) = q_{kl}(x, \mathbf{u})h^2/Q_h^k(x, \mathbf{u}),$$

where a_{ij}^{k+} and a_{ij}^{k-} represent the positive and negative parts of $a_{ij}^k(x)$, respectively.

After substituting and rearranging terms, we get the following difference equations:

$$v_j(x, k) = \left(\sum_{x'} p^k((x, k), (x', k)|\mathbf{u}) v_j(x', k) + \sum_{l \in E} p^k((x, k), (x, l)|\mathbf{u}) v_j(x', l) \right.$$

$$\left. + g(x, \mathbf{u}) \Delta t^h(x, \mathbf{u}) \right) \frac{1}{1 + \dfrac{\rho}{Q_h^k(x, \mathbf{u})}}, \qquad x \in \mathbb{R}_h^n, \qquad j \in M. \qquad (28)$$

This set of equations can be rewritten as a fixed point of a discrete-state dynamic programming operator

$$v_j(x, k) = (T_{i, \mathbf{u}} v_j(\cdot, \cdot))(x, k), \qquad x \in \mathbb{R}_h^n, \quad j \in M. \qquad (29)$$

The operator $T_{j, \mathbf{u}}$ is contracting. Therefore, if a feedback law $\mathbf{u}(\cdot)$ has been defined, the solution of the above fixed-point problem gives an approximation of the value functions of the players $j \in M$ defined on the grid points of $\mathbb{R}_h^n$.

It has been shown by Kushner that the Markov chain built according to the above scheme gives a converging approximation to the solution of the HJB equations associated with a given policy $\mathbf{u}(\cdot)$. The scheme would also converge, if one optimizes, in the discrete model, toward the optimal control of player j when the feedback policy of the other players is kept fixed.

An open problem (and probably not an easy one) would be to give conditions under which equilibria for the associated sequence of Markov games converge toward an equilibrium for the diffusion game.

7.2   A Procedure for Computing Approximate Equilibria

We propose below a procedure which could be easily implemented to try to approximate a feedback equilibrium in a stochastic differential game:

(Step 1) Take an initial set of value functions $v_j^0(s, k)$, $j = 1, \ldots, m$, for example, $\equiv 0$;

(Step 2) At iteration n compute the feedback rule resulting from the equilibrium conditions on the RHS of the HJB equations; call this feedback law $\mathbf{u}^n(x, k)$;

(Step 3) For a given feedback control $\mathbf{u}^n$ proceed with Kushner's discretization scheme and get an approximation of the associated value function, for the given grid $\mathbb{R}_h^n$;

(Step 4) Interpolate to get a new set of value functions $v_j^{n+1}(s, k)$, $j = 1, \ldots, m$;

(Step 5) If $\|v_j^{n+1}(s, k) - v_j^n(s, k)\| \le \varepsilon$ stop; we have obtained an ε-equilibrium. Otherwise go to step 2.

This procedure is obviously reminiscent of the Howard (1960) *policy improvement algorithm* for Markov decision processes. Since we compute equilibria, instead of simple optimization in step 2, the procedure is not always monotonous and contracting, and thus may fail to converge. One knows that there are no general procedures for computing equilibria in dynamic sequential games (see Breton et al. 1986). We can only hope that, by implementing various relaxation schemes, one may circumvent the difficulties created by the nonmonotonous behavior of this approximation scheme.

We refer the reader to Haurie, Krawczyk, and Roche 1992 for an example where this approach has been implemented with success.

8 Conclusion

Time is not always discrete, even in economic modeling. Stochastic differential games thus provide the most general framework to model competitive behavior in an environment where uncertainties occur at different time scales. Randomness can affect a system in two different ways, either continuously as a Brownian motion of infinitesimal perturbations or as sudden jumps that modify the operational mode of the system. The formalism of *stochastic diffusion games with random modal changes* captures these two facets of uncertainty in decision making. These modal jumps may also represent endogenous modifications of the mood of play (we could even consider modifications of the rules of the games).

Repeated games have been extremely useful to generate new solution concepts in the theory of games (e.g., equilibria with memory (trigger) strategies). The repetition of the same game structure makes all computations a lot easier. Sequential or Markov games and, ultimately, stochastic differential games can describe more faithfully the true economic context. Usually a concept proposed for repeated games can be extended to the sequential game context without much difficulty. In the differential game context some precautions have to be taken, due to the continuous-time setting. We have shown that these extensions are nevertheless possible.

There are obvious intrinsic limits to getting qualitative results in dynamic game models. Therefore one needs computational techniques to get the solutions of these models. Unfortunately, there are no good general algorithms for computing equilibria in sequential games.

In an operational context a solution concept (e.g., equilibrium) should be computationally feasible, that is, there should exist a practical way to compute a good approximation of the solution within a reasonable amount of computing time. Since time is essentially continuous, a stability with respect to time discretization is also a necessity in order for the solution concept to have an operational value. The formalism of Markov games provides a framework in which computationally feasible algorithms can eventually be designed. Recent experiments with a variety of such games show that one can expect good performance of algorithms computing Nash feedback equilibria, even though a general theory of convergence is still lacking (and probably impossible to obtain).

More experimentation with Kushner's approach in the realm of stochastic differential games is needed. The approach proceeds through a simultaneous approximation in time and space. As said before, the stability of the equilibrium solution obtained in the sequence of such approximations should be exhibited in order to obtain an operational concept.

As a final statement, we could propose the researchers interested in game theory the following alternative: Instead of only getting qualitative results on simplistic models, why not try to get approximate numerical solutions to more complex, nontrivial models?

Note

This work has been supported by grants from FNRS-Switzerland, NSERC-Canada, and FCAR-Quebec. The author thanks Michèle Breton, Jacek, Krawczyk, and Michel Roche for their helpful comments.

References

Başar, T., and A. Haurie. 1984. "Feedback Equilibria in Differential Games with Structural and Modal Uncertainties." In *Advances in Large-Scale Systems*, ed. José B. Gruz, Jr. 1:163–201.

Başar, T., and G. J. Olsder. 1982. *Dynamic Noncooperative Game Theory*. New York: Academic Press.

Breton, M. 1987. "Équilibres pour des Jeux Séquentiels." Ph.D. diss., University of Montreal.

Breton, M., J. Filar, A. Haurie, and T. A. Schultz. 1986. "On the Computation of Equilibria in Discounted Stochastic Games." In *Dynamic Games and Applications in Economics*, ed. T. Başar. Lecture Notes in Economics and Mathematical Systems, vol. 265. New York: Springer-Verlag.

Clark, C. W. 1980. "Restricted Access to Common-Property Resources: A Game-Theoretic Analysis." In *Dynamic Optimization and Mathematical Economics*, ed. P. Liu. New York: Plenum Press.

Cournot, A. 1838. *Recherches sur les principes mathématiques de la théorie des richesses*. Paris: Hachette.

Denardo, E. V. 1967. "Contraction Mappings in the Theory Underlying Dynamic Programming." *SIAM Review* 9(2):165–177.

Friedman, A. 1971. *Differential Games*. New York: Wiley-Interscience.

Friedman, J. W. 1971. "A Noncooperative Equilibrium for Supergame." *Review of Economic Studies* 38:1–12.

Friedman, J. W. 1977. *Oligopoly and the Theory of Games*. Amsterdam: North Holland.

Friedman, J. W. 1986. *Game Theory with Applications to Economics*. New York: Oxford University Press.

Green, E. J. and R. H. Porter. 1984. "Noncooperative Collusion under Imperfect Price Information." *Econometrica* 52:87–100.

Hamalainen, R., A Haurie, and V. Kaitala. 1985. "Equilibria and Threat in a Fishery Management Game." *Optimal Control Applications and Methods* 6:315–333.

Haurie, A. 1975. "A Note on Nonzero-Sum Differential Games with Bargaining Solutions." *Journal of Optimization Theory and Applications* 18:31–39.

Haurie, A. 1991. "Piecewise Deterministic and Piecewise Diffusion Differential Games." In *Decision Processes in Economics*, ed. G. Ricci. Lecture Notes in Economics and Mathematical Systems, vol. 353. New York: Springer-Verlag.

Haurie, A., J. B. Krawczyk, and M. Roche. 1992. "Monitoring Cooperative Equilibria in a Stochastic Differential Game." In *Proceedings 31st IEEE-CDC*, Tucson, Arizona.

Haurie, A., and B. Tolwinski. 1990. "Cooperative Equilibria in Discounted Stochastic Sequential Games." *Journal of Optimization Theory and Applications* 64(3):511–535.

Howard, R. A. 1960. *Dynamic Programming and Markov Processes*. Cambridge: MIT Press.

Krassovski, and A. I. Subbotin. 1977. *Jeux Différentiels*. Moscow: Mir.

Kushner, H. J. 1977. *Probability Methods for Approximation in Stochastic Control and for Elliptic Equations*. New York: Academic Press.

Lemke, J. E., and J. T. Howson. 1964. "Equilibrium Points of Bimatrix Games." *SIAM Journal of Applied Mathematics* 12:413–423.

Munro, G. R. 1979. "The Optimal Management of Transboundary Renewable Resources. *Canadian Journal of Economics* 12:355–376.

Nash, J. 1950. "The Bargaining Problem." *Econometrica* 18:155–162.

Nash, J. F. 1951. "Non-Cooperative Games." *Annals of Mathematics* 54:286–295.

Porter, R. H. 1983. "Optimal Cartel Trigger Strategies." *Journal of Economic Theory* 29:313–338.

Radner, R. 1980. "Collusive Behavior in Noncooperative ε-Equilibria of Oligopolies with Long but Finite Lives." *Journal of Economic Theory* 22:136–154.

Radner, R. 1981. "Monitoring Cooperative Agreement in a Repeated Principal-Agent Relationship." *Econometrica* 49:1127–1148.

Radner, R. 1985. "Repeated Principal-Agent Games with Discounting." *Econometrica* 53:1173–1198.

Rosen, J. B. 1965. "Existence and Uniqueness of Equilibrium Points for Concave N-Person Games." *Econometrica* 33:520–534.

Selten, R. 1975. "Reexamination of the Perfectness Concept for Equilibrium Points in Extensive Games." *International Journal of Game Theory* 4:25–55.

Shapley, L. 1953. "Stochastic Games." In *Proceedings of the National Academy of Science* 39:1095–1100.

Simaan, M., and J. B. Cruz, Jr. 1973. "Additional Aspects of the Stackelberg Strategy in Non-Zero-Sum Games." *Journal of Optimization Theory and Applications* 11:613–626.

Tolwinski, B., A. Haurie, and G. Leitmann. 1986. "Cooperative Equilibria in Differential Games." *Journal of Mathematical Analysis and Applications* 119:182–202.

Whitt, W. 1980. "Representation and Approximation of Noncooperative Sequential Games." *SIAM Journal of Control* 18(1):33–48.

10 Unraveling in Games of Sharing and Exchange

Steve J. Brams,
D. Marc Kilgour, and
Morton D. Davis

1 Introduction

Traditionally, "unravel" means "disengage or separate the threads" (*Webster's Ninth New Collegiate Dictionary*). More recently, "unraveling" has come to mean the coming apart of a situation—related to its traditional meaning of disentangling—but without the connotation of something's being cleared up in the process. Quite the contrary: unraveling now connotes breakdown or disintegration, with the presumption that matters have exceeded their normal bounds, gotten out of hand.

This is the meaning that we intend in the title of this paper. Our analysis focuses on strategic forces that cause unraveling to occur. Using several different games of sharing and exchange that model simplified social systems, we show that these forces can lead naturally to very different outcomes. Sometimes there is a kind of spiraling down so that no exchange or sharing ever occurs. Other times there can be an upward spiraling, whereby sharing or exchange always occurs. And there are also games with intermediate outcomes, in which there are limits on unraveling.

To illustrate what we mean by strategic unraveling, consider the following game, first proposed by Littlewood and reported in Bollobás (1986, 26):

There is an indefinite supply of cards marked 1 and 2 on opposite sides, and of cards marked 2 and 3, 3 and 4, and so on. A card is drawn at random by a referee and held between the players, *A* and *B*, so that each sees one side only. Either player may veto the round, but if it is played the player seeing the high number wins.

What winning means is unspecified, but assume it results in a positive payoff, whereas losing results in a negative payoff and a vetoed round in a zero payoff. The surprising result in this game is that, if the players behave "optimally," every round is vetoed. If A sees a 1 the other side is 2 and he must veto. If he sees a 2 the other side is 1 or 3; if 1 then B must veto; if he does not then A must. And so on by induction.

We would put the argument somewhat differently. A will certainly veto 1, so B's choice on seeing 2 has no effect if the card is 1–2; B loses nothing by vetoing. On the other hand, if the card is 2–3, B does have something to lose if he sees 2 and does not veto it, so his dominant strategy is to veto 2 whenever he sees it. (A strategy is *dominant* if and only if it never makes a player worse off, and may make him better off, no matter what strategy is chosen by his opponent(s).) Then, given that 2 is always vetoed, a player who sees 3 has a dominant strategy to veto it, and so on. Consequently, there is never any winner; this iteration of vetoes causes the process to unravel, always producing zero payoffs for the players.

It is the inferences that the players make from information they know they both possess—their common knowledge—that is the key to the unraveling in Littlewood's game. Similarly, in the sharing and exchange games that we introduce next, common knowledge has a cascading effect on players' strategy choices, as has been noted by other analysts in economic and related contexts (Milgrom and Stokey 1982; Ribeiro da Costa Werlang 1989; and Monderer and Samet 1990).

In our games of sharing and exchange, there are always two players. Each has an initial wealth, or endowment, determined randomly and known only to the player. However, the distributions from which the endowments are independently drawn are common knowledge. There is a fixed number s, satisfying $0 < s \leq 1$, specified in advance and called the *sharing fraction*. Each player's only decision is whether or not to offer to exchange the fraction s of the player's own endowment for the fraction s of the other player's. There are many possible exchange rules to determine whether the exchange actually takes place, as a function of both players' decisions. Our general objective is to investigate the effects of different exchange rules on "optimal" decision making.

When the sharing fraction s equals 1, the players simply exchange their entire endowments. When $s = \frac{1}{2}$, they share their joint wealth equally. As we shall see later, the value of s is generally irrelevant to optimal play of the game.

We assume throughout that each player's objective is to maximize the player's expected final wealth—the amount that the player possesses after the exchange, if there is one. Note that the exchange games described so far are explicitly constant-sum: if an exchange occurs, then whatever one player gains, the other must lose. But we shall also analyze a nonconstant-sum game, in which the exchange loser's losses may be reduced substantially, making the loser's wealth almost as great as the exchange winner's. Nevertheless, the greater incentive that the players have to exchange in this game does not affect their decisions, which are never to share or exchange if both must offer. But if only one must offer for an exchange to occur, the unraveling is always in favor of an exchange.

2   A One-Person Game of Sharing and Exchange

Consider first the situation of an individual A who draws a number x and has the option of exchanging sx for sY, where Y is a random variable distributed according to some known distribution. Then A's expected final wealth is x if there is no exchange, and

$$(1 - s)x + sEY$$

if there is one, where EY is the expectation of Y. It is easy to see that A prefers an exchange if and only if $x < EY$.

The policy of exchanging exactly when x is small benefits A considerably if A is the sole decision maker. For example, assume that $s = 1$ and that the distributions from which X and Y are drawn are both uniform on $[0, 1]$. A will then want to exchange if and only if $x < \frac{1}{2}$. This policy will net A the expected final wealth

$$\int_0^{1/2} EY\,dx + \int_{1/2}^1 x\,dx = \frac{1}{4} + \frac{3}{8} = \frac{5}{8}.$$

since $EY = \frac{1}{2}$. In general, if $F(\cdot)$ is the cumulative distribution function (cdf) of X, then A's a priori expected value is

$$EY \cdot F(EY) + \int_{EY}^{\infty} x\,dF(x) = EY + \int_{EY}^{\infty} (x - EY)\,dF(x),$$

which exceeds $EY < \infty$ as long as $F(EY) < 1$.

3   The AND Game

Now assume that player A draws X from the cdf $F(\cdot)$ and, independently, player B draws Y from the cdf $G(\cdot)$. In AND, sharing occurs if and only if both A and B (simultaneously) assent to it. As we shall see, the fact that there are two decision makers has an enormous effect on the outcome.

To simplify the presentation of this and future decision problems, we assume that both $F(\cdot)$ and $G(\cdot)$ are continuous. (In fact, analogous results can be obtained for the discrete case.) Further, assume player A knows the realized value $X = x$, but not the realized value $Y = y$.

Suppose that player B has adopted a strategy to offer to exchange with probability $w_B(y)$ whenever B observes $Y = y$. It follows that A's value remains x if A does not offer to exchange, and A's expected value is

$$EV_A = \int \{[1 - w_B(y)]x + w_B(y)[(1 - s)x + sy]\} \, dG(y)$$

$$= \int \{x + sw_B(y)[y - x]\} \, dG(y)$$

if it does.

Because A's decision is irrelevant if $Pr\{w_B(Y) > 0\} = 0$, assume otherwise. Taking expectations with respect to Y (and assuming that $w_B(\cdot)$ is suitably integrable and that $EY < \infty$) yields

$$EV_A = x + s(E[Yw_B(Y)] - xE[w_B(Y)]).$$

Clearly, A should offer to exchange whenever $EV_A > x$. (For notational convenience, we assume that a player prefers to stand pat unless the expected gain from sharing is strictly positive.) Because $s > 0$, it is easy to see that A should offer to exchange if and only if

$$x < \frac{E[Yw_B(Y)]}{E[w_B(Y)]} = a \tag{1}$$

Thus, A's optimal strategy will be a "threshold strategy," with threshold a defined by (1):

$$w_A^*(x) = \begin{cases} 1 & \text{if } x < a \\ 0 & \text{if } x \geq a \end{cases}.$$

Analogously, B's optimal strategy must be of the form

$$w_B^*(y) = \begin{cases} 1 & \text{if } y < b \\ 0 & \text{if } y \geq b \end{cases}$$

for an appropriate threshold b.

To explore the relationship between the optimal thresholds a and b, note that $E[w_B^*(Y)] = G(b)$ and that

$$E[Yw_B^*(Y)] = \int_{-\infty}^{b} b \, dG(y) = G(b) \int_{-\infty}^{b} y \, \frac{dG(y)}{G(b)} = G(b)E[Y|Y < b].$$

(Here our assumption that $Pr\{w_B^*(Y) > 0\} = G(b) > 0$ is critical.) Substituting in (1) yields

$$a = E[Y|Y < b] < b. \tag{2}$$

Furthermore, the calculations can all be reversed to show that B should optimally set $b < a$, on the assumption that $Pr\{w_A^*(X) > 0\} = F(a) > 0$.

But we have now shown, under the assumptions noted, that A's maximizing strategy satisfies $a < b$, and B's maximizing strategy satisfies $b < a$. A pair of strategies, each maximizing against the other, is called a *(Bayesian) equilibrium* (Rasmusen 1989, 59). It follows that at any equilibrium, $Pr\{w_B^*(Y) > 0\} = 0$. In other words, this is a *never-trade equilibrium*; there is never any exchange.

To see how this result represents unraveling, consider a specific example. Assume that $s = 1$ and that X and Y are uniformly distributed on $[0, 1]$. Fix B's threshold at b. A's value is x if A does not offer, and A's expected value is

$$EV_A = \int_0^b y \, dy + (1 - b)x = x + [b^2/2 - xb]$$

if it does. Clearly, A gains more by offering if and only if $x < b/2$. Thus, A should set its threshold at $a = b/2$. In the special case when $b = 0$, B is never willing to trade. Because A's final wealth does not depend on A's decision in this case, any choice of a is in equilibrium.

Thus, any equilibrium must have either $b = 0$ or $a = b/2$. Analogous consideration of EV_B proves that, at any equilibrium, either $a = 0$ or $b = a/2$. The intersection of these conditions is $a = b = 0$, so trading is a zero-probability event. At this never-trade equilibrium, $EV_A = EV_B = \frac{1}{2}$.

An intuitive way of thinking about this never-trade result is to imagine that one player (say, B) sets an initial threshold, b_1. Then if A should learn about b_1, A's best response is to set a threshold of $a_1 = b_1/2$. But B's best response to a_1, should B learn about a_1, is to set a new threshold $b_2 = a_1/2 = b_1/4$. Thereby, the best responses of each player to the other player's previous threshold unravel down to 0 (in the limit). Put another way, neither player can optimally respond to the other player's threshold except at $a = b = 0$, making this the unique equilibrium of the game, from which neither player would have an incentive to depart unilaterally.

The exchange game AND is a vivid example of how the presence of a second decision maker changes optimizing behavior drastically compared with the one-person game. We now generalize AND to illustrate the effects of other exchange rules, which can make for different, but equally drastic, changes in optimal behavior.

4 Generalized Exchange Games

To obtain the most general possible rule linking player choices—to offer to exchange or not—with whether or not an exchange occurs, let the probability of an exchange be

P_{AB}	if	A: Yes	and	B: Yes
P_A	if	A: Yes	and	B: No
P_B	if	A: No	and	B: Yes
P_0	if	A: No	and	B: No,

where "A: Yes" means A offers, etc. Thus AND is defined by $P_{AB} = 1$, $P_A = P_B = P_0 = 0$. To give the players some control over whether the exchange occurs, and to give meaning to their choices to assent or not, we define

$$\Delta_B = P_{AB} - P_B$$

$$\Delta_0 = P_A - P_0$$

and assume that both Δ_B and Δ_0 are nonnegative, and that at least one is strictly positive. We also make analogous assumptions for B.

Suppose that A knows x and is choosing the probability it will offer, $w_A = w_A(x)$. Assume that B's strategy is given by $w_B = w_B(Y)$. Then A's expected final value is the integral of

$$V_A = x + s\{w_A w_B P_{AB} + w_A(1 - w_B)P_A + (1 - w_A)w_B P_B$$

$$+ (1 - w_A)(1 - w_B)P_0\}(y - x)$$

$$= x + s\{P_0 + w_A(P_A - P_0) + w_B(P_B - P_0)$$

$$+ w_A w_B(P_{AB} - P_A - P_B + P_0)\}(y - x),$$

which equals

$$EV_A = x + s\{P_0 + w_A(P_A - P_0)\}(E[Y] - x)$$

$$+ s\{(P_B - P_0) + w_A(P_{AB} - P_A - P_B + P_0)\}$$

$$\times (E[Yw_B(Y)] - xE[w_B(Y)]).$$

Differentiating,

$$\frac{\partial EV_A}{\partial w_A} = s(P_A - P_0)(E[Y] - x) + s(P_{AB} - P_A - P_B + P_0)$$

$$\times (E[Yw_B(Y)] - xE[w_B(Y)])$$

$$= s\Delta_0(E[Y] - x) + s(\Delta_B - \Delta_0)(E[Yw_B(Y)] - xE[w_B(Y)]). \tag{3}$$

Clearly, this derivative is linear in x; the coefficient of x is

$$-s\Delta_0 - s(\Delta_B - \Delta_0)E[w_B(Y)] = -s\Delta_0(1 - E[w_B(Y)]) - s\Delta_B E[w_B(Y)],$$

which is strictly negative provided $0 < E[w_B(Y)] < 1$.

It follows that EV_A is an increasing function of w_A if x is less than some threshold, and a decreasing function of w_A if x exceeds that threshold. Hence, A's optimal strategy is again a threshold strategy (offer if and only if $x < a$). Analogously, B's optimal strategy is also a threshold strategy (offer if and only if $y < b$). To obtain an expression for the interrelationship of these thresholds, recall that because we assume that

$$0 < E[w_B^*(Y)] = G(b) < 1,$$

we can write

$$E[Yw_B^*(Y)] = G(b)E[Y|Y < b].$$

Substituting in (3), setting $\partial EV_A / \partial w_A = 0$, and solving for $x = a$ yields A's threshold:

$$a = \frac{\Delta_0 EY + (\Delta_B - \Delta_0)G(b)E[Y|Y < b]}{\Delta_0 + (\Delta_B - \Delta_0)G(b)}. \tag{4.1}$$

Note that a does not depend on s. Further manipulation yields other useful expressions, which we include for later reference:

$$a = \frac{\Delta_0(1 - G(b))E[Y|Y > b] + \Delta_B G(b)E[Y|Y < b]}{\Delta_0(1 - G(b)) + \Delta_B G(b)}, \tag{4.2}$$

$$a = \frac{\Delta_B \int_{-\infty}^{b} y \, dG(y) + \Delta_0 \int_{b}^{\infty} y \, dG(y)}{\Delta_B G(b) + \Delta_0(1 - G(b))}. \tag{4.3}$$

It is easy to verify that for AND, $\Delta_0 = 0$ and $\Delta_B = 1$, so (4.1) yields (2) immediately.

We next explore the implications of some other exchange rules. For convenience we will assume that the sharing fraction s equals one, since any level of sharing, $s < 1$, is strategically equivalent to full exchange, $s = 1$. In other words, individuals interested in maximizing their holdings should be willing to share with each other exactly when they would be willing to make a full exchange.

5 The OR Game

Consider the exchange rule determined by $P_{AB} = P_A = P_B = 1$, and $P_0 = 0$, so that an exchange occurs if and only if either player offers. This game we call OR because a trade is consummated if *either* player—or both—wants it. As we shall see, the equilibrium structure of OR is just as extreme as that of AND, but in the opposite direction.

Given that $0 < G(b) < 1$, substitution of $\Delta_B = 0$, $\Delta_0 = 1$ into (4.2) yields

$$a = E[Y|Y > b] > b.$$

As before, the assumption that $0 < F(a) < 1$ leads similarly to the conclusion that $b > a$. Again, this contradiction proves that there is no "intermediate" equilibrium, in which an exchange sometimes takes place and sometimes does not. It is easy to verify that any equilibrium of OR must have either $F(a) = 1$ or $G(b) = 1$. Thus, at least one player will always offer, so an exchange is certain to occur at this *always-trade equilibrium*.

In fact, what happens in OR is an upward unraveling, as can be illustrated with our example, in which X and Y are uniformly distributed on [0, 1]. Suppose that B's threshold is b. A's expected wealth is $EY = \frac{1}{2}$ if A does offer, and

$$EV_A = \int_0^b y \, dy + (1 - b)x = \frac{1}{2} + \left[(1 - b)x - \frac{1 - b^2}{2} \right]$$

if it does not. Clearly, A is better off not to offer if and only if $x > (1 + b)/2$. Of course, when $b = 1$, there will always be an exchange, making any choice of a in equilibrium in this special case.

Hence, any equilibrium must have either $b = 1$ or $a = (1 + b)/2$. Analogous consideration of EV_B shows that, at any equilibrium, either $a = 1$ or $b = (1 + a)/2$. The intersection of these conditions shows that the only possible equilibrium is $a = b = 1$, which makes an exchange certain. At this always-trade equilibrium, $EV_A = EV_B = \frac{1}{2}$.

The intuition behind this result is similar to that of AND, except that the unraveling based on best responses is in the opposite direction—the players will push trades up to the limiting threshold of 1. Only at $a = b = 1$ are the players responding optimally to each other's strategies, making this the unique equilibrium of OR.

The equilibrium results for both AND and OR can be viewed in another way: ex ante—before each player draws a number—the equilibrium strategies in these games are the only strategies that guarantee each player an expected value of at least $\frac{1}{2}$. In AND this value is assured by never trading, which each player can effect by never offering. In OR this value is assured by always trading, which each player can effect by always offering. The optimality of such conservative, guaranteed-return strategies is a distinguishing feature of constant-sum games.

6 MIX: A Probabilistic Exchange Game

In an effort to find a game that neither unravels downward (toward never trading) nor upward (toward always trading), we choose a symmetric but probabilistic exchange rule that lies between AND and OR. In MIX a number p satisfying $0 < p < 1$ is fixed. The exchange probabilities are then

$$P_{AB} = 1, \qquad P_A = P_B = p, \qquad P_0 = 0.$$

Thus, an exchange occurs for certain if both players offer, and with probability p if exactly one player offers, but never if neither player offers.

Because MIX falls within the class of generalized exchange games, A's best strategy will be a threshold strategy with threshold a, and B will similarly have an optimal threshold b. Further, if $0 < G(b) < 1$, then by (4.1),

$$a = \frac{pEY + (1 - 2p)G(b)E[Y|Y < b]}{p + (1 - 2p)G(b)} = H(b) \tag{5}$$

because $\Delta_0 = \Delta_{A|0} = p$ and $\Delta_B = \Delta_{A|B} = 1 - p$. It is obvious that in MIX with $p = \frac{1}{2}$, A's best strategy is the threshold $a = EY$. Furthermore, this is a *dominant* strategy for A, that is, A can never do better than $a = EY$, and could do worse, whatever strategy B chooses. (By comparison, the $a = b/2$ optimal threshold of AND obviously depends on b.) Similarly, $b = EX$ is a dominant strategy for B in MIX when $p = \frac{1}{2}$.

We next consider MIX Games between symmetric players—that is, we assume that $F(\cdot) = G(\cdot)$, so that X and Y are identically distributed. Of course, we already know that, for $p = \frac{1}{2}$, the optimal thresholds are $a = b = EX = EY$. We now search for equilibria for other values of p.

Any pair of equilibrium thresholds a and b must satisfy $a = H(b)$ and $b = H(a)$, where $H(\cdot)$ is as given by (5). Fix p so that $1 - 2p > 0$ (i.e., $0 < p < \frac{1}{2}$). Because of (4.3), an alternative representation of $H(\cdot)$ is

$$H(t) = \frac{(1 - p) \int_{-\infty}^{t} y \, dG(y) + p \int_{t}^{\infty} y \, dG(y)}{(1 - p)G(t) + p(1 - G(t))}. \tag{6}$$

Since we assume that EY is finite, $\lim_{t\to\infty} \int_{-\infty}^{t} y\, dG(y) = EY$, so $\lim_{t\to\infty} \int_{t}^{\infty} y\, dG(y) = 0$. This shows that

$$\lim_{t\to\infty} H(t) = EY,$$

and a parallel argument proves

$$\lim_{t\to-\infty} H(t) = EY.$$

Finally, fix t so that $0 < G(t) < 1$. It is clear that $E[Y\,|\,Y < t] < EY$, so

$$pEY + (1 - 2p)G(t)E[Y\,|\,Y < t] < [p + (1 - 2p)G(t)]EY,$$

which demonstrates, because of (5), that $H(t) < EY$.

We have shown so far that $H(t) < EY$ for $0 < G(t) < 1$, and that $H(t) \to EY$ as $t \to \infty$ or $t \to -\infty$. It is easy to verify that $H(t) \le EY$ for all t. We now find a value $t = t^*$ where $H(t)$ is a minimum.

From (6) the derivative of the numerator of $H(t)$ is

$$(1 - p)tg(t) - ptg(t) = (1 - 2p)tg(t),$$

where $g(t)$ is the probability density function (pdf) of $Y = X$. Analogously, the derivative of the denominator of $H(t)$ is $(1 - 2p)g(t)$. Therefore, the sign of $H'(t)$ is the same as that of

$$(1 - 2p)tg(t)\left\{(1 - p)\int_{-\infty}^{t} dG(y) + p\int_{t}^{\infty} dG(y)\right\}$$

$$- (1 - 2p)g(t)\left\{(1 - p)\int_{-\infty}^{t} y\, dG(y) + p\int_{t}^{\infty} y\, dG(y)\right\},$$

because the denominator of $H(t)$ is strictly positive. Consequently, whenever $g(t) > 0$, $H'(t)$ has the same sign as

$$(1 - p)\int_{-\infty}^{t} (t - y)\, dG(y) - p\int_{t}^{\infty} (y - t)\, dG(y). \tag{7}$$

Expression 7 is clearly negative for t small enough, and positive for t large enough. Furthermore, (7) is strictly increasing over the support of Y: if $t_0 < t_1$ and $0 < G(t_0) \le G(t_1) < 1$, then

$$(1 - p)\int_{-\infty}^{t_1} (t_1 - y)\, dG(y) - p\int_{t_1}^{\infty} (y - t_1)\, dG(y)$$

$$> (1 - p) \int_{-\infty}^{t_0} (t_1 - y)\, dG(y) - \int_{t_1}^{\infty} (y - t_0)\, dG(y)$$

$$> (1 - p) \int_{-\infty}^{t_0} (t_0 - y)\, dG(y) - \int_{t_0}^{\infty} (y - t_0)\, dG(y).$$

Therefore, there is a unique value t^* where (7) vanishes.

We have now shown that $H(t)$ is decreasing for $t < t^*$ and increasing for $t > t^*$. But there is more, because at $t = t^*$,

$$(1 - p) \int_{-\infty}^{t^*} y\, dG(y) + p \int_{t^*}^{\infty} y\, dG(y)$$

$$= (1 - p) \int_{-\infty}^{t^*} t^*\, dG(y) + p \int_{t^*}^{\infty} t^*\, dG(y)$$

$$= t^*\{(1 - p)G(t^*) + p(1 - G(t^*))\},$$

which shows, by (6), that $H(t^*) = t^*$.

In fact, the equation $H(t) = t$ has no solutions other than $t = t^*$. To verify this, note from (6) that $H(t) = t$ implies that expression (7) vanishes, or that $t = t^*$. Therefore, the unique symmetric equilibrium of the game is given by $a = b = t^*$.

Finally, we prove that symmetric MIX has no nonsymmetric equilibria. Assume that $a = H(b)$ and $b = H(a)$, where $a \neq b$. First $H(t)$ has its absolute minimum at $t = t^*$, so $a = H(b) \geq H(t^*) = t^*$. But $a = t^*$ implies $b = H(a) = H(t^*) = t^*$, so $a > t^*$ is required. Analogously, so is $b > t^*$. But $H(t) \leq t$ for $t > t^*$, so that

$$b = H(a) \leq a = H(b) \leq b.$$

The contradictory conclusion that $a = b$ proves that there are no non-symmetric equilibria.

If we had assumed $1 - 2p < 0$, all of the above conclusions would still follow, except that $H(t) \geq EY$, with $t = t^*$ the absolute maximum of $H(t)$. Thus, any symmetric MIX has a unique "intermediate" equilibrium, which involves sometimes offering and sometimes not.

To illustrate these ideas, we apply them to MIX when X and Y are uniformly distributed on $[0, 1]$. Suppose that A draws x and must decide whether to offer to exchange. Assume that B's threshold is b. If A does not offer, A receives x with probability $[1 - p \Pr\{Y < b\}]$ and Y otherwise, so A's expected value is

$$(1 - pb)x + pb^2/2.$$

If A does offer, A receives x with probability $[(1 - p)\,Pr\{Y \geq b\}]$ and Y otherwise, so A's expected value is

$$(1 - p)(1 - b)x + [\tfrac{1}{2} - (1 - p)(1 - b^2)/2].$$

Subtracting, A's expected gain from offering is

$$T(x) = (p + b^2 - 2pb^2)/2 - (p + b - 2pb)x.$$

Next suppose that $p = \tfrac{1}{2}$. Then $T(x) = \tfrac{1}{2}(\tfrac{1}{2} - x)$, which makes it clear that A should offer if and only if $x < \tfrac{1}{2}$. In other words, a threshold of $\tfrac{1}{2}$ is A's dominant strategy—it is best for A regardless of what B does.

But now suppose that $p \neq \tfrac{1}{2}$. Then $T(x)$ is positive if and only if

$$x < \frac{1}{2}\left(\frac{p + b^2 - 2pb^2}{p + b - 2pb}\right). \tag{8}$$

The right side of (8) is thus the threshold that is A's best response to b. In fact, by evaluating the integrals directly in (6), it can be shown that the right side of (8) is precisely $H(b)$. Figure 10.1 displays the graph of $H(t)$ for the case $p = 1/5$. Note that $H(0) = H(1) = EY = \tfrac{1}{2}$ for $0 < t < 1$, and that the absolute minimum of $H(t)$ occurs uniquely at the point $t = t^*$, where $H(t^*) = t^*$.

As we know from the analysis of symmetric MIX, the unique equilibrium of this game occurs at the thresholds $a = b = t^*$. In this case, $H(t) = t$ if and only if

$$Q(t) = (1 - p)t^2 + (2p)t - p = 0.$$

The zero of $Q(t)$, satisfying $0 < t < 1$, is

$$t^*(p) = \begin{cases} \dfrac{1}{2} & \text{if } p = \dfrac{1}{2} \\[2ex] \dfrac{-p + \sqrt{p - p^2}}{1 - 2p} & \text{if } p \neq \dfrac{1}{2}. \end{cases}$$

The graph of $t^*(p)$ is shown in figure 10.2. Note that any value of t^* can be achieved by the appropriate value of p.

To illustrate the effects of the choice of p, note that when $p = 1/5$, $t^* = 1/3$. The probability of an exchange in this case is

$$\left(\frac{1}{3}\right)\left(\frac{1}{3}\right) + 2\left[\left(\frac{1}{3}\right)\left(\frac{2}{3}\right)\right]\left(\frac{1}{5}\right) = \frac{1}{5}, \tag{9}$$

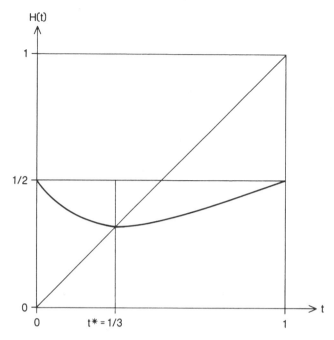

Figure 10.1
The function $H[t]$ when $p = 1/5$

or the sum of the probabilities that either (i) both players offer or (ii) one player offers and the other player does not (two cases—either player could make the offer) times the probability (p) that a single offer is sufficient for an exchange.

It is no accident that this probability equals $p = 1/5$. In fact, the equation $Q(t) = 0$ can be rewritten as

$$t^2 + 2[t(1 - t)]p = p,$$

which is identical in form to (9); it says that the solution $t = t^*$ given above ensures that when one player offers and the other player does not, the conditional probability that there will be an exchange p is equal to the unconditional probability of an exhange. In other words, an equilibrium exists exactly when there is equality between the conditional and unconditional probabilities—the former probability, in effect, does not depend on the conditioning factor.

We end this section with an example illustrating that the equilibexchange games are not always symmetric. Consider the exch

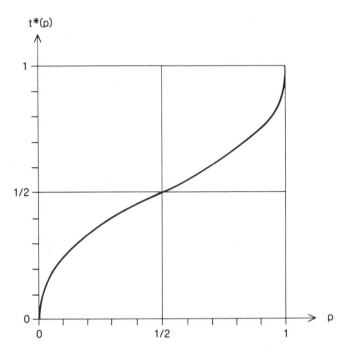

Figure 10.2
The function $t^*[p]$

$P_{AB} = 1$, $P_A = .5$, $P_B = P_0 = 0$. Using (4.2), it is easy to show that when X and Y are uniformly distributed on $[0, 1]$, this game has a unique equilibrium consisting of thresholds satisfying

$$a = \frac{1 + b^2}{2(1 + b)}, \qquad b = \frac{a}{2}.$$

Then unique root of this system of equations is

$$a = \frac{2\sqrt{7} - 4}{}05, \qquad b = \frac{\sqrt{7} - 2}{3} \cong .2153.$$

resholds of asymmetric games need not be equal.
e posit the nonconstant-sum exchange game PLUS,
sses from trading are attenuated. In encouraging
US also creates a dilemma for the players in their
es.

7   PLUS: A Nonconstant-Sum Exchange Game

Consider AND, and assume that there is an exchange: A receives y and B receives x after the exchange. We now modify AND so that if, say, y is the smaller number, A does not receive y but $x - k(x - y)$, where $0 \leq k \leq 1$ is a constant. (Hence, A cannot receive less than y.) We call this game—in which the loser does not generally receive the smaller initial endowment but instead has some deduction, $k(x - y)$, made from the larger one— "PLUS." If $k = 1$ (maximum deduction), PLUS is AND; if $k = 0$ (no deduction), both players end up with the larger wealth, x.

In section 3 we showed that never-trade is the unique equilibrium of AND. When $k = 0$, on the other hand, it is apparent that one equilibrium in PLUS is always-trade, because either player's deviation would prevent it from *always* receiving the larger of the two numbers drawn. Moreover, because the players never do worse, and sometimes do better, by always offering to trade when $k = 0$, their strategies associated with this equilibrium are dominant.

But what are the equilibria when $0 < k < 1$? As in MIX, are there intermediate thresholds that are in equilibrium? The answer, surprisingly, is no, even though PLUS is a nonconstant-sum game and both players can, on average, benefit by always offering to trade, at least ex ante.

Specifically, if $0 < k \leq 1$, the unique equilibrium is never-trade. We simplify the calculations by assuming that Y is uniformly distributed on $[0, 1]$, and that B has chosen a threshold b satisfying $0 \leq b \leq 1$.

Suppose that A's initial wealth is x. If A does not offer, its final wealth will be x. If A does offer, there will be an exchange if and only if $Y < b$. Suppose first that $x > b$. Then A will be the loser in any exchange, so its expected final wealth will be

$$x(1 - b) + \int_0^b [x - k(x - y)]\, dy = x(1 - kb) + kb^2/2.$$

But now suppose $x < b$. Then A will be the winner in an exchange, receiving final wealth Y whenever $x \leq Y < b$, whereas A will be the loser and receive $x - k(x - y)$ whenever $Y < x$. Thus, A's expected final wealth when $x < b$ will be

$$x(1 - b) + \int_x^b y\, dy + \int_0^x [x - k(x - y)]\, dy$$

$$= (1 - k)x^2/2 + x(1 - b) + b^2/2.$$

It follows that A's expected net gain from offering is

$$J(x) = \begin{cases} -kbx + kb^2/2 & \text{if } x > b \\ (1-k)x^2/2 - bx + b^2/2 & \text{if } x \leq b. \end{cases}$$

Now A should offer precisely when $J(x)$ is positive. Notice that $J(b) = -kb^2/2 < 0$ if $b > 0$. Furthermore, $J'(x) < 0$ for $x > b$, so clearly $J(x) < 0$ for $x \geq b$. On the other hand, $J(0) = b^2/2 > 0$; the fact that $J(x)$ is quadratic on $[0, b]$ thus means that there is a unique root a such that $J(x) \geq 0$ if and only if $x \geq a$, with equality if and only if $x = a$. In fact, the required root of the quadratic can easily be seen to be .

$$a = b\left[\frac{1 - \sqrt{k}}{1 - k}\right] = \frac{b}{1 + \sqrt{k}}.$$

Like AND, PLUS unravels, because $a < b$ whenever $k > 0$. Thus, in the symmetric game in which X is also uniformly distributed on $[0, 1]$, the only equilibrium is $a = b = 0$—never-trade. Thus, short of both players profiting equally when $k = 0$, the players in PLUS never trade at equilibrium.

At the never-trade equilibrium, the players' expected final values are $\frac{1}{2}$. But this unique equilibrium is *Pareto-inferior* in the sense that it is possible for both players to do better, on average, by credibly committing to trade sometimes.

How can a player guarantee more than $\frac{1}{2}$? Assume B *publicly* announces b, offering to exchange any number below this threshold. Moreover, assume that the choice of this strategy can be enforced, perhaps by having B show its number to some third party and having that third party select or confirm B's strategy choice.

Assume A responds optimally to B's announcement by choosing $a = b/(1 + \sqrt{k})$. A's expected payoff, based on the calculation for the case $x \leq b$, is

$$EV_A = \frac{1}{2} + \left(\frac{1}{2}\right)\left[\frac{b}{\sqrt{k}}\right]^3 (-2k + \sqrt{k} + 3),$$

which is greater than $\frac{1}{2}$ except when $b = 0$.

When we make the analogous calculation for B, we obtain

$$EV_B = \frac{1}{2} + \left(\frac{1}{6}\right)\left[\frac{b}{1 + \sqrt{k}}\right]^3 (-3k^2 - 3k^{3/2} - k + 1).$$

The sign of $EV_B - \frac{1}{2}$ is the same as that of

$$-3k^2 - 3k^{3/2} - k + 1,$$

which can be shown to have exactly one zero in $[0, 1]$, at $k \cong .288$. For $k < .288$, therefore, $EV_B > \frac{1}{2}$, so B maximizes EV_B by setting $b = 1$, or always offering to exchange. On the other hand, if $k > .288$, B maximizes EV_B by setting $b = 0$, or never offering to exchange.

Notice that this calculation is entirely consistent with our finding that the unique equilibrium of PLUS is never-trade. A public announcement by B of any threshold other than $b = 0$ is not in equilibrium, and B could do better by resetting its threshold to maximize against A. But if this process starts, the game will unravel back to never-trade. Hence PLUS may result in a Prisoner's Dilemma, whereby both players do better by "cooperating," but this outcome is not in equilibrium. Nevertheless, as we showed in the previous paragraph, a commitment always to offer by one player, with the other responding optimally, may yield the first player (as well as the responder) a greater payoff than at the unique equilibrium, never-trade.

8   Summary and Conclusions

We have analyzed four games, in each of which two players independently draw numbers that represent initial endowments. Each player can then choose to offer or not offer to exchange its number for the other player's. A player's payoff is the number (i.e., wealth) the player holds after all players have made their choices and a possible exchange has occurred (except in PLUS). We summarize the rules that determine the conditions for an exchange, each player's payoff, and the equilibrium outcomes in the different games:

(1) AND: Both players must offer to exchange in order for a trade to occur. The unique equilibrium is that neither player will ever offer, no matter how low the player's number is.

(2) OR: One player's offer is sufficient for a trade to occur. The unique equilibrium is that each player will always offer, no matter how high its number is.

(3) MIX: Both players must offer in order for a trade to occur with certainty; if only one player offers, a trade occurs with probability p. The unique equilibrium is for the players to select a particular common threshold —below which they will always offer—that is monotonically (but not linearly) increasing in p. When $p = \frac{1}{2}$, the players have dominant strategies of choosing a threshold of $\frac{1}{2}$. When $p = 0$, MIX is AND, and when $p = 1$, MIX is OR.

(4) PLUS: Same as AND, except the payoff to the loser if a trade occurs is a number between the lower and the higher numbers drawn. Hence, there is a subsidy to the loser, and the game is nonconstant-sum. Like AND, the unique Nash equilibrium in this game is for the players never to trade, except in the degenerate case when both receive a payoff equal to the higher number after the trade.

We demonstrated in PLUS that if the payoff to the loser after trading is sufficiently close to the higher number, a player can do better always offering to trade, even if exploited by its opponent. Thereby, PLUS highlights a conflict between the criterion of stability—as embodied in the concept of equilibrium—and the criterion of maximization of expected value. The latter, as we have shown, may be satisfied by choosing a non-equilibrium strategy, including the strategy of always offering to trade.

Unraveling surely occurs in the world, although perhaps not as inexorably or as completely as in the games we have analyzed. The direction and extent of unraveling are very sensitive to the game being played. AND and OR illustrate this, and MIX shows a combination in which both upward and downward unraveling are arrested to a degree. PLUS, on the other hand, indicates that strategic forces may be powerful enough to resist the effects of risk-reducing subsidies, leading once again to complete unraveling.

The games we have analyzed mirror simple and highly stylized exchanges. Nonetheless, with refinements they may be useful in modeling real-life strategic processes, enhancing our understanding of conditions under which unraveling is likely to occur.

References

Bollobás, Béla, ed. 1986. *Littlewood's Miscellany*. Cambridge: Cambridge University Press.

da Costa Werlang, Sergio Ribeiro. 1989. "Common Knowledge." In *The New Palgrave: Game Theory*, 74–85. New York: Norton.

Milgrom, Paul, and Nancy Stokey. 1982. "Information, Trade, and Common Knowledge." *Journal of Economic Theory* 26(1):17–27.

Monderer, Dov, and Dov Samet. 1990. "Proximity of Information Structures in Games with Incomplete Information." Working paper 63/9, Israel Institute of Business Research, Tel Aviv University.

Rasmusen, Eric. 1989. *Games and Information: An Introduction to Game Theory*. New York: Basil Blackwell.

11   Does Evolution Eliminate Dominated Strategies?

Larry Samuelson

1 Introduction

The requirement that weakly dominated strategies not be played is often considered an essential feature of both a theory of rational decision making and a refinement of the Nash equilibrium concept.[1] Kohlberg and Mertens (1986), for example, attach considerable importance to weak dominance. Many game theory texts (such as Moulin 1986) first present dominance and iterated dominance arguments as the obvious characterization of rational choice, and resort to constructions such as the Nash equilibrium only after dominance arguments are found not to solve all games. Dekel and Fudenberg (1991, 245) comment that the iterated deletion of weakly dominated strategies "clearly incorporates certain intuitive beliefs about rationality postulates." Normal-form perfection, one of the weakest refinements of Nash equilibrium, is equivalent (in two-player games) to requiring that one restrict attention to Nash equilibria in strategies that are not weakly dominated.

In spite of the intuitive appeal of weak-dominance arguments, a theoretical justification of weak dominance has been elusive. Kohlberg and Mertens (1986), for example, find it much easier to motivate strict than weak dominance. The small probabilities of a mistake that are often employed to drive weak-dominance arguments are not easily reconciled with the perfectly rational agents that appear in most formal game theory.

A common response is to suggest that evolutionary arguments will suffice to eliminate weakly dominated strategies. In particular, the strategies that are initially played in an evolutionary model (but are eventually eliminated by evolution) are said to be analogous to trembles, causing strategies that are weakly dominated to earn strictly lower payoffs than those which dominate them, and hence causing the former to be eliminated.

This chapter investigates the question: Does evolution eliminate weakly dominated strategies? We find that in general, the answer is no. Evolutionary models do not provide a foundation for the elimination of weakly dominated strategies. In light of this, the common insistence on weak-dominance arguments in equilibrium refinements may not be as intuitively obvious as it first appears.

Section 2 presents the model. We provide intuitive discussions of most results but only citations to proofs, which can be found elsewhere. We note that the common notion of an evolutionarily stable strategy precludes dominated strategies when it exists, but that it fails existence too often to provide a foundation for eliminating dominated strategies. In light of this, section 3 examines dynamic models of evolution. These dynamic models again fail to eliminate dominated strategies. However, dominated strategies appear to survive because the models make insufficient provision for mutations. Section 4 accordingly expands these models to make provision for mutations, but again finds that dominated strategies survive. Sections 5 and 6 investigate the forces that drive this result by examining a finite model. Section 7 concludes.

2   ESS and Dominated Strategies

We examine two-player normal-form games. We let such a game be denoted $(\{1, 2\}, I, J, \pi_1, \pi_2)$, where the players are denoted 1 and 2; the pure strategy sets for players 1 and 2 (respectively) are denoted I and J, and player i's ($i = 1, 2$) payoff function is given by $\pi_i : I \times J \to \mathbb{R}$. Let the cardinalities of I and J be denoted n_1 and n_2. We say that the game is *symmetric* if $I = J$ and $\pi_1(i, j) = \pi_2(j, i) \equiv \pi(i, j)$, and if strategy choices cannot be conditioned on whether one is player 1 or player 2. We say that strategy i *dominates* i' for player 1 (player 2 is similar) if, for all $j \in J$,

$$\pi_1(i, j) \geq \pi_1(i', j) \tag{1}$$

with strict inequality for at least one $j \in$ in J.[2]

We now think of this game as being embedded in an evolutionary system in which members of large populations of players 1 and 2 are randomly and repeatedly matched to play the game. We use the terms *population* and *player* interchangeably, and refer to the members of the populations as "agents."

We first consider the widely used notion of an *evolutionarily stable strategy*, or ESS (Maynard Smith 1982). For a symmetric game, a strategy i^* is an ESS if, for all $i \in I$,

$$\pi(i^*, i^*) \geq \pi(i, i^*) \tag{2}$$

$$\pi(i^*, i^*) = \pi(i, i^*) \quad \Rightarrow \quad \pi(i^*, i) > \pi(i, i). \tag{3}$$

To interpret these conditions, suppose that i^* is an ESS and that proportion ε of the population switches to the mutant strategy i. As long as ε is sufficiently small, conditions 2–3 ensure that strategy i^* will earn a higher payoff than i, presumably causing an unmodeled process of evolutionary selection to eliminate i from the population.

If the game is asymmetric, then it is common to "symmetrize" the game by embedding it in a larger, symmetric game in which nature first randomly assigns the players to roles, with each player equally likely to play either role. The ESS concept is then applied to this expanded game, where a strategy for a player includes a specification of what the player will choose in either role. Proposition 1 follows immediately from the definition of an ESS.

PROPOSITION 1　If i^* is an ESS in either a symmetric or asymmetric game, then i^* cannot be dominated.

Proposition 1 holds because if i' dominates i^*, then i^* must be at least as good a reply as i^* to both i^* and i', preventing (2) and (3) from holding.

Proposition 1 appears to provide an immediate, positive answer to the question of whether evolution eliminates dominated strategies. The difficulty, however, is that in many games an ESS fails to exist, which leads us to:

PROPOSITION 2　A Nash equilibrium in an asymmetric game is an ESS if and only if it is a strict Nash equilibrium (Selten 1983). A Nash equilibrium in a symmetric or asymmetric game that induces an equilibrium in an extensive-form game with unreached information sets fails to be an ESS (Swinkels 1990).

In many games that are important in economics, such as games with non-trivial extensive-form structures, an ESS will thus not exist.

A failure of existence by itself would not be cause for concern. For example, strictly dominant strategies often fail to exist, but this causes us no qualms about endorsing strictly dominant strategies when they do exist. The difficulty is twofold. First, consider asymmetric games. An ESS then fails to exist whenever interesting questions concerning dominated strategies arise. In particular, questions of dominance are most interesting when there exists a Nash equilibrium in which some player's strategy is dominated. In this case, the equilibrium will fail to be strict, and an ESS will generally not exist, so that the ESS concept provides no insight into the question of dominance.

Second, an ESS often fails to exist in games in which evolutionary arguments appear to have considerable force, suggesting that the ESS does not
appear to be an effective model of evolution. Consider the following game,
which will be a standard example throughout this paper:

$$
\begin{array}{c|cc}
 & \multicolumn{2}{c}{2} \\
 & L & R \\
\hline
T & 1,1 & 1,0 \\
B & 1,1 & 0,0 \\
\end{array}
$$

This asymmetric game has no strict Nash equilibrium, and hence no ESS.
Notice, however, that L strictly dominates R for player 2. One would then
expect an evolutionary process to eliminate R from population 2. The
outcome for population 1 is less clear. T dominates B, but the dominance
is only weak, with the payoff difference disappearing as population 2
agents switch to L. Will evolution yield an outcome in which all population
1 agents play L, or an outcome in which some population 1 agents play R?
This is precisely the question of weak dominance in which we are interested. Evolution thus appears to have something to say in games that fail
to have an ESS, but it is not clear what implications evolution has for
dominated strategies in such games. We pursue these implications in the
following section by constructing a dynamic model.

3   Dynamics

The comments of the previous section suggest that we require a more
effective model of evolutionary considerations than the ESS. The obvious
place to turn is to dynamic models of the evolutionary process. Let x_t be a
vector in the n_1-dimension simplex that identifies the proportions of the
agents in population 1 playing each of the pure strategies in I at time t. Let
y_t be a vector in the n_2-dimension simplex giving the proportion of agents
in population 2 playing each of the pure strategies in J at time t. Then we
examine dynamic systems of the form:

$$
\frac{dx_i(t)}{dt} = f_i(x(t), y(t)), \qquad i \in I \tag{4}
$$

$$
\frac{dy_j(t)}{dt} = g_j(x(t), y(t)), \qquad j \in J, \tag{5}
$$

where $f_i(x, y)$ and $g_j(x, y)$ are assumed to be Lipschitz-continuous, to equal
zero for strategies played by no agents in the population, to be such

that the system remains within the simplex, and to be such that $\lim_{x_i \to 0} f_i(x, y)/x_i$ and $\lim_{y_j \to 0} g_j(x, y)/x_j$ exist and are finite for all $i \in I$ and $j \in J$. The process given by (4)–(5) is said to be a *selection dynamic*.

Game-theoretic considerations enter this model through assumptions on the characteristics of the functions $f_i(x, y)$ and $g_j(x, y)$. We assume that $f_i(x, y)$ and $g_j(x, y)$ are *monotonic* (see Samuelson and Zhang 1992), which is to say, that if strategy i for player 1 currently earns a higher average payoff than i', then the growth rate of i (derived from (4)) exceeds that of i'. Hence, more successful strategies tend to prosper at the expense of less successful strategies. Perhaps the best-known example of a monotonic system is the replicator dynamics, borrowed from biology (see Hofbauer and Sigmund 1988).

It is well known that every ESS is asymptotically stable under the (monotonic) replicator dynamics, while the converse of this statement does not hold.[3] The limiting outcomes of monotonic selection dynamics thus provide a more general model of evolutionary considerations than does the ESS, just as we require. How do dominated strategies fare under monotonic selection dynamics? We require a stability notion to address this.

We will state that an outcome (x^*, y^*) is *stable* if, for every neighborhood V of (x^*, y^*), there exists a neighborhood U with $(x^*, y^*) \in U \subseteq V$ such that if the dynamic process begins in U, then its path remains in V. The outcome (x^*, y^*) is *asymptotically stable* if there exists a neighborhood U with $(x^*, y^*) \in U$ such that if the dynamic process begins in U, then it converges to (x^*, y^*). It is now easy to show

PROPOSITION 3   The set of stable outcomes under any monotonic selection mechanism for game G1 is the set of all outcomes (x, y) in which y allocates unitary probability to L. The set of asymptotically stable outcomes for (G1) under a monotonic selection dynamic is empty.

To see why the set of asymptotically stable outcomes is empty, notice that the only candidates for such points are those in which all population 2 agents play L. However, one possible perturbation of such a point consists of slightly altering the proportion of population 1 agents playing B. As long as all population 2 agents continue to play L, then no pressure for movement will be created by this perturbation and the system will not converge back to the point of departure. This precludes asymptotic stability and ensures that the set of asymptotically stable outcomes is empty. Next notice that any outcome in which all population 2 agents play L is stable because any slight perturbation away from such a point, including one to a state in which some population 2 agents play R, will result in convergence to a new point in which all population 2 agents again play L, and therefore the proportion of population 1 agents playing B will not be too different (given the continuity of the selection mechanism) from the point of departure.

Monotonic selection dynamics for game G1 thus give either an empty outcome or an outcome that embraces dominated strategies. This result is not limited to game G1. In general, the requirements for asymptotic stability are only slightly weaker than those for a strict Nash equilibrium (for example, Samuelson and Zhang (1991) show that any pure-strategy asymptotically stable outcome must be strict), so that asymptotically stable outcomes do not exist in many interesting games. In addition, stable outcomes do not preclude dominated strategies in general.

The interpretation of these results depends upon which stability notion is thought to be appropriate. If one requires asymptotic stability, then there can be little progress beyond the nonexistence problems of the ESS. Embracing stability as the preferred notion alleviates the existence problem, but we must then conclude that evolutionary outcomes do not preclude dominated strategies.

4   Dynamics with Error

It may initially be surprising that stable outcomes under a monotonic selection dynamic, such as a replicator dynamic, can include dominated strategies. If we make the innocuous assumption that the dynamics begin at an interior point, so that all strategies are played by some proportion of the population, then the continuity of the growth rates derived from equations 4–5 ensures that all strategies will *always* be played by some (possibly very small) proportion of the population, with strategies only asymptotically eliminated. The possibly small proportions of the populations playing each of the game's pure strategies are reminiscent of the small trembles that appear in the notion of a normal-form perfect equilibrium, and might similarly be expected to banish dominated strategies. How can dominated strategies then survive?

The stable outcomes for game G1 include any outcome in which all population 2 agents play L. Among these outcomes, the outcome in which all population 1 agents play T appears to be "more stable" than the rest. To see this, consider an outcome, denoted (x', y'), in which population 2 agents all play L and population 1 agents are split between T and B. Consider a system that begins at (x', y') and then suffers a small disturbance that (temporarily) introduces agents into population 2 who play R. The evolutionary dynamics will converge to a point near (x', y'), with R being eliminated, but in the process of this convergence there will be selection pressure against strategy B. The new point will then feature fewer agents playing B than (x', y'). A succession of such shocks will push the system ever closer to the outcome (x^*, y^*) in which population 1 (2) agents play T (L). The outcome (T, L) thus appears to be "more stable" than the other stable outcomes.

The succession of shocks in this story might be interpreted as mutations in an evolutionary model. Notice that monotonic selection dynamics such as the replicator dynamics capture a stylized learning process, but make no provision for mutation. It appears to be precisely the addition of mutations that is needed to banish dominated strategies.

In light of this, we expand our model to make provision for mutations. We modify the dynamics given by (4)–(5) to:

$$\frac{dx_i(t)}{dt} = (1 - \delta_1)f_i(x, y) + \delta_1(\xi_i - x_i) \tag{6}$$

$$\frac{dy_j(t)}{dt} = (1 - \delta_2)g_j(x, y) + \delta_2(\eta_j - y_j), \tag{7}$$

where $\xi_i, \eta_j \in (0, 1)$ and $\sum_{i \in I} \xi_i = \sum_{j \in J} \eta_j = 1$. We think of δ_k as being the death rate of population k. From (6)–(7) we see that the distribution of strategies among surviving members of the population evolves according to a monotonic selection dynamic. However, these members die at the rate δ_k and are replaced by entrants whose strategies are given by the distribution ξ or η.

Let (x^*, y^*) be called a "rest point" of (6)–(7) if (x^*, y^*) gives $dx^*/dt = dy^*/dt = 0$. We are interested in cases in which mistakes in transmission occur but do so relatively infrequently. The appropriate object for study is then the limit of the rest points of the system as the δ_k approach zero. Let such points be called "limit rest points."

It is now interesting to consider the following variant of game G1:

		2	
		L	R
1	T	1, 1	1, 1
	B	1, 1	0, 0

Game G2 has a single equilibrium in undominated strategies, given by (T, L). Samuelson and Zhang (1991) show the following:

PROPOSITION 4.   Let the selection mechanism be monotonic. Then

(4.1) Any limit rest point is a Nash equilibrium, but a limit rest point need not be perfect (i.e., need not exclude dominated strategies).

(4.2) Consider the replicator dynamics and let δ_{1n} and δ_{2n} be sequences such that $\lim_{\delta \to \infty} \delta_{1n}/\delta_{2n} \equiv \Lambda$. Then the limit rest point in (G1) is (T, L) if and only if $\Lambda = \infty$. The limit rest point in (G2) is (T, L) if and only if $\Lambda = (1 - \eta_R)/(1 - \xi_B)$.

To see why this result holds, consider statement 4.2 and game G2. Without trembles an outcome in which the dominated strategy R is played can appear because there will be selection pressure against R only if some members of population 1 play B. However, B may be eliminated in the limit, removing the pressure against R and allowing R to survive. The mutations embedded in (6)–(7) address this by ensuring that some members of population 1 always tremble to B, maintaining the pressure against R. Unfortunately, these trembles have the effect of introducing pressure not only *against* R but also *toward* B. The elimination of dominated strategies requires that both R and B be banished from the system, and this can occur only if the trembles to B are large enough to eliminate R, but not so large to preserve B. Similarly, the trembles to R must be large enough to eliminate B, but not so large as to preserve R. These objectives can be simultaneously satisfied only in the special case in which the tremble probabilities are chosen so that $\Lambda = (1 - \eta_R)/(1 - \xi_B)$.

Hence, the addition of mutations to our model produces an outcome that eliminates dominated strategies only if the probabilities of these mutations take a very specific form. Furthermore, this form must be tailored to the game in question, as is seen in the differing results for games G1 and G2. A theory that evolutionary considerations will eliminate dominated strategies if, but only if, a specific evolutionary process is constructed for each game does not provide a convincing argument for the elimination of dominated strategies. We are again left with the conclusion that evolutionary arguments do not suffice to eliminate dominated strategies.

5   Markov Dynamics

The previous section shows that the addition of mutations to our evolutionary model does not suffice to purge the limiting outcome of dominated strategies. Notice, however, that we have added these mutations in a quite mechanical way. In particular, we began with a deterministic system of differential equations. These are presumably generated by a stochastic matching process, with some sort of (unspecified) law-of-large-numbers argument transforming this stochastic matching process into deterministic dynamics. We then observed that the resulting system does not make adequate provision for random events. We responded by explicitly introducing a mutation process to capture these random events, but this introduction took the form of attaching a deterministic "error term" onto the deterministic replicator dynamics. It is then not at all clear that we have actually captured the desired random mutation process.

What is needed is to more carefully model the stochastic nature of the evolutionary process rather than to sweep this under the law-of-large-numbers rug. This section constructs a finite model featuring an explicit, stochastic mutation process. The model exploits techniques introduced in Kandori, Mailath, and Rob 1990.

5.1 Selection

We again have two populations, although it is now more convenient to denote strategy sets by S_1 and S_2. We assume that each population is composed of Δ identical agents, where Δ is finite. Let t index the iterations of the matching process and play of the game. At each time t, each agent will be characterized by a pure strategy. The state of the system at time t then identifies, for each population $\alpha \ (= 1, 2)$ and each strategy $x \in S_\alpha$, the number of agents of population α playing pure strategy x (denoted $\theta_{\alpha x}$ or $\theta_{\alpha x}(t)$, but with t generally suppressed). Hence, a state is an element of the form $((\theta_{11}, \ldots, \theta_{1|S_1|}), (\theta_{21}, \ldots, \theta_{2|S_2|}))$ the property that for all $\alpha \in N$ and all $x \in S_\alpha$, $\theta_{\alpha x}$ is nonnegative and $\sum_{x \in S_\alpha} \theta_{\alpha x} = \Delta$. We let θ denote the set of states. We use θ, i, j, and k to refer to states. We assume that the matching process is specified by a uniform distribution over each of the possible matching configurations, that is, over each of the possible ways that the Δ agents of each population can be matched into pairs containing one agent from each population.

As the agents play the game, they may switch strategies in light of their experience. Let the process by which agents switch between strategies be called a "selection mechanism." A selection mechanism is then a transition matrix defined on the state space θ that identifies, for each state that the system might occupy at time t, the probability that the system moves to each of the various states in θ in period $t + 1$. Hence, a selection mechanism is a transition matrix

$$P \equiv \left\{ p_{ij}, i, j, \varepsilon \Theta : p_{ij} \geq 0, \sum_{j \in \theta} p_{ij} = 1 \right\}. \tag{8}$$

Notice that transition probabilities depend on all of the information contained in the current state, which includes a specification of the number of agents of each population playing each strategy, so that the probability of players in population α switching from strategy x_α to y_α can depend upon factors such as the number playing x_α, the number playing y_α, and the payoffs of x_α, y_α, and other strategies.

The transition probabilities will generally be linked to payoffs, and it is again through this link that familiar game theoretic considerations enter the analysis. It may be helpful to consider an example of a selection mechanism. Suppose that in each period t, each agent in each population takes an independent draw from a binomial random variable. With probability $1 - \mu$, this draw produces the outcome "do not learn" or "do not adjust," and the agent does not change strategies. With probability μ, this draw produces the outcome "learn" or "adjust," in which case the agent switches to a best response to the period t actions of the agents in other populations. (If there is more than one best response, the agent switches to each of them with positive probability). From this model of individual agent behavior the probabilities p_{ij} that describe the aggregate behavior of the system can be calculated. We refer to this as the "best-response dynamics with inertia." We find the best-response dynamics with inertia intuitively appealing, although our results below require weaker restrictions on the selection mechanism.

5.2   Mutation

We now add mutations to this model. Intuitively, we think of the evolutionary process as proceeding as follows. At time t, nature chooses a matching of agents from the probability distribution over such matchings. The agents then play the game and receive their payoffs. Giving this matching and payoffs, the selection mechanism causes some agents to switch strategies. Mutations then occur. Formally, mutations will take the form of further switches in agents' strategies. We can think of this as agents actually mutating (or experimenting) to new strategies or as agents leaving the game and being replaced by new agents whose strategies are chosen according to the mutation process.

We assume that the process of mutation is independent across agents. Consider an agent from population α playing strategy $x_\alpha \in S_\alpha$ at the end of period t (i.e., after selection has occurred). With probability $1 - \lambda$, for $\lambda \in (0, 1)$, no mutation occurs on this agent, and the agent continues to play strategy x_α. With probability λ, this agent undergoes a mutation, in which case the agent switches to each strategy $y_\alpha \in S_\alpha$ with probability $f_\alpha(x_\alpha, y_\alpha) > 0$, where $f_\alpha : S_\alpha \times S_\alpha \to (0, 1)$.

The conjunction of the selection and mutation mechanisms gives us an overall transition matrix between states which we denote Γ. To construct the elements of Γ, define $P(i) \equiv \{k \in \theta : p_{ik} > 0\}$, so that $P(i)$ is the set of states which are reached with positive probability from state i under the selection mechanism alone. Then $P(i)$ must be nonempty, and we have

$$\gamma_{ij} = \sum_{k \in P(i)} p_{ik} q_{kj}. \tag{9}$$

Notice that because $q_{kj} > 0$ for all $k, j \in \theta$, we also have $\gamma_{ij} > 0$ for all i, $j \in \theta$.

The state space θ and the transition matrix Γ define a Markov process, and we would like to examine the stationary distributions of this process. The first question concerns the existence and uniqueness of such a distribution. The key here is to recall that Γ has only strictly positive elements. Straightforward results from the theory of Markov processes (see, for example, Billingsley 1986 and Seneta 1981) give

LEMMA 1

(1.1) The Markov process defined by Γ has a unique stationary distribution; namely, a probability measure z^* on θ such that $z^*\Gamma = z^*$;

(1.2) z^* is stable, that is, for any initial distribution z, $z\Gamma^t \to z^*$ as $t \to \infty$;

(1.3) z^* is ergodic, that is, if θ_t denotes the state at time t and if χ_i is an indicator function given by $\chi_i(\theta_t) = 1$ if $\theta_t = i$ and zero otherwise, then $T^{-1} \sum_t^{T=1} \chi_i(\theta_t) \to z_i^*$ almost surely as $T \to \infty$.

Hence, independent of the initial condition, the distribution of the population is asymptotically given by z^*. This stationary distribution can be interpreted both as the proportion of time that any realization of the process spends in each state and as the probability that the process will be in each state at any (sufficiently distant) future time.

We are interested in an evolutionary process with *rare* mutations. Noting that the transition matrix Γ and stationary distribution z^* depend upon λ (which we occasionally denote by $\Gamma(\lambda)$ and $z^*(\lambda)$), we are accordingly interested in the limit of the distribution $z^*(\lambda)$ as λ goes to zero.

Finally, notice that the selection mechanism P, without mutations, also defines a Markov process on θ. The Markov process defined by the selection mechanism is likely to have a number of stationary distributions. The transition probability p_{ij} will equal zero for many states i and j under many selection mechanisms, since there will be strategy changes that some mechanisms will not induce agents to make, and since Markov processes whose transition matrices contain zeros often admit multiple stationary distributions. The stationary distribution induced by the γ_{ij} will be one of the stationary distributions under p_{ij}, so that the mutations provide a means of selecting a stationary distribution.

5.3   Limiting Results

We now examine the limit of $z^*(\lambda)$ as λ approaches zero. One possibility would be to fix a game, calculate $z^*(\lambda)$, and take the limit as λ approaches zero. However, we find it more helpful to develop a general characterization of this limit. First, we introduce a class of directed graphs on the state space, θ.

DEFINITION 1   Let θ be a state in θ. Then a θ-graph on θ is a tree with each state in θ as a node and with θ as its initial node.

For each θ, denote the set of θ-graphs by H_θ.

We now construct the following vector. For a fixed θ and for each θ-graph, associate with each (i, j) (i.e., with each arrow from state i to j) in the graph the transition probability from i to j, or γ_{ij}. Then take the product of all of these probabilities for the graph, and sum these products over the set of all θ-graphs. This gives a number of the form

$$Z_\theta = \sum_{h \in H_\theta} \prod_{(i,j) \in h} \gamma_{ij}. \tag{10}$$

We can collect these numbers to construct a vector of the form $Z(\lambda) \equiv (Z_1, \ldots, Z_{|\theta|})$. Then the basic result is

LEMMA 2 $z^*(\lambda)$ is proportional to $Z(\lambda)$.

A proof is given by Freidlin and Wentzell (1984, 177, lemma 3.1) and in Kandori, Mailath, and Rob 1990. The (very rough) intuition behind this result is that Z_θ is part of the solution to a system of linear equations. This solution can be computed via Cramer's rule, and (10) corresponds to the expansion of the determinant which appears in the numerator of the resulting expression.

Lemma 2 allows us to infer properties of $z^*(\lambda)$ and the limit of $z^*(\lambda)$ as λ approaches zero by examining the Z_θ. To do this, we must calculate Z_θ more explicitly. From (2) and (3), we have

$$Z_\theta = \sum_{h \in H_\theta} \prod_{(i,j) \in h} \sum_{k \in P(i)} p_{ik} q_{kj}. \tag{11}$$

Attention thus turns to an expression for q_{kj}. This term identifies the probability that mutations take the system from states k to j. To calculate q_{kj}, we must identify the possible combinations of mutations that can change the state from k to j, and then sum the probability of these combinations. To accomplish the first of these tasks, we define M_{kj} as a set of vectors of dimension $2|S_1|^2 x 2|S_2|^2$, where each element $m_{kj} \in M_{kj}$ identifies for each population α and each pair of strategies x_α and y_α in S_α a number of mutations of members of population α from strategy x_α to y_α; where m_{kj} has the property that the specified mutations are feasible (i.e., m_{kj} never calls for more α agents to mutate from strategy x_α to y_α than the number of agents who play x_α in state k); and where the effect of the mutations specified by m_{kj} is to move the state of the system from k to j. M_{kj} then identifies the various combinations of mutations that can move the state from k to j.

Turning now to the probability of mutations, we define $\psi(\alpha, m_{kj})$ to be the total number of mutations required of agents in population α under m_{kj}. We also let $C(\alpha, m_{kj})$ be the total number of ways that these population α mutants can be drawn from population α, given state k, and let $F(\alpha, m_{kj})$ be the product of the terms $f(x_\alpha, y_\alpha)$ for the mutations required of population α under m_{kj}. Then we have

$$q_{kj} = \sum_{M_{kj}} \prod_{\alpha \in N} C(\alpha, m_{kj}) F(\alpha, m_{kj}) \lambda^{\psi(\alpha, m_{kj})} (1 - \lambda)^{\Delta - \psi(\alpha, m_{kj})}, \tag{12}$$

and from (3), we have

$$Z_\theta = \sum_{h \in H_\theta} \left[\prod_{(i,j) \in h} \left(\sum_{k \in P_i} p_{ik} \left(\sum_{m_{kj} \in M_{kj}} \right. \right. \right.$$
$$\left. \left. \left. \prod_{\alpha \in N} C(\alpha, m_{kj}) F(\alpha, m_{kj}) \lambda^{\psi(\alpha, m_{kj})} (1 - \lambda)^{\Delta - \psi(\alpha, m_{kj})} \right) \right) \right]. \tag{13}$$

We use this expression for Z_θ to characterize the limiting distribution. First, let

$$\eta(i, j) = \min_{k \in P_i} \left[\min_{m_{kj} \in M_{kj}} \sum_{\alpha \in N} \psi(\alpha, m_{kj}) \right]. \tag{14}$$

$\eta(i, j)$ is interpreted as the least number of mutations required to get from i to j, in the sense that there is positive probability that, starting from i, the selection mechanism will move the system to a state k, from which $\eta(i, j)$ mutations can move the system to state j (with a similar statement holding for no number less than $\eta(i, j)$). Then Samuelson (1991) proves the following:[4]

LEMMA 3

(3.1) $\lim_{\lambda \to 0} z^*(\lambda)$ exists (and is unique);

(3.2) Let $\lim_{\lambda \to 0} z^*(\lambda) \equiv z^{**}$. Then $z^{**}(\theta) > 0$ if and only if θ satisfies

$$\theta \in \underset{\Theta}{\text{argmin}} \left(\min_{h \in H_\theta} \sum_{(i,j) \in h} \eta(i,j) \right). \tag{15}$$

To see why lemma 3 holds, note that $z^{**}(\theta)$ will be positive only for those θ for which $Z_\theta(\lambda)$ approaches zero most slowly (as λ approaches zero). As λ becomes small, the rate of convergence of the $Z_\theta(\lambda)$ to zero will be determined by the exponents attached to λ in (13). Those θ for which $Z_\theta(\lambda)$ approaches zero most slowly, and hence $z^{**}(\theta) > 0$, will be those θ with the smallest exponents attached to θ. From (14) this consists of those θ satisfying (15).

Lemma 3 indicates that results on the limiting distribution z^{**} will be derived from counting arguments, where the counting concerns the least number of mutations (highest power attached to $(1 - \lambda)$) required to accomplish the transitions contained in a θ-graph. The fewer the mutations, the more likely θ is to appear in the limit distribution. Notice also that the only relevant property of the selection probabilities p_{ij} in this calculation is whether they are zero (yielding $\eta(i,j) > 0$) or positive ($\eta(i,j) = 0$), with the magnitude of a positive p_{ij} being irrelevant. Hence, we can say that the transition (i,j) "requires $\eta(i,j)$ mutations." Similarly, (i, j) "does not require a mutation" for the purposes of this calculation if and only if $p_{ij} > 0$.

To make use of lemma 3, it is helpful to examine more closely the set of states Θ.

DEFINITION 2   Let $Q \subseteq \Theta$ be nonempty. Then Q is an *absorbing set* if,

(2.1) for any $i \in Q$ and $j \in \Theta \setminus Q$, $p_{ij} = 0$;

(2.2) no nonempty set $Q' \subseteq Q$ satisfies (2.1).

The interpretation of an absorbing set is that if one begins in this set, then the process of *selection* cannot take one out of the set (although mutations may still move the system out of an absorbing set.)

Let $\Theta^{**} \subseteq \Theta$ be the set of states for which z^{**} is positive. Then it is easily shown that the limiting distribution includes only elements of absorbing sets.

LEMMA 4   If $\theta \in \Theta^{**}$, then θ is an element of an absorbing set.

The intuitive interpretation of lemma 4 is that the selection mechanism more easily moves the system into absorbing sets than out of them, and hence the limiting distribution (as λ becomes small) is concentrated on absorbing sets.

We next show that all members of an absorbing set are created equal, in the sense that if one is a limiting outcome, then all are.

LEMMA 5   If Q is an absorbing set, $\theta \in Q$ and $\theta' \in Q$, and $\theta \in \Theta^{**}$, then $\theta' \in \Theta^{**}$.

To see why lemma 5 holds, we note that if θ and θ' are members of an absorbing set Q, then it must be the case that with positive probability the selection mechanism leads from state θ to θ' (and vice versa, although in each case not necessarily in a single step), and hence that the selection mechanism yields cycles on the set Q. In particular, if such a cycle did not exist, then Q could be decoupled into two or more absorbing sets, vitiating the minimality assumption in (2.2). The ease with which the selection mechanism moves through the cycle on Q then ensures that if the limiting outcome selects one element of Q, it must select all of them.

We have transformed the question of which states will appear in the limiting distribution to a question of which absorbing sets will appear. Intuitively, the absorbing sets that appear in the limit will be those which can be reached with the fewest mutations. More specifically, to check if absorbing set Q will be in the limit, we construct paths from all other absorbing sets to Q and find the fewest number of mutations required to traverse such paths. Those Q which have the minimum such "fewest muta-tion paths" will appear in the limiting distribution.

Instead of presenting this general result formally, we introduce a notion that will be especially helpful in our examination of dominated strategies.

DEFINITION 3   Absorbing sets Q and Q' are *adjacent* if there exists $i \in Q$ and $j \in Q'$ such that a single mutation can change state i to state j. The set $\mathcal{F} = \{Q_1, \ldots, Q_n\}$ of absorbing sets is *totally adjacent* if, for every two elements Q_i and Q_j of $\mathcal{F}$, one can construct a sequence of elements of $\mathcal{F}$ beginning with Q_i and ending with Q_j with the property that each pair of sets in the sequence is adjacent.

Two absorbing sets are thus adjacent if one can, with only one mutation, move from an element of one of the absorbing sets to an element of the other. Notice that if a single mutation can move the system from state i to state j, then a single mutation can also move the system from j to i, so that the relationship of adjacency is a symmetric one.

The next result states that if an absorbing set appears in the limiting distribution, so do any adjacent absorbing sets.

LEMMA 6

(6.1) Let Q and Q' be adjacent absorbing sets with $Q \subseteq \Theta^{**}$. Then $Q' \subseteq \Theta^{**}$.

(6.2) Let $\mathcal{F}$ be totally adjacent and $Q \subseteq \Theta^{**}$ for some $Q \in \mathcal{F}$. Then $Q' \subseteq \Theta^{**}$ for all $Q' \in \mathcal{F}$.

The intuition behind this result is that if states θ and θ' are adjacent, then mutations can move the system from θ to θ' as easily as from θ' to θ, and hence (since limiting outcomes are those which require the fewest mutations to reach), one will appear in the limit if and only if the other does.[5] This result will be important in our examination of dominated strategies in the next subsection, because dominated strategies will often give rise to adjacent Nash equilibria.

5.4   Evolutionary Stability and Dominated Strategies

We now derive the implications of these results for the outcomes of evolutionary games. We must first introduce some game-theoretic considerations into the model by placing some restrictions on the selection mechanism. To do this, let the state of the system be given by k and consider an agent in population α who plays strategy x_α in state k. The matching process is assumed to make all possible opponents of this agent equally likely. Together with the specification contained in k of the numbers of opponents playing each possible strategy, this allows us to calculate an expected payoff to the agent playing x_α in state k, which we denote $\pi(x_\alpha, k)$. This expected payoff is identical to that of a player in the game G who plays pure strategy x_α and who faces opponents playing mixed strategies that match the population proportions induced by k.

We then require that, for any state k,

$$[\exists \alpha \in N, \exists x_\alpha, y_\alpha \in S_\alpha \text{ s.t. } k_{\alpha x_\alpha} > 0, \pi(x_\alpha, k) < \pi(y_\alpha, k)]$$

$$\Leftrightarrow \quad [\exists j \in \Theta, k \neq j, \text{ s.t. } p_{kj} > 0]. \tag{16}$$

From statement 16, there is a positive probability that the state of the system changes if and only if some strategy x_α for some agent of population α currently earns a lower expected return than does another strategy y_α. Equivalently, we assume that agents switch strategies (via the learning mechanism) if and only if there is a payoff-based reason for doing so, that is, if and only if some agent is not currently playing a best response.

We impose (16) because we have in mind a situation in which players who contemplate switching strategies are able to collect information on the current state of play and hence on the payoffs of various strategies, and thus will be drawn to switch strategies if and only if this information reveals that they are playing a suboptimal strategy.[6]

We will also require

DEFINITION 4   The selection mechanism is *weakly monotone* if, for any state k, there exists $j \in \Theta$ with $p_{kj} > 0$ such that

$$[\forall \alpha \in N, \forall x_\alpha \in S_\alpha, [\pi(x_\alpha, k) > \pi(y_\alpha, k) \; \forall y_\alpha \in S_\alpha] \wedge [k_{x_\alpha} < \Delta]]$$

$$\Rightarrow \quad [j_{\alpha x_\alpha} > k_{\alpha x_\alpha}]. \tag{17}$$

Condition 17 requires that if population α has a strict best reply to the current state in which not all agents of population α are playing, then the number of population α agents playing that strategy increases. This again appears to be a mild condition, and is certainly consistent with the type of decision making we suggested as motivating (16).

This lemma allows us to derive our first basic result. Recall that Θ^{**} denotes the support of z^{**}, the limiting distribution of the evolutionary process.

PROPOSITION 5   Let (16) hold. If $\Theta^{**} = \{\theta\}$ for some $\theta \in \Theta$ (i.e., Θ^{**} is a singleton), then θ is a Nash equilibrium.

To see why this holds, suppose that θ is the only element of Θ^{**}. Then, from lemma 4, we know that θ is an element of an absorbing set, say Q; and from lemma 5 we know that Q is a singleton. (16)–(17) ensure that any singleton absorbing set is a Nash equilibrium.

Proposition 5 is another form of the "folk theorem" of evolutionary games that "stability implies Nash." In this case, the stability condition takes the form of the requirement that the limiting outcome be a singleton.

Proposition 5 could obviously be extended to the statement that if the limiting support consists of a collection of singleton absorbing sets (as in game G1, discussed below), then the limit distribution will attach positive probability only to Nash equilibria. Notice, however, that we have stopped short of saying that in all cases the support of the limiting distribution will consist of Nash equilibria. This statement may fail if nonsingleton absorbing sets appear in the limit.[7] We could easily show that the limit contains only Nash equilibria if we imposed a requirement similar to Young's (1991) assumption that the game is weakly acyclic.

The next result follows directly from lemma 6, and addresses dominated strategies.

PROPOSITION 6   Let (17) hold. If θ is a Nash equilibrium and $\theta \in \Theta^{**}$, then every Nash equilibrium that can be constructed by changing some agents of some populations to alternative best replies is also contained in Θ^{**}.

Proposition 6 holds because the set of Nash equilibria created by repeatedly switching some agents to alternative best replies will be totally adjacent, so that one member of this set appears in the limit if and only if all do.

An immediate implication of proposition 6 is that the limiting outcomes of this model will often include dominated strategies. In particular, suppose that a Nash and normal-form perfect equilibrium s^* is included in the limiting outcome. Suppose further that there exists an alternative best reply to this Nash equilibrium for player 1, but that this alternative best reply is dominated. Then there will exist a continuum of other equilibria in which player 1 allocates some probability to the dominated strategy. Our limiting outcome will include all of these equilibria, and hence will include states in which some agents play dominated strategies.

For example, consider game G1. Let the selection mechanism be any mechanism satisfying (16)–(17). Then the absorbing sets for this game are all singletons and include any state in which all of population 2 plays L. These absorbing sets are totally adjacent, and hence the limiting outcome for this game will be a distribution over all of the absorbing sets, including the state in which all of population 1 plays B. The limiting distribution thus includes all of the game's Nash equilibria, all but one of which include dominated strategies.

6   Trembles and Mutations

The previous section again finds limiting outcomes that allocate positive probability to dominated strategies. This may again be somewhat surprising, because the "completely mixed" mutations built into the model bear a resemblance to the trembles of trembling hand perfection. How do mutations and trembles differ? In this section we investigate this by adding choice trembles to our model.

Consider first an example built around game G1. We have seen that the limiting distribution for (G1), that is, for any selection mechanism satisfying (16)–(17), includes every state in which all population 2 agents play L, including outcomes in which some (or all) population 1 agents play the dominated strategy B.

Will choice trembles eliminate the states in which dominated strategies are played? To answer this, we specify a selection mechanism and a pattern of choice trembles. We choose the choice trembles so as to "rig" the specification of the model, as far as possible, to achieve a limit that excludes dominated strategies. We find, however, that dominated strategies are excluded only if choice trembles become arbitrarily more likely than mutations in the limit as both become small.

We assume that each population consists of only one agent. Player 1's strategy choices are not subject to trembles. Player 2's choice of R is similarly not subject to trembles. However, player 2's choice of L does involve a tremble, with an intended choice of L yielding a play of L with probability $(1 - \delta)$ and a choice of R with probability δ. These trembles ensure that T receives a higher expected payoff than B in every state. The trembles thus appear ideally suited to the task of eliminating dominated strategies from the limiting distribution.

The selection mechanism is specified as follows. If player 2 plays R in period t, we assume that player 2 switches to L in period $t + 1$. Player 1 switches strategies only if a payoff of 0 is received, in which case player 1 switches to T. The state space for this system is the set $\{TL, TR, BL, BR\}$, where TL (for example) denotes the state in which player 1 plays T and 2 plays L.

In the absence of trembles, the selection mechanism is given by

	TL	TR	BL	BR
TL	1	0	0	0
TR	1	0	0	0
BL	0	0	1	0
BR	1	0	0	0

Notice that {BL} are {TL} are both singleton absorbing sets and are adjacent, so that the limiting distribution will include BL and TL (in the absence of trembles). Recalling our tremble specification, which is specially designed to eliminate outcomes in which B is played, the selection mechanism with trembles becomes

	TL	TR	BL	BR
TL	1	0	0	0
TR	1	0	0	0
BL	δ	0	$1-\delta$	0
BR	1	0	0	0

In the presence of trembles, $\{TL\}$ is now the only absorbing set, and hence the only element in the limiting distribution.

We have then apparently achieved a limiting outcome that excludes dominated strategies. However, we are interested in the limit as both δ and λ approach zero, so that both choice trembles and mutations are rare. To examine this limit, notice that the complete transition matrix, with mutations, is given by

	TL	TR	BL	BR
TL	$(1-\lambda)^2$	$(1-\lambda)\lambda$	$(1-\lambda)\lambda$	λ^2
TR	$(1-\lambda)^2$	$(1-\lambda)\lambda$	$(1-\lambda)\lambda$	λ^2
BL	$(1-\delta)(1-\lambda)\lambda$ $+\delta(1-\lambda)^2$	$(1-\delta)\lambda^2$ $+\delta(1-\lambda)\lambda$	$(1-\delta)(1-\lambda)^2$ $+\delta(1-\lambda)\lambda)$	$(1-\delta)(1-\lambda)\lambda$ $+\delta\lambda^2$
BR	$(1-\lambda)^2$	$(1-\lambda)\lambda$	$(1-\lambda)\lambda$	λ^2

Let us now examine the θ-graphs associated with TL and BL. For TL, the θ-graph that maximizes the product of transition probabilities is given by $\{(TR, TL), (BL, TL), (BR, TL)\}$, for a product of transition probabilities of

$$\beta_{TL} \equiv [(1-\lambda)^2]^2[(1-\delta)(1-\lambda)\lambda + \delta(1-\lambda)^2]. \tag{18}$$

For BL, the θ-graph that maximizes the product of transition probabilities is given by $\{(TL, BL), (TR, TL), (BR, TL)\}$, for a product of transition probabilities of

$$\beta_{BL} \equiv [(1-\lambda)^2]^2[(1-\lambda)\lambda]. \tag{19}$$

We are now interested in the limits of these expressions as λ and δ approach zero. The state BL will be excluded from the limit if and only if

$$\lim_{\delta \to 0, \lambda \to 0} \frac{\beta_{BL}}{\beta_{TL}} = 0. \tag{20}$$

From (18) and (19), we see that (20) will hold if and only if

$$\lim_{\delta \to 0, \lambda \to 0} \frac{1}{(1 - \delta) + (\delta/\lambda)(1 - \lambda)} = 0. \tag{21}$$

(21) in turn will hold if and only if

$$\lim \frac{\delta}{\lambda} = \infty. \tag{22}$$

Hence, in the limit choice trembles must be arbitrarily more likely than mutations. This example then suggests that choice trembles can be effective in eliminating dominated strategies, unlike mutations, but can do so only if they are "large" in the sense that they are arbitrarily more likely than mutations.

The result that choice trembles will matter only if they are arbitrarily larger than mutation probabilities will generalize. To formulate the generalization, fix a selection mechanism p_{ij}. Let the transition probabilities with trembles be given by $p_{ij}(\delta)$, where $\lim_{\delta \to 0} p_{ij}(\delta) = p_{ij}$. Let $p_{ij}(\delta)$ be polynomial in δ. Let Θ^{**} be the support of the limiting distribution (as mutations become rare) under p_{ij} and $\Theta^{**}(\delta)$ be the support of the limiting distribution (as mutations become rare, and δ approaches zero) under $p_{ij}(\delta)$. Finally, let δ, $\lambda \to 0$ and let $\delta(\lambda)$ be a polynomial that describes the relationship between δ and λ. Samuelson (1991) proves

PROPOSITION 6 Suppose Θ^{**} contains the adjacent Nash equilibria θ and θ'. Let $\theta \in \theta^{**}(\delta)$ but $\theta' \notin \Theta^{**}(\delta)$. Then $\lim_{\delta, \lambda \to 0} \delta/\lambda = \infty$.

Proposition 6 states that if the addition of trembles succeeds in eliminating one, but only one, of an adjacent pair of Nash equilibria from the limiting distribution, then in the limit trembles must become arbitrarily more likely than mutations. The intuition behind this result is that choice trembles matter because they create new selection mechanism links between states; namely, they yield $p_{ij}(\delta) > 0$ for states i and j that have $p_{ij} = 0$ without trembles, and hence allow some paths in the state space to be traversed with fewer mutations. However, in the limit a selection mechanism link saves on mutations only if it is of a probability that is an order of magnitude higher than that of a mutation.

We thus find that an evolutionary system with trembles can eliminate dominated strategies, but only if the trembles are large in the sense of being arbitrarily more likely than mutations. The trembles that appear in trembling-hand perfection may thus not be as small as they first appear, and it is again not clear that we have a useful justification for eliminating dominated strategies.

7 Conclusion

We have examined a succession of evolutionary models. In spite of our best efforts to capture evolutionary considerations designed to eliminate dominated strategies, we find that dominated strategies persist in the outcome of the evolutionary process. While one cannot preclude the possibility that other, more suitable models exist which will eliminate dominated strategies, the apparent conclusion from our investigation is that if one embraces the evolutionary approach to games, then it is not clear that one should insist on equilibrium concepts which respect weak dominance.

Notes

The author is grateful to Ken Binmore for his helpful comments.

1. See van Damme 1991 for a survey of the refinements literature.

2. We will be concerned only with weakly dominated strategies throughout this paper, and will take "dominated" to mean "weakly dominated." A number of papers establish the result that evolutionary selection models will eliminate strictly dominated strategies or impose the iterated elimination of strictly dominated strategies. See, for example, Nachbar 1990; Samuelson and Zhang 1992; and Milgrom and Roberts 1991.

3. See Bomze and van Damme 1990 for a complete discussion of the relationship between the ESS concept and the replicator dynamics.

4. All subsequent results are proved in Samuelson 1991.

5. One must be careful in making such *pairwise* comparisons between absorbing sets. Pairwise comparisons are not informative in general, but do suffice for the special case of adjacent sets. See Samuelson 1991 for details.

6. If (16) does not hold, the possibility remains that agents will persist forever in playing suboptimal strategies without making adjustments.

7. The inability to establish that the limiting distribution will always consist of Nash equilibria should be no surprise. Many evolutionary models have established that evolutionary outcomes will be Nash equilibria if they exhibit some stability property, but evolutionary systems need not yield stable outcomes in general, and nonstable outcomes need not be Nash equilibria. Our results are similar, with the condition that the limiting absorbing sets be singletons taking the place of the stability requirement.

References

Billingsley, Patrick. 1986. *Probability and Measure*. New York: Wiley.

Bomze, I. M., and E. van Damme. 1990. "A Dynamical Characterization of Evolutionarily Stable States." CentER discusion paper 9045, University of Tilburg.

Dekel, Eddie, and Drew Fudenberg. 1991. "Rational Behavior with Payoff Uncertainty." *Journal of Economic Theoy* 52:243–267.

Freidlin, M. I., and A. D. Wentzell. 1984. *Random Perturbations of Dynamical Systems.* New York: Springer-Verlag.

Hofbauer, Josef, and Karl Sigmund. 1988. *The Theory of Evolution and Dynamical Systems.* Cambridge: Cambridge University Press.

Kandori, Michihhiro, George J. Mailath, and Rafael Rob. 1990. "Learning, Mutation, and Long-Run Equilibria in Games." University of Pennsylvania. Mimeo.

Kohlberg, Elon, and Jean-François Mertens. 1986. "On the Strategic Stability of Equilibria." *Econometrica* 52:1003–1038.

Maynard Smith, John. 1982. *Evolution and the Theory of Games.* Cambridge: Cambridge University Press.

Milgrom, Paul, and John Roberts. 1991. "Adaptive and Sophisticated Learning in Normal Form Games." *Games and Economic Behavior* 3:82–100.

Moulin, Hervé. 1986. *Game Theory for the Social Sciences.* 2d ed. New York: New York University Press.

Nachbar, John H. 1990. "'Evolutionary' Selection Dynamics in Games: Convergence and Limit Properties." *International Journal of Game Theory* 19:59–89.

Samuelson, Larry. 1991. "How to Tremble if You Must." University of Wisconsin. Mimeo.

Samuelson, Larry, and Jianbo Zhang. 1992. "Evolutionary Stability in Asymmetric Games." *Journal of Economic Theory* 57:363–391.

Selten, Reinhard. 1983. "A Note on Evolutionarily Stable Strategies in Asymmetric Animal Conflicts." *Journal of Theoretical Biology* 84:93–101.

Seneta, E. 1981. *Non-Negative Matrices and Markov Chains.* New York: Springer-Verlag.

Swinkels, Jereon. 1990. "Evolutionary Stability with Equilibrium Entrants." Stanford University. Mimeo.

van Damme, Eric. 1991. "Refinements of Nash Equilibrium." In *Advances in Economic Theory: Sixth World Congress of the Econometric Society*, ed. J. J. Laffont. Cambridge: Cambridge University Press.

Young, P. 1991. "Conventional Equilibria." University of Maryland. Mimeo.

12 Equilibrium Selection in Stag Hunt Games

Hans Carlsson and Eric van Damme

1 Introduction

A weakness of the Nash equilibrium concept for noncooperative games is that it frequently does not generate a unique outcome. In the literature, therefore, a great many concepts have been introduced that refine the Nash concept by imposing additional rationality restrictions or by requiring additional robustness properties. However, frequently even the strongest refinements that have been proposed—such as Kohlberg and Mertens's (1986) stability concept—do not succeed in determining unique solutions. This is true, in particular, for any game that has several strict Nash equilibria since all such equilibria survive any of the established refinement tests.

Many economic situations give rise to games with multiple strict Nash equilibria. As an example, consider the game displayed in figure 12.1. (Various economic scenarios that can be associated with this game are described in section 2.) In the game $g(x)$ each player has to choose among two strategies: α is a safe strategy that yields x, irrespective of what the opponent does. The strategy β might yield the higher payoff of 1—if the opponent chooses β as well—but it is risky since it yields only 0 if the opponent chooses the safe strategy. It is easily seen that $g(x)$ has two strict Nash equilibria, namely, $\bar{\alpha}$ (both players choose α) and $\bar{\beta}$ (both choose β). Hence, when playing this game, players face a coordination problem. The dilemma is whether one should go for the equilibrium $\bar{\beta}$ with the highest possible payoff or whether, in view of the strategic uncertainty, one should rather play according to the safe equilibrium $\bar{\alpha}$.

Many game theorists would argue that the Pareto-dominant equilibrium $\bar{\beta}$ is the natural focal point in the game $g(x)$. In support of this view, they might invoke Schelling's principle of tacit bargaining: since the players know that they would talk each other into $\bar{\beta}$ if they could communicate, they will also be able to reach this conclusion without actually communi-

	α	β
α	x x	0 x
β	x 0	1 1

Figure 12.1
Game $g(x)$ $(0 < x < 1)$

cating. (see Schelling 1980) From the viewpoint of a strict methodological individualism, however, these arguments in favor of $\bar{\beta}$, which almost amount to simply postulating collective rationality, are not wholly convincing. A satisfactory solution to the equilibrium selection problem should have a better foundation in individual decision making.

One can also question whether $\bar{\beta}$ is always the intuitively most appealing solution. For instance, would you accept a bet where you win $10,000 in case another person B, with whom you cannot communicate, accepts a similar bet, but lose $90,000 if B declines the bet? We believe many people would hesitate to accept *even if* prior communication with the opponent was allowed. Finally, one can note that subjects participating in experiments frequently do not succeed in coordinating on the Pareto-dominant equilibrium (see Cooper et al. 1990; Van Huyck, Battalio, and Beil 1990).

The above discussion indicates the hazards of taking short cuts in matters of equilibrium selection and the need for a more fundamental approach where solutions to the selection problem are derived from individualistic assumptions. In view of the importance of games with multiple strict equilibria, there have been remarkably few contributions to this approach. Recently, however, the theory of equilibrium selection has received a strong impetus from Harsanyi and Selten's (1988) book. Apart from the Harsanyi-Selten theory, we will here discuss modifications to that theory by Güth and Kalkofen as well as our rather different approach initiated in Carlsson and Van Damme 1990.

A common feature of these approaches is that the selection of a particular equilibrium results from the individual players' strategic uncertainty. There are, however, considerable differences: theorists within the Harsanyi-Selten approach content themselves to postulate a specific form of uncertainty, typically a uniform prior in some fixed scheme of expectations formation, but in our approach the uncertainty is derived from more fundamental assumptions about how the players' information is generated. Hence, while in the former approach the equilibrium selection rule has a somewhat ad hoc character, we derive the selection rule within a strictly noncooperative framework by perturbing the game to be solved and embedding it in a game of incomplete information.

A drawback of our 1990 paper is that it only covers 2×2 games and hence, does not describe a general equilibrium selection theory. Here, however, we demonstrate that some properties we derived can be generalized to a certain class of n-person symmetric binary choice problems. In particular, we show that introducing slight payoff uncertainty allows the equilibrium selection problem to be resolved by a process of iterative elimination of strictly dominated strategies (proposition 4.1). In our 1990 paper we showed that for two-player 2×2 games equilibrium selection on the basis of Harsanyi and Selten's (1988) risk-dominance criterion[1] can be justified by considerations of slight payoff uncertainty. Our aim in this chapter is to show that these approaches do no longer yield the same solutions if the number of players exceeds two. Along the way we also show that the modifications of the Harsanyi-Selten theory that have been proposed by Güth (1990) yield still different outcomes.

The remainder of the paper is organized as follows. Section 2 describes the class of n-person binary choice games that we will study and mentions some contexts in which these games arise. The approaches to equilibrium selection that have been proposed in Harsanyi and Selten 1988; Güth and Kalkofen 1989 and Güth 1990 are outlined in section 3, while section 4 is devoted to extending the approach to equilibrium selection that has been put forward in Carlsson and van Damme 1990. This section contains the paper's main result (proposition 4.1). Section 5 concludes the paper with a general discussion on equilibrium selection and an illustration of the fact that different forms of payoff uncertainty may give rise to very different results.

2   Stag Hunt Games

We consider games where n identical players are to choose simultaneously between two actions, α and β. The players' identical preferences are determined by a parameter x $(0 < x < 1)$ and a nondecreasing function $p : [0, 1]$ $\rightarrow [0, 1]$ with $p(0) = 0$ and $p(1) = 1$. If a player chooses action α, his payoff is x no matter what his opponents' choices are. If he chooses β, then his payoff is $p(k/n)$, where k is the number of players that choose β. The normal form game described by the above data is denoted by $g(n, x, p)$ and will be called a "Stag Hunt Game." In the remainder of the chapter we will restrict ourselves to the case where

$$x \neq p(k/n) \quad \text{for all } k \in \{0, 1, \ldots, n\} \tag{2.1}$$

in order to avoid uninteresting case distinctions. In this case we have

PROPOSITION 2.1   The Stag Hunt Game $g(n, x, p)$ has two Nash equilibria in pure strategies, namely, $\bar{\alpha}$, and $\bar{\beta}$. Both equilibria are strict.

Proof   Let s be a pure strategy combination in $g(n, x, p)$ and let k be the number of players choosing β. If $x > p(k/n)$, then a player choosing β (if there is any) has an incentive to switch to α. If $x < p(k/n)$, then a player choosing α (if there is any) can gain by unilaterally deviating to β. Hence, a necessary condition for a pure equilibrium is $k = 0$ or $k = n$. Straightforward verification shows that both possibilities do indeed yield strict equilibria.   □

The Stag Hunt Game $g(n, x, p)$ can be viewed as a formalization of a dilemma described in Rousseau's *Discours sur l'origine et les fondements de l'inégalité parmi les hommes* (Rousseau 1971; also see Lewis 1969; Aumann 1990; and Crawford 1991). Suppose each member of a group of hunters has to decide independently whether to cooperate with the others in hunting a stag (action β) or instead, to go off on his own and hunt hares (action α). While the latter does not require cooperation of the others, the probability that the stag hunt is successful depends, on the number of hunters that does not chase hares and is increasing in this number.

The Stag Hunt Game $g(n, x, p)$ can also be viewed as a stylized model of many other interesting economic and political situations. For example, α may be interpreted as consuming own production and β may be interpreted as going to a market place to trade own production for more desired products. The attractiveness of the latter strategy depends on the chance of finding a trading partner, that is, on how many people adhere to the same strategy. Alternatively, α may be interpreted as shirking, while β stands for spending effort in a situation of team production: one's own effort is wasted unless a sufficient number of other people spend effort as well. The game $g(n, x, p)$ also arises in models of public goods. Assume that people have to decide whether to contribute to a public good (action β) or not (action α). If noncontributors can be excluded from consuming the public good, if contributions are not refunded and if the public good is provided only if enough people contribute, then, for interesting parameter values, the situation is represented by a game that is strategically equivalent to a Stag Hunt Game (see Harrison and Hirschleifer 1989). Finally, games with the Stag Hunt structure have been used as models to explain the occurrence of Keynesian coordination failures (Cooper and John 1988; Van Huyck, Battalio, and Beil 1990), while in the international relations literature a model of this type is known as the Security Dilemma (Jervis 1978).

Proposition 2.1 shows that, in $g(n, x, p)$, Pareto efficiency is compatible with equilibrium play. (Note that, since $x < 1$, the unique Pareto-efficient outcome is $\bar{\beta}$.) Hence, it is not necessary to make binding agreements in order to reach an efficient outcome. However, it is not clear whether players will be able to reach this outcome in a noncooperative context where no direct communication is possible. Choosing the cooperative action β is risky in the sense that it only pays if there are enough people who follow this action. If you expect only few other people to choose β, you are better off choosing α even though such expectations—if they are generally held—will lead the players to coordinate on the Pareto-inferior equilibrium $\bar{\alpha}$. Intuitively, one would think that the larger the value of x, the greater the chance that players will indeed end up in this (inefficient) equilibrium. The experimental results reported in Van Huyck, Battalio, and Beil 1990 concerning similar games indeed point in this direction, but formal game theory provides no support: both $\bar{\alpha}$ and $\bar{\beta}$ are strict equilibria—that is, each player is strictly worse off is she deviates unilaterally—so each of these equilibria survives the most stringent refinements that have been proposed to date. To resolve the player's dilemma in $g(n, x, p)$ we, therefore, turn to theories of *equilibrium selection* in the following sections.

3 Equilibrium Selection

In this section we discuss some principles of equilibrium selection that are based on comparisons of riskiness of equilibria. All are variations of Harsanyi and Selten's (1988) concept of risk dominance and all yield the same result if the number of players is equal to two.[2] Specifically, if $n = 2$, then the game $g(n, x, p)$ is given in figure 12.1, and the risk-dominant equilibrium is the one with the largest Nash product, that is, the one for which the product of the deviation losses is largest. Hence, if $n = 2$, then $\bar{\alpha}$ risk-dominates $\bar{\beta}$ if $x^2 > (1 - x)^2$, that is, if $x > \frac{1}{2}$, while $\bar{\beta}$ risk-dominates $\bar{\alpha}$ if the reverse (strict) inequality is satisfied. However, as we will see, the various equilibrium selection theories generate different outcomes as soon as the number of players exceeds two. The discussion that follows may also give some insight in the relative merits and drawbacks of the various concepts.

We first discuss the idea of equilibrium selection on the basis of maximal unilateral deviation stability that has been put forward in Güth 1990. Suppose that each player i believes that he is the only player who does not know what the unique solution of $g(n, x, p)$ is. All players, however, know that the solution is unique and that it is either $\bar{\alpha}$ or $\bar{\beta}$. Two players i and j may then represent their decision problem by means of a reduced game in which each player i believes that each player $k \notin \{i, j\}$ will take the same choice as player j. Since $g(n, x, p)$ is symmetric, the derived game does not depend on which players i and j are selected from the original player set and is represented by the bimatrix from figure 12.1. Assuming that the players i and j consider their decision problem in $g(n, x, p)$ to be equivalent to that in the game of figure 12.1 and that the players use risk dominance as the selection criterion in 2×2 games, the players will choose $\bar{\alpha}$ whenever $x > \frac{1}{2}$. Güth (1990) argues that $\bar{\alpha}$ is more stable against unilateral deviations than $\bar{\beta}$ if $x > \frac{1}{2}$. Hence, Güth advocates $\bar{\alpha}$ as the solution of $g(n, x, p)$ if $x > \frac{1}{2}$, and he advocates $\bar{\beta}$ as the solution if $x < \frac{1}{2}$. Clearly, the selection rule proposed by Güth corresponds to choosing that equilibrium with the largest Nash product. This implies, in particular, the somewhat counterintuitive property that the equilibrium selected does not depend on the number of players in the game. Güth himself remarks that selection on the basis of Nash products may not reflect all strategic aspects of the situation and that this might be viewed as a major deficiency of such a selection rule. Nevertheless, the rule may still serve as a benchmark against which other selection rules may be compared.

Next, we discuss selection on the basis of Harsanyi and Selten's (1988) risk-dominance concept. The definition of risk dominance is based on a hypothetical process of expectation formation starting from the initial situation, where it is common knowledge that either $\bar{\alpha}$ or $\bar{\beta}$ will be the solution but where players do not yet know this solution. Harsanyi and Selten postulate a process in which players first, on the basis of a preliminary theory, form priors on the strategies played by their opponents. Thereafter, players gradually adapt their prior expectations to final equilibrium expectations by means of the tracing procedure (see Harsanyi and Selten 1988, 207–209).

According to Harsanyi and Selten, the players' prior beliefs q_i about player i's strategy should coincide with the prediction of an outside observer who reasons in the following way about the game:

(i) Player i believes that his opponents will either all choose α or that they all choose β; he assigns a subjective probability z_i to the first event and $1 - z_i$ to the second.

(ii) Whatever the value of z_i, player i will choose a best response to his beliefs.

(iii) The beliefs (i.e., the z_i) of different players are independent, and they are all uniformly distributed on $[0, 1]$.

From (i) and (ii) the outside observer concludes that player i chooses α_i if $z_i > 1 - x$, and that he chooses, β_i if $z_i < 1 - x$. Hence, using (iii), the outside observer forecasts player i's strategy as

$$q_i = x\alpha + (1 - x)\beta, \tag{3.1}$$

with different q_i being independent. Harsanyi and Selten assume that the mixed strategy vector $q = (q_1, \ldots, q_2)$ describes the players' prior expectations in the game $g(n, x, p)$. Since q is not a Nash equilibrium, this expectation is not self-fulfilling, and thus has to be adapted. Adaptation is achieved by using the tracing procedure; namely, by following a distinguished path in the graph of the correspondence

$$\lambda \rightarrow E((1 - \lambda)g(q) + \lambda g(n, x, p)) \quad (\lambda \in [0, 1]) \tag{3.2}$$

from the unique equilibrium of the game $g(q)$ associated with $\lambda = 0$ to an equilibrium of the game $g(n, x, p)$ that corresponds to $\lambda = 1$. In (3.2), E denotes the set of Nash equilibria and $g(q)$ is the game where each player j computes his payoffs from the matrix $g(n, x, p)$ by assuming that his opponents are committed to use q as in (3.1). Hence, in $g(q)$ a player's optimal strategy does not depend on the strategies of his opponents. In the special case at hand, tracing is easy: the process comes to an end at the first iteration, except in degenerate cases. The reason is simply that, since the situation is symmetric, either all players will have α as the unique best response against q, in which case $\bar{\alpha}$ is the distinguished equilibrium in (3.2), or they will all have β as the unique best response against q, and in this case the result of the tracing procedure is $\bar{\beta}$. (See Harsanyi and Selten 1988, lemma 4.17.7.)

Write $B_n^p(t)$ for player i's expected payoff associated with β in $g(n, x, p)$ when each of the opponents chooses β with probability t, that is,

$$B_n^p(t) = \sum_{k=1}^{n} \binom{n-1}{k-1} t^{k-1} (1 - t)^{n-k} p(k/n). \tag{3.3}$$

If the players' prior q is as in (3.1), then the expected payoff associated with β is $B_n^p(1 - x)$, and each player's best response against q is α if $x > B_n^p(1 - x)$, while the best response is β if $x < B_n^p(1 - x)$. Hence, if $x > B_n^p(1 - x)$ (resp. $x < B_n^p(1 - x)$), then the outcome of the tracing procedure is $\bar{\alpha}$ (resp. $\bar{\beta}$). In this case Harsanyi and Selten say that $\bar{\alpha}$ *risk-dominates* $\bar{\beta}$ (resp. that $\bar{\beta}$ risk-dominates $\bar{\alpha}$). To derive a more convenient characterization of risk dominance we state the following lemma.

LEMMA 3.1

(i) $B_n^p(t)$ is nondecreasing in t for any n;

(ii) If p is continuous, then $B_n^p(t) \to p(t)$ as $n \to \infty$ for any t.

Proof   Direct computation shows that

$$\frac{\partial}{\partial t} B_n^p(t) \geq 0$$

since p is nondecreasing. By a simple manipulation it is seen that

$$t B_n^p(t) = \sum_{k=0}^{n} \binom{n}{k} t^k (1-t)^{n-k} p(k/n) k/n. \tag{3.4}$$

Now for a function f, the polynomial

$$B_n(f; t) = \sum_{k=0}^{n} \binom{n}{k} t^k (1-t)^{n-k} f(k/n)$$

is known as the Bernstein polynomial of order n of f. Hence, (3.4) can be rewritten as $t B_n^p(t) = B_n(f, t)$, where $f(x) = x p(x)$ for $x \in [0, 1]$. By Bernstein's theorem (Klambauer 1975, 332) $B_n(f, \cdot) \to f$ uniformly on $[0, 1]$ as $n \to \infty$ if f is continuous. It follows that $t B_n^p(t) \to t p(t)$ uniformly as $n \to \infty$, so that $B_n^p(t) \to p(t)$ for all $t \to [0, 1]$. $\square$

Lemma 3.1 allows us to conclude that there exists a unique $x^* = x^*(n, p)$ for which $x^* = B_n^p(1 - x^*)$. Thus $\bar{\alpha}$ risk-dominates $\bar{\beta}$ if $x > x^*$ and $\bar{\beta}$ is risk-dominant if the reverse strict inequality is satisfied. The lemma also implies that, as $n \to \infty$, $x^*(n, p) \to x^*(p)$, where $x^*(p)$ is the unique solution of the equation $x = p(1 - x)$. Hence, we get the intuitive comparative statics result that $x^*(p) \leq x^*(p')$ if $p \leq p'$. Furthermore, direct computation shows that, if $p(x) = 0$ for $x < 1$ and $p(1) = 1$, then $x^*(n, p) \to 0$ as $n \to \infty$. All in all, it seems that the risk-dominance notion is more in agreement with the intuition than Güth's selection on the basis of Nash products is.

To conclude this section, we discuss selection on the basis of resistance avoidance as proposed in Güth and Kalkofen 1989. Player i's *resistance* against $\bar{\beta}$ at $\bar{\alpha}$ is defined as the maximum probability that each opponent may assign to β such that, if players randomize independently, player i still prefers α to β. Formally,

$$r_i(\bar{\alpha}, \bar{\beta}) = \max\{z \in [0, 1]; x \geq B_n^p(z)\}. \tag{3.5}$$

Similarly, player i's resistance against $\bar{\alpha}$ at $\bar{\beta}$ is defined as

$$r_i(\bar{\beta}, \bar{\alpha}) = \max\{z \in [0, 1] : B_n^p(1 - z) \geq x\}. \tag{3.6}$$

Note that, since the game is symmetric, these resistance values are indepen-
dent of the player under consideration, so that we may speak of $r(\bar{\alpha}, \bar{\beta}) = r_i(\bar{\alpha}, \bar{\beta})$ as the resistance of $\bar{\alpha}$ against $\bar{\beta}$. Güth and Kalkofen (1989) say that
$\bar{\alpha}$ is *resistant-dominant* if $r(\bar{\alpha}, \bar{\beta}) > r(\bar{\beta}, \bar{\alpha})$ and that $\bar{\beta}$ is resistant-dominant if
the reverse inequality is satisfied. Now lemma 3.1 implies that $r(\bar{\beta}, \bar{\alpha}) = 1 - r(\bar{\alpha}, \bar{\beta})$; therefore $\bar{\alpha}$ is resistant-dominant if and only if $r(\bar{\alpha}, \bar{\beta}) < \frac{1}{2}$, or
equivalently if $x > B_n^p(\frac{1}{2})$. Hence, Güth and Kalkofen pick $\bar{\alpha}$ as the solution
of $g(n, x, p)$ whenever each player prefers to play α if he expects all others
to randomize equally over both actions, while they choose $\bar{\beta}$ as the solu-
tion if a player prefers to play β in this case. Writing $x^{**} = x^{**}(n, p) = B_n^p(\frac{1}{2})$ and using lemma 3.1, we see that $x^* \to p(\frac{1}{2})$ as $n \to \infty$ and that
$x^{**} < x^*$ if and only if $x^* < \frac{1}{2}$. Hence, resistance dominance also seems to
capture the intuition about the effect of strategic uncertainty in $g(n, x, p)$,
but in general the concept may lead to a recommended action that differs
from one governed by risk-dominance considerations. In particular, depending on the shape of the function p, the area where α is resistant-
dominant may be either larger or smaller than the area where α is risk-
dominant.

The following proposition summarizes the discussion from this section.

PROPOSITION 3.1   In the game $g(n, x, p)$:

(i) $\bar{\alpha}$ is most stable against unilateral deviations (Güth 1990) if and only if
$x > \frac{1}{2}$;

(ii) $\bar{\alpha}$ is risk-dominant (Harsanyi and Selten 1988) if and only if $x > x^*$,
where x^* is the solution to $x^* = B_n^p(1 - x^*)$; and

(iii) $\bar{\alpha}$ is resistant-dominant (Güth and Kalkofen 1989) if and only if
$x > B_n^p(\frac{1}{2})$.

4   Global Payoff Uncertainty

In this section we will show that the equilibrium selection problem in
a Stag Hunt Game can be solved using our approach in Carlsson and van
Damme 1990, which is based on the idea that the payoff parameters of a
game can only be observed with some noise. To be specific, assume that all
data of the Stag Hunt Game $g(n, x, p)$ are common knowledge, except for
the payoff x associated with the safe action α. Each player i will receive a
signal x_i that provides an unbiased estimate of x, but the signals are noisy

so the true value of x will not be common knowledge. It should be noted that in Carlsson and van Damme 1990 attention is restricted to 2×2 games, and players are allowed to be imperfectly informed about more than one (possibly even all) parameters. In our 1990 paper we derive a justification of the risk dominance selection criterion for 2×2 games, by showing that, under some rather weak conditions, considerations of iterated dominance will force the players to play the risk-dominant equilibrium for every possible observation as the noise vanishes. It is quite remarkable that in the 2×2 games this result is to a large extent independent of the players' prior beliefs and of the distributions of the observation errors. We will not seek the same degree of generality here, but will confine ourselves to analyzing the special case where the prior on x is uniform and the players' observation errors are identically and independently distributed. As we will see, the results obtained differ from any of those discussed in the previous section.

Let X be a random variable that is uniformly distributed on an interval that strictly contains $[0, 1]$ and let $(E_i)_{i=1}^n$ be an n-tuple of mutually independent, identically distributed random variables, each having zero mean. The E_i are assumed to be independent of X, to allow a density and to have support within $[-1, 1]$. For $\varepsilon > 0$ write $X_i^\varepsilon = X_i + \varepsilon E_i$. As our model for the situation where each player i observes the true value of x in $g(n, x, p)$, only with some slight noise, we will consider the incomplete information game $g^\varepsilon(n, p)$ described by the following rules:

(1) A realization $(x, x_1, \ldots, x_n)$ of $(X, X_1^\varepsilon, \ldots, X_n^\varepsilon)$ is drawn;

(2) Player i is informed about x_i and chooses between α and β;

(3) Each player i receives payoffs as determined by $g(n, x, p)$ and the choices in rule 2.

We now address the question of which choice of player i is rational in $g^\varepsilon(n, p)$ at the observation x_i. Note that player i will certainly choose α if $x_i > 1$. Since the expected value from choosing α at x_i is $E(X|X_i^\varepsilon = x_i) = x_i$, player i knows that α is strictly dominant at each such observation. For the same reason β will be chosen when $x_i < 0$. The following proposition shows that considerations of iterated dominance allow player i to solve his decision problem for all observations but one. Let p^* denote the expected value from choosing β when the number of opponents choosing β is uniform on $\{0, \ldots, n - 1\}$; then

$$p^* := \sum_{k=1}^n p(k/n)/n.$$

And we have

PROPOSITION 4.1   In any strategy that survives iterative elimination of strictly dominated strategies in $g^\varepsilon(n, p)$, player i chooses α if he observes $x_i > p^*$, and β if he observes $x_i < p^*$.

Proof   Assume that α has already been shown to be iteratively dominant for each player j at each observation $x_j > \bar{x}$. (By the above, such an $\bar{x}$ exists in $[0, 1]$.) Now let us assume player i observes $x_i = \bar{x}$ and let us derive an upper bound for his expected payoff from playing β, provided that no opponent uses an iteratively dominated strategy. Thus any opponent j can choose β only if $x_j \leq \bar{x}$. Let s be the strategy vector in which each player chooses β if $x_j \leq \bar{x}$ and α if $x_j > \bar{x}$. Since the function p is nondecreasing, player i's expected payoff from β cannot exceed the payoff that β yields against s as long as the opponents do not play dominated strategies. To compute the expected payoff of β against s, we have to know, for each $k \in \{0, 1, \ldots, n - 1\}$, the probability that exactly k opponents will make observations that do not exceed $\bar{x}$, that is, we have to know

$$P(X_j^\varepsilon < \bar{x} \text{ for exactly } k \text{ opponents } j | X_i^\varepsilon = \bar{x}). \tag{4.1}$$

The fact that the prior distribution of X is uniform allows us to conclude that the probability in (4.1) is independent of $\bar{x}$, as long as $\bar{x}$ is at least ε inside the support of X. (The formal proof is by direct computation; see also Carlsson and van Damme 1990). The intuition, however, is obvious: if the prior is uniform, such observations do not give new information.) The fact that the probability in (4.1) is independent of $\bar{x}$ allows us to conclude that this probability must be equal to the a priori probability E_i is the $(k + 1)$th smallest among the errors. Hence, the probability in (4.1) is equal to

$$P(E_j < E_i \text{ for exactly } k \text{ opponents } j). \tag{4.2}$$

Obviously, this probability is the same for any player. On the other hand, ties between different E_j are zero-probability events, so we know that exactly one player's error will be the $(k + 1)$th smallest. Therefore the probability in (4.2) must equal $1/n$. Consequently, as long as the opponents do not play (iteratively) dominated strategies, the expected payoff of β at $\bar{x}$ cannot exceed p^*. Since the expected payoff of α at $\bar{x}$ is $E(X | X_i^\varepsilon = \bar{x}) = \bar{x}$, it follows that the range where α is strictly (iterative) dominant for each player i may be extended below $\bar{x}$ if $\bar{x} > p^*$. This shows the first part of the proposition. The proof of the second part is completely analogous. $\square$

It is remarkable that the result described in proposition 4.1 does not depend on the scale parameter ε of the observation errors. In particular, the result remains valid for observation errors that are infinitesimally small. However, as ε tends to zero, the players' observations become perfectly correlated and in the limit they coincide with the value of x that actually prevails in the game. Hence, if one accepts the game $g^\varepsilon(n, p)$ with infinitesimal ε as an accurate model of the situation in which $g(n, x, p)$ has to be played, but x can only be observed with a small amount of noise, then one will also have to accept that the game should be played as described in proposition 4.1. Consequently, adding some noise allows us to solve the equilibrium selection problem. Comparing the switching point $\bar{x} = \bar{x}(n, p)$ in proposition 4.1 with the cutoff levels x^* and x^{**} obtained in section 3 we see that they generally will differ. Hence, although all the approaches that have been discussed yield the switching point $x = \frac{1}{2}$ if $n = 2$, they typically lead to different answers if $n > 2$.

5 Discussion

5.1 Equilibrium Selection

The foundations of equilibrium selection theory were laid in the seminal papers of Nash on bargaining (Nash 1950, 1953). Nash initiated what is nowadays called the Nash program, noting that cooperative games may be reformulated as noncooperative ones, by modeling explicitly the bargaining process through which agreements may be reached. Nash proposed that every bargaining game be solved by selecting one of the equilibria of its noncooperative representation as the solution, and he suggested unanimity games as noncooperative models of bargaining situations. In such games players simultaneously propose an outcome, and an outcome is implemented if and only if it has been proposed by all players; all other cases result in the status quo. A unanimity game indeed has many (strict) equilibria and, thus, Nash was forced to address the equilibrium selection problem. He proposed to select as the solution that equilibrium for which the product of the deviation losses was largest, and he offered an axiomatic as well as a noncooperative justification for this selection rule. The latter is based on a perturbation argument. The unanimity game is "smoothed" by introducing some uncertainty (about the size of the pie that is to be divided), and it is shown that only one equilibrium of the original game is a necessary limit of equilibria of the smoothed game as the amount of smoothing approaches zero. Nash writes:

Thus the equilibrium points do not lead immediately to a solution of the game. But if we discriminate between them by studying their relative stabilities we can escape from this troublesome nonuniqueness (Nash 1953, 132)

The approaches to equilibrium selection discussed in the previous sections were all inspired by Nash's ideas and can be viewed as attempts to extend the solution obtained by Nash beyond the class of unanimity games.[3] For example, Harsanyi and Selten write:

Our attempts to define risk dominance in a satisfactory way have been guided by the idea that it is desirable to reproduce the result of Nash's cooperative bargaining theory with fixed threats. The Nash property is not an unintended by-product of our theory. (Harsanyi and Selten 1988, 215)

Although all the solutions considered in this chapter indeed reproduce the outcome proposed by Nash for the special class of unanimity games, the example of the Stag Hunt Game shows that they no longer coincide outside this restricted class. The discussion in the previous sections has made clear that different outcomes result because the approaches differ in their assumptions on what players believe about the amount of correlation in the beliefs and/or strategies of their opponents. The main difference between the equilibrium selection approaches in section 3 and the payoff uncertainty approach in section 4 is that the former rely on more or less ad hoc thought processes to model the players' reasoning about the game, while the latter—in the spirit of the Nash program—is based on a fully specified noncooperative game.

In connection with the payoff uncertainty approach, several important questions remain to be answered. In particular, one would like to know how robust the result is with respect to the distributional assumptions and to the parametrization of the underlying class of games. Naturally, one would also like to know whether the approach can be extended to other classes of games. At present we are not able to answer these questions in a satisfactory way. As far as robustness is concerned, we can point to our 1990 paper, in which we show that, for the special class of 2×2 games, the results obtained are independent both of distributional assumptions and of which parameters are allowed to vary, at least as long as the ex ante uncertainty is sufficiently large so that players consider the various types of dominance solvable games to be possible. Of course it is still an open question whether this independence result generalizes to other classes of games.

5.2   The Stag Hunt

It should be clear that the result of proposition 4.1 is driven by the fact that the areas where $x > 1$ (resp. $x < 0$) exert a remote influence on any x that is inside the interval $(0, 1)$. In the context considered by Rousseau, x might be viewed as a measure of the number of hares in the forest. The model described in section 4 then assumes that each hunter, by looking around, can make an unbiased estimate x_i of x, and the intuitive argument underlying the proof of proposition 4.1 is as follows. (For simplicity, assume $p(x) = 0$ if $x < 1$ and $p(1) = 1$, so that the stag hunt is successful only if all hunters cooperate.) If $x_i > 1$, then hunter i thinks that there are so many hares around that it is simply not worthwhile to continue the stag hunt. If $x_i < 1$, but $x_i \approx 1$, player i believes that it is very likely that some other hunter j thinks that hunting the stag is not worthwhile, and hence decides not to cooperate, so that player i concludes that stag hunting is not worthwhile for himself either. This reasoning process may continue to very low values of x_i. As long as player i thinks that some player j may think that some player k may think that ... some player l does not cooperate in the stag hunt, player i will not cooperate himself. Presenting the argument in this way makes clear that what is driving the result is the lack of common knowledge (Aumann 1976) in the perturbed game. Although in the game $g^\varepsilon(n, p)$ player i has very precise *knowledge* about X if he observes x_i (i.e., he knows that $X \in [x_i - \varepsilon, x_i + \varepsilon]$), there is no *common knowledge* about X among the players, except for the prior distribution of this random variable. This lack of common knowledge forces the players to take a global perspective in solving the perturbed game: in order to know what to do at the observation x_i, one should also know what to do at observations that are far away from x_i. This is why the regions $x_i > 1$ and $x_i < 0$ exert a remote influence.[4]

In all honesty we are compelled to say that Rousseau attributes much less rationality to the players than we do in the proof of proposition 4.1. He writes:

Voilà comment les hommes purent insensiblement acquérir quelque idée grossière des engagements mutuels, et de l'avantage de les remplir, mais seulement autant que pouvait l'exiger l'intérêt présent et sensible; car la prévoyance n'était rien pour eux; et, loin de s'occuper d'un avenir éloigné, ils ne songeaient pas même au lendemain. S'agissait-il de prendre un cerf, chacun sentait bien qu'il devait pour cela garder fidèlement son poste; mais si un lièvre venait à passer à la portée de l'un d'eux, il ne faut pas douter qu'il ne le poursuivît sans scrupule, et qu'ayant atteint sa proie il ne se souciât fort peu de faire manquer la leur à ses compagnons. (Rousseau 1971, 229)[5]

The above quotation also suggests a quite different perturbation of the game $g(n, x, p)$; namely, the probability of being confronted with a hare may be independent across hunters. For the sake of simplicity assume that the stag hunt is successful only if all players cooperate ($p(x) = 0$ if $x < 1$, $p(1) = 1$); let the hunter's utility of consuming his part of the stag be normalized to 1; interpret $\underline{x} \in (0, 1)$ as the disutility of the effort spent in hunting; and let $\bar{x} - \underline{x}$ (with $\bar{x} > 1$) be the utility of consuming a hare. Then, if each hunter encounters a hare with probability ε, and if the probabilities associated with different players are independent, the situation may be represented by the following game $g^\varepsilon(n, \underline{x}, \bar{x})$:

(1) For each i a realization x_i of X_i is drawn, where X_i takes the value $\underline{x}$ with probability $1 - \varepsilon$, and the value $\bar{x}$ with probability ε, and where $(X_i)_{i=1}^n$ are mutually independent;

(2) Player i learns x_i and chooses between α and β;

(3) If player i chooses α, his payoff is x_i; if he chooses β, his payoff is 1 if all opponents also choose β, otherwise it is 0.

The analysis of this game yields a result that is completely different from that of the game $g^\varepsilon(n, p)$ discussed in section 4; in $g^\varepsilon(n, \underline{x}, \bar{x})$, cooperation may be feasible even for high values of $\underline{x}$. Specifically, as long as

$$(1 - \varepsilon)^{n-1} \geq \underline{x}, \tag{5.1}$$

the game $g^\varepsilon(n, \underline{x}, \bar{x})$ has an equilibrium where each player i chooses β if $x_i = \underline{x}$. (Note that this game also has an equilibrium where each player i always, i.e., for each realization of X_i, chooses β.) Whether or not condition (5.1) can be satisfied depends on whether or not ε is small in relation to n, so it matters in which order limits are taken. For fixed ε, condition (5.1) will not be satisfied for n sufficiently large, but if ε is infinitesimally small, then (5.1) is satisfied for all n.

The game $g^\varepsilon(n, \underline{x}, \bar{x})$ is a special case of a game with independent randomly disturbed payoffs, as considered originally in Harsanyi 1973. Harsanyi's main result is that *each* equilibrium (be it pure or mixed) of a "generic" unperturbed game can be approximated by the pure equilibria of games in which there is slight payoff randomness. Hence, Harsanyi's approach offers a justification for the set of all equilibria, and does not enable us to select particular equilibria. The aim of this chapter has been to show that selection becomes possible if players' payoffs (or at least players' observations, see Carlsson and van Damme 1990) are correlated. An obvious question, therefore, is which approximation method (correlated or independent) is most appropriate. In our view, this question cannot be answered in the abstract, but must be related to specific contexts. We believe that both the independent and the correlated case yield valuable insights concerning the stability and the selection of equlhbrla.

Notes

The authors gratefully acknowledge Pieter Kop Jansen for drawing their attention to Bernstein polynomials.

1. It is important to note that the theory of Harsanyi and Selten does not rely on risk dominance alone but also invokes the principle of payoff dominance. Although the authors are aware of its questionable justification, they decide to rank payoff dominance above risk dominance (see Harsanyi and Selten 1988, secs. 10.11 and 10.12.)

2. For the special class of 2×2 games, the risk-dominance relation is characterized by a convincing set of axioms (Harsanyi and Selten 1988, sec. 3.9).

3. Nash also considered only two-person games.

4. A similar action from a distance occurs in Rubinstein's (1989) electronic mail game.

5. That is the way by which men could unconsciously acquire some rough idea of mutual commitments, and of the advantage of keeping to them, but only insofar as their present and perceivable interests dictated; because foresight meant nothing to them; and, far from concerning themselves with the long-term future, they did not even think of tomorrow. In a stag hunt, each one knew that he had to stay faithfully in his allotted place; but if a hare happened to pass by within reach of one of them, there can be no doubt that he would pursue it without any scruples, and that after reaching his quarry he would worry very little about depriving his fellows of their share of it.

References

Aumann, R. J. 1976. "Agreeing to Disagree." *The Annals of Statistics* 4:1236–1239.

Aumann, R. J. 1990. "Nash Equilibria Are Not Self-Enforcing." In *Economic Decision-making: Games, Econometrics and Optimisation,* ed. J. J. Gabszewicz, J.-F. Richard, and L. A. Wolsey. New York: Elsevier.

Carlsson, H., and E. van Damme. 1990. "Global Games and Equilibrium Selection." CentER Discussion Paper 9052,

Cooper, R., and A. John. 1988. "Coordinating Coordination Failures in Keynesian Models." *Quarterly Journal of Economics* 103:441–463.

Cooper, R. W., D. V. DeJong, R. Forsythe, and T. W. Ross 1990. "Selection Criteria in Coordination Games: Some Experimental Results." *American Economic Review* 80:218–233.

Crawford, V. P. 1991. "An 'Evolutionary' Interpretation of Van Huyck, Battalio, and Beil's Experimental Results on Coordination." *Games and Economic Behavior* 3:25–59.

Güth, W. 1985. "A Remark on the Harsanyi-Selten Theory of Equilibrium Selection." *International Journal of Game Theory* 14:31–39.

Güth, W. 1990. "Equilibrium Selection by Unilateral Deviation Stability." Working paper, University of Frankfurt/M.

Güth, W., and B. Kalkofen. 1989. *Unique Solutions for Strategic Games*: Lecture Notes in Economic and Mathematical Systems, vol. 328. Berlin: Springer Verlag.

Harrison, G. W., and J. Hirschleifer 1989. "An Experimental Evaluation of Weakest Link/Best Shot Models of Public Goods." *Journal of Political Economy* 97:201–225.

Harsanyi, J. C. 1973. "Games with Randomly Disturbed Payoffs: A New Rationale for Mixed-Strategy Equilibrium Points." *International Journal of Game Theory* 2:1–23.

Harsanyi, J. C., and R. Selten. 1988. *A General Theory of Equilibrium Selection in Games*. Cambridge: M.I.T. Press.

Jervis, R. 1978. "Cooperation under the Security Dilemma." *World Politics* 30:167–214.

Klambauer, G. 1975. *Mathematical Analysis*. New York: Marcel Dekker.

Kohlberg, E., and J.-F. Mertens. 1986. "On the Strategic Stability of Equilibria." *Econometrica* 54:1003–1039.

Lewis, D. 1969. *Convention: A Philosophical Study*. Cambridge: Harvard University Press.

Nash, J. F. 1950. "The Bargaining Problem." *Econometrica* 18:155–162.

Nash, J. F. 1953. "Two-Person Cooperative Games." *Econometrica* 21:128–140.

Rousseau, J.-J. 1971. *Discours sur l'origine et les fondements de l'inégalité parmi les hommes*. Vol. 2 of *Oeuvres complètes*. Paris: Editions du Seuil.

Rubinstein, A. 1989. "The Electronic Mail Game: Strategic Behavior Under 'Almost Common Knowledge.'" *American Economic Review* 79:385–391.

Schelling, T. C. 1980. *The Strategy of Conflict*. 2nd ed. Cambridge: Harvard University Press.

Van Huyck, J. B., R. C. Battalio, and R. O. Beil. 1990. "Tacit Coordination Games, Strategic Uncertainly, and Coordination Failure." *American Economic Review* 80:234–248.

13 Variable Universe Games

Michael Bacharach

1 Introduction

1.1 Blockmarking

The game of Blockmarking is played like this. Two players are shown some children's wooden playblocks on a tray. They are told that each in turn must make a secret mark on one of them, and that they will both receive a prize of £100 if they turn out to have marked the same one, and otherwise nothing.

Here are three variants:

Blockmarking 1: There are five blocks, and there is no obvious way to distinguish them: they seem identical in color, shape, size, material, and so on.[1]

Blockmarking 2: Once again there are five blocks. One is red and the rest yellow; otherwise they are as alike as in Blockmarking 1.

Blockmarking 3: There are 20 blocks, of which 2 are red and 18 yellow. Otherwise they are as alike as in Blockmarking 1, but for one thing: if you look you can see that the grain of the wood isn't the same in all of them; in one of them (a yellow one) it's wavy, and in all the others it's straight.

How is it rational to choose in these three games? I think that our intuitions are clear, at least about the first two. In Blockmarking 1 there is nothing to choose between the five blocks, and one might as well choose at random. In Blockmarking 2 one should most certainly mark the red block. In Blockmarking 3 the answer, for a player who has noticed the patterns in the wood grain, depends on her assessment of how likely it is that her partner will have noticed them, too. We are inclined to say that if this is high enough she should mark the wavy-grained block; and that if not she should mark one of the two red blocks. In this chapter 1 shall give game-theoretic arguments that these intuitions are sound.

The intuitive solutions agree broadly with the prescription: "In coordination problems, choose salient options." This suggests that my analysis may help solve the unsolved problem of how to give a game-theoretic rationale for choosing the salient. It does so.[2]

But my principal purpose here is not this. It is, rather, to introduce a new representation of multiperson decision problems, to be called a "variable universe game" (VU-game). The main novelty about variable universe games is that one specifies *the way players conceive their situation* and how this varies. By contrast, in standard representations such as the extensive and normal forms the way players conceive their situation is not treated as a variable, and indeed is not explicitly specified at all.[3]

I shall use the Blockmarking games as illustrations of what can be done with this representation. But the representation may be applied not only to Blockmarking and such isomorphs of Blockmarking as Rendezvous, and not only indeed to games of coordination, but to multiperson decision problems quite generally. And I conjecture that for many of these, of diverse structures, its application may prove to be of value.

1.2 Traditional Theory Misspecifies the Payoff Matrices

The traditional way of analyzing Blockmarking 1–2 is this: There are five blocks. Let us call them "B1," ..., "B5." Setting the utility of the £100 prize equal to 10, the payoff matrix for Blockmarking 1 is as in table 13.1 (where B1 denotes the action of marking B1, and so on). The payoff matrix of Blockmarking 2 is the same. The traditional analysis next identifies five pure Nash equilibria ((B1, B1), etc.) and finally asks if there are valid solution concepts which allow us to select one of these as the solution, perhaps, in the case of Blockmarking 2, by invoking the salience of (Bk, Bk), where Bk is the red block.

Table 13.1
Traditional payoff matrix for blockmarking 1 and 2

	B1	B2	B3	B4	B5
B1	10, 10	0, 0	0, 0	0, 0	0, 0
B2	0, 0	10, 10	0, 0	0, 0	0, 0
B3	0, 0	0, 0	10, 10	0, 0	0, 0
B4	0, 0	0, 0	0, 0	10, 10	0, 0
B4	0, 0	0, 0	0, 0	0, 0	10, 10

In the approach I shall offer here, the payoff matrices for Blockmarking 1 and Blockmarking 2 turn out to be quite different both from that of 13.1 and from each other. They are shown in table 13.2a and 2b, respectively.

This respecification is the key to the game-theoretic argument I shall give for the intuitive solutions. Given these matrices, we have only to invoke the so-called Principle of Coordination (the principle that in a pure coordination game with multiple equilibria, it is rational to play one's part in the unique Pareto-optimal equilibrium if there is one).[4]

1.3 Belief-Spaces as Variables

Quite generally, a given question may or may not *occur to* an agent facing a decision problem; she may or may not *think of* it. This phenomenon gives rise to variations in agents' belief systems of a more radical sort than those to be found in the familiar Bayesian model. In the Bayesian model the different belief states of a person (produced in her by this or that evidence) merely redistribute the weights she attaches to the propositions (or events) of some fixed set (the sigma field of some fixed probability space). Here, by contrast, it is the set of propositions about which she has beliefs at all—her *belief-space*—that varies. Variable universe games model such variations: thus they represent games as a species of what Binmore (1987) calls "open universe" problems[5]

It may seem an odd suggestion that there is any indeterminacy about what game players, of all people, think about. For in game theory all that the players think about is the "rules of the game" and their consequences, and we take it for granted that the "rules" are unambiguously given to the players. These "rules" may include descriptions of objectives (such as "being the first to go out"), of ranges of permitted acts at a given stage (such as "Move any pawn one square forward"), and of possible outcomes, together with specifications of probability distributions over these elements. Or they may be given more abstractly, in terms of payoffs and of acts defined merely by their payoff vectors or as branches in a game tree. Either

Table 13.2
Payoff matrices for blockmarking 1 and 2 as VU games

	2, 2	2, 2	2, 2
2, 2	2,2	10, 10	0, 0
	2, 2	0, 0	2.5, 2.5
(a)		(b)	

way, the idea of unmistakable rules is extremely restrictive. Its easy assumption may have been fostered by the prominence of parlor games in
the development of game theory: in parlor game theory it's natural to
suppose the "rules" known, because the game is defined in a book of rules,
and arguably players must know them for it to be true that they're playing
that game. In sharp contrast, the "rules" are not unambiguously given to
players of games arising "in the field." Such players must derive "rules"—
formulate their problem to themselves as a certain game—from some
initial apprehension of their situation. In a given problem situation, as we're
about to see, there are multiple possibilities as to how they may do so.

It is hardly surprising that some familiar properties of games fail in
VU-games. For example, in general players do not not know their own
alternative strategies, and so cannot choose one (so VU-games in general
lack normal forms). For suppose a player has a possible future information
state in which she believes that p_1 and that p_2 and that . . . . Now suppose
that one of the p's doesn't belong to her current belief-space; then she
cannot now specify what to do when in the above-defined information
state.[6] This absence of strategies known to players will force us to devise
a new notion of equilibrium for VU-games.

In most problem situations there are some questions that are bound to
occur to a normal person, others that are less obvious, others that it would
be positively peculiar to think of. I have little to say here about what
rationality requires of us in this respect. What I do offer is a rudimentary
descriptive model of the process that brings questions to the minds of
players and the consequences of this process.

This model gives us probabilities for players' having various belief-
spaces. It allows us, too, to say something about the beliefs which a player
with one belief-space has about the belief-spaces of others; and this is vital
if we are to have a theory of encounters between such players that's worth
calling a theory of games between them.

The process revolves around the fact that different thoughts involve
common concepts, and the broad hypothesis that when one thought involving given concepts occurs to someone, related thoughts involving the
same concepts are likely to, also: for instance, if it occurs to me that there
is only one block touching the edge, it's likely to occur to me also that I can
mark the block touching the edge, that the block touching the edge is one
of the white ones, to wonder whether you have noticed that there is one
block touching the edge, and so on. Concepts also give structure to the set
of belief-spaces in another way: they *hang together*. There are clusters of
concepts such that if propositions involving one member occur to me,

related propositions involving other members are likely to occur to me also: for instance, if I notice that some of the blocks are square, I am likely to notice that others are triangular, when this is so. But such clusters vary widely in the probability, in a given problem situation, that thoughts involving them occur to a player: for instance, one conjectures that in Blockmarking 3 color thoughts are more likely to occur than grain-pattern thoughts.[7]

The membership, and the probability of "firing," of clusters of concepts are (stylized) facts about the players' culture: wood-grain patterns may be more important in the lives of the Ashanti than in those of Oxford dons, and wood-grain thoughts may occur more readily to Ashanti playing Blockmarking; the cluster of color concepts may be richer in the white range among the Eskimos; and so forth. But within one culture the parameters of the conceptual scheme—its membership, its clustering, and the readiness to mind of the clusters in a given situation—are essentially shared. Furthermore, they are shared in this strong sense: not only does everyone have certain conceptual competences by virtue of belonging to the community, but every member knows that every member has them.[8]

2   Variable Universe Games

2.1   Variable Universe Games Defined

In this subsection I describe briefly a formal model of games—"variable universe games"—in which players' belief-spaces vary in the sort of way I have been describing. The model I present here contains some special assumptions (for example, that there are two players, with identical feasible act sets and identical payoffs); but it will be clear enough how the same ideas may be applied in other cases.

The primitive elements of a VU-game are as follows. First, the labels "P1" and "P2" of the two players. Next, a set A of *verbal phrases*, interpreted as describing a set of feasible acts. Thus, in a VU-game intended to model Blockmarking 2, A contains *mark the red block*, but not *mark the white block*. A is called the *act-description set*. Next, a *utility function* U defined on pairs of elements of A: $U(a, a')$ is interpreted as the common payoff of $P1$ and $P2$.

The next element is a set F of disjoint sets of concepts called "families." Typical families applicable to physical objects are the set $C = \{$blue, brown, buff, ...$\}$ of (ordinary English) color concepts, the set S of shape concepts, and so on. We shall assume presently that, for each F in F, in thinking about her situation a player uses all or none of the concepts of F: hence the term *family*. A set of families we shall call a "repertoire" (of concepts), and we'll write $\mathbb{R}$ for the set of nonempty repertoires. If r, r' are repertoires and $r \subseteq r'$, r is called a "subrepertoire" of r'.

The next element is a function V, the *availability function*, defined on both families and repertoires, and taking values between 0 and 1. The interpretation of V is as follows. For each family F and each player Pi there is a single Bernoulli trial, trial (F, i), in which a success is interpreted as the outcome that F *occurs to* Pi. All the trials are independent. $V(F)$ is interpreted as the probability of a success in trial (F, i) $(i = 1, 2)$. We shall say that Pi *has the repertoire* r if the event that F occurs to Pi is realized just for $F \in r$. The independence assumption implies that the probability Pi has repertoire r is $V(r)$, where

$$V(r) = \prod_{F \in r} [V(F)] \prod_{F \in F \setminus r} [1 - V(F)]. \tag{1}$$

The last element of a VU-game is a function A from $\mathbb{R}$ to subsets of $\mathbb{A}$, the *coverage function*. We construct A thus: the phrases in $A(r)$ are those which involve, of the concepts belonging to families, only those belonging to families in r. For example, suppose that $\mathbb{F} = \{C, S\}$ and the act-description set $\mathbb{A} = \{$*mark the red, mark the yellow, mark the round, mark the square*$\}$; then if, say, r is the singleton repertoire $\{C\}$ we set $A(r) = \{$*mark the red, mark the yellow*$\}$. (We introduce A as a *primitive* in order to avoid having to define formally the delicate notion of "involving a concept.") Given the construction of A, it follows from our interpretation of a player having a repertoire that it she has repertoire r, the only act descriptions about which she has beliefs are the members of $A(r)$; and so we shall assume.

One restrictive feature of VU-games as here defined, implicit in the fact that the range of A is $\mathbb{A}$, is that variations in players' belief-spaces are assumed to be confined to their beliefs about actions. But there is nothing to stop one from considering, in contexts where it's called for, analogous effects on the scope of players' beliefs about, for example, outcomes.

I assume that the beliefs players have about actions are as follows. If player has repertoire r, then for each a in $A(r)$ she believes that she can a if she does no other act,[9] and for each a not in $A(r)$ she has no belief as to whether she can a if she does no other act. That is, writing $C_i a$ for the proposition Pi *can a if she does no other act*, and $\mathbb{B}_i$ for the *belief-space* of Pi:

(i) If Pi has r, $C_i a$ belongs to $\mathbb{B}_i$ if and only if $a \in A(r)$;

(ii) If $C_i a$ belongs to $\mathbb{B}_i$, then Pi believes $C_i a$.

$$\tag{2}$$

Call an act description a such that Pi believes $C_i a$ an "option" for Pi, and the set of Pi's options Pi's "option set." (2) implies that

If Pi has r, Pi's option set is $A(r)$.   (3)

Similarly, writing $(a_1, a_2) \mapsto u$ for the proposition *if P1 a_1s and P2 a_2s, then each has payoff u*, we assume

(i) If Pi has r, $(a_1, a_2) \mapsto U(a_1, a_2)$ belongs to $\mathbb{B}_i$ if and only if
$a_1, a_2 \in A(r)$;

(4)

(ii) If $(a_1, a_2) \mapsto U(a_1, a_2)$ belongs to $\mathbb{B}_i$, then Pi believes that
$(a_1, a_2) \mapsto U(a_1, a_2)$.

Lastly, we make an assumption about players' knowledge of (3) and (4). It says in essence that (for each i) a player has a belief about (3) just if r is a subrepertoire of her own repertoire, and if so she believes (3); similarly for (4).

(i) If Pj has r', for $i = 1, 2$, proposition 3 (resp. (4)) belongs to $\mathbb{B}_j$
if and only if $r \subseteq r'$;

(5)

(ii) For $i = 1, 2$, if (3) (resp. (4)) belongs to $\mathbb{B}_j$, Pj believes (3)
(resp. (4)).

Note that all the beliefs players have about acts are true.

The specification of players' beliefs is completed by a collection $\{\pi_r | r \in \mathbb{R}\}$ of subjective probability functions (the same for both players) over the subrepertoires of r. For each $r' \subseteq r$, $\pi_r(r')$ is known as the "probability of r' modulo r," and is interpreted as the subjective probability that a player having repertoire r assigns to the other player's having r'. I assume that players are "naive" in the following way: Pi implicitly assumes that Pj's repertoire ($j \neq i$) is some subrepertoire of hers; that is, if she has r, she implicitly assigns probability 0 to his having occur to him any family not in r. We shall see in section 4.2 that this naïveté is likely to make no difference to behavior, and the assumption spares us some apparatus. To be precise, we assume that

$$\pi_r(r') = \prod_{F \in r'} [V(F)] \prod_{F \in r \backslash r'} [1 - V(F)] \quad \text{if } r' \subseteq r$$

$$\text{undefined} \qquad\qquad\qquad \text{otherwise.} \qquad (6)$$

Hence, from (1),

$$\pi_r(r') = V(r') / \prod_{F \in \mathbb{F} \backslash r} [1 - V(F)], \qquad (7)$$

which is the conditional probability that Pj's repertoire is r' given that it contains no family outside r. (Thus the $\pi_r(r')$ ($r' \subseteq r$) sum to unity.)

These being the primitive elements in the definition of a VU-game, and since the player labels are fixed over all VU-games, we can define a *VU-game* as a 5-tuple $\langle \mathbb{A}, U, \mathbb{F}, V, A \rangle$, where $\mathbb{A}$ is the *act-description set*, U is the *utility function*, $\mathbb{F}$ is the *set of families*, V is the *availability function*, A is the *coverage function*, and these elements are defined as above.

2.2 Modeling Blockmarking 3 as a VU-Game

In some cases, choosing appropriate parameters $\mathbb{A}$, U, $\mathbb{F}$, V, A to represent a problem situation as a VU-game is a trivial matter. For most parlor games we mechanically transcribe the rules: $\mathbb{A}$ is simply the set of options as described in the rules; there is only one repertoire (the set of all families), which has availability 1 and is mapped by A into $\mathbb{A}$. But when the problem situation is known to us in story form, or from observing life, modeling demands judgment.

The core of the modeling problem is the question: How are the players likely to describe their choice situation to themselves and to describe each other describing it to themselves? Although there is no general mechanical method for answering this question, the exercise is not quite unprincipled. As the example I shall now give illustrates, we can make use of certain general considerations about how agents understand situations and understand each other to understand them, considerations built on the notion of "normality."

First, let's fill out a little the story of Blockmarking 3 in section 1. The players are, we may presume, two normal English-speakers who know of each other no more than that they are just that. They are publicly told that each can mark any one block, that they each get a prize of £100 if and only if they mark the same one, and that they will each have a minute, say, to examine the blocks before they must make their choices. Normal people are unhandicapped, so our players can't help noticing the color distribution, and the probability is 1 that each will believe that there are 2 reds and 18 yellows and infer that each can mark either one of the reds or mark any one of the 18 yellows. Assume that all normal players have ways of "picking" at random one object from a definite set of objects (independently of any such randomization by the other player). Then each player will further conclude that each can mark a red at random in this way, or mark a yellow at random in this way. These then are options resulting from noticing the color distribution. Because what's required for these options to result is merely that the players are normal, the players also know that the options result in each other from noticing the distribution.[10] Similarly, because the probability of any normal player's noticing is 1, each player knows that the probability is 1 that the other notices.

On the other hand, it is by no means certain that a normal player notices the grain patterns. Simplifying somewhat, we may suppose that there's a definite probability, v, that an arbitrary normal player in this situation does so. As before, because the players are normal, they are in a position to know *this* fact about normals. However, they only know it (in the sense of "know" required for it to belong to their belief-spaces) if the question occurs to them. It's natural to assume that it won't if they don't notice the grain patterns, and it will if they do.

These observations underlie the following representation of Blockmarking 3 as a VU-game (VUG3).

2.3   Blockmarking 3 as a VU-game (VUG3)

Write b = *block*, r = *red*, y = *yellow*, s = *straight-grained*, w = *wavy-grained*, $C = \{r, y, \ldots\}$ for the color family, $G = \{s, w, \ldots\}$ for the grain-pattern family, and $B = \{b, \ldots\}$ for the family that contains *block*. Write Mx for *mark the* x and $M\tilde{x}$ for *mark an* x *at random* ($x \in \{b, r, y, s, w\}$). Set $\mathbb{A}$, U, $\mathbb{F}$, V, A thus

$$\mathbb{A} = \{M\bar{b}, M\bar{r}, M\bar{y}, M\bar{s}, Mw\}.$$

U as in table 13.3. The independence of the randomizing actions implies that if P1 marks one of the 20 blocks at random, the probability that P1 marks the same block as P2 is 1/20 whatever the act of P2. If P1 marks one of the 2 reds at random, and P2 marks one of the 19 straights at random, then since both reds are straight, the coordination probability is 1/19; and so forth.

Table 13.3
Payoff matrix for VUG3

	$M\bar{b}$	$M\bar{r}$	$M\bar{y}$	$M\bar{s}$	Mw
$M\bar{b}$	0.5	0.5	0.5	0.5	0.5
$M\bar{r}$	0.5	5	0	0.526	0
$M\bar{y}$	0.5	0	0.556	0.497	0.556
$M\bar{s}$	0.5	0.526	0.497	0.526	0
Mw	0.5	0	0.556	0	10

$\mathbb{F} = \{B, C, G\}$; thus $\mathbb{R} = \{B, C, G, BC, BG, CG, BCG\}$, in obvious nota-tion. $V(B) = V(C) = 1$, $V(G) = v < 1$. We shall largely work not with $\mathbb{R}$ but with $\mathbb{R}^+ =_{df} \{r | r \in \mathbb{R}, V(r) > 0\}$. From (1) and the V-assignment

$$\mathbb{R}^+ = \{BC, BCG\}$$

$$A(C) = \{M\bar{b}, M\bar{r}, M\bar{y}\}, \qquad A(BCG) = \mathbb{A}.$$

Thus from (3), (4), (5) if Pi has repertoire BC (if G does not occur to her) her option set is $\{M\bar{b}, M\bar{r}, M\bar{y}\}$, she is aware only of the submatrix of figure 13.3 consisting of its first three rows and columns, and she knows that if the other player has repertoire BC, he too will be aware of just these facts about his options and about the payoffs to act pairs. If G *does* occur to Pi, her option set is $\mathbb{A}$; she is aware of the whole matrix, and knows that if Pj has BC, he will have the limited option set and matrix knowledge described above, and that if Pj has BCG, he will have the option set and matrix knowledge that she herself does.

Further, if Pi has repertoire BC, from (6) Pi has subjective probability $\pi_{BC}(BC) = 1$ that Pj has BC and $\pi_{BC}(r) = 0$ that Pj has $r = B, C$; and if Pi has BCG, Pi's subjective probabilities for Pj's repertoire r are

$$\pi_{BCG}(r) = 1 - v \quad \text{for } r = BC, v \text{ for } r = BCG, \text{ and } 0 \text{ for all other } r \in \mathbb{R}^+_{BCG}.$$

3   Solution Theory for Variable Universe Games

3.1   Variable Universe Equilibria

In seeking solutions of VU-games I adopt, in this chapter, the conventional approach: that is, I characterize solutions in terms of certain equilibria. The connection between being an equilibrium and being a solution of a VU-game is given by applying to these games the indirect argument—the general argument that being an equilibrium is a necessary condition for being a solution *if* there is a determinate theory of rational play (von Neumann and Morgenstern 1944; Luce and Raiffa 1957; and Bacharach 1987). The notion of a theory of rational play needs generalizing in the context of VU-games. A determinate theory of rational play known by a rational player indicates to the player the right action to choose, that is, brings such a player to believe that a certain action is the right one. This means that such a theory for a VU-game $\mathscr{T}$, say, must have the following property: when a player has conceptual repertoire r, $\mathscr{T}$ indicates an action in $A(r)$. For when she has r, the player has no thought involving acts outside $A(r)$, and a fortiori no beliefs that she should choose such an action. Thus the output of such a theory of rational play for a VU-game is a function from repertoires to feasible act descriptions; I shall call such a function an "indicator."

For the same reason, a player cannot, when she has repertoire r (other than $\mathbb{F}$), know the indicator thrown up by the rational theory (nor, for that matter, any other indicator). She can know at most that part of it which involves no concepts outside her repertoire; that is, the restriction of the indicator to her actual repertoire and its subrepertoires. (Her position may be likened to that of an agent entrusted with a principal's strategy in the form of a pack of envelopes, one for each information set, who is only able to open envelopes as and when she finds herself in the information sets to which the envelopes relate.) So an equilibrium cannot be a pair of indicators each of which is a subjective best reply to the other. We need notions of "best reply" and "equilibrium," which are first defined partially, relatively to repertoires, then somehow combined.

Formally, an *indicator* σ is a function from $\mathbb{R}^+$ (the set of repertoires with positive probability) to $\mathbb{A}$ which satisfies $\sigma(r) \in A(r)$. Say that σ *indicates a in r* if $\sigma(r) = a$. Note that what an indicator indicates to a player is independent of the player (with no loss of generality in view of the symmetries of VU-games). If σ is an indicator, say that a player *follows* σ if, for all r, she chooses the act $\sigma(r)$ if her repertoire is r. Write $\mathbb{R}_r^+ = \{r' | r' \in \mathbb{R}^+, r' \subseteq r\}$ for the set of subrepertoires of r that have positive probability. Call a function ρ from $\mathbb{R}_r^+$ to $\mathbb{A}$ such that $\rho(r) \in \mathbb{A}(r)$ an "r-indicator." If ρ is an r-indicator, say that Pi *follows* ρ if, for all $r' \subseteq r$, she chooses $\rho(r')$ if she has r'. Lastly, if σ is an indicator, write σ_r for the r-indicator that is the restriction of σ to $\mathbb{R}_r^+$.

Let ρ be any r-indicator. For any option $a \in A(r)$, define the *payoff modulo r against ρ of a* as

$$EU_r(a, \rho) := \sum_{r' \in \mathbb{R}_r^+} [\pi_r(r') U(a, \rho(r'))]. \tag{8}$$

Note that, from (7), the sum in (8) is equal to the sum taken over all $r' \subseteq r$. So if Pi has repertoire r, $EU_r(a, \rho)$ is simply her conditional subjective expected utility conditioned on her choosing a and Pj's following ρ.

If ρ is a r-indicator, say that an option $a \in A(r)$ is a *best-reply modulo r against ρ* if a maximizes over $A(r)$ the payoff modulo r against ρ, that is, if

$$a \in \text{argmax}_{a \in A(r)} EU_r(a, \rho).$$

Suppose that there is a determinate theory of play, $\mathcal{T}$, that best describes rational play in our game, and suppose it contains the theorem that rational play for P1, P2 is given by the indicator τ. Call (τ, τ) the "solution" of the game. Assume that P1 and P2 are rational, and that rational players maximize subjective expected utility. Then we may make the following formal assumptions (in which $i, j = 1, 2; i \neq j$). Each ascribes a property of rationality to a player *relative to* the belief-space she has given her current repertoire.[11]

(A1) Pi follows τ;

(A2) If Pi has r, she knows that Pj follows the r-indicator τ_r (all $r \in \mathbb{R}_r^+$);

(A3) If Pi has r, and knows that Pj follows the r-indicator ρ, then Pi chooses a best reply modulo r against ρ.

It follows immediately from (A1)–(A3), in generalization of the indirect argument, that

The solution of a VU-game is a variable universe equilibrium,   (9)

where *variable universe equilibrium* is defined as follows. Call a symmetric pair (ρ, ρ) of r-indicators an "equilibrium modulo r" if $\rho(r)$ is a best reply modulo r against ρ. A symmetric pair (σ, σ) of indicators is a *variable universe (VU-) equilibrium* if (σ_r, σ_r) is an equilibrium modulo r for each r in $\mathbb{R}^+$.[12]

3.2   The Principle of Coordination and Admissible Equilibria

Write Eq_r for the set of r-indicators ρ such that (ρ, ρ) is an equilibrium modulo r. If $\rho \in Eq_r$, say that (ρ, ρ) is *admissible modulo* r (and that ρ itself is *admissible modulo* r) just if $EU_r(\rho, \rho) < EU_r(\rho', \rho')$ for no ρ' in Eq_r. Say also that a VU-equilibrium (σ, σ) is *admissible* just if (σ_r, σ_r) is an admissible equilibrium modulo r for each r in $\mathbb{R}^+$.

I shall adopt the following version of the Principle of Coordination. Let (τ, τ) be the solution of a VU-game.

(A4) If (ρ, ρ) is an equilibrium modulo r that is not admissible, $\tau_r \neq \rho$.

It follows at once from (9) and (A4) that

The solution of a VU-game is an admissible VU-equilibrium.   (10)

4   Solving the Blockmarking Problems

4.1   Blockmarking 1 and 2

Blockmarking 1 and 2 may be represented as the VU-games "VUG1" and "VUG2," which I now define. The acts $M\tilde{b}$, and so on, and the families C, and so on, are defined as in subsection 2.3.

VUG1   Define $\mathbb{A} = \{M\tilde{b}\}$, U by $U(M\tilde{b}, M\tilde{b}) = 0.2$, $\mathbb{F} = \{B\}$, $V(B) = 1$, and A by $A(B) = \{M\tilde{b}\}$. We have

THEOREM 1   The solution of VUG1 is (σ, σ) where σ is the indicator defined by $\sigma(B) = M\tilde{b}$.

The proofs of the theorems are in the chapter appendix.

VUG2   We set $\mathbb{A} = \{M\tilde{b}, Mr, M\tilde{y}\}$ and U as in table 13.2b. The quantities in table 13.2b follow from the story and the independence of the randomizing actions. We define $\mathbb{F} = \{B, C\}$, and V by $V(B) = V(C) = 1$, whence $\mathbb{R}^+ = \{BC\}$. Finally, we define A by $A(BC) = \{M\tilde{b}, Mr, M\tilde{y}\}$. Then we have

THEOREM 2   The solution of VUG2 is (σ, σ), where σ is the indicator defined by $\sigma(BC) = Mr$.

4.2   The Source of the Solutions

In each of VUG1 and VUG2 there is only one possible repertoire, so it cannot be the stochastic variation of repertoires allowed for in VU-games that does the work in rationalizing the intuitive solutions of Blockmarking 1 and 2. But the fundamental fact that what options a player has depends on what concepts she has *is* responsible. It is this which accounts for the payoff matrices being the 1×1 and 3×3 matrices of figure 13.2, rather than the 5×5 matrix of figure 13.1. The former matrices then easily imply the intuitive solutions, in the case of Blockmarking 2 via the Principle of Coordination.

The fact that the matrices are the 1×1 and 3×3 ones depends on "what concepts Pi has" in the sense that it depends on what concepts are *available* to Pi, that is, on the function V. V in turn is given by the culture to which the players belong. Suppose all the blocks are red. If the range of color concepts of normal players were very refined—as refined as that of a painter—it is easy to see that the matrix would comprehend that of figure 13.1, with acts like *mark the magenta block*. The converse—that not having more refined concepts means players face the 1×1 matrix— involves a more subtle point. The essence of the argument is this. Consider any one of the blocks in Blockmarking 1—say $B4$. To decide to mark $B4$, a player must have some way of thinking about it as a particular block. If there were some concept x that distinguished it for her from the others—as "the one that is x"—she could decide on an act which would be (coextensive with) an act of marking $B4$, by deciding to *mark the one that is x.*[13] But *ex hypothesi* there is no such x; she has no way of thinking about the particular block $B4$[14] and so she cannot decide to mark *it*. By the same token, *none* of the options implicit in the 5×5 matrix of figure 13.1 exists. All that is left is to decide to mark one block at random.

4.3   Blockmarking 3: Rarity versus Availability

Solution as a VU-game
Let us generalize the story of Blockmarking 3 a bit, so that instead of 20 blocks of which 2 are red and 18 are yellow, there are N blocks of which m are red and n yellow, where

$$m + n = N, \quad 0 < m < n. \tag{11}$$

Everything else is as before: the one wavy-grained block is of the more numerous color, yellow. In the representation of the problem as a VU-game, VUG3* say, $\mathbb{A}$, $\mathbb{F}$, V, A are as before, and U is given in table 13.4. Define the indicators σ_2, σ_5 by

$$\sigma_2(BC) = M\tilde{r}, \quad \sigma_2(BCG) = M\tilde{r}$$

$$\sigma_5(BC) = M\tilde{r}, \quad \sigma_5(BCG) = Mw.$$

Then we have

Table 13.4
Payoff matrix for VUG3*

	$M\tilde{b}$	$M\tilde{r}$	$M\tilde{y}$	$M\tilde{s}$	Mw
$M\tilde{b}$	10/N	10/N	10/N	10/N	10/N
$M\tilde{r}$	10/N	10/m	0	10/(N − 1)	0
$M\tilde{y}$	10/N	0	10/n	10(n − 1)/n(N − 1)	10/n
$M\tilde{s}$	10/N	10/(N − 1)	10(n − 1)/n(N − 1)	10/(N − 1)	0
Mw	10/N	0	10/n	0	10

THEOREM 3   The solution of VUG3* belongs to $\{(\sigma_2, \sigma_2), (\sigma_5, \sigma_5)\}$, and is (σ_2, σ_2) if $v < 1/m$, and (σ_5, σ_5) if $v > 1/m$.

Theorem 3 tells us that however likely or unlikely players are to have beliefs about the grain patterns, for a player who hasn't got any the rational thing to do is to mark a red at random. If she *has* thoughts about the grain patterns, then the rational thing to do depends on the parameters. Since $1/m$ measures the rarity of red blocks relative to wavy blocks, the theorem says that a grain-aware player should mark the wavy block if the probability that the other is grain-aware exceeds the relative rarity of red blocks, and should mark the red one if it falls short of it.

Explanation
Here, intuitively, is how our assumptions entail theorem 3. If a player Pi is unaware of the grain patterns (has repertoire BC), she takes both players to have the options $M\bar{b}$, $M\tilde{r}$, $M\tilde{y}$; as in VUG2, each of these options gives an equilibrium modulo BC, but of these only $(M\tilde{r}, M\tilde{r})$ is admissible, so only $M\tilde{r}$ is rational.

Consider now a player who *is* aware of the grain patterns. She is pulled by conflicting reasons. On one hand, she *has* the option of marking the wavy block (she believes that the action so described is a feasible act for her), and she has a good reason for choosing it: if both she and the other player do so, her utility is 10, while the next best option to coordinate on, marking a red at random, has payoff of only $10/m$. This merit of Mw is due to the rarity of wavy blocks relatively to red blocks. On the other hand, it may be that her partner is grain-unaware. In that case he doesn't have marking the wavy block on his list of options, and there is no reason to think that he will mark it unless by chance; while he certainly has thoughts involving the colors and is considering "picking" a red. Indeed, picking a red will appear to him the best option to coordinate on. So it is riskier to mark the wavy block than to pick a red, because of the low relative availability of the grain-pattern concepts, measured by v. The low relative rarity $1/m$ of red blocks, and the low relative availability v of the grain-pattern concepts, pull against each other. The balance of reasons favors marking the wavy block if and only if v is great enough compared with $1/m$.

Sophisticated Players
Suppose we assume that the players are "sophisticated"—that is, each player Pi assigns some positive probability to the proposition *one or more families other than* $F_1, F_2, \ldots$ *have occurred to* Pj (where $F_1, F_2, \ldots$ are the families of Pi's own repertoire). If we assume this, we must make a further

assumption, about Pi's "blind conjecture," that is, her conjecture as to how Pj would choose in this case. The result is unaffected if we make the most natural assumption, namely that the blind conjecture is that the partner is equally likely to choose each of the blocks.[15]

5   Discussion

5.1   Salience

Our solutions of the VU-game representations of the three Blockmarking problems corroborate the so-called Focal-Point Principle (in a coordination game one should choose the *salient* Nash equilibrium when there is one).

Lewis (1969) defines a *salient item* in a group as "one that stands out from the rest by its uniqueness in some conspicuous respect." Salience thus defined has two dimensions: *conspicuousness* or noticeability of some feature, and *unique instantiation* of this feature. These are logically independent, although they frequently appear in amalgam in discussions of salience. Now a feature of blocks is "conspicuous" just if the associated concept is highly *available* in the sense of this chapter. So an equilibrium[16] is salient just if it's of the form (Mx, Mx), and x is highly available. In Blockmarking 2 *mark the red* is the only such option, and in Blockmarking 1 there is none.

Our analysis shows not only *that* rational choice agrees with the Focal-Point Principle but explains *why* it does in these two examples. The two dimensions of salience play radically different roles: the conspicuousness of redness is responsible for an act description involving redness *being an option at all*; the uniqueness of the red block makes the action be the *only admissible one* (modulo the unique repertoire) among the options.

The case of Blockmarking 3 is more complex. On Lewis's definition, both $M\bar{r}$ and Mw fail to be salient, for *red* isn't uniquely instantiated, and *wavy-grained* isn't conspicuous; the link between Lewis's salience and rational choice present in Blockmarking 1 and 2 is thus broken in Blockmarking 3. However, the spirit of Lewis's notion is preserved if we gloss it to admit, as we certainly should, degrees of salience, and make these depend positively on degree of conspicuousness and degree of rarity. On this account both $M\bar{r}$ and Mw *may* be highly salient: the former if m is small enough; the latter if v is large enough. And theorem 3 can then be put in this way: If a player has repertoire BCG, she should choose the most salient of her options. That is, she should obey a focal-point principle. This principle is not, however, the Focal-Point Principle, but the latter relativized to the player's repertoire and belief-space. But so it should be, for if a player has no thoughts involving G, she *cannot* choose Mw, however much more salient than $M\tilde{r}$ it may be; and it *can* be much more salient without her having thoughts involving G.

5.2   The Status of the Present Theory

I have shown that the representation of certain multiperson decision problems as VU-games gives a game-theoretic basis for intuitive solutions that have previously lacked one. The key to doing so has been to extend game theory backwards to include a theory, however skeletal, of the player's conception of her situation. As we have seen, insisting on this reveals that the outcome of a given interactive problem situation can vary dramatically with the conceptual resources of the players. We have observed that there are two levels of such variation: the stochastic variations of the "coming to mind" process parametrized by the availability function V, and the possibility of alternative values of the parameters of V itself. The latter variation models effects of culture. VU-games may therefore be seen as a tool for giving precise expression to the emerging view (see, for example, Kreps 1990) that the rational solutions of some games depend on the culture of the players.

Appendix

Proof of Theorem 1 σ is the only indicator, and is a best reply modulo B to $\sigma(B)$. Hence (σ, σ) is the unique equilibrium modulo B and so the unique admissible VU-equilibrium.   □

Proof of Theorem 2 $\mathbb{R}^+ = \{BC\}$ and the only indicators are σ, σ', σ'', where $\sigma(BC) = M\tilde{r}$, $\sigma'(BC) = M\tilde{y}$, $\sigma''(BC) = M\tilde{b}$. Each gives an equilibrium modulo BC and so a VU-equilibrium, but only σ is admissible modulo BC and so (σ, σ) is the unique admissible VU-equilibrium.   □

Proof of Theorem 3   To find the solution, if any, of MG3 we first find the admissible equilibria modulo r for $r = BC$.

(a) *Analysis for repertoire BC.* $\mathbb{R}^+_{BC} = \{BC\}$ and $\mathbb{A}_{BC} = \{M\tilde{b}, M\tilde{r}, M\tilde{y}\}$. The BC-indicators are thus ρ_1, ρ_2, ρ_3, given by $\rho_1(BC) = M\tilde{b}$, $\rho_2(BC) = M\tilde{r}$, $\rho_3(BC) = M\tilde{y}$.

From (8), if ρ is a BC-indicator ρ and $x \in \mathbb{A}_{BC}$, $EU_{BC}(x, \rho(BC)) = \pi_{BC}(BC)U(x, \rho(BC)) = U(x, \rho(BC))$, since $\mathbb{R}^+_{BC} = \{BC\}$ and $\pi_{BC}(BC) = 1$. Thus (ρ_1, ρ_1) is an equilibrium modulo BC), since $M\tilde{b}$ maximizes

$U(x, M\tilde{b})$, from figure 13.4. Similarly, (ρ_2, ρ_2) is an equilibrium modulo BC since $m < N$ by (11), and so $M\tilde{r}$ maximizes $U(x, M\tilde{r})$. So, too, is (ρ_3, ρ_3), since Mw maximizes $U(x, Mw)$.

But $EU_{BC}(\rho_2, \rho_2) > EU_{BC}(\rho_3, \rho_3) > EU_{BC}(\rho_1, \rho_1)$ from figure 13.4, since $(1/m) > (1/n) > (1/N)$. Thus the unique admissible equilibrium modulo BC is (ρ_2, ρ_2).

(b) *Analysis for repertoire BCG.* The BCG-indicators are the 25 functions from $\mathbb{R}^+_{BCG} = \{BC, BCG\}$ to $\mathbb{A}_{BCG} = \{M\tilde{b}, M\tilde{r}, M\tilde{y}, M\tilde{s}, Mw\}$. But we don't need to consider all these in order to find the admissible VU-equilibria. For each BCG-indicator σ, (σ, σ) is one just if σ_r is admissible modulo r for all $r \in \mathbb{R}^+_{BCG}$; that is, just if

(i) σ_{BC} is admissible modulo BC, and

(ii) σ_{BCG} is admissible modulo BCG.

From (a), (i) is so just if σ_{BC} is ρ_2, that is, $\sigma(BC) = M\tilde{r}$, that is, writing $\sigma \mapsto (x, y)$ when $\sigma(BC) = x$, $\sigma(BCG) = y$, just if σ is one of the indicators $\sigma_1, \ldots, \sigma_5$ given by

$\sigma_1 \mapsto (M\tilde{r}, M\tilde{b})$; $\sigma_2 \mapsto (M\tilde{r}, M\tilde{r})$; $\sigma_3 \mapsto (M\tilde{r}, M\tilde{y})$;

$\sigma_4 \mapsto (M\tilde{r}, M\tilde{s})$; $\sigma_5 \mapsto (M\tilde{r}, Mw)$.

We now determine which of these satisfies (ii) for what values of v. $(\sigma_{BCG}, \sigma_{BCG})$ is an equilibrium modulo BCG (not necessarily admissible) if $\sigma(BCG)$ maximizes, over $x \in \mathbb{A}_{BCG}$,

$$\sum_{r \in \mathbb{R}^+_{BCG}} [\pi_{BCG}(r) U(x, \sigma(r))] = (1 - v) U(x, \sigma(BC)) + v U(x, \sigma(BCG)),$$

since $\pi_{BCG}(BC) = 1 \times (1 - v)$ and $\pi_{BCG}(BCG) = 1 \times v$, from (6).

Thus σ_1 satisfies (ii) if and only if $M\tilde{b}$ maximizes $(1 - v) U(x, M\tilde{r}) + v U(x, M\tilde{b})$ over $\mathbb{A}_{BCG}$, that is, from table 13.4, if and only if

$$1/N = \max\{1/N, [(1 - v)/m] + (v/N), v/N, v/N,$$

$$[(1 - v)/(N - 1)] + v/N, v/N\}.$$

But this is false, since $v < 1$ and $m < N$.

σ_2 satisfies (ii) if and only if $M\tilde{r}$ maximizes $(1 - v) U(x, M\tilde{r}) + v U(x, M\tilde{r}) = U(x, M\tilde{r})$, which is true, since $m < N - 1$.

σ_3 satisfies (ii) if and only if $M\tilde{y}$ maximizes $(1 - v) U(x, M\tilde{r}) + v U(x, M\tilde{y})$, that is, if and only if

$$(v/n) = \max\{(1 - v)/m, v/n, v/n, [1 - (v/n)]/(N - 1), v/N\}.$$

This is so if and only if $v \geq n/N$.

σ_4 satisfies (ii) if and only if $M\bar{s}$ maximizes $(1 - v)U(x, M\bar{r}) +$ $vU(x, M\bar{s})$, that is, if and only if

$$1/(N - 1) = \max\{1/N, [(1 - v)/m] + [v/(N - 1)], v(n - 1)/n(N - 1),$$

$$1/(N - 1), 0\}.$$

This is false, since $v < 1$ and $m < N - 1$.

σ_5 satisfies (ii) if and only if Mw maximizes $(1 - v)U(x, Mw) +$ $vU(x, Mw)$, that is, if and only if

$$v = \max\{1/N, (1 - v)/m, v/n, (1 - v)/(N - 1), v\}.$$

This is so if and only if $v \geq 1/(m + 1)$.

Thus (ii) is satisfied, and (σ, σ) is an equilibrium modulo BCG just for σ_2, for σ_3 if $v \geq n/N$, and for σ_5 if $v \geq 1/(m + 1)$. But

$$EU_{BCG}(\sigma_2, \sigma_2) = 1/m, \qquad EU_{BCG}(\sigma_3, \sigma_3) = v/n, \qquad EU_{BCG}(\sigma_5, \sigma_5) = v$$

so the unique admissible indicator modulo BCG is σ_2 or σ_5 according as $v < 1/m$ or $v > 1/m$. Since both σ_2 and σ_5 are admissible modulo BC unconditionally, the unique admissible VU-equilibrium is (σ_2, σ_2) or (σ_5, σ_5) according as $v < 1/m$ or $v > 1/m$. The theorem follows, by (10). $\square$

Notes

The author is grateful to Robin Cubitt, Elizabeth Fricker, Peter Gärdenfors, Alan Gibbard, Margaret Gilbert, David Gauthier, Martin Hollis, Hyun Song Shin, and Robert Sugden for discussions and for comments on earlier versions of this paper.

1. For instance, they are distributed higgledy-piggledy in such a way that there is no obvious positional feature to distinguish them either.

2. Elsewhere (Bacharach 1991) I focus on how it does. See also section 5.1.

3. One previous study that makes the way players conceive their situation explicit is Gauthier's important 1975 paper; see note 8 on the difference between Gauthier's approach and mine.

4. See, for example, Luce and Raiffa 1957; Gauthier 1975; and Anderlini 1990 for various statements and arguments in favor of this principle. Whether or not it describes the outcomes of interactions between ideal spirits, it is strongly commended by common sense.

5. But "variable" is better than "open" here. Binmore has in mind a learning situation in which the believer cannot tell now how the believer's belief-space may evolve with experiences that may force changes in the believer's fundamental theory; I am concerned with contemporaneous alternatives.

6. I assume that if one has a belief about the truth of "if I believe that ... and p and ... then I'll ...," then one has beliefs about the truth of p.

7. In Blockmarking problems the thoughts in question have perceptual content, and their occurrence is a matter of "noticing." But the points in the text are perfectly general. Consider an isomorph of Blockmarking in which players must write down the name of the same nineteenth-century British monarch: gender thoughts and length-of-reign thoughts are, I submit, more likely to occur than thoughts about, say, the spelling of the monarch's name.

8. Of course, individuals' competences may depart widely from the "by virtue" competences in some respects. But someone playing against someone having "nonbasic" concepts in general has no ground for knowing he has them. For further discussion of these questions see Bacharach 1992.

In contrast to my model, Gauthier (1975) describes the players as "choosing" ways of conceiving them. There is certainly a voluntary element in conceptualization: one may deliberately search for new ways of describing one's problem. But *what* this search produces is essentially out of one's hands, determined by sub-personal mechanisms. We can make some allowance for such a search within the present model: if the players' problem situation gives them time to engage in it, the values of the occurrence probabilities will be correspondingly higher.

9. When the umpire says, "Go," or whatever.

10. The theory of the acquisition of mutual beliefs among normal agents is discussed in detail in Bacharach 1992. At the heart of it is the Axiom of Double Sufficiency, namely: if being normal suffices for some ability, then being normal also suffices for knowing that it suffices for this ability.

11. (A1) expresses the idea that rational players know the rational theory; (A2) the idea that each knows the other to be rational and knows (A1) to be true of rational players; (A3) specifies part of the substance of rationality.

12. (9) is the analogue for VU-games of the proposition that a unique rational solution of a normal-form game must be a Nash equilibrium. We may say that (τ, τ) is a VU-equilibrium just if τ is "subjectively best against itself." But note that following τ may be, in some conceptual states, not objectively best, given that the other player is following τ, since when Pi has r, Pi has, literally, no idea of what Pj is up to, if Pj is in a condition outside $\mathbb{R}_r^+$.

13. One can only decide on an act as described in some way; acts regarded as objects of decision are differentiated by their descriptions. But two act descriptions may be "coextensive": that is, they may, as it happens, refer to the same event. See Davidson 1980; Macdonald and Pettit 1981.

14. The latter action may be described as "marking the one that comes up" if it's $B4$ that happens to come up, but this phrase doesn't express a way of thinking about a particular one.

It may be objected that the story of Blockmarking 1 allows players to have "private" individuating descriptions. We can generalize VU-games to model this possibility. But it does not change the rational outcome. For suppose the grain of one of the blocks reminds P1 of the face of an aged uncle. Although this gives P1 a way of thinking about it, and an option, it does nothing to make that option rational, for she has no reason to suppose that P2 will have a private description that picks out this block rather than another.

15. On this assumption the sophisticated player's maximand $EU_r^{soph}(x, \rho)$ mixes $qU(x, M\bar{b})$ into $EU_r(x, \rho)$, where q is her probability that her partner has thoughts that she hasn't. But $U(x, M\bar{b})$ is constant over x, so the maximizer, and the best reply map, are unaffected.

16. In Blockmarking problems an *option* is a way of marking a block, and I take it that an option, and the corresponding equilibrium, are salient if and only if it is a way of marking a salient *block*.

References

Anderlini, Luca. 1990. "Communication, Computability, and Common-Interest Games." Working paper. St John's College, Cambridge University.

Bacharach, Michael. 1987. "A Theory of Rational Decision in Games." *Erkenntnis* 27:17−55.

Bacharach, Michael. 1991. "Games with Concept-Sensitive Strategy Spaces." Working paper. Institute of Economics and Statistics, University of Oxford.

Bacharach, Michael. 1992. "The Acquisition of Common Knowledge." In *Knowledge, Belief, and Strategic Interaction*, ed. C. Bicchieri and B. Skyrms. Cambridge: Cambridge University Press.

Davidson, Donald. 1980. *Essays on Actions and Events*. Oxford: Clarendon Press.

Gauthier, David. 1975. "Coordination." *Dialogue* 14:195−221.

Kreps, David. 1990. *Game Theory and Economic Modelling*. Oxford: Oxford University Press.

Lewis, David. 1969. *Convention: A Philosophical Study*. Cambridge: Harvard University Press.

Luce, Duncan, and Howard Raiffa. 1957. *Games and Decisions: Introduction and Critical Survey*. New York: Wiley.

Macdonald, Graham, and Philip Pettit. 1981. *Semantics and Social Science*. London: Routledge and Kegan Paul.

Sugden, Robert. 1991. "Rational Bargaining." In *Foundations of Decision Theory*, ed. Michael Bacharach and Susan Hurley. Oxford: Basil Blackwell.

von Neumann, John, and Oskar Morgenstern. 1944. *Theory of Games and Economic Behavior*. Princeton: Princeton University Press.

14   Aspects of Rationalizable Behavior

Peter J. Hammond

1 Introduction

1.1. Common-Expectations Equilibrium

For much of its history, game theory has been pursuing an enormously ambitious research program. Its aim has been nothing less than to describe equilibrium outcomes for every game. This involves not only a specification of each player's behavior or choice of strategy, but also of what beliefs or expectations justify that behavior. The crucial feature of equilibrium expectations is that they correspond to a single *common* joint probability distribution over all players' strategy choices. This makes it natural to speak of "common-expectations equilibrium." Moreover, these expectations must be *rational* in the sense that each player is believed to play, with probability 1.0, some optimal strategy, given the conditional joint probability of all the other players' strategies. Indeed, this is the essential idea behind Aumann's (1987) notion of "correlated equilibrium." If one also imposes stochastic independence between the probability beliefs concerning strategy choices by different players, then each common expectations or correlated equilibrium with this property is a Nash equilibrium, and conversely. Thus, the crucial feature of both Nash and correlated equilibrium is the existence of common "rational" expectations. In the case of games of imperfect information, the same is true of a Bayesian Nash equilibrium with a common prior, as considered by Harsanyi (1967–68). Refinements of Nash equilibrium, including subgame-perfect, trembling-hand-perfect, proper, sequential, and stable equilibria, all incorporate the same common expectations hypothesis a fortiori.

1.2   Battle of the Sexes, and Holmes vs. Moriarty

The restrictiveness of such common expectations equilibrium can be illustrated by two classic games. The first is Battle of the Sexes, as presented by Luce and Raiffa (1957) and often considered since. As is well known, this game between the two players Row (R) snd Column (C) has three Nash equilibria in which

(1) Row and Column play (A, a) and get (2, 1);

(2) Row and Column play (B, b) and get (1, 2);

(3) Row and Column play the mixed strategies $(\frac{2}{3}A + \frac{1}{3}B, \frac{1}{3}a + \frac{2}{3}b)$, and get expected payoffs $(\frac{2}{3}, \frac{2}{3})$.

Knowing that these are the three Nash equilibria does little to help select among them. Moreover, while observing the strategy choices (A, a) or (B, b) might help to reinforce our belief in equilibrium theory, how are we to interpret an observation of (B, a) or of (A, b)? Did these anomalous observations arise because the players followed the mixed strategies of the third Nash equilibrium and experienced misfortune on this occasion? Or if (A, b) is observed, is that because R hoped that the equilibrium would be (A, a), whereas C hoped that it would be (B, b)? And if (B, a) is observed, is that because R feared that the equilibrium would be (B, b), while C feared it would be (A, a)?

A second classic game is von Neumann and Morgenstern's (1953, 176–178) simple model of one small part of the story concerning Sherlock Holmes's attempts to escape being murdered by Professor Moriarty before he could get the professor and his criminal associates arrested.[1] According to this simple model, Moriarty wants to catch Holmes, while Holmes wants to escape to Dover and then to the Continent. As Holmes boards a train heading from London to Dover, he sees Moriarty on the platform and sees that Moriarty sees him, and sees him seeing Moriarty, and so on.[2]

	C			
		a		b
A	2	1	0	0
B	0	0	1	2

Figure 14.1
Battle of the sexes

Holmes knows that Moriarty will hire a special train to overtake him. The regular train has just one stop before Dover, in Canterbury. Given the payoffs that von Neumann and Morgenstern chose in order to represent Holmes's and Moriarty's preferences, this involves the two-person zero-sum bimatrix game shown. Here H denotes Holmes, M denotes Moriarty, and each has the strategy D or d of going on to Dover, as well as the strategy C or c of stopping in Canterbury.

The unique equilibrium of this simplified game has Moriarty stop his special train in Canterbury with probability 0.4, but go on to Dover with probability 0.6, while Holmes should get off the ordinary train in Canterbury with probability 0.6 and go directly to Dover with probability 0.4. In fact, Conan Doyle had Holmes (and Watson) get out at Canterbury and take hiding, as Moriarty's special train rushed through the station on its way to Dover. Von Neumann and Morgenstern observe that this is the closest pure-strategy profile to their mixed-strategy Nash equilibrium, but that the latter gives Holmes only a 0.52 chance of escaping. In fact, who is to say that Holmes did not do better? Holmes predicted that Moriarty would head straight to Dover, thinking perhaps that Moriarty had to reach it at all costs in time to intercept Holmes before he could escape quickly, while believing (correctly) that Moriarty could still catch Holmes later even if Holmes did get off at Canterbury and proceed more slowly to the Continent. What this shows, I suppose, is partly that von Neumann and Morgenstern's model is excessively simplified. But it also calls into question their advocacy of mixed strategies in such complex situations. Although pursuit games can involve bluff, just as poker does, there is much else to consider as well.

In the first of these two games there is as yet no good story of how one of the three Nash equilibria is to be reached. In the second, even though there is a single Nash equilibrium in mixed strategies, it is by no means obvious that this describes the only possible set of rational beliefs which the players might hold about each other.

	M			
		c		d
H	C	-100 $\quad$ 100	0 $\quad$ 0
	D	50 $\quad$ -50	-100 $\quad$ 100

Figure 14.2
Holmes v. Moriarty

1.3   Rationalizable Strategic Behavior

Fortunately, work on "rationalizable strategic behavior" initiated during
the early 1980s by Bernheim (1984, 1986) and Pearce (1984) (and in their
earlier respective Ph.D. dissertations) offers us a way out of the predicament. Actually, their approach is quite closely related to Farquharson's
(1969, chap. 8 and app. 2) earlier idea (in his 1958 D.Phil. dissertation) that
one should eliminate all (weakly) dominated strategies repeatedly, and consider anything left over as a possible strategy choice. A partial link between
these ideas will be discussed in section 3 below. In both Battle of the Sexes
and Morgenstern's version of Holmes vs. Moriarty, *any* pair of strategy
choices by both players is rationalizable. However, before we can say what
is really rational, we have to say much more about players' beliefs, and
about whether they are sensible. This seems entirely right. A Nash equilibrium is indeed plausible when there is good reason for the players to have
the particular common expectations underlying that equilibrium. But if
there is no particularly good reason for them to have such common expectations, a Nash equilibrium has no more obvious claim to our attention than
does any other profile of rationalizable strategies with associated divergent
beliefs for the different players.

1.4   Outline of Chapter

The rest of this chapter will study some implications of relaxing the hypothesis that expectations are held in common by all players, and so of
allowing that any profile of rationalizable strategies could occur. Section 2
begins by considering iteratively undominated strategies. It provides a
concise definition of rationalizable strategies, and explains how they form
a subset of those strategies that survive iterative deletion of strictly dominated strategies. An example shows that this rationalizability is too weak a
criterion, however, because it allows players to use strategies that are
strictly dominated in subgames, but not in the whole game. Accordingly,
Pearce's (1984) more refined concept of "cautious rationalizability" is reca-
pitulated for later use. It is also shown how strategies are cautiously rationalizable only if they survive a "cautious" version of iterative deletion of
weakly dominated strategies.

Section 3 considers correlated strategies, and argues that there is more
scope for these in connection with divergent expectations than with the
common expectations that underlie a correlated equilibrium. It is somewhat
implausible for players to believe, even in the absence of a correlation

device, that their own strategies are correlated with those of other players. But it is entirely reasonable for one player to believe that strategies of other players are correlated with each other. The common-expectations hypothesis forces these two kinds of correlation to be synonymous, but in games with three or more players the ideas are quite different when players' expectations are allowed to diverge. Moreover, the set of all correlated rationalizable strategies can be found by removing all strictly dominated strategies for each player iteratively. And the set of all correlated cautiously rationalizable strategies can be found by "cautiously" iterating the rule of removing weakly dominated strategies.

Although rationalizability appears to be a coarsening instead of a refinement of Nash equilibria, there are cases when it helps to establish a refined equilibrium, as both Bernheim (1984, 1023) and Pearce (1984, 1044) have pointed out. Indeed, as section 4 explains, the arguments behind forward induction make much more sense when players are allowed to be uncertain about what happens in a subgame, instead of having in mind some definite Nash or sequential equilibrium. The arguments that help sustain forward induction, however, also point to a serious weakness of orthodox game theory. For it turns out that players' expectations in a subgame may well be influenced by the opportunities that they know other players have forgone in order to reach the subgame. Indeed, such is the essence of forward induction. But then it follows that the subgame is not adequately described by the strategy sets and payoff functions, or even by its extensive-form tree structure. Important information about what happened before the subgame started is missing from the usual description of a game, and such information could also be relevant to the whole game, since that is presumably a subgame of some larger game started earlier.

Iterative removal of all weakly dominated strategies has often been criticized as leading to implausible outcomes. Some of these objections are based on examples from van Damme (1989) and also from Ben-Porath and Dekel (1992) of how the opportunity to "burn money" at the start of a game can significantly influence its outcome, even though that opportunity is never actually used. Dekel and Fudenberg (1990) discuss another similar example. Although cautious rationalizability is generally different from iterative removal of all weakly dominated strategies, in these particular examples it actually leads to identical outcomes. Accordingly, section 4 also provides a brief discussion of the examples. It is claimed that appropriate forward-induction arguments make the disputed outcomes less implausible than has previously been suggested.

Section 5 offers some brief concluding remarks.

2 Iteratively Undominated and Rationalizable Strategies

2.1 Iteratively Undominated Strategies

Consider a normal-form game (N, A^N, v^N), where N is a finite set of players who each have specified finite (action) strategy spaces A_i, and A^N denotes the Cartesian product space $\prod_{i \in N} A_i$ of strategy profiles, while $v^N = (v_i)_{i \in N}$ is a list of all individuals' payoff functions $v_i : A^N \to \mathbb{R}$ that depend on the strategy profile $a^N \in A^N$.

As general notation, given any measurable set T, let $\Delta(T)$ denote the set of all possible probability distributions over T.

Given any product set $K^N = \prod_{i \in N} K_i \subset A^N$ of strategy profiles, any player $i \in N$, and any pure strategy $a_i' \in K_i$, say that a_i' is "strictly dominated relative to K^N" if there exists $\mu_i \in \Delta(K_i)$ such that $\sum_{a_i \in K_i} \mu_i(a_i) v_i(a_i, a_{-i}) > v_i(a_i', a_{-i})$ for all combinations $a_{-i} = (a_j)_{j \in N \setminus \{i\}} \in K_{-i} := \prod_{j \in N \setminus \{i\}} K_j$ of all the other players' pure strategies. And say that a_i' is "weakly dominated relative to K^N" if there exists $\mu_i \in \Delta(K_i)$ such that $\sum_{a_i \in K_i} \mu_i(a_i) v_i(a_i, a_{-i}) \geq v_i(a_i', a_{-i})$ for all $a_{-i} \in K_{-i}$, with strict inequality for at least one such a_{-i}. Then let $S_i(K^N)$ (resp. $W_i(K^N)$) denote the members of K_i that are not strictly (resp. weakly) dominated relative to K^N. Also, let $S(K^N)$ and $W(K^N)$ denote the respective product sets $\prod_{i \in N} S_i(K^N)$ and $\prod_{i \in N} W_i(K^N)$.

Next, for each positive integer $k = 1, 2, 3, \ldots$, let $S^k(K^N) := S(S^{k-1}(K^N))$ be defined recursively, starting from $S^0(K^N) := K^N$. In the case when $K^N = A^N$, write S^k for $S^k(A^N)$, and let S_i^k denote player i's component of the product space $S^k = \prod_{i \in N} S_i^k$; it is the set of all i's strategies that remain after k rounds of removing all the strictly dominated strategies of every player. Evidently

$$\varnothing \neq S_i^k \subset S_i^{k-1} \subset \cdots \subset S_i^1 \subset S_i^0 = A_i \quad (k = 3, 4, \ldots).$$

Therefore, because each player's A_i is a finite set, the limit set

$$S_i^\infty := \lim_{k \to \infty} S_i^k = \bigcap_{k=0}^{\infty} S_i^k$$

must be well defined and nonempty. Actually, there must exist some finite n for which $S_i^k = S_i^n$ for all $i \in N$ and all integers $k \geq n$. Moreover, the same arguments apply to the sets W_i^k of strategies that survive k rounds of removing all the weakly dominated strategies of every player, and for the limit sets W_i^∞.

Finally, to prepare the ground for the later discussion of cautious rationalizability, another iterative rule for removing dominated strategies needs to be considered. This involves the recursive definition that starts from $(WS^\infty)^0(A^N) := A^N$ and continues with

$$(WS^\infty)^k(A^N) := W(S^\infty((WS^\infty)^{k-1}(A^N))) \quad (k = 1, 2, 3, \ldots),$$

where $S^\infty(K^N) := \bigcap_{k=0}^\infty S^k(K^N)$, of course. Also, $(WS^\infty)^k(A^N)$ can be written as the Cartesian product $\prod_{i \in N} (WS^\infty)_i^k$. Arguing as before, this recursion converges in a finite number of steps, so that each player $i \in N$ has a well-defined nonempty limit set

$$(WS^\infty)_i^\infty := \bigcap_{k=0}^\infty (WS^\infty)_i^k.$$

In what follows, $(WS^\infty)_i^\infty$ will be described as the set of i's strategies that survive *cautious iterative deletion of dominated strategies*. Evidently, the construction of this limit set begins with removing strictly dominated strategies iteratively, in order to arrive at S_i^∞ for each player. But whenever the process of removing strictly dominated strategies gets stuck because there are no more to remove, the procedure passes on to the next stage, which consists of just *one* round of removing *all* the weakly dominated strategies of *every* player. After this single round, it reverts immediately to removing strictly dominated strategies iteratively. Since the process can get stuck many times, in fact strategies that are only weakly dominated may have to be removed repeatedly. But such weakly dominated strategies are removed only "cautiously," in the sense that they must remain inferior even after strictly dominated strategies have been removed iteratively as far as possible.

2.2   Definition and Basic Properties of Rationalizable Strategies

For any probability distribution $\pi_i \in \Delta(A_{-i})$ which represents player i's beliefs about other players' strategies $a_{-i} \in A_{-i}$, let

$$U_i(a_i, \pi_i) := \mathbf{E}_{\pi_i} v_i(a_i, a_{-i}) := \sum_{a_{-i} \in A_{-i}} \pi_i(a_{-i}) v_i(a_i, a_{-i})$$

denote, for each $a_i \in A_i$, the expected value of v_i with respect to π_i. Then i's *best-response correspondence* is defined by

$$B_i(\pi_i) := \arg \max_{a_i \in A_i} \{U_i(a_i, \pi_i)\}.$$

The sets R_i ($i \in N$) of *rationalizable strategies* are now constructed recursively as follows (see Pearce 1984, 1032, def. 1; and compare Bernheim 1984, 1015). First, let $R_i^0 := A_i$ for each player i. Then let

$$R_i^k := B_i\left(\prod_{j \in N \setminus \{i\}} \Delta(R_j^{k-1})\right) \quad (i \in N; k = 1, 2, \ldots).$$

Thus R_i^1 consists of all player i's possible best responses, given the various beliefs that i might have about the strategies chosen by the other players from the sets $R_j^0 = A_j$ ($j \neq i$). Next, R_i^2 consists of all i's possible best responses given the various beliefs about the strategies chosen by other players from R_j^1 ($j \neq i$), and so on. Evidently, $\emptyset \neq R_i^k \subset R_i^{k-1}$ ($k = 1, 2, \ldots$), as can readily be proved by induction on k. It follows that each player $i \in N$ has a well-defined limit set

$$R_i := \lim_{k \to \infty} R_i^k = \bigcap_{k=0}^{\infty} R_i^k.$$

This completes the construction. Indeed, because each set A_i is finite, the limit R_i is reached after a finite number of iterations, and is nonempty. Since there is a finite number of players, moreover, there is a finite integer n, independent of i, for which $k \geq n$ implies $R_i = R_i^k$ (all $i \in N$). But then

$$R_i = B_i\left(\prod_{j \in N \setminus \{i\}} \Delta(R_j)\right),$$

so that rationalizable strategies are best responses to possible beliefs about other players' rationalizable strategies. The following result is also easy to prove:

THEOREM   Every strategy which is used with positive probability in some Nash equilibrium must be rationalizable. That is, if $E \subset \prod_{i \in N} \Delta(A_i)$ denotes the set of possible Nash equilibrium beliefs that players can hold about each other, and if for any player $i \in N$, the set E_i is defined as $\{a_i \in A_i | \exists \pi^N = (\pi_i)_{i \in N} \in E : \pi_i(a_i) > 0\}$, then $E_i \subset R_i$.

Proof   Let $\bar{\pi}^N = \prod_{i \in N} \bar{\pi}_i$ be any Nash equilibrium, where $\bar{\pi}_i \in \Delta(\bar{A}_i)$ (all $i \in N$). Let $\bar{A}_i := \{a_i \in A_i | \bar{\pi}_i(a_i) > 0\}$ be the set of strategies used by i with positive probability in this Nash equilibrium. Then $\bar{A}_i \subset B_i(\bar{\pi}_{-i})$, where $\bar{\pi}_{-i} := \prod_{j \in N \setminus \{i\}} \bar{\pi}_j$. Since $R_i^0 = A_i$, obviously $\bar{A}_i \subset R_i^0$ (all $i \in N$). Now suppose that the induction hypothesis $\bar{A}_i \subset R_i^{k-1}$ (all $i \in N$) is satisfied. Then

$$\bar{A}_i \subset B_i(\bar{\pi}_{-i}) \subset B_i\left(\prod_{j \in N \setminus \{i\}} \Delta(\bar{A}_j)\right) \subset B_i\left(\prod_{j \in N \setminus \{i\}} \Delta(R_j^{k-1})\right) = R_i^k.$$

Thus $\bar{A}_i \subset R_i^k$ for $k = 1, 2, \ldots$, by induction on k, and so $\bar{A}_i \subset R_i$ as required.   □

So all Nash strategies are rationalizable. But, as Bernheim's (1984, 1024–1025) Cournot oligopoly example clearly shows, other non-Nash strategies are often rationalizable, too.

Since a strictly dominated strategy is never a best response, for $k = 1$, $2, \ldots$ it must be true that all strictly dominated strategies for player i are removed from R_i^{k-1} in reaching R_i^k. It follows easily by induction on k that R_i^k is a subset of S_i^k, the set of i's strategies that survive k iterations of removing strictly dominated strategies. Taking the limit as $k \to \infty$ implies the R_i must be a subset of S_i^∞, the set of all i's strategies that survive iterative removal of strictly dominated strategies. Generally, however, $R_i \neq S_i^\infty$, although the two sets are always equal in two-person games (see Fudenberg and Tirole 1991, 50–52 and 63).

2.3   Refinements

Rationalizability on its own fails to exclude some very implausible strategy choices. In the example shown, d is evidently an optimal strategy for player II whenever the subgame is reached. But D is player I's best response to d, and a is one of player II's best responses to D, while A is player I's best response to a. Thus all strategies are possible best responses and so rationalizable in this game. In the normal form, moreover, there are no strictly dominated strategies. Yet a is not a credible choice by player II. In fact, a is strictly dominated in the subgame which starts with player II's move. If only d is really rationalizable for player II, however, then only D is for player I, so the only really rationalizable choices are (D, d). This illustrates *subgame rationalizability* (Bernheim 1984, 1022).

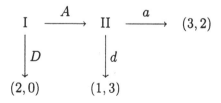

Figure 14.3
A simple extensive form

The argument of the above paragraph exploited the extensive-form structure of the game. But there are similar normal-form arguments such as that used by Bernheim (1984, 1022) to discuss "perfect rationalizability." This chapter, however, will instead make use of Pearce's (1984) idea of refining rationalizable to "cautiously rationalizable" strategies. To explain Pearce's construction, first let $\Delta^0(T)$ denote, for any finite set T, the interior of $\Delta(T)$—that is, the set of all probability distributions attaching positive probability to every member of T. Also, given any subset $A_i' \subset A_i$, player i's *constrained best-response correspondence* is defined by

$$B_i(\pi_i|A_i') := \underset{a_i \in A_i'}{\arg \max} \{U_i(a_i, \pi_i)\}.$$

Now start with $\hat{A}_i^0 = A_i$, the set of all i's possible strategies, and $\hat{R}_i^0 := R_i$, the set of all i's rationalizable strategies. Then construct the sequences of sets $\hat{P}_i^k$, $\hat{A}_i^k$, $\hat{R}_i^k$ ($k = 1, 2, \ldots$) recursively so that

$$\hat{P}_i^k := \prod_{j \in N \setminus \{i\}} \Delta^0(\hat{R}_j^{k-1}),$$

while $\hat{R}_i^k$ is the set of rationalizable strategies in the restricted normal-form game, where each player $i \in N$ is only allowed to choose some strategy a_i in the set

$$\hat{A}_i^k := B_i(\hat{P}_i^k|\hat{R}_i^{k-1}) \subset \hat{R}_i^{k-1}$$

of what Pearce called "cautious responses" within $\hat{R}_i^{k-1}$ to expectations concerning other players' strategies in the sets $\hat{R}_j^{k-1}$ ($j \neq i$). Provided that the sets $\hat{R}_i^{k-1}$ ($i \in N$) are nonempty, the construction will continue to yield nonempty sets $\hat{A}_i^k$, $\hat{R}_i^k$ ($i \in N$) that because of the definition of rationalizable strategies, must satisfy

$$\hat{R}_i^k = B_i(\bar{P}_i^k|\hat{A}_i^k) \subset \hat{A}_i^k \quad \text{where} \quad \bar{P}_i^k := \prod_{j \in N \setminus \{i\}} \Delta(\hat{R}_j^{k-1}) = \text{cl } \hat{P}_i^k.$$

It follows by induction on k that

$$\varnothing \neq \hat{R}_i^k \subset \hat{A}_i^k \subset \hat{R}_i^{k-1} \subset \hat{A}_i^{k-1} \subset \cdots \subset \hat{R}_i^0 \subset \hat{A}_i^0 = A_i \quad (k = 1, 2, \ldots).$$

Now, repeating the argument used for rationalizable strategies shows that there must be a finite integer n for which $k \geq n$ implies that $\hat{A}_i^k = \hat{A}_i^n = \hat{R}_i^k = \hat{R}_i^n$ (all $i \in N$). The set

$$\hat{R}_i := \bigcap_{k=0}^{\infty} \hat{R}_i^k = \hat{R}_i^n \subset \hat{R}_i^0 = R_i$$

must therefore be a well-defined and nonempty subset of R_i. Call $\hat{R}_i$ the "set of cautiously rationalizable strategies" for player i. Evidently $\hat{A}_i^k = \hat{R}_i$ for all $k \geq n$, and so

$$\hat{R}_i = B_i(\hat{P}_i | \hat{R}_i) \quad \text{where} \quad \hat{P}_i := \prod_{j \in N \setminus \{i\}} \Delta^0(\hat{R}_j) \quad \text{(all } i \in N).$$

Thus any player's cautiously rationalizable strategies are indeed (cautious) best responses to nondegenerate probability beliefs about other players' cautiously rationalizable strategies. But it is not required that all such best responses be included in the set of cautiously rationalizable strategies.

Because only strategies that are best responses to *interior* probability distributions are retained in passing from the sets $\hat{R}_i^{k-1}$ to $\hat{A}_i^k$, it follows that all *weakly* dominated strategies in $\hat{R}_i^{k-1}$ are eliminated. Thus $\hat{A}_i^k$ must be a subset of $W_i(\hat{R}_i^{k-1})$, and the product set $\hat{A}^k := \prod_{i \in N} \hat{A}_i^k$ must be a subset of $W(\hat{R}^{k-1})$, where $\hat{R}^{k-1} := \prod_{i \in N} \hat{R}_i^{k-1}$. Thereafter, all strategies among $W(\hat{R}^{k-1})$ that would be removed by iterative strict dominance must also be removed from $\hat{A}^k$ in order to arrive at strategies in the product set $\hat{R}^k$ that are rationalizable in the game where each player $i \in N$ is artificially restricted to choosing some strategy in $\hat{A}_i^k$. It follows that $\hat{R}^k \subset S^\infty(\hat{A}^k)$. So $\hat{R}^k$ must be a subset of the set $S^\infty(W(\hat{R}^{k-1}))$ of those strategies that survive the removal of *all* weakly dominated strategies at the first stage, followed by iterated removal of all strictly dominated strategies at each later stage. Ultimately, moreover, each $\hat{R}_i$ must be a subset of the set $(WS^\infty)_i^\infty$ of i's strategies that survive cautious iterative removal of dominated strategies.[3]

Note that, in the above construction of the sets $\hat{R}_i^k$, it is *not* enough to replace $\hat{A}_i^k$ by the whole unrestricted best-response set $A_i^k := B_i(\hat{P}_i^{k-1})$. This is because, even though $\hat{R}_j^k \subset \hat{R}_j^{k-1}$, it is not generally true that $\Delta^0(\hat{R}_j^k) \subset \Delta^0(\hat{R}_j^{k-1})$, and so this alternative construction does not guarantee that $A_i^{k+1} \subset A_i^k$. Indeed, for the counterexample normal-form game shown, this it would result in a different sequence of sets $\tilde{R}_i^k$ given by

$$\tilde{R}_I^k = A_I^k = \begin{cases} \{U, D\} & \text{if } k \text{ is even;} \\ \{U\} & \text{if } k \text{ is odd;} \end{cases} \qquad \tilde{R}_{II}^k = A_{II}^k = \begin{cases} \{L, R\} & \text{if } k \text{ is even;} \\ \{L\} & \text{if } k \text{ is odd.} \end{cases}$$

		II		
		L	R	
I	U	1 1	1 1	
	D	1 1	0 0	

Figure 14.4
A counterexample

The difference is that, in the kth step of Pearce's construction of the sets $\hat{R}_i^k$, only cautious responses among the sets $\hat{A}_i^k$ of surviving strategies are considered. Strategies which have already been eliminated at a previous step as not cautiously rationalizable should never be readmitted into the set of cautiously rationalizable strategies.[4]

For similar reasons, the limit sets do not generally satisfy the condition $\hat{R}_i = B_i(\hat{P}_i)$ that was investigated by Börgers and Samuelson (1992, 20). In particular, whereas Pearce's definition (the one used here) ensures both existence and uniqueness of the set of cautiously rationalizable strategies, neither is guaranteed with this alternative condition.

Nevertheless, in the chapter appendix it will be shown that $B_i(\pi_i | \hat{A}_i^k) = B_i(\pi_i) \cap \hat{A}_i^k$ for all $\pi_i \in \bar{P}_i^k$. From this it follows that

$$\hat{A}_i^{k+1} = B_i(\hat{P}_i^k | \hat{R}_i^k) = B_i(\hat{P}_i^k | B_i(\bar{P}_i^k | \hat{A}_i^k)) = B_i(\hat{P}_i^k | \hat{A}_i^k)$$

$$= B_i(\hat{P}_i^k) \cap \hat{A}_i^k = \bigcap_{q=0}^{k} B_i(\hat{P}_i^q) \quad (k = 0, 1, 2, \ldots),$$

where the last equality follows from recursion. In addition,

$$\hat{R}_i^{k+1} = B_i(\bar{P}_i^k | \hat{A}_i^k) = B_i(\bar{P}_i^k) \cap \hat{A}_i^k = B_i(\bar{P}_i^k) \cap \left[\bigcap_{q=0}^{k-1} B_i(\hat{P}_i^q)\right] \quad (k = 0, 1, 2, \ldots).$$

Thus each set $\hat{R}_i^{k+1}$ and $\hat{A}_i^{k+1}$ consists of *unconstrained* best responses, but only those which remain "cautiously rationalizable" after k steps of the construction.

2.4   Rationalizable Expectations

In the following I shall use the obvious notation

$$R_{-i} := \prod_{j \in N \setminus \{i\}} R_j; \qquad \hat{R}_{-i} := \prod_{j \in N \setminus \{i\}} \hat{R}_j$$

for the sets of all possible profiles of rationalizable (resp. cautiously rationalizable) strategies that the players other than i are able to choose. Now, if a strategy $s_i \in R_i$ is rationalizable, it is because there exists a probability distribution $\pi_i \in \Delta(R_{-i})$ over other players' rationalizable strategies such that $s_i \in B_i(\pi_i)$. Similarly, if a strategy $s_i \in \hat{R}_i$ is cautiously rationalizable, it is because there exists an interior probability distribution $\pi_i \in \Delta^0(\hat{R}_{-i})$ over other players' cautiously rationalizable strategies such that $s_i \in B_i(\pi_i)$. Therefore, if player i has a subjective probability distribution satisfying $\pi_i \in \Delta(R_{-i})$, then i will be described as having "rationalizable expectations." This accords with the terminology introduced by Bernheim (1984,

1025). Similarly, if in fact $\pi_i \in \Delta^0(\hat{R}_{-i})$, then i will be described as having "cautiously rationalizable expectations." Moreover, given any $\pi_i \in \Delta(R_{-i})$ for which the strategy $s_i \in B_i(\pi_i)$ is a best response, the expectations π_i will be described as "rationalizing" that strategy.

3   Correlated Strategies

3.1   Background

Aumann (1987) has proposed an interesting extension to Nash equilibrium. A *correlated equilibrium* is a joint probability distribution $\bar{\pi} \in \Delta(A^N)$, possibly with correlation between different players' strategies, with the property that, for all $i \in N$, whenever $\bar{a}^N \in A^N$ satisfies $\bar{\pi}(\bar{a}^N) > 0$, then

$$\bar{a}_i \in \arg\max_{a_i \in A_i} \left\{ \mathbb{E}_{\pi(\cdot \mid \bar{a}_i)} v_i(a_i, a_{-i}) \right\}.$$

Here $\pi(\cdot \mid \bar{a}_i) \in \Delta(A_{-i})$ denotes the conditional distribution of other player's strategies, given that player i chooses $\bar{a}_i$. As Aumann points out, this notion of correlated equilibrium is consistent with the two players in Battle of the Sexes choosing (A, a) with probability $\frac{1}{2}$ and (B, b) with probability $\frac{1}{2}$.

Although Aumann argues quite persuasively for this "coarsening" of the usual Nash equilibrium concept, it does create some serious conceptual problems. For how can the two players ensure that their strategy choices are perfectly correlated, as they must be in the above-correlated equilibrium of Battle of the Sexes? Effectively, after all, player R is required to believe that whatever causes player R choose A also causes C to choose a, and vice versa. Similarly for B and b. These beliefs appear highly implausible in the absence of a correlation device. Of course, if there really is a correlation device, such as traffic lights at a busy crossroads, then that should be modeled as an explicit feature of the game, so that players' strategies can be conditioned by the information provided by the correlation device. Brandenburger and Dekel (1987) do suggest that it is legitimate to consider correlated strategies even where it is understood only implicitly that there may be a correlation device not explicitly modeled within the game. This, however, seems unsatisfactory because it is not clear how much correlation is really possible on the basis of the unmodeled device.

Actually, the beliefs behind correlated equilibria are somewhat reminiscent of those that underlie "causal decision theory," as discussed by Nozick (1969) and others (see Campbell and Sowden 1985, as well as Gärdenfors and Sahlin 1988, pt. 5). There is, however, an important difference between correlated equilibrium and causal decision theory. In Newcomb's problem, for instance, it is assumed that one player's choice can somehow *cause* the choice of a second player to change, even though the second player has to move before observing the first player's choice. If such causation were really possible, it would obviously be rational for players to take it into account. Therefore, causal decision theory suggests that each player $i \in N$ should choose an $\bar{a}_i$ to maximize $\mathbb{E}_{\pi(\cdot|a_i)} v_i(a_i, a_{-i})$ with respect to a_i, instead of maximizing $\mathbb{E}_{\pi(\cdot|\bar{a}_i)} v_i(a_i, a_{-i})$, as the above definition of correlated equilibrium would require. The difference is whether the relevant expectations are described by $\pi(\cdot|a_i)$, which the action a_i causes to vary, or by $\pi(\cdot|\bar{a}_i)$ instead, which remains fixed even as a_i varies within the set A_i.

3.2   Correlated Rationalizability

Neither causal decision theory nor correlated equilibrium makes much sense to me, at least. Still, as Pearce (1984, 1048), Bernheim (1986) and many others have realized, that does not rule out the possibility of each player's strategy choice being rationalized by correlated beliefs about all the *other* players' strategies. Indeed, consider the game shown, in which player III's intial choice of strategy α or β determines whether the left or the right trimatrix will occur. In this game, it makes very good sense for player III to take a view regarding how likely it is that players I and II can coordinate their strategies and choose either (U, l) or (D, r) with high probability. A player III who thinks this is likely will want to choose α and go to the left-hand trimatrix; but one who thinks it unlikely will want to choose β and go to the right-hand trimatrix instead. Constraining player III's beliefs to exclude any such possibility of correlation does not seem reasonable, since player III may believe that there really is some common causation behind players I and II's behavior, even if there is no correlation device or other means of communication. For instance, players I and II may

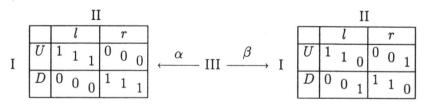

Figure 14.5
Correlated rationalizability

be identical twins, who are always observed to make matching choices. Or player III may know that players I and II were able to communicate at some time in the past, before the start of this game.[5]

The important point to realize is this. With common expectations, if any two players $i, j \in N$ have correlated strategy choices, then i must believe that the likelihood of j's choice is conditioned on i's own choice. Without common expectations, however, any two players can believe that what they choose is independent of the other's strategy, even though any third player may regard their choices as stochastically dependent. As an example, identical twins probably feel that they are always choosing independently, even though outside observers and third players only see them making identical choices. And suppose there is a group of people who, because they have agreed in the past about what to do in a game that confronts them later, are believed by outsiders to be playing correlated strategies. Nevertheless, this group will not actually be able to correlate their choices in that game, unless its structure explicitly allows further communication.

Allowing correlated beliefs about the strategies of others makes more strategies rationalizable, of course. Indeed, it weakens rationalizability so that it becomes what Brandenbuger and Dekel (1987) called "correlated rationalizability." It has become well known that this is equivalent to iterated removal of strictly dominated strategies (see, for example, Fudenberg and Tirole 1991, 52). In other words, the set R_i of rationalizable strategies expands to become equal to S_i^∞. Allowing correlated beliefs also weakens cautious rationalizability, so that $\hat{R}_i$ becomes equal to $(WS^\infty)_i^\infty$—as can be seen from the fact (Pearce 1984, 1049, lemma 4) that a strategy is not weakly dominated if and only if it is a cautious best response. Pearce proves this only for two-person games, but remarks how the same proof would work for n-person games if correlated beliefs about other players' strategies were allowed.

To summarize, therefore, we have the following characterization:

THEOREM   A strategy is correlated rationalizable if and only if it survives iterative removal of strictly dominated strategies, and is cautiously correlated rationalizable if and only if it survives cautious iterative removal of dominated strategies.

4   Forward Induction and Conditional Rationalizability

Forward induction was first introduced by Kohlberg and Mertens (1986). The discussion here begins, therefore, with a special case of the example

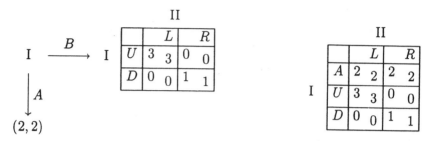

Figure 14.6
A team version of Kohlberg's example

they present in figure 3 on page 1008. I have taken $x = 0$ to make the example into a "team decision problem" (Marschak and Radner 1972) with both players sharing the same payoffs. An earlier example by Kohlberg with some of the same features (although not a team decision problem) was discussed by Kreps and Wilson (1982, 885), Bernheim (1984, 1023), Pearce (1984, 1044) and McClennan (1985).

In this example, the obvious strategy choices (U, L) form one Nash equilibrium, but (A, R) is another. Indeed, both (U, L) and (A, R) are sequential equilibria. The strategies A, U for player I and L, R for player II are therefore rationalizable. Now, for player I strategy D is strictly dominated by A. Yet, after the strictly dominated strategy D has been eliminated, R becomes a weakly dominated strategy for player II, and so an incautious best response. After it has been eliminated next, then A becomes a strictly dominated strategy for player I. So iterative deletion of all weakly dominated strategies among those which remain rationalizable leads ultimately to (U, L) as the only possible outcome. By our previous theorem, this is also the only cautiously rationalizable outcome.

The forward-induction argument of Kohlberg and Mertens (1986, 1013), however, seems quite different, at least to begin with. They write that "a subgame should not be treated as a separate game, because it was preceded by a very specific form of preplay communication—the play leading to the subgame." Yet, according to the standard view of Nash equilibrium and, more particularly, of sequential equilibrium, there is no reason for such preplay communication to be relevant at all. Indeed, the sequential equilibrium that the players are supposed to be following prescribes beliefs in every possible subgame, and as long as these fulfil all the requirements of sequential equilibrium, there is nothing more that equilibrium theory can say.[6] In fact, Kohlberg and Mertens expect player II, when required to move, to be influenced by the fact that player I has given up an opportunity to get a payoff of 2. Although their argument is rather sketchy, it seems that we are expected to conclude that it is reasonable for player II, faced with the move, to believe that player I was expecting to get at least 2 in the subgame. Yet, according to sequential equilibrium theory, there really is no reason for player II to abandon the beliefs that sustain player (A, R) as the anticipated sequential equilibrium; instead, player I's playing B is seen as a mere "tremble."

It seems to me, therefore, that this kind of forward-induction argument makes much more sense when we think of rationalizable strategies. The same point, in fact, was suggested by Bernheim and Pearce themselves, and also appears more recently in Battigalli 1991. The theory of rationalizability allows us to recognize that player II may not be certain after all what will happen in the subgame where there is a move to make, and will be looking for clues concerning what is likely to happen. In the subgame all strategies are rationalizable, and so player II has no information within the subgame itself that helps decide whether player I is more likely to play U or D. However, there is crucial information from outside the subgame— namely, the fact that player I has chosen B rather than A, so giving up the opportunity to get 2 for sure. In the framework of rationalizability, the above quotation from Kohlberg and Mertens makes excellent sense— much more, it seems to me, than if one considers only sequential equilibria, where it is presumed that players already have equilibrium beliefs, and so cannot possibly be influenced by any form of "preplay communication." In fact, knowing that player I has forgone the opportunity to get a payoff of 2, it is plausible for player II to believe that player I is expecting a payoff of at least 2 in the subgame. This is only possible, however, if player I expects to play U in the subgame, regarding it as sufficiently likely that player II will play L. So player II, also expecting player I to play U in the subgame, should play L.

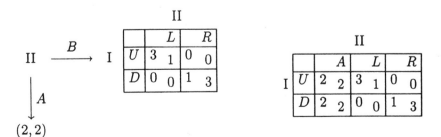

Figure 14.7
Battle of the sexes with a correlation option

The conclusion is that, once the subgame has been reached, only (U, L) is "conditionally rationalizable," in the obvious sense that it is rationalized by rationalizable expectations satisfying the condition that player I's expected payoff in the subgame should be at least 2. Of course, if player I foresees that this will be the outcome of the subgame, then player I will indeed choose to play B and then U, and so the "sensible" outcome is indeed achieved.

Another rather similar example is a slight variation on one that was first discussed by van Damme (1989, 479).[7] The game can be regarded as an extension of Battle of the Sexes in which player II is given the option of setting up beforehand a correlation device that will ensure the symmetric correlated equilibrium payoffs (2, 2). For this example, the set of cautiously rationalizable strategies can be found by iteratively deleting dominated strategies as follows. First, A strictly dominates L for player II. But this is the only strict dominance relation, so U, D remain as rationalizable strategies for player I, as do A, R for player II. However, after L has been eliminated, D weakly dominates U for player I; again, this is the only dominance relation at this stage. Finally, after U has also been eliminated, R strictly dominates A for player II, and so we are left with (D, R) as the only possible outcome.

In this example, the forward-induction argument leads to the same result. If player II forgoes the correlation option and chooses B, this can only be rationalized by the belief that player II expects to get a payoff of at least 2 in the subgame. Thus player II must be intending to play R in the belief that, with probability at least $\frac{2}{3}$, player I will choose D. This leads to (D, R) as the only possible conditionally rationalizable outcome in the subgame. So player II is induced to enter the subgame and play Battle of the Sexes without a correlation device in the expectation of achieving this preferred outcome.

The same game can be used to illustrate the inconsistency of this kind of forward induction or iterated elimination of dominated strategies with Harsanyi and Selten's theory of equilibrium selection[8]—see Harsanyi and Selten (1988, sect. 10.8) and van Damme (1990) for other examples making a similar point. For Harsanyi and Selten's theory imposes symmetry upon the (unique) solution to all symmetric games such as Battle of the Sexes. It follows that the only Harsanyi-Selten equilibrium in the subgame is the mixed-strategy symmetric equilibrium $(\frac{3}{4}U + \frac{1}{4}D, \frac{1}{4}L + \frac{3}{4}R)$ yielding expected payoffs $(\frac{3}{4}, \frac{3}{4})$. In the full game with a correlation option this would encourage player I to choose A, and so lead to the (mixed-strategy) equilibrium $(A, \frac{1}{4}L + \frac{3}{4}R)$. This contradicts the conclusion of the previous paragraph, of course, and so demonstrates the claimed inconsistency.

The game we have just been discussing is actually a subgame of another, considered by Dekel and Fudenberg (1990, 265−266, fig. 7.1), which can be regarded as a version of Battle of the Sexes allowing two correlation options. Indeed, compared with the previous example, player I has now also been given the option of using a correlation device, but a somewhat costly one, since using it reduces the payoffs to (1.5, 1.5). As is easy to check, cautious iterated deletion of dominated strategies now leads to (X, R) as the unique cautiously rationalizable outcome. There is one other Nash equiiibrium (U, A) that also happens to be subgame-perfect.

Yet Dekel and Fudenberg (1990, 265) claim that (D, A) is also reasonable in this example. The reason they give is that, "if player II accepts the $[(X, R)]$ solution (which is based on the intuition of forward induction) and then is given the opportunity to play, II must conclude that 'something basic has changed,' and II might conclude that I's payoffs will lead I to violate the $[(D, R)]$ outcome in the subgame." In fact, there is a really interesting tension here between player I's attempt, by playing Y, to convince player II that player I expects a payoff of at least 1.5, and player II's attempt, by playing B, to convince player I that player II expects a payoff

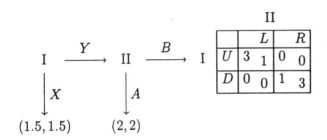

Figure 14.8
Battle of the sexes with two correlation options

of at least 2. Without a correlation device, there is simply no way to fulfill both expectations simultaneously. Quite a likely outcome of the second subgame is that player I will choose U while player II plays R, each thinking it likely that the other will play the alternative strategy, and each expecting a higher payoff than what would result from their forgone opportunities to play X and A, respectively.

Nevertheless, the outcome in which player I plays X still makes the most sense to me. After choosing Y first, will player I really proceed with U if player II plays B? Or is player I more likely to realize at the last minute that player II really must be intending R, and so play D in the end? It seems that player II has an advantage in the first subgame from having the last move before the second subgame starts.[9] Anyway, compared to standard equilibrium theory, rationalizability clearly allows a much richer discussion of what players can reasonably expect of each other.

In the examples discussed so far, it was easy to find a forward-induction argument yielding the same unique outcome as iterated elimination of all weakly dominated strategies. This will not be so easy in the next example.

	II L_B	II R_B
I U	3 1	-2 0
D	-2 0	-1 5

$\xleftarrow{\;B\;}$ I $\xrightarrow{\;N\;}$

	II L_N	II R_N
I U	5 1	0 0
D	0 0	1 5

	II $L_B L_N$	II $L_B R_N$	II $R_B L_N$	II $R_B R_N$
BU	3 1	3 1	-2 0	-2 0
BD	-2 0	-2 0	-1 5	-1 5
NU	5 1	0 0	5 1	0 0
ND	0 0	1 5	0 0	1 5

(I)

Figure 14.9
Ben-Porath and Dekel's "money burning" example

In the form given here, this is originally from Ben-Porath and Dekel 1992, although it is based on an idea of van Damme's (1989, 488–490) that is also discussed by Myerson (1991, 194–195); see also Fudenberg and Tirole (1991, 461–464).[10] The game begins with player I having a choice between B, to be interpreted as "burning money" that leads to a loss of 2 units of utility for player I, and N, to be interpreted as not burning money. After N the basic payoffs are given by the right-hand bimatrix, which is a modified form of Battle of the Sexes. After B the payoffs are given by the left-hand bimatrix. Compared with the right-hand bimatrix, player I's payoff have all been reduced by 2, but player II's payoffs are exactly the same.

In the corresponding normal form of this game, BU, BD, NU, ND are the four strategies for player I, while $L_B L_N$, $L_B R_N$, $R_B L_N$, $R_B R_N$ are the four strategies for player II. Of player I's strategies, ND strictly dominates BD, and so BD can be eliminated, but all other strategies of both players remain rationalizable. After BD has been eliminated, $L_B L_N$ weakly dominates $R_B L_N$ for player II, and $L_B R_N$ weakly dominates $R_B R_N$. So $R_B L_N$ and $R_B R_N$ are eliminated, leaving $L_B L_N$ and $L_B R_N$. Once it is known that player II will choose L_B, however, BU strictly dominates ND for player I, and so ND can be eliminated. This leaves only BU and NU as possible cautiously rationalizable strategies for player I. However, of player II's remaining strategies, $L_B L_N$ weakly dominates $L_B R_N$, leaving $L_B L_N$ as player II's only cautiously rationalizable strategy. This leaves NU as player I's only cautiously rationalizable strategy, and $(NU, L_B L_N)$ as the only cautiously rationalizable outcome, with $(9, 6)$ as the resulting payoffs.

To establish $(NU, L_B L_N)$ as the only conditionally rationalizable outcome in this game, the corresponding forward induction argument has to pass backwards and forwards between the two different possible subgames that can occur after player I's first move. Notice first how, by choosing ND, player I can guarantee a payoff of at least 0. So if player I were to play B, it could only be in the expectation of obtaining at least 0 in the left-hand subgame. With conditionally rationalizable strategies, this is only possible if player I were to choose U expecting player II to play L_B. Thus, if player I were to choose B, it would be in the expectation of getting a payoff of 3. Now, however, if player I were to choose N instead, this could only be rationalized if player I were expecting a payoff of at least 3 in the right-hand subgame following that first move. This, however, is only possible if player I intends to play U and expects player II to choose L_N with a sufficiently high probability. Conditional rationalizability then requires player II to choose L_N, so yielding $(NU, L_B L_N)$ as the only possible outcome of forward induction.

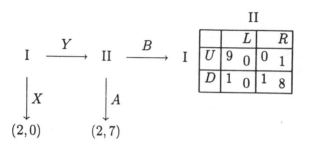

II

	A		BL		BR	
X	2	0	2	0	2	0
YU	2	7	9	0	0	1
YD	2	7	1	0	1	8

I (to the left of the table)

Figure 14.10
Myerson's example

It should be pointed out that Ben-Porath and Dekel regard it as surprising that giving player I the opportunity to "burn money" in this way should confer an advantage in the subgame that occurs after no money has been burnt. They also consider a large class of games in which a similar phenomenon arises. But is this really any more surprising than the possibility that Schelling (1980, 24) noticed—namely, that the potential buyers of a house could influence the outcome of a bargaining process with the sellers by first making a large enough bet with an outside party that they would not pay more than a specified price? Of course, the (forgone) opportunity to burn money does only affect conditionally rationalizable beliefs, whereas Schelling's house buyers' bet affects payoffs directly. Yet both affect *expected* payoffs, which are what rationalize behavior.

My last example is from Myerson (1991, 192–193). It illustrates that there is as yet no generally accepted concept of forward induction. To quote (with some changes to reflect different notation):

Unfortunately, some natural forward-induction arguments may be incompatible with other natural backward-induction arguments. [In the example shown, a] forward-induction argument might suggest that, because YD is a weakly dominated strategy for player I, player II would expect player I to choose U [in the last subgame] if he chose Y [originally]; so player II should choose A. On the other hand, backward induction determines a unique subgame-perfect equilibrium (XD, BR) in which player II would choose B [for his first move].... Forward induction corresponds to interatively eliminating weakly dominated strategies in the order: first YD for player I, then BL and BR for player II, leaving the equilibria (X, A) and (YU, A).

In fact (X, A) is the unique cautiously rationalizable outcome. For in the game as a whole there are no strictly dominated strategies, so all strategies are rationalizable. Thereafter, on the first round of eliminating weakly dominated strategies, both YD for player I and BL for player II get eliminated. This leaves (U, R) as the only possible outcome of the last subgame. Then there are still no strictly dominated strategies. But both YU for player I and BR for player II get eliminated on the second round of eliminating weakly dominated strategies, leaving (X, A) as the only possibility.

As for Myerson's alternative outcome (YU, A), however, it is really only credible as an outcome of this game if more reliance is placed on the logic of forward induction on the basis of player I's first move than on that of either subgame rationalizability or forward induction on the basis of player II's first move. For R strictly dominates L in the last subgame, so subgame rationalizability leaves (D, R) as the only possible outcome of the last subgame. Only if player II believes rather strongly that player I is likely to choose U in the subgame, presumably expecting player II to play the dominated strategy L, will player II choose A over B. Moroever, the logic of forward induction allows player I to infer from the choice of B that player II's expected payoff in the subgame is at least 7, so reinforcing the claim that only (D, R) is really rationalizable in the last subgame. This leads me to claim that (XD, BR) is the only convincing outcome of this game. Of course, this outcome both differs from and makes more sense than the unique cautiously rationalizable outcome (X, A). So forward induction can suggest different strategy combinations from cautious rationalizability, even though the consequences of (XD, BR) and (X, A) are, of course, entirely the same in this example.

That concludes the series of examples that make up this section. They show how powerful forward-induction arguments can be, but they still need to be formalized for general extensive- and normal-form games before any of their general implications can be deduced. As yet, I know of no general theorems relating forward induction to cautious rationalizability.

Nor do I know of an accepted definition of forward induction, even though Hillas (1990, 1368), for example, offers one that works well enough for his purposes.

One clear conclusion does emerge, however. In each of the subgames discussed in this section, what is conditionally rationalizable after applying forward induction depends on which options and what resulting payoffs the players in the subgame had renounced beforehand. An adequate description of the subgame therefore requires specifying these forgone options, as well as the usual extensive form of the subgame. By itself, that may not be too controversial even though, as van Damme (1989) points out, it amounts to admitting that phenomena like "sunk costs" may be relevant after all in subgames. Notice, however, that a subgame is itself a game. The fact that the extensive form is an inadequate description of a subgame therefore suggests that it may not be an adequate description of a full game either. Indeed, faced with a particular game in extensive form to analyze, the examples of this section suggest that the game theorist should at least be asking what outside options the players may have given up in the past, before the game even started, since these forgone options will influence players' (conditionally) rationalizable expectations concerning what should happen in the course of the game itself. Of course, forgone options are only one of a host of extraneous features that may help to determine rationalizable expectations in the game. One of the benefits of replacing equilibrium analysis with considerations of rationalizability is precisely that such considerations, which do seem to influence the outcomes of actual games, can be brought into the game-theoretic analysis. The obvious disadvantage is that much less precise conclusions are possible, yet such precision should not replace realism.

5   Conclusions

Harsanyi and Selten (1988, 342–343), amongst others, clearly point out how equilibrium theory sets itself the worthy goal of determining both what actions and also what "rational" or equilibrium expectations should arise in general noncooperative games. Usually, this goal is not achievable, even in games with unique Nash equilibria (Bernheim 1986). Instead, the less demanding requirement of rationalizability seems much more reasonable, since it permits each player to be uncertain about what other players believe, unlike the straitjacket of equilibrium. Besides, it is just enough to allow individual players to have appropriate "rationalizable" expectations concerning everything about which they are uncertain in the game, including both the strategies and the expectations of all the other players (see Tan and Werlang 1988). Correlated strategies and forward induction also appear to make more sense in the context of rationalizable rather than rational expectations. In addition, when each player is allowed to have correlated expectations regarding the strategies of all the other players, then rationalizable strategies are precisely those which survive iterated removal of strictly dominated strategies, whereas "cautiously" rationalizable strategies are those which survive "cautious" iterated removal of dominated strategies. And the intuition of forward induction seems to be well captured in a form of "conditional rationalizability" that excludes all beliefs giving a lower expected payoff to any player than the best outside option which that player is known to have passed up beforehand.

Rationalizability therefore removes some difficulties that equilibrium theory has created unnecessarily. Several anomalies remain, however. For example, the prevalence of tit for tat in finite repetitions of the Prisoner's Dilemma is no more consistent with rationalizability than with equilibrium theory. This and other related anomalies may well need explaining by some "bounded" version of rationalizability instead, recognizing players' inability to formulate excessively complicated models of the game they are playing (cf. Hammond 1990). In particular, it is once again easier to contemplate bounds on rationalizable models rather than on rational or equilibrium models that represent each player's expectations concerning the game. As always, however, there is much work left to do, partly on bounded rationalizability, but also on unbounded rationalizability, which was the subject of this paper.

Appendix

LEMMA $B_i(\pi_i | \hat{A}_i^k) = B_i(\pi_i) \cap \hat{A}_i^k$ for all $\pi_i \in \bar{P}_i^k$.

Proof   By induction on k. For $k = 0$ one has $B_i(\pi_i | \hat{A}_i^0) = B_i(\pi_i) \cap \hat{A}_i^0 = B_i(\pi_i)$ because $\hat{A}_i^0 = A_i$. As the induction hypothesis, suppose that $B_i(\tilde{\pi}_i | \hat{A}_i^{k-1}) = B_i(\tilde{\pi}_i) \cap \hat{A}_i^{k-1}$ for all $\tilde{\pi}_i \in \bar{P}_i^{k-1}$.

Suppose now that $\pi_i \in \bar{P}_i^k$ and $\hat{a}_i \in \hat{A}_i^k \backslash B_i(\pi_i)$. Then there exist $\varepsilon > 0$ and $a_i \in A_i$ such that

$$U_i(a_i, \pi_i) > U_i(\hat{a}_i, \pi_i) + 2\varepsilon.$$

Because $\bar{P}_i^k$ is a subset of the closure of $\hat{P}_i^{k-1}$, there exists a sequence $\langle \pi_i^\nu \rangle_{\nu=1}^\infty$ in $\hat{P}_i^{k-1}$ that converges to $\pi_i \in \bar{P}_i^k$. Construct a corresponding sequence

$$a_i^\nu \in B_i(\pi_i^\nu | \hat{A}_i^{k-1}) = B_i(\pi_i^\nu) \cap \hat{A}_i^{k-1} \quad (\nu = 1, 2, \ldots),$$

where the equality follows from the induction hypothesis. After choosing an appropriate subsequence if necessary, there will exist $a_i^* \in \hat{A}_i^{k-1}$ such that $a_i^v = a_i^*$ for all large v, while $\pi_i^v \to \pi_i$ as $v \to \infty$.

For all large v, since $a_i^v \in B_i(\pi_i^v)$, one has

$$U_i(a_i^*, \pi_i^v) = U_i(a_i^v, \pi_i^v) \geq U_i(a_i, \pi_i^v) > U_i(\hat{a}_i, \pi_i^v) + \varepsilon.$$

Taking the limit as $v \to \infty$ implies that $U_i(a_i^*, \pi_i) \geq U_i(\hat{a}_i, \pi_i) + \varepsilon$. Since

$$a_i^* = a_i^v \in B_i(\pi_i^v | \hat{A}_i^{k-1}) \subset B_i(\hat{P}_i^{k-1} | \hat{A}_i^{k-1}) = \hat{A}_i^k$$

for all large v, it follows that $\hat{a}_i \notin B_i(\pi_i | \hat{A}_i^k)$.

So, for all $\pi_i \in \bar{P}_i^k$, it has been proved that $\hat{a}_i \in \hat{A}_i^k \setminus B_i(\pi_i)$ implies $\hat{a}_i \notin B_i(\pi_i | \hat{A}_i^k)$. Hence $B_i(\pi_i | \hat{A}_i^k) \subset B_i(\pi_i) \cap \hat{A}_i^k$. Since it is trivially true that $B_i(\pi_i) \cap \hat{A}_i^k \subset B_i(\pi_i | \hat{A}_i^k)$ even when the former set is empty, it follows that $B_i(\pi_i | \hat{A}_i^k) = B_i(\pi_i) \cap \hat{A}_i^k$ for all $\pi_i \in \bar{P}_i^k$. The proof by induction is complete. $\square$

Notes

The author is grateful to Luigi Campiglio of the Università del Sacro Cuore in Milan and to Piero Tani of Florence for making possible the lectures at which some of these ideas were originally presented. In addition, Piero Tani coaxed me into giving a talk at the Florence conference, provided me time to write up the ideas presented, and has been remarkably good-humored throughout the whole process. A useful interchange with Giacomo Costa of the University of Pisa did much to convince me of the interest of forward induction. Pierpaolo Battigalli kindly pointed out a serious error in earlier versions, and passed on more good suggestions than I have so far been able to explore.

1. I am indebted to Kenneth Arrow for reminding me of this example, which I had forgotten long ago. For the full story, including Holmes's finding himself in Florence sometime in May 1891, see "The Final Problem" in Sir Arthur Conan Doyle's *Memoirs of Sherlock Holmes*, followed by "The Adventure of the Empty House" in the same author's *The Return of Sherlock Holmes*. Morgenstern seems to have been fond of this example, since he had already used it twice before (see Morgenstern 1928, 98, and 1935, 343, and note that the reference to the latter in von Neumann and Morgenstern 1953, 176, is slightly inaccurate).

2. Actually, in "The Final Problem" it is not at all clear that Moriarty does see Holmes, who had after all taken the precaution of disguising himself as "a venerable Italian priest" so effectively as to fool his constant companion, Dr. Watson. Nevertheless, Moriarty acted as though he knew Holmes really was on the train, and he would surely expect to be seen by Holmes.

3. Dekel and Fudenberg (1990) justify the strategy set $S^\infty W(A^N)$ as the implication of modifying iterative deletion of *all* weakly dominated strategies at each round so as to allow each player to be a little uncertain about other players' payoffs. Although the motivation would have to be different, $(WS^\infty)^\infty W(A^N)$ is

a refinement of their concept, and is obviously related to a slightly different version of Pearce's notion of "cautious rationalizability."

4. For this example I am indebted to Pierpaolo Battigalli. The games in examples 3 and 4 of Börgers and Samuelson 1992 could both be used to make the same point.

5. In fact, as Pierpaolo Battigalli has pointed out to me, in this game, where each player has only two strategies, the sets of rationalizable and correlated rationalizable strategies must be identical. So must the sets of cautiously rationalizable and correlated cautiously rationalizable strategies. The reason is that, whenever a player has only two strategies, one of those strategies is never a best response if and only if it is strictly dominated by the other (and is never a cautious best response if and only if it is weakly dominated by the other). So the process of successively eliminating never (cautious) best responses is equivalent to that of iterative deletion of dominated strategies. In view of the theorem stated below, this establishes the claim. Yet the discussion in the main text concerns only the expectations regarding other players' strategies that may rationalize a particular rationalizable strategy. The set of such expectations is obviously expanded by allowing correlation.

6. It should be emphasized that neither Kreps and Wilson (1982) nor McClennan (1985) really contradict this, since they use the earlier version of Kohlberg's example only to argue that it may be desirable to impose additional restrictions on players' sequential equilibrium beliefs.

7. The only difference is that van Damme lets player II have a payoff of 5 instead of 2 if player I chooses the strategy A. It is easy to see that this makes no difference to the argument presented below for this particular game.

8. Such inconsistencies were kindly pointed out to me by Giacomo Costa, but with a different example, similar to the one used by Harsanyi and Selten themselves.

9. Ben-Porath and Dekel (1992, 46) have an example that displays a similar "vulnerability to countersignals."

10. Actually, one of the payoffs given in Ben-Porath and Dekel (1992, fig. 1.2) is a 4, when a 5 is clearly intended. The change is irrelevant to the argument, however.

References

Aumann, R. J. 1987. "Correlated Equilibrium as an Expression of Bayesian Rationality." *Econometrica* 55:1–18.

Battigalli, P. 1991. "On Rationalizability in Extensive Games." Preprint, Istituto di Economia Politica, Università Commerciale "L. Bocconi," Milan.

Ben-Porath, E., and E. Dekel. 1992. "Signaling Future Actions and the Potential for Sacrifice." *Journal of Economic Theory* 57:36–51.

Bernheim, B. D. 1984. "Rationalizable Strategic Behavior." *Econometrica* 52:1007–1028.

Bernheim, B. D. 1986. "Axiomatic Characterizations of Rational Choice in Strategic Environments." *Scandinavian Journal of Economics* 88:473–488.

Börgers, T., and L. Samuelson. 1992. "'Cautious' Utility Maximization and Weak Dominance." *International Journal of Game Theory* 21:13–25.

Brandenburger, A., and E. Dekel. 1987. "Rationalizability and Correlated Equilibria." *Econometrica* 55:1391–1402.

Campbell, R., and L. Sowden, eds. 1985. *Paradoxes of Rationality and Cooperation.* Vancouver: University of British Columbia Press.

Dekel, E., and D. Fudenberg. 1990. "Rational Behavior with Payoff Uncertainty." *Journal of Economic Theory* 52:243–267.

Farquharson, R. 1969. *Theory of Voting.* Oxford: Basil Blackwell.

Fudenberg, D., and J. Tirole. 1991. *Game Theory.* Cambridge: MIT Press.

Gärdenfors, P., and N. E. Sahlin, eds. 1988. *Decision, Probability, and Utility: Selected Readings.* Cambridge: Cambridge University Press.

Hammond, P. J. 1990. "A Revelation Principle for (Boundedly) Bayesian Rationalizable Strategies." Working paper no. ECO 90/4, European University Institute.

Harsanyi, J. C. 1967–68. "Games with Incomplete Information Played by 'Bayesian' Players, I–III." *Management Science* 14:159–182, 320–334, 486–502.

Harsanyi, J. C., and R. Selten. 1988. *A General Theory of Equilibrium Selection in Games.* Cambridge: MIT Press.

Hillas, J. 1990. "On the Definition of the Strategic Stability of Equilibria." *Econometrica* 58:1365–1390.

Kohlberg, E., and J.-F. Mertens. 1986. "On the Strategic Stability of Equilibria." *Econometrica* 54:1003–1037.

Kreps, D., and R. Wilson. 1982. "Sequential Equilibrium." *Econometrica* 50:863–894.

Luce, R. D., and H. Raiffa. 1957. *Games and Decisions: Introduction and Critical Survey.* New York: John Wiley.

McLennan, A. 1985. "Justifiable Beliefs in Sequential Equilibrium." *Econometrica* 53:889–904.

Marschak, J., and R. Radner. 1972. *Economic Theory of Teams.* New Haven: Yale University Press.

Morgenstern, O. 1928. *Wirtschaftsprognose: Eine Untersuchung ihrer Voraussetzungen und Möglichkeiten [Economic Forecasting: An Investigation of its Presuppositions and Possibilities].* Vienna: Julius Springer.

Morgenstern, O. 1935. "Vollkommene Voraussicht und wirtschaftliches Gleichgewicht" "Perfect Foresight and Economic Equilibrium". *Zeitschrift für Nationalökonomie* 6:337–357.

Myerson, R. B. 1991. *Game Theory: Analysis of Conflict.* Cambridge: Harvard University Press.

Nozick, R. 1969. "Newcomb's Problem and Two Principles of Choice." In *Essays in Honor of C. G. Hempel,* ed. N. Rescher et al., 114–146. Dordrecht: D. Reidel.

Pearce, D. 1984. "Rationalizable Strategic Behavior and the Problem of Perfection." *Econometrica* 52:1029–1050.

Schelling, T. C. [1960] 1980. *The Strategy of Conflict.* Cambridge: Harvard University Press.

Tan, T. C.-C., and S. R. da C. Werlang. 1988. "The Bayesian Foundations of Solution Concepts of Games." *Journal of Economic Theory* 45:370–391.

van Damme, E. 1989. "Stable Equilibria and Forward Induction." *Journal of Economic Theory* 48:476–498.

van Damme, E. 1990. "On Dominance-Solvable Games and Equilibrium Selection Theories." CentER discussion paper no. 9046, University of Tilburg.

von Neumann, J., and O. Morgenstern. [1943] 1953. *Theory of Games and Economic Behavior* 3d ed. Princeton: Princeton University Press.

15   Normative Validity and Meaning of von Neumann–Morgenstern Utilities

John C. Harsanyi

1   The Problem

Payoffs in game theory are usually expressed in von Neumann–Morgenstern (vNM) utilities. Yet there is a lot of experimental evidence that people's behavior often fails to conform to the vNM axioms. This empirical fact is part of the more general observation that people do not consistently follow *any one* of the rationality requirements of economic theory, and deviate even from such very basic ones as extensionality[1] and transitivity (see Tversky and Kahneman 1981; Arrow 1982; and Schoemaker 1982).

The observed deviations from the vNM axioms pose two different problems. One concerns the *predictive value of these axioms* and of economic models based on these axioms. The other concerns the *normative validity* of the axioms as rationality requirements. In this chapter I shall restrict my discussion to the latter, quite different problem. For even if we decided that the vNM axioms had full normative validity, we should not be surprised if natural selection failed to provide us with an instinctive ability to make rational and efficient choices between often quite complicated lotteries in accordance with the vNM axioms, since our animal and early human ancestors were never confronted with such problems, and obviously did not suffer any evolutionary disadvantage by lacking the instinctive ability to make such choices in a proficient manner. Nobody doubts the normative validity of arithmetic, yet most children cannot solve arithmetic problems of any complexity without special training.

I shall argue that the vNM axioms do have full normative validity as rationality axioms—but that this is true only under some very specific motivational assumptions.

2 Notations

I shall distinguish between *pure* and *mixed* alternatives, depending on whether they do, or do not, include risk and/or uncertainty. Pure alternatives will be regarded as degenerate special cases of mixed alternatives. I shall use also the term *lotteries* to describe mixed alternatives.

Strict preference, equivalence, and *nonstrict preference* will be denoted as $\succ$, $\sim$, and $\succsim$, respectively.

Let L be a lottery yielding alternative A_k if event e_k occurs, with $k = 1, \ldots, n$. Then I shall write

$$L = (A_1|e_1; \ldots; A_n|e_n). \tag{1}$$

The alternatives A_k will also be called "prizes" or "outcomes." The events e_k will be called "conditioning events." It will be assumed that these events are mutually exclusive and exhaust all possibilities.

Suppose the decision maker knows the objective probabilities $p_1, \ldots, p_n$ associated with the events $e_1, \ldots, e_n$. Then I shall write

$$L = (A_1, p_1; \ldots; A_n, p_n) \tag{2}$$

and shall call L a "risky" lottery. Of course, all these probabilities must be nonnegative and must add up to unity. On the other hand, a lottery will be called an "uncertain" lottery if it is *not* a risky lottery under this definition.

3 A Simplified and Generalized Version of the von Neumann–Morgenstern Axioms

Von Neumann and Morgenstern's (1947) theory was restricted to the case where all probabilities were *objective* probabilities *known* to the decision maker, that is, the case of *risky* lotteries. But most economists use Savage's (1954) theory, which employs only *subjective* probabilities (which he called *personal* probabilities). Therefore, it also cover the general case, where objective probabilities may be unknown or may be even undefined. Anscombe and Aumann (1963) proposed still another theory, likewise covering the general case, but using much simpler axioms. Their theory, however, has to use *both* objective and subjective probabilities. (But all the objective probabilities they need may be generated by *one* random device whose statistical behavior is known to the decision maker.)

What makes the vNM axioms rather complicated is the fact that some of them simply *restate* certain propositions of probability theory. In order to simplify my axioms—and in order to make it clear what the logical status of each axiom is—I have separated my four rationality postulates, to be called simply *axioms*, from my two *background assumptions*, whose only purpose is to enable us to use the theorems of the propositional calculus and of the probability calculus in any mathematical proof. My two background assumptions are

ASSUMPTION 1   The conditional statements defining a lottery (as stated in the sentence preceding equation 1) follow the laws of the propositional calculus.

ASSUMPTION 2   The objective probabilities defining a *risky* lottery (as in equation 2) follow the laws of probability calculus.

I need assumption 1 because I want to use Anscombe and Aumann's "reversal of order" postulate, without making it into a separate axiom. The postulate assumes that the "roulette lottery" and the "horse lottery" will be conducted *consecutively* but that it makes no difference if their time order is *reversed*. But we can just as well assume that the two lotteries will be conducted *simultaneously*. Once this assumption is made, the postulate becomes a corollary of a well-known theorem of the propositional calculus. If we write $p \to q$ for the statement "If p, then q," and write $=$ for logical equivalence, then the relevant theorem can be written as

$$p \to (q \to r) = q \to (p \to r). \tag{3}$$

I need assumption 2 because, in order to compute the final probability of each outcome in a two-stage lottery, I want to use the addition and the multiplication laws of the probability calculus, without making them into separate axioms.

I also need the following four rationality axioms.

AXIOM 1 (Complete Preordering)   The relation $\succsim$ (nonstrict preference) is a complete preordering over the set of all lotteries (that is to say, $\succsim$ is both transitive and complete).

AXIOM 2 (Continuity)   Suppose that $A \succsim B \succsim C$. Then there exists some probability mixture

$$L(p) = (A, p; C, 1 - p) \tag{4}$$

of A and C with $0 \le p \le 1$ such that $B \sim L(p)$.

AXIOM 3 (Monotonity in Prizes)   Suppose that $A_k^* \succsim A_k$ for $k = 1, \ldots, n$. Then also $L^* \succsim L$, where

$$L^* = (A_1^*|e_1; \ldots; A_n^*|e_n) \qquad \text{and} \qquad L = (A_1|e_1; \ldots; A_n|e_n). \tag{5}$$

(This axiom is a version of the sure-thing principle.)

AXIOM 4 (Probabilistic Equivalence)   Let *Prob* denote objective probability. Define the lotteries L and L' as

$$L = (A_1|e_1; \ldots; A_n|e_n) \quad \text{and} \quad L' = (A_1|f_1; \ldots; A_n|f_n). \tag{6}$$

Suppose the decision maker *knows* that

$$Prob(e_k) = Prob(f_k) \quad \text{for } k = 1, \ldots, n. \tag{7}$$

Then, for this decision maker, we must have

$$L \sim L'. \tag{8}$$

In other words, a rational decision maker will be indifferent between two lotteries yielding the *same prizes*, and yielding each prize with the *same objective probability*—regardless of the physical mechanisms the two lotteries use to generate these probabilities. In particular, the decision maker must be indifferent between a one-stage and a two-stage lottery yielding the same prizes with the same probabilities.

We can now state the following theorem.

THEOREM   Given assumptions 1 and 2, an individual i whose preferences satisfy axioms 1 to 4 will have a utility function U_i that equates the utility $U_i(L)$ of any lottery L to the *expected utility* of this lottery so that

$$U_i(L) = \sum_{k=1}^{n} p_k U_i(A_k), \tag{9}$$

where $p_1, \ldots, p_n$ are *either* the *objective* probabilities of the conditioning events $e_1, \ldots, e_n$ *known* to the decision maker, *or* are his own *subjective* probabilities for these events.

If a utility function U_i satisfies (9), then it is said to possess the *expected-utility property*, and is called a *von Neumann–Morgenstern utility function*.

Given assumption 2, our axioms are equivalent to the vNM axioms, which means that they can be used to prove the above theorem for *risky* lotteries. On the other hand, as Anscombe and Aumann have shown, we can extend the theorem to *all* lotteries by using our axioms, after adding as new axioms the theorem itself, restricted to risky lotteries, and Anscombe and Aumann's "reversal of order" postulate, derived from equation 3 by means of assumption 1 (as explained above).

In view of the above theorem, we can now extend the notation used in equation 2 also to *uncertain* lotteries if we reinterpret the probabilities $p_1, \ldots, p_n$ as the decision maker's *subjective* probabilities for the conditioning events $e_1, \ldots, e_n$.

It is easy to verify that the *converse* of the theorem is likewise true: If a person's choices among lotteries consistently maximize the expected value of some utility function then his behavior will satisfy axioms 1 to 4.

4   Need for an Outcome-Oriented Attitude

I shall now consider the *normative validity* of our four axioms as rationality requirements. To start with axiom 1 (complete preordering), this is a rationality axiom used in all parts of economic theory. Its normative validity is rather uncontroversial.[2]

On the other hand, axiom 2 (continuity) is basically a regularity assumption, rather than a rationality requirement. Even in the absence of axiom 2, we can show the existence of a utility indicator with the expected-utility property by using our other three axioms. But this utility indicator will not be a real-valued (scalar-valued) utility function, but rather will be a *utility vector* with two or more lexicographically ordered components (see Hausner 1954). We need a continuity axiom (like axiom 2) only to ensure the existence of a *scalar-valued* utility function.

Thus, the real question is how much normative validity our axioms 3 and 4 have. To answer this question, I propose to divide the utilities associated with choices involving risk and/or uncertainty into *outcome utilities* and *process utilities*. The former are the (positive and negative) utilities the chooser derives from the various possible *outcomes* (or prizes) of each lottery. The latter are the (positive and negative) utilities the chooser derives from the chooser's *psychological experiences* before, during, and after the act of gambling itself. These experiences include the nervous tension produced by gambling; the joy of winning and the sorrow of losing; the pride or the regret of having made what has turned out to be the right choice or the wrong choice; the favorable or unfavorable reactions by other people to the final outcome and to the chooser's purported responsibility for this outcome; and so on.

When people gamble for entertainment, they tend to do so both in the hope of winning valuable prizes and also in the hope of having a good time, which means that they are guided *both* by their outcome utilities and by their process utilities. But this may not be true when the stakes are *very high,* or when the participants are business executives or political leaders gambling with *other people's* money (or even with other people's lives). In such cases, the decision makers will have very good reasons, based both on self-interest and on moral considerations, to concentrate on trying to achieve the best possible *outcomes* both for themselves and for their constituents, without being diverted from this objective by the pleasant or unpleasant subjective experiences they derive from the process of gambling itself.

This suggests the following definition. I shall say that decision makers take a strictly *outcome-oriented* attitude if they are guided solely by his *outcome utilities,* that is, by the utilities they assign to the various possible outcomes of each lottery, and by their *outcome probabilities,* that is, by the probabilities they associate with these outcomes. I shall argue that our axioms 3 and 4 are perfectly *valid normative rationality requirements* for decision makers with strictly *outcome-oriented* attitudes but are *not* valid rationality requirements for *other* decision makers, who are wholly or partly guided by their *process utilities* derived from the process of gambling itself.

Let me first discuss axiom 4 (probabilistic equivalence). As we have seen, this axiom implies that a rational decision maker will be indifferent between a one-stage and a two-stage lottery if both yield the same prizes with the same probabilities. Since, by definition, strictly outcome-oriented decision makers will be interested only in the possible outcomes and their probabilities, and these two pieces of information will be the *same* for both lotteries, they will have to be indifferent between the latter, as required by our axiom.

On the other hand, axiom 4 is *not* a valid rationality requirement for decision makers guided wholly or partly by their process utilities derived from the process of gambling itself. For a one-stage and a two-stage lottery may generate very *different* psychological experiences and therefore also very *different* process utilities, even if they both yield the same possible prizes with the same probabilities. For instance, a one-stage lottery will give rise only to *one* period of nervous tension, whereas a two-stage lottery will give rise to *two* such periods. As a result, other things being equal, among people who give some weight to their process utilities, some will tend to prefer *one-stage* lotteries because they derive higher process utilities from them, while others will tend to prefer *two-stage* lotteries because they derive higher process utilities from the latter. In both cases, this will be a *rational* preference—even though it will violate our axiom 4.

Similar considerations apply to our axiom 3 (monotonity in prizes). The axiom considers two lotteries L and L^*. Lottery L^* is obtained by replacing each prize A_k of L by a prize A_k^* *at least as desirable* as A_k itself from the decision maker's point of view. The axiom asserts that, under these assumptions, the decision maker will find the new lottery L^* itself also *at least as desirable as* the original lottery L was. The reason is that participation in lottery L^* will always yield the decision maker an outcome as good or better than participation in lottery L would have yielded. As this argument is based on comparing the possible *outcomes* of lottery L^* with those of lottery L, it shows that axiom 3 is in fact a valid rationality requirement for any decision maker with a strictly *outcome-oriented* attitude.

Yet, it is *not* a valid rationality requirement for decision makers wholly or partly guided by their process utilities. To verify this, let me assume that the prizes $A_1, \ldots, A_n$ of lottery L are *pure alternatives* whereas the prizes A_1^*, $\ldots, A_n^*$ are themselves *lotteries* (lottery tickets). Under this assumption, L will be always a *one-stage* lottery because it will end as soon as one of its possible prizes, say, A_k, has been selected as outcome. In contrast, L^* will be a *two-stage* lottery, where at stage 1 one of the prizes A_k^* will be selected whereas at stage 2 the outcome of the lottery A_k^* itself will be decided. This means that a decision maker who derives higher *process utilities* from one-stage than from two-stage lotteries may actually *prefer L to L^**, even though the decision maker prefers the *prizes* of the latter to the corresponding prizes of the former—and this may be a perfectly rational preference from the decision maker's point of view. In other words, decision makers who give some weight to their process utilities may reasonably assign a *different utility* to a lottery A_k^* when it *is* embedded in a larger lottery L^* than when it is *not* so embedded.

5 Von Neumann-Morgenstern Utility Functions, Outcome Utilities, and Process Utilities

As we have seen, only people with a strictly outcome-oriented attitude will act consistently in accordance with the vNM axioms. By definition, these will be people guided only by their outcome utilities (and by the probabilities they assign to various outcomes) but paying no attention to their process utilities. Yet, by our theorem and its converse, both stated in section 3, only people with these characteristics will have vNM utility functions. This in turn implies that the decision makers' vNM utility function, if they have any, can express *only their outcome utilities* and cannot but disregard their process utilities, which will have no influence on their choice behavior.

An even simpler way of verifying this is by inspection of equation 9 in section 3, which defined the utility $U_i(L)$ of a lottery L solely in terms of its *outcome utilities* $U_i(A_k)$ and the outcome probabilities p_k, without reference to any process utilities.

Let me add that von Neumann and Morgenstern (1947, esp. 28 and 632) were perfectly aware of the fact that their axioms *excluded* what they called the "utility of gambling," and what I am calling "process utilities." But they apparently felt that exclusion of these utilities was simply a *shortcoming* of their theory, one to be removed eventually by devising a set of more powerful axioms. Of course, a formal theory covering also process utilities would be an important advance. Yet, in my own view, even though von Neumann and Morgenstern's original theory does not cover process utilities, it is an analytically very valuable theory because the vNM utility functions defined by it have very attractive mathematical properties, including that of being *cardinal* utility functions (see section 7 below).

6 Von Neumann–Morgenstern Utility Functions and Attitudes toward Risk

We often read in the literature that vNM utility functions express people's attitudes toward *risk taking*, that is, toward *gambling*.[3] Yet, without proper qualifications, this is a very *misleading* statement. If we do not assume strictly outcome-oriented attitudes, then people's willingness to take risks will depend on two factors:

(i) On their like or dislike for *gambling* as such, as determined by the positive and negative *process utilities* they associate with gambling;

(ii) On the utilities and probabilities they assign to various possible *outcomes*.

For the sake of simplicity, I shall describe factor (i) as a person's *intrinsic attitude* toward gambling while describing factor (ii) as the person's *instrumental attitude* toward the latter. (In the latter case I shall speak of an *instrumental* attitude because it is not based on the person's like or dislike for gambling *as such* but rather refers to the person's willingness to gamble for the sake of the various possible outcomes.)

As we have seen, in the case of people who have vNM utility functions at all, factor (i) will be completely inoperative, so that their only reason for gambling will be *instrumental*, based on their desire to achieve some specific outcomes.

Yet, when it is claimed that vNM utility functions express people's attitudes toward *gambling* without any qualification, it is natural to assume that their *intrinsic* attitude toward gambling—that is, their *intrinsic* like or dislike for gambling—is being meant, even though, as we have seen, people's vNM utility functions cannot be affected by this attitude at all.

7 Von Neumann–Morgenstern Utilities as *Cardinal* Utilities

I now propose to argue that v.N.M. utility functions are cardinal utility functions. There are two basic differences between merely *ordinal* and *cardinal* utility functions. One is that the former allow meaningful comparisons only between the relevant individual's *utility levels* but not between their *utility differences*, whereas the latter allow both kinds of comparisons in a meaningful way. Thus, regardless of whether U_i is an ordinal or a cardinal utility function of individual i, the preference statement $A \succ B$ will be represented by the inequality $U_i(A) > U_i(B)$, whereas the indifference statement $A \sim B$ will be represented by the equation $U_i(A) = U_i(B)$.

On the other hand, if U_i is merely an *ordinal* utility function then inequalities and equalities between utility differences such as

$$\Delta U_i(A, B) = U_i(A) - U_i(B) \quad \text{and} \quad \Delta U_i(C, D) = U_i(C) - U_i(D)$$
(10)

will have no introspective or behavioral meaning. In contrast, if U_i is a *cardinal* utility function then such inequalities and equalities will be meaningful. (As we shall see, in the special case where U_i is a vNM utility function, such inequalities and equalities will tell us something about i's preferences and indifferences between certain lotteries.)

The other difference is that an ordinal utility function U_i tells us only *what* i's preferences are whereas, if U_i is a cardinal utility function, then it will also permit us to *compare* i's different preferences as to their *intensities* or, equivalently, as to their *relative importance* for i.

The relevant mathematical facts will be stated in the form of the following:

LEMMA   Consider the inequality

$$\Delta U_i(A, B) > \Delta U_i(C, D).$$
(11)

This inequality will hold if and only if

$$L_1(A, \tfrac{1}{2}; D, \tfrac{1}{2}) \succ L_2 = (B, \tfrac{1}{2}; C, \tfrac{1}{2}).$$
(12)

Moreover, the lemma remains true even if in (11) and in (12) the signs $>$ and $\succ$ are replaced by the signs $=$ and $\sim$, respectively.

To verify the first two sentences of the lemma, note that, in view of (10), inequality (11) can be written also in the form

$$\tfrac{1}{2}U_i(A) + \tfrac{1}{2}U_i(D) > \tfrac{1}{2}U_i(B) + \tfrac{1}{2}U_i(C). \tag{13}$$

Yet (13) implies, and is also implied by, statement (12). The last sentence of the lemma can be verified in a similar way.

The lemma shows how statements about one utility difference $\Delta U_i(A, B)$ being *larger than*, or being *equal to*, another utility difference $\Delta U_i(C, D)$ can be reduced to statements about i's *preference* for some lottery L_1 over some lottery L_2, or about i's *indifference* between the two lotteries. It also shows how, conversely, statements about i's preferences and indifferences can be reduced to inequalities and equalities between utility differences.

I now propose to show that, in view of our lemma, if i prefers A to B but prefers C to D, then the utility differences $\Delta U_i(A, B)$ and $\Delta U_i(C, D)$ can be used to measure the intensities of these two preferences by i, or, equivalently, the *relative importance* of these two preferences for i.

Again consider the two lotteries

$$L_1 = (A, \tfrac{1}{2}; D, \tfrac{1}{2}) \qquad \text{and} \qquad L_2 = (B, \tfrac{1}{2}; C, \tfrac{1}{2}).$$

We can obtain L_1 from L_2 by making two moves:

Move 1: Replace prize B by prize A in lottery L_2;

Move 2: Replace prize C by prize D.

Since by assumption we have $A \succ B$ but $C \succ D$, move 1 will amount to replacing a given prize by a *preferred* prize while move 2 will amount to replacing a given prize by a *less preferred* prize. It is natural to assume that i will prefer lottery L_1 to lottery L_2 if and only if i's preference for A over B has *greater intensity* or, equivalently, if it has *greater importance* for i, than i's preference for C over D.

Yet, by our lemma, i will prefer L_1 over L_2 if and only if $\Delta U_i(A, B)$ is *larger* than $\Delta U_i(C, D)$. This means that i's preference for A over B will have *greater intensity* and will have *greater importance* for i if and only if $\Delta U_i(A, B)$ is *larger* than $\Delta U_i(C, D)$. In other words, the two utility differences $\Delta U_i(A, B) = U_i(A) - U_i(B)$ and $\Delta U_i(C, D) = U_i(C) - U_i(D)$ can be used as *measures* for the *intensities* and for the relative *importance* of i's preference for A over B, and of i's preference for C over D. This is of course an intuitively very plausible result: the mere fact that i prefers A to B is indicated by the piece of information that the utility difference $\Delta U_i(A, B)$ is *positive*. Thus, it is not surprising to find that the *magnitude* of this utility difference indicates the *intensity* of this preference and its *importance* for i.

8 Marginal Utilities, Complementarity, and Substitution

Economists use vNM utilities primarily in analyzing choices involving risk and uncertainty. Other things being equal, the *more concave* a person's vNM utility function for money, that is, the more strongly it displays *decreasing marginal utilities*, the less willing the person will be to take risks; and the *more convex* the person's vNM utility function for money, that is, the more strongly it displays *increasing marginal utilities*, the more willing the person will be to take risks (cf. Friedman and Savage 1948).

Yet, once vNM utility functions are available, they can be used also in other branches of economic theory. For instance, they can be used to replace the well-known Hicks-Allen definitions for complements and for substitutes (see Hicks 1939) by much simpler definitions. Let A and B denote specific amounts of commodities α and β. Let U_i be i's vNM utility function. Let $U_i(A \& B)$ denote the utility that i derives from consuming A and B together, and let $U_i(A)$ and $U_i(B)$ denote the utilities he derives from consuming A and B *separately*.

Then, A and B will be *complements* if

$$U_i(A \& B) > U_i(A) + U_i(B); \tag{14}$$

and they will be *substitutes* if

$$U_i(A \& B) < U_i(A) + U_i(B). \tag{15}$$

Under these definitions, i's vNM utility function for money will display *concavity*, that is, *decreasing marginal utilities*, in those income ranges where among the commodities consumed by i *substitution* relations predominate. The opposite will be true in those income ranges where among these commodities *complementarity* relations predominate. (For this purpose, indivisibilities must be considered to be special cases of complementarities.)

These conclusions usefully supplement those we reached in sections 6 and 7. There we concluded that a person's vNM utility function has nothing to do with the person's *intrinsic* like or dislike for gambling. Rather, it expresses the person's *instrumental* attitude toward risk taking and is itself determined by the person's *cardinal utilities* (outcome utilities) for various alternatives (such as alternative commodity baskets). Now we have found that these cardinal outcome utilities themselves depend on the *substitution* and *complementarity* relations existing among the commodities consumed by the relevant individual.

In any case, it is the decision makers' *cardinal utilities* (outcome utilities) for various alternatives that determine their (instrumental) *willingness to take risks* in order to obtain some desirable alternatives. These cardinal utilities determine their attitude toward risk taking, rather than the other way around.

9 Conclusion

In game theory, payoffs are usually expressed in vNM utilities. Yet, experiments show that many people repeatedly deviate from the vNM axioms as well as from other rationality axioms. This raises the question whether the vNM axioms have even *normative validity* as rationality requirements. To make it easier to answer this question, I proposed a simplified form of the vNM axioms, based on the Anscombe-Aumann (1963) approach to decision theory. Then, I proposed to divide the (positive and negative) utilities people derive from risky choices into *outcome utilities* and *process utilities*. The former are the utilities people assign to the various possible outcomes of any lottery, whereas the latter are the utilities they derive from the process of gambling itself.

I argued that, in many choice situations involving risk, some people will have good reasons to *disregard* their process utilities and to be guided solely by the utilities and the probabilities they assign to the various possible outcomes. This attitude I described as a strictly *outcome-oriented* attitude.

I suggested that the vNM axioms have full normative validity as rationality requirements—but only for people taking this particular attitude. This, however, means that, if a person has a vNM utility function at all, this utility function can express only the person's *outcome utilities* and cannot but disregard his *process utilities*. Already von Neumann and Morgenstern realized this fact (though they spoke of "the utility gambling" rather than of "process utilities").

It is often claimed that vNM utility functions express people's attitudes toward *gambling*. But the truth is that these utility functions have nothing to do with people's intrinsic attitudes toward gambling, that is, with their intrinsic like or dislike for gambling as such. What they do express is people's *instrumental* attitudes toward risk taking, that is, their willingness to take risks in order to obtain some desirable outcomes.

Then I tried to show that vNM utility functions are *cardinal* utility functions, which permit us to make meaningful comparisons, not only between *utility levels* but also between *utility differences*, and which also permit us to compare a person's different preferences as to their *intensities* or, equivalently, as to their relative *importance* for the individual in question.

Finally, I proposed definitions for *complementarity* and for *substitution* in terms of a person's vNM utility function, and argued that the convexity or the concavity of a person's vNM utility function for money in any given income range depends on whether complementarity or substitution relations predominate among the commodities the person consumes.

Notes

1. I shall follow Arrow (1982) in describing as *extensionality* the requirement that people's choices between two alternatives should not depend on the way these are described to them as long as these descriptions are logically clearly equivalent. As we all know, in actual fact people do not satisfy this requirement. For instance, their willingness to undergo an operation may be quite different if they are told that this operation has a survival rate of 95 percent than if they are told that it has a fatality rate of 5 percent.

2. Yet we know from experimental studies that, in choices of some complexity, people's behavior often fails to conform to this axiom (mainly because they may make *intransitive* choices; but see May 1954 for an interesting discussion).

3. In what follows, for convenience I shall follow colloquial usage and use the term *risk* so as to cover both "risk" and "uncertainty."

References

Anscombe, F. J., and R. J. Aumann. 1963. "A Definition of Subjective Probability." *Annals of Mathematical Statistics* 34:199–205.

Arrow, K. J. 1982. "Risk Perception in Psychology and Economics." *Economic Inquiry* 20:1–9.

Friedman, M., and L. J. Savage. 1948. "The Utility Analysis of Choices Involving Risk." *Journal of Political Economy* 56:279–304.

Hausner, M. 1954. "Multidimensional Utilities." In Thrall et al., eds., *Decision Processes,* 167–180. New York: Wiley.

Hicks, J. R. 1939. *Value and Capital.* Oxford: Oxford University Press.

May, K. O. 1954. "Intransitivity, Utility, and the Aggregation of Preference Patterns." *Econometrica* 22:1–13.

Savage, L. J. 1954. *The Foundations of Statistics.* New York: Wiley.

Schoemaker, P. 1982. "The Expected Utility Model: Its Variants, Purposes, Evidence, and Limitations." *Journal of Economic Literature* 20:529–563.

Tversky, A., and D. Kahneman. 1981. "The Framing of Decisions and the Psychology of Choice." *Science* 211:453–458.

von Neumann, J., and O. Morgenstern. 1947. *Theory of Games and Economic Behavior*. Princeton: Princeton University Press.

16   De-Bayesing Game Theory

Ken Binmore

... the look before you leap principle is preposterous if carried to extremes ...
Leonard Savage, *Foundations of Statistics*

1 Bayesianism

Debasing the coinage is a serious offense. De-Bayesing game theory would be even worse if it meant denying game theorists the use of Bayes's rule. How would we make a living if deprived of the most fundamental of the tools of our trade? It therefore needs to be explained that this chapter is not an attack on Bayesian decision theory as commonly used in analyzing particular games. I am a Bayesian myself in such a context. The chapter is an attack on *Bayesianism*, which I take to be the philosophical principle that Bayesian methods are always appropriate in all decision problems. I want to argue in particular that Bayesianism is an inappropriate standpoint from which to view the foundations of game theory. My own hopes for progress on this front depend on importing evolutionary ideas into game theory. However, I shall have nothing to say about such alternative approaches.

The word "Bayesianismist" will be used to describe an adherent of the creed of Bayesianism. I freely admit that few serious researchers would react with pride if such a label were pinned on them. But I do not think I am merely attacking a straw man. What matters for this purpose is not so much what people say about their philosophical attitudes, but what models they choose to construct. As Robert Aumann likes to say of game-theoretic concepts in general: "By their fruits shall ye know them."

There is an exception to the rule that Bayesianism is an underground creed. This is provided by the economics profession. For many young economists just out of graduate school, it is almost a heresy to argue that alternatives to Bayesian decision theory might ever make any sense. The defense against charges of heresy is to refer to the Scriptures. In the case of Bayesianism, the appropriate text is Savage's *Foundations of Statistics*. (1951). Savage is very clear that his is a "small world" theory.[1] Others speak of a "closed universe," but for reasons that will emerge, I prefer to refer instead to a "completable universe."

Savage makes the distinction between a small and a large world in a folksy way by quoting the proverbs "Look before you leap" and "Cross that bridge when you come to it." You are in a small world if it is feasible always to look before you leap. You are in a large world if there are some bridges that you cannot cross before you come to them. As Savage comments, when proverbs conflict, it is proverbially true that there is some truth in both. The words of the prophet therefore seem quite clear. Some decision situations are best modeled in terms of a completable universe; others are not. Savage rejects the idea that *all* universes are completable as both "ridiculous" and "preposterous."

My view is that the foundational problems of game theory are not completable universe problems, and hence are not amenable to a Bayesianismist methodology along the lines proposed by Robert Aumann (1987, 1989) and others. On the contrary, I see one of the major purposes of studying foundational questions as being that of finding appropriate ways of closing the universe of discourse so as to *legitimize* the use of Bayesian methods in analyzing particular games.

I am well aware that a formal theory of rational decision making in an incompletable universe seems likely to remain as elusive in the near future as it always has in the past. To maintain otherwise would be to maintain that the problem of scientific induction is on the point of being solved. However, I would prefer to work with a game theory that has no foundations at all, than to operate using foundational principles based on a flawed methodology.

2 Using Savage's Theory

This section reiterates the reasons given in Binmore (1987a) for rejecting unqualified Bayesianism as naive. Savage's theory is entirely and exclusively a *consistency* theory. It says nothing about how decision makers come to have the beliefs ascribed to them; it asserts only that, if the decisions taken are consistent (in a sense made precise by a list of axioms), then they act *as though* maximizing expected utility relative to a subjective probability distribution. Objections to the axiom system can be made, although it is no objection when discussing rational behavior to argue, along with

Allais (1953) and numerous others, that real people often contravene the axioms. People also often get their sums wrong, but this is no good reason for advocating a change in the axiomatic foundations of arithmetic. In any case, it is not Savage's consistency axioms that are to be attacked here.

What is to be denied is that Savage's passive *descriptive* theory can be reinterpreted as an active *prescriptive* theory at negligible cost. Obviously, a reasonable decision maker will wish to avoid inconsistencies. A Bayesianismist therefore assumes that it is enough to assign prior beliefs to a decision maker and then forget the problem of where beliefs come from. Consistency then forces any new data that may appear to be incorporated into the system via Bayesian updating. That is, a posterior distribution is obtained from the prior distribution using Bayes's rule. The näiveté of this approach does not consist in using Bayes's rule, whose validity as a piece of algebra is not in question. It lies in supposing that the problem of where the priors came from can be quietly shelved. Some authors even explicitly assert that rationality somehow *endows* decision makers with priors, and hence that the problem does not exist at all.

Savage did argue that his descriptive theory of rational decision making could be of practical assistance in helping decision makers form their beliefs, but he did not argue that the decision maker's problem was simply that selecting a prior from a limited stock of standard distributions with little or nothing in the way of soul-searching. His position was rather that one comes to a decision problem with a whole set of subjective beliefs derived from one's previous experience. This belief system may or may not be consistent. In a famous encounter with Allais, Savage himself was trapped into expressing inconsistent beliefs about a set of simple decision problems. The response he made is very instructive. He used his theory to adjust his beliefs until they became consistent. Luce and Raiffa (1957, 302) explain the process by means of which such a consistent set of final beliefs is obtained as follows:

Once confronted with inconsistencies, one should, so the argument goes, modify one's initial decisions so as to be consistent. Let us assume that this jockeying— making snap judgments, checking on their consistency, modifying them, again checking on consistency, etc.—leads ultimately to a bona fide, *a priori* distribution.

For Savage therefore, forming beliefs was more than a question of attending to gut feelings. It was a matter for *calculation*—just as the question of whether you or I prefer 17×29 to 19×23 is a matter for calculation.

But why should we wish to adjust our gut feelings using Savage's methodology? In particular, why should a rational decision maker wish to be consistent? After all, scientists are not consistent, on the grounds that it is not clever to be consistently wrong. When surprised by data that show current theories to be in error, they seek new theories that are inconsistent with the old theories. Consistency, from this point of view, is only a virtue if the possibility of being surprised can somehow be eliminated. This is the reason for distinguishing between incompletable and completable universes. Only in the latter is consistency an unqualified virtue.

One might envisage the process by means of which decision makers achieves a consistent set of subjective beliefs in a completable universe as follows. The decision makers know that subjective judgments need to be made, but prefer to make such judgments when their information is maximal rather than minimal. They therefore ask themselves, for every conceivable possible course of future events: What would my beliefs be *after* experiencing these events? Such an approach automatically discounts the impact that new knowledge will have on the basic model that the decision makers use in determining their beliefs—that is, it eliminates the possibility that the decision makers will feel the need to alter their basic model after being surprised by a chain of events whose implications they had not previously considered. Next comes the question: Is this system of *contingent* beliefs consistent? If not, then the decision makers may examine the relative *confidence* that they have in the "snap judgments" they have made, and then adjust the corresponding beliefs until these *are* consistent.[2] With Savage's definition of consistency, this is equivalent to asserting that the adjusted system of contingent beliefs can be deduced, using Bayes's rule, from a single prior.

At the end of the story, the situation is as envisaged by Bayesianismists: the final "massaged" posteriors can indeed be formally deduced from a final "massaged" prior using Bayes's rule. This conclusion is guaranteed by the use of a complex adjustment process that operates until consistency is achieved. As far as the massaged beliefs are concerned, Bayes's rule has the status of a *tautology*—like $2 + 2 = 4$. Together with the massaged prior, it serves essentially as an indexing system that keeps track of the library of massaged posteriors. However, what is certainly false in this story, is the Bayesianismist view that one is *learning* when the massaged prior is updated to yield a massaged prior. On the contrary, Bayesian updating only takes place *after* all learning is over. The actual learning takes place while the decision makers are discounting the effect that possible future surprises may have on the basic model that they use to construct their beliefs, and continues as they refine their beliefs during the massaging process. Bayesianismists therefore have the cart before the horse. Insofar as learning consists of deducing one set of beliefs from another, it is the massaged *prior* that is deduced from the unmassaged *posteriors*.

A caveat is necessary before proceeding. When the word "learning" is used in the preceding paragraph, it is intended in the sense of "adding to one's understanding" rather than simply "observing what happens." Obviously, people with perfect recall will have more facts at their disposal at later times than at earlier times, and it is certainly true that there is a colloquial sense in which they can be said to "learn" these facts as time goes by. However, it seems to me that this colloquial usage takes for granted that, whoever they are, people "learning" the facts are also sorting and classifying them into some sort of orderly system with a view to possibly making use of their knowledge in the future. Otherwise it would not seem absurd to say that a video camera is "learning" the images it records. In any case, it is not the simple recording of facts that is intended when "Bayesian learning" is discussed. Any proposal for a rational learning scheme will presumably include recording the facts (if the cost of so doing is negligible). What distinguishes "Bayesian learning" from its alternatives must therefore be something else.

In spite of this caveat about what I intend when speaking of learning, the suggestion that Bayesian updating in a completed universe involves no learning at all commonly provokes expressions of incredulity. Is it being said that we can only learn when deliberating about the future, and never directly from experience? The brief answer is no, but I have learned directly from experience that a longer answer is necessary.

In the first place, the manner in which you and I (and off-duty Bayesian-ismists) learn things about the real world is not necessarily relevant to the way a Bayesian learns. Still less is it relevant to the way in which a Bayesianismist learns when on duty. Experimental evidence offers very little evidence in favor of the proposition that we are natural Bayesians of any kind. Indeed, what evidence there is seems to suggest that, without training, even clever people are quite remarkably inept in dealing with simple statistical problems. In my own game theory experiments, no subject has ever given a Bayesian answer to the question: Why did you do what you did?, when surveyed after the experiment—even though, in most cases, the populations from which the subjects were drawn consisted entirely of students who had received training in Bayesian statistics. I therefore think introspection is unlikely to be a reliable guide when considering what learning for a Bayesian may or may not be.

The fact that real people actually learn from experience is therefore not relevant to whether Bayesian updating in a completed universe should count as genuine learning. The universes about which real people learn are almost always incomplete and, even when they are confronted with a completable universe, they almost never use Bayesian updating. Of course, Bayesian statisticians are an exception to this generalization. They use Bayesian updating all the time, but, just like real people, they are almost never working in a completed universe. That is to say, they have not asked themselves why a knee-jerk adherence to consistency requirements is appropriate, but simply update from a prior distribution chosen on a priori grounds. I do not argue that such a procedure is necessarily nonsensical. On the contrary, it often leads to descriptions of the data that provide much insight. Nor do I argue that a Bayesian statistician who updates from a prior distribution chosen on a priori grounds is not learning. All I have to say to such a Bayesian statistician is that I see no grounds for him to claim that he is learning *optimally*, or that his methodology is *necessarily* superior to those of classical statistics.[3]

The problem of how "best" to learn in an incompletable universe is unsolved. Probably it is one of those problems which have no definitive solution. But, until the problem of scientific induction is solved, any learning procedures that we employ in the context of an incompletable universe will necessarily remain arbitrary to some extent.

Recall that we are still not through with the question of whether Bayesian updating in a completed universe can properly count as learning. So far, it has been argued that the fact that real people clearly learn from experience is irrelevant to this question. The same is true of Bayesian statisticians operating in a universe that is incompletable, or which they have not chosen to complete. This leaves us free to focus on what is genuinely at issue. For this purpose, I want to draw an analogy between how a Bayesian using the massaging methodology I have attributed to Savage learns, and how a child learns arithmetic. It is true that the Bayesian is envisaged as teaching himself, but I do not think this invalidates the comparison.

When a child learns arithmetic at school, the child's teacher does not know what computations life will call upon the child to make. Amongst other things, the teacher therefore teaches him an algorithm for adding numbers. This algorithm requires that the child memorize some addition tables. In particular, the child must memorize the answer to $2 + 3 = ?$ The teacher, if good, will explain *why* $2 + 3 = 5$. The child, if apt, will understand the teacher's explanation. One may then reasonably say that the child has learned that, should the need ever arise to compute $2 + 3$, then the answer will be 5. Now consider the child, as an adult, trying to complete an income tax form. In filling out the form, the adult is faced with the problem of computing $2 + 3$, and so writes down the answer 5. Did the adult just learn that the answer to this problem is 5? Obviously not. All that one can reasonably say that the adult "learned" in filling the form is that filling the form requires computing $2 + 3$. But such simple registering of undigested facts is excluded by the caveat that identifies learning with "adding to one's understanding." Of course, there may be children who are such poor students that they grow to maturity without learning their addition tables. Such people might perhaps use their fingers to reckon with and thereby discover or rediscover that $2 + 3 = 5$ while filling out the tax form. They would then undoubtedly have learned something. But they would not be operating in a completed universe within which all potential surprises have been predicted and evaluated in advance of their occurrence.

How is it that Bayesianismists succeed in convincing themselves that rational learning consists of no more than the trivial algebraic manipulations required for the use of Bayes's rule? My guess is that their blindness is only a symptom of a more serious disease that manifests itself as a worship of mathematical formalism. A definition-axiom-theorem-proof format is designed to close the mind to irrelevant distractions. But the aspects of the learning process that are neglected by Savage's formalism are not irrelevant. How decision makers form and refine their subjective judgments really does matter. But the fact that Savage's theory leaves these aspects of the learning process utterly ummodeled creates a trap into which Bayesianismists are only too ready to fall. The trap is to proceed as though anything that is not expressed in the formalism to which one is accustomed does not exist at all.

In game theory, however, the question of where beliefs come from cannot sensibly be ignored. Bayesianismist decision theory provides an adequate account of why we should study equilibria, but fails to make any headway at all with the problem of equilibrium *selection*. Game theorists therefore cannot afford to fall victim to Bayesianismist "newspeak"[4] if they hope to break out of the bridgehead they currently occupy.

3 Bayesianism in Game Theory

This section looks very briefly at two approaches to the problem of founding game theory on Bayesian principles. One approach, that of Robert Aumann (1987) hangs together very much better than the other. But this is because Aumann's approach does not attempt to do more than justify game theorists' obsession with the notion of an equilibrium. However, the other approach aims to say things about which equilibrium should be selected.

Although Harsanyi and Selten's (1988) theory is without doubt the best known of the avowedly Bayesian approaches to the problem of equilibrium selection, it is too baroque a theory to lend itself to easy discussion in a chapter like this. In brief, the notion of a "tracing procedure" lies at the heart of Harsanyi and Selten's model. Their procedure seeks to trace the manner in which Bayesian players will reason their way to an equilibrium. Other authors offer alternative accounts of how such reasoning might proceed. Skyrms (1990) gives a particularly clean description of how he sees the deliberative process operating inside the head of a Bayesian player.

Skyrms (1990) follows Harsanyi and Selten and others in supposing that, while deliberating, the players assign interim subjective probabilities to the actions available to their opponents. If these subjective probabilities are common knowledge,[5] along with the fact that everyone is a maximizer of expected utility, then an inconsistency will arise—unless the players' beliefs happen to be in equilibrium. When such an inconsistency arises, the players are assumed to update their subjective probabilities using Bayes's rule. Various candidates for the likelihood function can be considered (of which Skyrms offers a small sample). However, the modeling judgment made at this level is irrelevant to the point I want to make.

My criticism of this and similar models will be clear. By hypothesis, the players have *not* looked ahead to preview all possible lines of reasoning they might find themselves following in the future. They are therefore operating in a universe that is definitely incomplete. In such a universe, no special justification for the use of Bayesian updating exists. One might seek to rescue the special status of Bayesian updating by departing from Skyrms's story and postulating that the players have indeed previewed all the possible lines of reasoning open to them. But, after the previewing is over, there would be no scope for Bayesian updating because there would then be no new information to incorporate into the system when the player began to reason for real. In summary, one might say, the conditions that justify the use of Bayes's rule in this context are satisfied if and only if there is nothing for Bayes's rule to update.

One cannot make the same criticism of a recent paper by Kalai and Lehrer (1990). They envisage a game being played repeatedly in real time. The circumstances under which the repetition takes place need not concern us. For our purposes, it is enough that the players use Bayes's rule to update their beliefs after each repetition, and that Kalai and Lehrer give conditions under which there is convergence on a Nash equilibrium. What does such a conclusion mean? It is certainly a very reassuring consistency result for those like myself who regard Nash equilibrium as the basic tool of game theory. But is the result also a contribution to equilibrium selection theory? It is certainly true, as Kalai and Lehrer remark, that the limit equilibrium is a function of the players' prior beliefs,[6] but it seems to me that much care is necessary in interpreting this piece of mathematics. If we take seriously the notion that a players' prior beliefs are simply a summary of a set of massaged posterior beliefs, we have to abandon the idea that the players in Kalai and Lehrer's model are *learning* which equilibrium to play as the future unfolds. The players *already know* what equilibrium will be played under all possible future contingencies. Their initial snap judgments necessarily incorporate *preconceptions* on this subject that the model leaves unexplained. Any learning takes place during the unmodeled introspection period *before* the play of the game, when the players previewed all possible courses the game might take and predicted how the game would end up being played after each of these possible sets of common experience.

It should be emphasized that the last thing I wish to do is to criticize anyone for seeking to model the *process* by means of which equilibrium is achieved. Indeed, I have contributed to this literature myself (Binmore 1987b). Far from decrying such work, I believe the reason game theorists have made so little progress with the equilibrium selection problem is that they are reluctant to confront such questions. I do not even object to Bayesian updating being used as a learning rule in this context, *provided* that nobody is claiming any special status for it beyond the fact that it possesses some pleasant mathematical properties. However, other learning rules also have virtues, and the decision to use Bayes' rule in the context of an incomplete universe is no less ad hoc than the decision to use one of the rival rules. My own preferred research strategy on this subject is not to make any a priori choice at all of a learning rule, but to let one emerge endogenously as a consequence of the operation of evolutionary pressures. However, this is an approach fraught with many difficulties.

Aumann's (1987, 1989) attempt to provide Bayesian foundations for game theory is very different in character from the work discussed so far in this section. Nobody learns anything or even decides anything in Aumann's very static model. Things are "just the way they are," and we are offered the role of a passive observer who sits on the sidelines soliloquizing on the nature of things. Such a model is not well adapted to the equilibrium selection problem. Its purpose is to clarify what kinds of equilibria should lie in the set from which a selection needs to be made.

In brief, Aumann postulates a universe of discourse whose states are *all-inclusive*. A description of such a state includes not only what players know and believe about the world and the knowledge and beliefs of other players, but also what all the players will *do* in that state. In such a framework, it becomes almost tautological that players whom fate has decreed will be Bayesian-rational in every state will necessarily operate some kind of equilibrium. Aumann (1987) then notes that, if what the players know always includes what strategy they find themselves using,[7] then they will necessarily be frozen into what he calls a "subjective correlated equilibrium."

The preceding paragraph is a scant assessment of how Aumann proceeds. A longer and more detailed account appears in Binmore 1991. However, what has been said is perhaps enough to make it clear that Aumann's universe is definitely not a small world. Indeed, his universe is as large as a universe could possibly be, since its states encompass everything that matters. However, Aumann evades the traps that await the Bayesianismist by refusing to classify his theory either as descriptive or as prescriptive. He describes his model as "analytic" to indicate that all the action takes place in the head of an otherwise passive observer. The model certainly cannot be prescriptive because there is no point in offering advice to players who "just do what they happen to do" and "believe what they happen to believe." Nor can the model be descriptive of a world in which people make conscious choices after transferring their experience into subjective judgments about the way things are. However, it seems to me that the latter is precisely the kind of world with which game theory needs to grapple.

I want to argue now that such a world is *necessarily* large in Savage's sense. The case for this is even stronger than the standard claim that the universe within which physics is discussed is incompletable. Or, to say the same thing more flamboyantly, inner space is necessarily even more mysterious than outer space. The reason is that, if the thinking processes of a player are to be modeled, then we are no longer free to envisage that all possible mental processes have been completed. A player *cannot* exhaustively evaluate all contingencies in a universe that includes the player's own internal deliberations and those of the other players. The issue is more fundamental than whether Bayesianism is applicable or not, since one cannot even rely on the *epistemology* that Bayesianismists take for granted.

Bayesians usually work with possibility sets in[8] specifying what a person knows. The possibility set $P(\omega)$ consists of the set of all states that the decision maker thinks possible when the true state is ω. Equivalently, it is the event that the decision maker perceives in state ω. But suppose we model players as Turing machines[9]—that is, as programs run on computers that have no storage constraints. Then we have to take on board the fact that possibility questions must be settled algorithmically.

To explore this issue, imagine that, for each *all-inclusive* state ω, possibility questions are resolved by a Turing machine $S = S(\omega)$ that sometimes answers no to questions which begin: Is it possible ...? Unless the answer is no, possibility is conceded. (Timing issues are neglected.)

Consider a specific question concerning the Turing machine N. Let the computer code for this question be $\lceil N \rceil$. Let $\lfloor M \rfloor$ be the computer code for the question: Is it possible that M will answer no to $\lceil M \rceil$? Finally, let T be a Turing machine that outputs $\lfloor x \rfloor$ when its input is $\lceil x \rceil$. Then the program $R = ST$, which consists of first operating T and then operating S, responds to $\lceil M \rceil$ as S responds to $\lfloor M \rfloor$.

Suppose that R responds to $\lceil R \rceil$ with no. Then S reports that it is *impossible* that R responds to $\lceil R \rceil$ with no. If what I know is true, it must therefore be that R never responds $\lceil R \rceil$ with no. But, if we as observers know this, why don't we replace S with a better program: one that accurately reflects our knowledge? Either our algorithm for determining what is possible is "incomplete" in that it allows as possible events we know to be false, or it is "inconsistent" in that it rejects as impossible events we know to be true.

This echoing of Gödel is no accident. The halting problem for Turing machines, from which the preceding example is adapted, is closely related to part of Gödel's reasoning. Note, in particular, the self-reference involved in asking a machine how it will respond to a question about how it responds to questions.

If the implications of taking an algorithmic view of knowledge acquisition are taken seriously, then the consequences for Bayesian epistemology run very deep. Binmore and Shin (1990) give some (not very profound) arguments why the modal logic (S5) that characterizes knowledge for Bayesians would need to be replaced by the modal logic (G) that Solovay (1976) showed to represent the "provable principles of probability" in Peano arithmetic. (See also Shin 1987 and Artemov 1990.)

One escape from such difficulties is to abandon the requirement that states be all-inclusive, so that self-referential questions that trouble knowledge algorithms can be disbarred. That is, one can seek to *complete* the universe of discourse. But self-reference is intrinsic to game theory, which is *about* chains of reasoning that go, "If I think that he thinks that I think ...." Papers that exploit the self-referential difficulties that arise in this specific context are Binmore 1987a, Anderlini 1988, and Canning 1988.

Anderlini offers a particularly insightful observation for those Bayesians who like to argue that game theory is based on the assumption that it is common knowledge that the players are rational. Such observations are thrown into the ring with no thought as to the nature of the universe of discourse. We are not even told what sort of entity a player is.[10] However, if a player is a Turing machine and "rationality" is defined in a natural way, Anderlini notes that the latter is not an effectively computable concept. That is, one can know every instruction in the computer program of the opponent and still not be able to tell whether the opponent is "rational."

4 Modeling Players

In this section the need for modeling the players in game theory will be taken for granted. Some reasons are given in Binmore (1990, 1991), but perhaps the most persuasive reason is the manner in which game theorists of all stripes have been driven, almost in spite of themselves, to the study of "bounded rationality."

Once a player has been modeled, one can say things about his complexity. In particular, one can compare the player's complexity to that of the player's environment. One might summarize this chapter so far by saying that, if the player's environment is sufficiently complex compared with the complexity of the player's mental apparatus, then a Bayesianismist view of the player's predicament is untenable.

I do not have any ism to offer as an alternative to Bayesianism for decision making in incompletable universes. I want only to make a plea for the issue to be returned to the research agenda from which it was displaced by the triumph of Bayesianism in the economics profession. It is worth noting that those who knew and worked with Savage in the fifties were under no illusions about the importance of the problem. Luce and Raiffa (1957), for example, list a number of systems for making decisions "under complete ignorance" in which the incompleteness of the universe of discourse is explicitly acknowledged. The existence of such systems indicates that the problem of decision making in an incompletable universe is not a featureless desert about which one can hope to say nothing at all. I do not feel able to endorse any of these systems, since they all appeal to axioms that I find it hard to evaluate in the abstract. Instead, I plan to describe some simple structural observations that seem to me to follow from little more than the requirement that a decision maker be modeled as a computing machine.

4.1   A Belief Machine

Let us simplify the problem to be considered by allowing only two consequences, winning and losing. Which of these will occur depends on some process about which the decision maker is only partially informed. A Turing machine M will be used to model the manner in which the decision maker evaluates his partial information. The input to M is therefore the data D available to the decision maker about the unknown process. Since this chapter is directed at Bayesianismists who believe that all ignorance can and should be quantified using subjective probabilities, let us restrict the output of the machine M to probabilistic statements. More specially, imagine that the machine M has k output devices $H_1, H_2, \ldots, H_k$, each of which corresponds one of the intervals $I_1, I_2, \ldots, I_k$ in a partition of $[0, 1]$. Each output device may or may not eventually type no. When the output device H_j types no, the understanding is that this answers the question: Is it possible that the notional probability π of winning lies in the interval I_j? It must be remembered that nothing guarantees that a Turing machine will stop calculating at all.

We presumably wish to exclude the possibility that all output devices will eventually print no. But, if we are to take incompletable universes seriously, it must be recognized that we cannot simultaneously insist that only *one* output device will fail to output no. If the set of admissible inputs D is not artificially restricted, then sometimes M will calculate forever without succeeding in tying π down to a single interval I_j.[11]

4.2.   Upper and Lower Probabilities

Such considerations lead very naturally to the notion of upper and lower probabilities with which many decision theorists have toyed. All that is needed, in addition to what has already been assumed, is the assumption that the subset S of $[0, 1]$ that remains after all the intervals I_j that are going to be excluded have been excluded should necessarily be convex. One may then argue that all that is known about the notional probability π is that it lies between the upper and lower limits of the interval S. The idea of a probability π therefore has necessarily to be supplemented by allowing intervals $[\underline{\pi}, \overline{\pi}]$ in which $\overline{\pi}$ is an *upper probability* and $\underline{\pi}$ is a *lower probability*.[12]

No-nonsense subjectivists like to debunk their critics by insisting that the critics compare bets on events to which the critics are reluctant to assign subjective probabilities with bets on events for which the appropriate probabilities are uncontroversial. In the case of a decision maker who uses the machine M, they would therefore seek two situations between which the decision maker is indifferent—one in which M outputs π and one in which M outputs $[\underline{\pi}, \overline{\pi}]$. However, even if the decision maker expresses such an indifference, it does not follow that the decision maker regards the output $[\underline{\pi}, \overline{\pi}]$ from M as being equivalent to the output π. The decision maker is expressing a *preference* not a *belief*. It is true that, with Savage's consistency axioms, these ideas merge. But Savage's consistency axioms are not designed for application in an incompletable universe, and it is therefore no longer possible to take for granted that a person's von Neumann–Morgenstern *utility* for a process that can lead only to winning or losing may be identified with the person's subjective *probability* of winning.

Von Neumann–Morgenstern utilities are mentioned because there seems no particular reason why one should not ask that the preferences a decision maker has over lotteries in which the prizes are objects of the form $[\underline{\pi}, \overline{\pi}]$ should not satisfy the von Neumann–Morgenstern rationality axioms. If so, it will make sense to speak of the von Neumann–Morgenstern utility $u[\underline{\pi}, \overline{\pi}]$ of a process. One will presumably wish to insist that

$$u[\underline{\pi}, \underline{\pi}] \leq u[\underline{\pi}, \overline{\pi}] \leq u[\overline{\pi}, \overline{\pi}],$$

and to normalize so that $u[p, p] = p$, but it is not clear what further rationality requirements are appropriate. One possibility is to ask that the decision maker evaluate $\overline{\pi}$ and $\underline{\pi}$ "separately."[13]

An argument of Keeney and Raiffa then shows that $u[\underline{\pi}, \overline{\pi}]$ must take one of the two forms:

$$\underline{u}(\underline{\pi}) + \overline{u}(\overline{\pi}) \qquad \text{or} \qquad \underline{u}(\underline{\pi}) \times \overline{u}(\overline{\pi}).$$

Thus, for example, it could be that

$$u[\underline{\pi}, \overline{\pi}] = \alpha\underline{\pi} + \beta\overline{\pi} \qquad \text{or} \qquad u[\underline{\pi}, \overline{\pi}] = \underline{\pi}^{\alpha}\overline{\pi}^{\beta},$$

where $\alpha \geq 0$, $\beta \geq 0$ and $\alpha + \beta = 1$.

4.3   Updating Upper and Lower Probabilities

Consider now three processes with respective data D_1, D_2, and D_3. Let D_3 be the process in which decision makers win if and only if they win in both D_1 and D_2. It is then natural to say that D_1 and D_2 should be regarded as independent processes if $\underline{\pi}_3 = \underline{\pi}_1\underline{\pi}_2$ and $\overline{\pi}_3 = \overline{\pi}_1\overline{\pi}_2$. One can then deal with conditioning by writing $D_2|D_1$ instead of D_2. It then seems that, although we may not be able to assign probabilities to all events in an incompletable universe, nevertheless Bayes's rule is still with us as the appropriate method for updating upper and lower probabilities.

I think this conclusion is correct, provided that one is not naive about the circumstances in which the procedure is used. In reaching the conclusion that upper and lower probabilities should be updated using Bayes's rule, I implicitly made use of *consistency* assumptions. However, earlier in the chapter it was argued that such consistency assumptions only make good sense in a completable universe. If upper and lower probabilities are to be updated by Bayes's rule, we therefore need to be able to argue that the relevant universe for this particular operation is completable. Among other things, we need to be confident that the machine M would not respond differently to the input D_1 after being asked to evaluate $D_2|D_1$ than it did before. If the machine were to operate like a human decision maker following Savage's methodology, this would be assured if the machine's massaging activities, while originally assessing the data D_1, were sufficiently wide ranging as to include the possibility that it might later be offered the data $D_2|D_1$. However, in an incompletable universe will not be possible for the machine to anticipate what the effect of *all* possible future data will be on the manner in which it processes data. Like ourselves, the machine will not only learn, it will learn how to learn as it gathers experience, and it is impossible for the machine to predict how it might possibly reprogram itself under all future contingencies.

4.4   Upper and Lower Probabilities in Games?

It is necessary to round off this section by indicating how the ideas it presents would work in a game-theoretic setting. I hope, however, that what comes next will not be regarded as an attempt to construct a new theory of games. It merely aims to discomfort Bayesianismists by bringing to their attention what they would have to believe if they genuinely sought to implement their ideas algorithmically.

Figure 16.1 shows a payoff matrix for a version of a well-known "toy" game called the "Battle of the Sexes." It comes with a story about a husband (player 1) and a wife (player 2) who did not agree at breakfast whether to go to a boxing match or a ballet performance in the evening. Later in the day, they get separated and hence have to make the decision of where to go in the evening independently.

According to a traditional analysis, the game has three Nash equilibria[14] (see figure 16.1). There are two Nash equilibria in pure strategies: namely (Boxing, Boxing) and (Ballet, Ballet). However, unless some way can be found to break the symmetry, neither can be the "solution" of the game, since any argument in favor of one of the pure strategy equilibria is equally an argument in favor of the other. The third Nash equilibrium calls for both players to use mixed strategies. That is, each player randomizes over his or her pure strategies. To be precise, the husband and wife each choose "boxing" independently with respective probabilities $\frac{3}{5}$ and $\frac{2}{5}$. However, this third Nash equilibrium is not a very attractive candidate for the "solution" of the game, because each player's solution payoff would then be no more than his or her security level.[15]

However, we perhaps ought to ask ourselves whether we have really exhausted all the Nash equilibria. Is it not possible, for example, that the wife might employ a decision process in deciding what action to take whose data, when taken as input for the husband's assessment machine, lead it to produce the output $[\underline{\pi}_2, \overline{\pi}_2]$ when questioned about the notional probability with which she will use "boxing"?

To simplify the situation, imagine that the husband's ultimate aim is to win a prize, and the wife's is to win a second and separate prize. One may then take the entries in the payoff matrix of figure 16.1 to be the probabilities with which the players will win their respective prizes for each of the four possible pure-strategy combinations. If player 1 now uses a decision process with data D_1, and player 2 independently uses a decision process with data D_2, then we can symbolically represent the process that decides whether player 1 wins his ultimate prize as

$$(D_1 \wedge D_2) \vee (\neg D_1 \wedge \neg D_2 \wedge D),$$

where D is the data for a process, independent of D_1 and D_2, that is assessed at $\frac{2}{3}$. If we make Bayesian assumptions about how such combinations of processes should be manipulated, the husband's machine will assess the combination as

$$[\underline{\pi}_1 \underline{\pi}_2 + \tfrac{2}{3}(1 - \overline{\pi}_1)(1 - \overline{\pi}_2), \overline{\pi}_1 \overline{\pi}_2 + \tfrac{2}{3}(1 - \underline{\pi}_1)(1 - \underline{\pi}_2)].$$

	Boxing	Ballet
Boxing	$\frac{2}{3}$ / 1	0 / 0
Ballet	0 / 0	1 / $\frac{2}{3}$

Figure 16.1
Battle of the sexes

To proceed further, it is necessary to make assumptions about the utility functions with which the players evaluate such assessments. I want only to observe that if both players have utility functions defined by

$$u[\underline{\pi}, \overline{\pi}] = \{\underline{\pi}\}^{1/2}\{\overline{\pi}\}^{1/2},$$

then the Battle of the Sexes not only has Nash equilibria other than those traditionally considered, it has Nash equilibria that generate payoffs for both players that are better than the $\frac{2}{3}$ the players get when the traditional mixed equilibrium is used.

5   Summary

This chapter has been an attack on Bayesianism, which I see as a metaphysical doctrine that hinders advances in the foundations of game theory. The chapter began with an appeal to the authority of Savage. It continued with an attempt to explain how it can be shown that certain universes of discourse *cannot* be completable in the sense required to legitimize a Bayesianismist methodology. It concluded with a brief discussion of some of the implications of looking seriously at the idea that decision making should be described in terms of algorithms.

Notes

1. There is room for confusion here for those who are well-read in the Scriptures. I do not intend when speaking of small worlds to refer to Savage's attempt to explain how a small world, which he calls a "microcosm" in this context, may be embedded in a grand world. This attempt does not seem to me to be very successful. I intend the concept of a small world to be interpreted in the wider, nontechnical sense of the earlier portion of his book.

2. Gärdenfors's *Knowledge in Flux* (1988) assesses the considerations that will control how such adjustments are made.

3. Which is not the same as saying that there may not be *empirical* grounds for preferring Bayesian methods to classical methods.

4. Recall from George Orwell's *1984* that "newspeak" is an invented language in which politically incorrect statements cannot be made.

5. As a consequence of the players' duplicating the reasoning processes of their opponents.

6. In general, the limit equilibrium will also depend on random events that occur during play.

7. This is not such an innocent assumption as it may appear. When the players are modeled as self-correcting computing machines, it becomes more than a little problematic (Binmore 1987b).

8. Game theorists refer to an elaboration of the idea of a possibility set as an "information set" (Binmore 1991).

9. The Church-Turing hypothesis asserts that any formal calculation possible for a human mathematician can be aped by a Turing machine. Penrose (1989) bravely puts the case for humans being able to transcend the limitations of such machines. Those who are constitutionally inclined to this view should read his book to find out what they are letting themselves in for in the way of assumptions about how the human mind works.

10. Whatever the definition of a player may be, it must certainly be rich enough in structure to admit the possibility of a player being irrational. Otherwise the statement would be empty.

11. One might argue that the decision maker might be able to tie things down further if the decision maker were allowed to examine a transcript of the calculations made by M. But the ground rules are that any such examination would need to be expressible algorithmically. We could then construct a Turing machine that does the same thing as the decision maker and run this along with M. We would then be making our judgments with a Turing machine again, albeit a larger Turing machine than M.

12. I am ignoring two issues. The first is that only approximations to probabilities can emerge from such a procedure. The second is that one cannot wait for ever to learn for sure which output devices are going to fail to print no.

13. This requires, for example, that $[\underline{\pi}, \bar{\pi}] \preceq [\underline{\pi}, \bar{q}] \Leftrightarrow [q, \bar{\pi}] \preceq [q, \bar{q}]$ whenever the expressions are meaningful. Not only this, the relationship must survive when lotteries are taken over $\bar{\pi}$ and $\bar{q}$. Moreover, everything must be the same when it is the second argument that is held constant in comparisons, rather than the first.

14. In a Nash equilibrium, each player's strategy choice is optimal given the strategy choices made by the other players.

15. Player 1's security level is his expected payoff if he acts on the assumption his opponent will guess his choice of mixed strategy in advance and respond by choosing a strategy herself that minimizes his payoff.

References

Allais, M. 1953. "Le Comportement de l'Homme Rationnel Devant le Risque: Critique des Postulats et Axiomes de l'École Américaine." *Econometrica* 21:503–546.

Anderlini, L. 1988. "Some Notes on Church's Thesis and the Theory of Games." Economic theory discussion paper, Cambridge University.

Artemov, S. 1990. "Kolmogorov's Logic of Problems and a Probability Interpretation of Intuitionistic Logic." In R. Parikh, ed., *Theoretical Aspects of Reasoning about Knowledge.* San Mateo, Calif.: Morgan Kaufmann.

Aumann, R. 1987. "Correlated Equilibrium as an Expression of Bayesian Rationality." *Econometrica* 55:1–18.

Aumann, R. 1989. "Interactive Epistemology." Working paper, Cowles Foundation, Yale University.

Binmore, K. 1987a. "Modeling Rational Players I." *Economics and Philosophy* 3:9–55.

Binmore, K. 1987b. "Modeling Rational Players II." *Economics and Philosophy* 4:179–214.

Binmore, K. 1990. *Essays on Foundations of Game Theory.* Oxford: Basil Blackwell.

Binmore, K. 1991. *Fun and Games.* Lexington, Mass.: D. C. Heath. Lexington.

Binmore, K., and H. Shin. 1990. "Algorithmic Knowledge and Game Theory." Discussion paper, University of Michigan.

Canning, D. 1988. "Rationality and Game Theory when Players are Turing Machines." Discussion paper 88/183, London School of Economics ST/ICERD.

Gärdenfors, P. 1988. *Knowledge in Flux.* Cambridge: MIT Press.

Harsanyi, J., and R. Selten. 1988. *A General Theory of Equilibrium Selection in Games.* Cambridge: MIT Press.

Kalai, E., and E. Lehrer. 1990. "Rational Learning Leads to Nash Equilibrium." Discussion paper 895, Northwestern University.

Luce, R., and H. Raiffa. 1957. *Games and Decisions.* New York: Wiley.

Penrose, R. 1989. *The Emperor's New Mind.* Oxford: Oxford University Press.

Savage, L. 1951. *The Foundations of Statistics.* New York: Wiley.

Shin, H. 1987. "Logical Structure of Common Knowledge, I and II." Nuffield College, Oxford.

Skyrms, B. 1990. *The Dynamics of Rational Deliberation.* Cambridge: Harvard University Press.

Solovay, R. 1976. "Provability Interpretation of Modal Logic." *Israel Journal of Mathematics* 25:287–304.

Contributors

Steve Alpern
Department of Mathematics, London School of Economics, London (UK)

David Austen-Smith
Department of Political Science, University of Rochester NY (USA)

Michael Bacharach
Christ Church, University of Oxford, Oxford (UK)

Ken Binmore
University College London (UK), University of Michigan (USA)

Steven J. Brams
Department of Politics, New York University, New York (USA)

Vincent Brousseau
European University Institute, Firenze (Italy)

Colin F. Camerer
Graduate School of Business, University of Chicago (USA)

Hans Carlsson
University of Gothenburg and University of Lund (Sweden)

Alan Kirman
European University Institute, Firenze (Italy)

Michael Maschler
The Hebrew University of Jerusalem (Israel)

Hervé Moulin
Duke University, Durham, North Carolina (USA)

Jos Potters
University of Nijmegen (The Netherlands)

Talia Rymon
Department of Marketing, The Wharton School, University of Pennsylvania (USA)

Larry Samuelson
Department of Economics, University of Wisconsin, Madison, Wisconsin (USA)

Sankar Sen
Department of Marketing, The Wharton School, University of Pennsylvania (USA)

Piero Tani
Centro Interuniversitario per la Teoria dei Giochi e le Applicazioni, Università di Firenze (Italy)

Stef Tijs
University of Nijmegen (The Netherlands)

Morton D. Davis
Department of Mathematics, City College of New York, New York (USA)

Françoise Forges
F.N.R.S., CORE, Louvain-la-Neuve (Belgium)

Joseph Greenberg
Department of Economics, McGill University, and C.R.D.E. Université de Montreal (Canada)

Peter J. Hammond
Department of Economics, Stanford University, California (USA)

John C. Harsanyi
University of California at Berkeley (USA)

Alain Haurie
Département d'économie commerciale et industrielle, Université de Genève (Switzerland)

Eric J. Johnson
Department of Marketing, The Wharton School, University of Pennsylvania (USA)

D. Marc Kilgour
Department of Mathematics, Wilfrid Laurier University, Waterloo, Ontario (Canada)

Eric van Damme
CentER for Economic Research, Tilburg University (The Netherlands)

Shlomo Weber
York University, Toronto (Canada)

Index